James Maidment, W. H. (William Hugh) Logan

A Pedlar's Pack of Ballads and Songs.

With Illustrative Notes

James Maidment, W. H. (William Hugh) Logan

A Pedlar's Pack of Ballads and Songs.
With Illustrative Notes

ISBN/EAN: 9783744777018

Printed in Europe, USA, Canada, Australia, Japan

Cover: Foto ©Thomas Meinert / pixelio.de

More available books at **www.hansebooks.com**

A

PEDLAR'S PACK

OF

BALLADS AND SONGS.

WITH ILLUSTRATIVE NOTES,

By W. H. LOGAN.

EDINBURGH: WILLIAM PATERSON.

MDCCCLXIX.

" Goe, tell the poets that their pedling rimes
    Begin apace to grow out of request,
While wanton humours in these idle times
    Can make of love but as a laughing jest:
And tell prose-writers, stories are so stale
That penny ballads make a better sale."
                            Breton's Pasquil's Nightcap.—1600.

"Come, pretty maydens, what is't you buy?
    See, what is't you lack ?
If you can find a toy to your mind,
    Be so kind view the pedlar's pack.
                Pedlar's Song from " Catch who catch can."—1652.

TO

JAMES MAIDMENT, ESQUIRE,

IN THE HAPPY REMEMBRANCE OF A FRIENDSHIP

WHICH HAS ENDURED UNINTERRUPTEDLY

FOR A LONG SERIES OF YEARS,

This Volume

IS AFFECTIONATELY INSCRIBED.

PREFACE.

A TASTE for the stupendous and extensive, combined with an assumption of wisdom and knowledge which our more sage ancestors never dreamt of, has led to an entire revolution in the manners and customs of the peasantry of this country. With a spurious desire to avoid what might be deemed "vulgar," the present generation have repudiated many things which formerly used to be regarded as institutions. Compare, for instance, a Country or Statute Fair of our time with the fairs of even twenty years ago, and mark well the difference. No stir, no bustle, no fun. Such a want of heart about everything; such a listlessness; and, notwithstanding the increased population, such a comparatively poor attendance. Learned Pigs, Spotted Indian Youths, White-haired Ladies, Fat Boys, the Speaking Fish, and other wonders of that kind, which were once reckoned great attractions to the common people, seem for ever banished. Dwarfs and Giants, also, which were only to be seen in itinerant shows on high days and holidays, have set about throwing off all connection with meanness and vulgarity, and now aim at raising their social position by assuming a style of grandeur and magnificence, and by putting a greater value, if that were possible, upon themselves. Their keeper, too, instead of being that honest-looking Yorkshireman in highlows, or that glib-tongued Irishman, who had just, by dint of a praiseworthy persevering spirit, emancipated himself from the thraldom of an agricultural "artist plying his *sickle-y* trade," now appears in the person of a fine gentleman with mustachios, a soft poetic voice, and arrayed in vestments which even the Prince of Wales might not object to. Instead of a Wooden Booth upon wheels surmounted by exaggerated daubs of the Giant " standing eight feet high " on his stocking-soles, and of the Dwarf reckoning only two feet and a half in his tiny top-boots (which by the way were in company with a baby house too small to hold him, always hung up to air in sight of the general public outside during the intervals of non-performance in order to beget an interest in what was going forward within), we find the best halls in London, and the most aristocratic rooms in country towns, hardly good enough for the reception of the distinguished exhibitors. No touter at the door invites you to " walk up ! step up ! just a-going to begin," nor does any stout lady with a muff sit for you in the moneytaker's box to ask you as you come out, how you have been pleased with the performance. Neither is there any stipulation that " your money will be returned " if everything is not as has been stated. No, everything is done upon the grand ; an "agent in advance," having hired the rooms, causes advertisements to be inserted in the *Times* and the other chief papers of the kingdom ; Photographic Portraits of the coming wonders are exhibited in prominent windows ; influence is made in every available quarter to obtain a command for the *lusus naturæ* to appear and exhibit themselves before some member of the Royal Family, and trading upon this stamp, they modestly ask you to pay half a crown for a sight, which, some few years ago, would have been estimated at about just as many pence as is now demanded in the shape of shillings.

In Equestrian Exhibitions as well, instead of ostlers in dingy red jackets leading in the horses as of old, and assisting the clown to hold up the hoops, balloons, and long cloths for the star rider's leap, we have now a large number of gentlemen clad in blue long-tailed coats and white waistcoats, from which a casual spectator might imagine he had come into the presence of the Directors of the Bank of England out on a lark for that particular evening.

Our street ballad singers are now also no more. They likewise have assumed the magnificent, and betaken themselves
to gigantic places of public resort, adorned with mirrors
and Dutch metal, grandiloquently termed "Music Halls,"
wherein they exercise their vocation (at a large fixed weekly
stipend) amid the fumes of tobacco, the sound of corks being
drawn, and a mixed aroma of bad (rummified) brandy, saw-
dust, and perspiration, from the hours of eight in the evening,
till "the wee short hour ayont the twal," the music and words
of their minstrelsy being of the very thinnest description,
adapted of course, in a peculiar degree, to suit the taste of
their degenerate audience.

"I'd rather be a kitten and cry 'mew !'
Than one of these same metre ballad mongers."

Another and a greater symptom of the growing desire for
"the grand" is the entire absence from lanes and alleys of
Broadsheet Ballads and of Flying-Stationers. To see such
vulgar things as common songs disfigure the walls could not
possibly be tolerated. Have we not our more wholesome
cheap literature to instruct the nation? Our lives of Heroic
Highwaymen, in penny numbers. Our adventures of Detec-
tive Officers. Our sea-stories, to induce boys to disobey their
parents and run away from home. Our Nicholas Nicklebys,
to teach boys to despise and assault their teachers. And
above all, have we not our newspapers full of descriptions of
prize-fights, details of murders, the art of garotting and its
defects,—in cases where the clumsy perpetrators have been
discovered,—reports of Divorce Cases, Seductions, and
Breaches of Promise, Burglaries, and "other articles too
numerous to mention?"—all so much in excellence (to say
nothing of the advantage in price) superior to hawkers'
Broadsides, and tending to make people more "knowing"
than there is any occasion for, so that as time goes on,
intending murderers and house-breakers may so improve
upon past atrocities, as to narrow the means of detection.

The vulgar Broadsheet Ballad thus being thrust from its
legitimate ground by more pretentious, and in too many

instances more questionable, literature, if we are compelled to
truckle to the prevailing taste for the magnificent, there is no
resource left, in order to preserve such old-fashioned legends,
than to follow the footsteps of the Giants and the Dwarfs,
and to appear before the public in a grander form and with
a more popular aspect than of yore.   There are happily still
left amongst us very many beings who delight in such
effusions, and who, like those who go to see our modern
Giant, will not object to the higher price, in consideration of
the superior manner in which our collection of ballads is now
placed before them.

   This collection was formed upwards of twenty years ago,
it having been my intention to present it as my contribution
to the members of the Abbotsford Club, to which I had then
the honour to belong.   Circumstances, however, having led
to a change of residence from Edinburgh to Berwick-on-
Tweed, my attention was for awhile directed to other matters,
and having seceded from the Abbotsford Club, which was
shortly afterwards broken up, and the MS. having fallen
aside, my intentions as to printing were for a while abandoned.

   Most of the ballads are from original Broadsides in the
possession of Mr Maidment, a gentleman eminent as a collector of antiquarian lore, as an extensive contributor to that
class of literature, and who is the chief Peerage Lawyer at present in Scotland.   The late Mr C. K. Sharpe, known as the
editor of Law's Memorials, Kirkton's Church History, and as
a gentleman who, having figured in the best society of Edinburgh about the beginning of the present century, was full of
much contemporaneous information and anecdote, having
obtained a loan of a portion of Mr Maidment's collections to
beguile the tedium of a few weeks when confined to the house
by indisposition, took occasion to mark those Ballads which
were deemed worthy of preservation, and suggested that they
would make a desirable volume.   Upon this hint, I had the
ballads transcribed, and I have now much pleasure in presenting them, with some additions from other sources, for the
acceptance of the more enlightened of the general public.

It is somewhat remarkable that the volumes from which the bulk of these ballads has been extracted, twice escaped being destroyed by fire.   On the first occasion, in February 1823, when the premises of Mr Abraham Thomson, the celebrated Bibliopogist, situated in the Old Fish Market Close, Edinburgh, were almost entirely consumed, and when a large amount of literary property left in his possession for binding was utterly lost.   In particular, the reprint, by Mr David Laing, of Chepman and Millar's unique volume in black letter, preserved in the Library of the Faculty of Advocates, was so much destroyed that very few copies could be made up, and even these required to be partially inlaid, which renders the volume, when a copy occurs in the market, of very high pecuniary value.   The second time was when the Great Fire in Edinburgh took place, in November 1824, the volumes having been in the hands of Mr Lockhart Frame, Bookbinder, as patterns.

W. H. L.

BERWICK-ON-TWEED,
    31st Dec. 1868.

TABLE OF CONTENTS.

xii CONTENTS.

POPULAR MINSTRELSY.

CAPTAIN WARD.

THE present version of Captain Ward is from a broadside, printed and sold by J. Pitts, 14 Great St. Andrew Street, Seven Dials, *circa* 1821. It has been collated with two other copies, one issued about 1817 from the same popular establishment; the other in "Early Naval Ballads," in the Percy Society's Publications, edited by James Orchard Halliwell, Esq., 1841, "from the British Museum Collection of Old Ballads." Mr. Halliwell gives no indication of the date of the copy he used, nor any information as to the subject of the ballad itself. He merely informs us that it was "Licensed and entered, London: Printed by and for W. Onley, and are to be sold by the booksellers." The different readings which are of any moment are given in the foot-notes.

In what collection first appeared "A Famous Sea-Fight between Captain Ward and the Rainbow," (as the title runs in the two copies cited,) we have been unable to trace. The time at which the event occurred was evidently during the early years of the reign of King James I. and VI. The king, in his despair of ever capturing the pirate, Ward, laments the loss of his "jewels three," any one of whom, had he then existed, he says, "would have gone unto the seas, and brought proud Ward to me." The first he mentions is "Lord Clifford, Earl of Cumberland," —that is, George Clifford, the celebrated Earl of Cumberland, remarkable for naval adventures in the reign of Queen Elizabeth, and who died at the age of forty-five, within three years after King James' accession. "Eleven days before his death," Brydges remarks in his Memoirs of the Peers of England, 8vo., 1802, vol. i. p. 21, "which happened at the Savoy on Oct. 30, 1605, he settled all his castles and large estates upon his brother, Francis, charging them with a portion of £15,000 to his daughter, with remainder of the estates themselves to her, on failure of issue male of his brother. This daughter, afterwards so well known as Countess of Dorset and Montgomery, came accordingly in 1643 to the inheritance of this powerful property." The Earldom of Cumberland in the Cliffords became extinct in 1643, and the Estates and Barony of De Clifford passed to the heirs of line, the Thanet family, 12th Dec., 1691. The Peerage is now held by one of the Russell family.

A

The family De Clifford were staunch adherents of the Lancastrians, and were very obnoxious to the Yorkists, in consequence of the death, by the hands of Lord Clifford, of the Earl of Rutland, the younger brother of Edward IV.—an act of barbarity which admits of no palliation. When the white rose became in the ascendant, every exertion was used by the conqueror to avenge the death of the boy ; and as Lord Clifford had himself fallen during the wars of the rival houses, leaving an infant son, every endeavour was made to obtain possession of the child to further that purpose. Lady Clifford, who had married a second time, with the assistance of her husband changed the place of her son's residence from time to time, till at last she placed him under the care of a shepherd, with whom he remained until the death of Richard III., which restored the fortunes of the house of Lancaster ; and upon the accession of Henry VII. the heir of the De Cliffords was advanced to his proper rank. He was then about thirty years of age, and could neither read nor write. Nevertheless he afterwards educated himself sufficiently to take his place amongst the nobility. He was created Earl of Cumberland by Henry VIII. He was greatly addicted to the study of astronomy, and, it is said, erected a tower on one of his estates for the better observing the motions of the heavenly bodies.

The second "jewel" the king had lost was "Lord Mountjoye." Charles Blount, Lord Mountjoye, had distinguished himself, particularly as Lord-Lieutenant of Ireland, towards the close of Queen Elizabeth's reign. He was second son of James, sixth Lord Mountjoye, came to Court at twenty years of age, was Knighted in 1586, and served in the English fleet against the Spanish armada. To the high office of Lord-Lieutenant he was re-appointed by King James, who made him a Knight of the Garter, and bestowed on him the Earldom of Devonshire. "In reward of his great services," remarks Brydges, "his majesty made him Master of the Ordnance in England, gave him Kingston-hall in Dorsetshire, £200 a-year old rent of Assize out of the Exchequer, and as much more out of the Dutchy, for him and his heirs for ever, besides the County of Lecal in Ireland, together with other lands in the Pale there, which were to fall to the Crown upon the death of the Countess of Kildare, for want of heirs male of her body." He subsequently achieved other honours. Cambden styles him "a person famous for conduct ; and so eminent for courage and learning, that in those respects he had no superior, and but few equals." And his secretary, Fynes Moryson (author of the Itinerary), characterizes him as "beautiful in his person as well as valiant, and learned as well as wise." His transactions in Ireland are recorded in Dr Leland's History of that Country, vol. ii. p. 371-417.

"Moryson," says Dr Birch, "has drawn his lordship's character with great judgment and candour, not concealing his defects, and acknowledging that in the last period of his life, after the Irish wars, 'grief of unsuccessful love brought him to his last end." He had been engaged, while a lad, to the Earl of Essex's sister, Penelope, before she was married to Robert, Lord Rich, in 1580. She left her husband, and had several children by him while Earl of Devonshire, and, on his return from Ireland, finding that she had been divorced, he married her. This connection, under all the circumstances, wounded his reputation in such a degree, that the impression which the disgrace made upon him was believed to have shortened his life. He died in 1606, at the age of forty-three. Samuel Daniel, the poet, wrote a Funeral poem upon him, which will be found *ad longum* in Brydges' Peers of England, vol. i., reprinted from the edition of Daniel's works—London, 1623, 4to. The Earl figures in Sir Walter Scott's "Kenilworth" as Sir Charles Blount.

The third and last of the king's "lost jewels" was Robert Devereux, Earl of Essex, "who blazed the comet of a season, the favourite equally of his countrymen and his queen,—the warrior and statesman, who played a conspicuous part in almost every event of the last sixteen years of Elizabeth's reign,—the patron and friend of men of genius, himself one of the first writers of pure and elegant English, and almost equally distinguished for the classical purity of his Latin letters,—a character composed of the most admirable qualities that can adorn a man, with the most fiery passions, and the most startling weaknesses."—See Lives and Letters of the Devereux, Earls of Essex, by the Honble. W. B. Devereux, London, 1853, 8vo., vol. i. The Earl was educated at Cambridge, where he afterwards received the degree of M.A. In 1584, at the age of seventeen, he, with "stiff aversation," entered the Court circle, under the auspices of the Earl of Leicester, whom he thereafter accompanied in his expedition to the Low Countries. Winstanley, in his "Worthies of England," says, that the Earl of Leicester brought Essex to Court, not so much out of love to him, as to be a counterpoise to Sir Walter Raleigh, who was then in high favour with the Queen. Essex' ultimate fate is well known.

Ward, the hero of our ballad, appears to have been a very notorious rover of the seas during the reign of Queen Elizabeth, as well as during the early part of that of King James ; and in addition to "honourable mention" being made of him in the present ballad, his fame was sounded by other contemporaneous minstrels. The "famous sea-fight," by Mr. Halliwell's account, was sung "to the tune of Captain Ward, &c.;" and in the same collection of Naval ballads referred to, he gives us "the Song of Dansikar, the Dutchman," "from an old black letter copy, preserved in Anthony à Wood's collection at Oxford, No. 401." In this occur the following stanzas, which embody a portion of Ward's history :—

"Now many a worthy gallant,
    Of courage now most valiant,
        With him hath put their fortunes to the sea ;

All the world about have heard
Of Dansekar and English Ward,
  And of their proud adventures every day.
    *   *   *   *   *

"They make children fatherless,
Woful widows in distresse:
  In shedding blood they take too much delight;
Fathers they bereave of sons,
Regarding neither cries nor moans,
  So much they joy to see a bloody fight.
    *   *   *   *   *

"Of Hull the Bonaventer,
Which was a great frequenter,
  And passer of the straits to Barbary;
Both ship and men late taken were
By pyrates Ward and Dansekar,
  And brought by them into captivity.

"English Ward and Dansekar
Begin greatly now to jar
  About dividing their goods;
Both ships and soldiers gather head,
Dansekar from Ward is fled,
  So full of pride and malice are their bloods.

"Ward doth only promise
To keep about rich Tunis,
  And be commander of those Turkish seas;
But valiant Dutch-land Dansekar
Doth hover neer unto Argier,
  And there his threat'ning colours now displays."
    *   *   *   *   *

The editor of "Notes and Queries" (3d S. xi., p. 419), with his usual politeness, has referred us " for particulars of Captain Ward, to 'a True and Certaine Report of the Beginning, Proceedings, Overthrowes, and now present Estate of Captain Ward and Dansekar, the two late famous Pirates. By Andrew Barker. Lond., 4to, 1609.' This work was dramatized by Robert Daborn, in a tragedy entitled, 'a Christian turn'd Turke; or, the Tragical Lives and Deaths of the two famous Pyrates, Ward and Dansiker. Lond., 4to, 1612.' The Roxburghe ballad, reprinted by the Percy Society, has the conjectured date of 1650."

From Daborn's Play, we gather that "Heroicke Captaine Ward,

Lord of the Ocean, terror of Kings, Landlord to Merchants, rewarder of Man-hood, conqueror of the Western World, to whose followers the lands and seas pay tribute, and they to none, but once in their liues to the Manor of Wapping, and then are free euer after," emanated from Kent, where in his early youth his vocation was to cry, "herrings seuen a penny." Francisco, the Captain of another free trader, who casts this in his teeth, thus goes on to taunt him further :—

> "Poor fisher's brat, that neuer didst aspire
> Aboue a musle boate, that wert not borne
> Vnto a fortune boue two cades of sprats,
> And those smoakt in thy father's bed-chamber.
> That by a beggar in meere charity,
> Being made drunke, 'steed of a mariner
> Wert stole aboard, and being awake didst smell
> Worse than thy shell commodity at midsummer ;—
> That desperate through feare wert made a Captaine,
> When to haue bene a shoare againe, thou wouldst haue turn'd
> Swabber vnto a Peter-man."

Touching at Tunis, as was his wont when he had a cargo to dispose of, there being certain Jews there greedy of ill-gotten gear, Ward was solicited by the Governor and other Turks to become Mahomedan, in order that they might secure his services in a Naval capacity. Although, like most daring adventurers, he had not much religion in him, yet had one belief in common with the Turks and Calvinists—that of Fatalism,— he hesitated to comply with their desire :—

> "What's mine of prowesse, or art, shall rest by you
> To be dispos'd of : but to abiure
> My name, and the beliefe my Ancesters
> Left to my being, I do not loue so well
> The earth that bore me, to lessen my contempt
> And hatred to her, by so much advantage
> So oblique act as this should giue to her."

One of the Turks named Crosman suggests to the Governor that female influence should be called in, and hints that his sister will manage matters judiciously. Crosman says :—

> "He enioyes too much by promise to be won,
> 'Tmust be a woman's act, to whom ther's nought
> That is impossible : what Devils dare not moue
> Men to accomplish, women work them to."

Voada, Crosman's sister, prevails, despite all friendly remonstrance, and Ward, who is already wealthy, is presented with "the Captainship of our strong Castle," as Voada's portion. His ambition has full scope as "the Sultaun's Admirall." Through the instrumentality, however, of Voada, who has formed an illicit passion for another, he is falsely accused of murdering her lover, and this, coupled with the usual revenge-ful feelings of envious compeers, leads to his ultimate disgrace.

> "*Governour.* His monument in brass wee'l thus engraue,
> Ward sold his country, turn'd Turke, and died a slaue."

The play itself contains many spirited and poetical passages, while in its arrangement it is very dramatic. The ceremony of Ward turning Turk is minute in its detail. It is represented in "dumb show with Chorus." There is a sensation scene,—the burning of the Jew's house by Dansiker and his crew, while Agar (his wife, a Turkish woman) had just received a promiscuous lover in the upper chamber by means of a rope ladder. It will be held in mind that this play was represented during Shakespeare's time.

Prior to his being led off, Ward recapitulates all that he had done for the Turks, ending with a denunciation in these lines :—

> "Vngrateful curs, that haue repaid me thus
> For all the seruice that I haue done for you;
> He that hath brought more treasure to your shore
> Than all Arabia yeelds,—he that hath showne you
> The way to conquer Europe, did first impart,
> What your forefathers knew not, the seaman's art ;
> Which had they attein'd, this vniuerse had bene
> One Monarchy :—May all your seed be damn'd !
> The name of Ottoman be the onely scorne
> .And by-word to all nations ; may his owne slaues
> Teare out the bowels of the last remaines
> Vnto his bloud-propt throne. May ye cut each other's throats;
> Or may—oh may the force of Christendom
> Be reunited, and all at once require
> The liues of all that you haue murdered,
> Beating a path out to Ierusalem
> Over the bleeding breasts of you and yours."

Dansiker, whose name is linked with that of Ward, does not appear to have been extensively connected with him in his marauding expedi-tions. He appears to have traded more upon his own account. In Daborn's play he does not hold a very prominent part, and has little to

do with the progress of the plot. He is thus spoken slightingly of by
"the Gouernour" of Tunis when addressing Ward :—

> "You are the man we couet, whose valor
> Hath spake you, so impartiall worthy,
> We should do wrong to merit, not gracing you.
> Beleeue me, sir, you haue iniur'd much your selfe.
> Vouchsafing familiarity with those
> Men of so common ranke as Dansiker—
> Your hopes should fly a pitch aboue them."

At the date of the action of the play, Dansiker has, seemingly, been
only four years pursuing his desperate vocation, and by letters from his
wife he is assured of pardon for himself and crew, "on condition they
henceforth for the state of France employ their lives and service."

The name Dansiker evidently implies a Danish extraction.

Captain Ward and the Rainbow.

STRIKE up, ye lusty gallants,
  With music beat of drum,
For we have got a rover,
  Upon the sea is come.*

His name is Captain Ward,
  Right well it now appears,
There hath not been such a rover
  Found out these thousand years.

For he hath sent unto the king,
  The sixth of January,
Desiring that he might come in
  With all his company.

---

* " With musick and sound of drum,
    For we have descryed a rover," &c.—*Halliwell.*
  " With music's sound of drum,
    For there is such a rover," &c.—*Pitt.*

And if the king* will let me come
    Till I my tale have told;
I will bestow, for my ransom,
    Full thirty ton of gold.

"O nay, O nay," then said the king,
    "O nay, this must not be,
To yield to such a rover
    Myself will not agree.

"He hath deceived the Frenchmen,
    Likewise the King of Spain;
Then how can he be true to me,
    Who has been false to twain?"

With that our king provided
    A ship of worthy fame;
The Rainbow she is called,
    If you would know her name.

And now the gallant Rainbow
    She rolls,† upon the sea,
Five hundred gallant seamen
    To keep‡ her company.

The Dutchman and the Spaniard
    She made them for to flee,
Also the bonny Frenchman
    As she met them on the sea.

When as the gallant Rainbow
    Did come where he did lye;
"Where is the captain of that ship?"
    The Rainbow she did cry.

---

* "Your king."—*Halliwell.*   † "Roves."—*Ib.*   ‡ "Bear."—*Ib.*

"O ! that I am," said Captain Ward,
    "There's no man bids me lie,
And if thou art the king's fair ship,
    Thou art welcome unto me."

"I'll tell you what," said the Rainbow,
    "Our king is in great grief,
That thou shouldst lie upon the seas,
    And play the arrant thief.

"You will not let our merchantmen*
    Pass as they did before ;
Such tidings to our king is come,
    Which grieves his heart full sore."

With that the gallant Rainbow
    She shot, out of her pride,
Full fifty gallant† brass pieces,
    Charged on every side.

And yet these gallant shooters
    Prevailed not a pin ;
Though they were brass on the outside,
    Brave Ward was steel within.

"Shoot on, shoot on," said Captain Ward,
    "Your sport well pleaseth me,
And he that first gives over,
    Shall yield unto the sea.

"I never wronged an English ship,
    But Turk and King of Spain,
Likewise the blackguard‡ Dutchman,
    Which I met on the main.

---

* "And will not let our merchants' ships."—*Halliwell.*
† "Good."—*Pitt.*   ‡ "Jovial."—*Halliwell.*

" If I had known your king
　　But two or three days before,*
I would have saved Lord Essex' life,
　　Whose death does grieve me sore.

" Go tell the King of England,
　　Go tell him this from me,
If he reigns king of all the land,
　　I will reign king at sea."

With that the gallant Rainbow shot,
　　And shot and shot in vain,
Then left the rover's company,
　　And home returned again.

" Oh! Royal King of England,
　　Your ship's returned again ;
For Captain Ward he is so strong,†
　　He never will be ta'en."

" Oh, everlasting!" said the king,
　　" I have lost jewels three,
Which would have gone unto the seas,
　　And brought proud Ward to me.

" The first was Lord de Clifford,
　　Great Earl of Cumberland,
The second was the Lord Mountjoy,
　　As you may understand.

" The third was brave Lord Essex,
　　From foe‡ would never flee,
Who would have gone unto the seas,
　　And brought proud Ward to me."

---

* " But one two years before."—*Halliwell.*
† " For Ward's ship is so strong,
　　　It never," &c.—*Ib.*　　　　　　‡ Field."—*Halliwell and Pitt.*

THE TURKISH LADY.

THE copy from which this has been transcribed was printed as one of
"Four Excellent New Songs: 1. The Turkish Lady; 2. Get Married
Betimes; 3. The Lady in the Wood; 4. The Female Press-gang.
Entered according to order, 1782."

"The Turkish Lady" does not appear to have been printed in any
other collection. Its date is conjectured to be about the middle of the
seventeenth century. The main incident of the story occurs in several other
ballads. In Deloney's "Garland of Goodwill" (edition 1678), there is
"The Spanish Lady's Love to an Englishman," which has frequently
been reprinted, and which formed the subject of a musical entertainment
by Thomas Hull, produced at Covent Garden Theatre in 1765.
"This beautiful old ballad," says Percy, "most probably took its rise
from one of those descents made on the Spanish coast in the time of
Elizabeth," and in all likelihood during the investment of Cadiz by the
Earl of Essex. It has apparently been "founded on fact," but who the
gallant was has been a matter of doubt. That question has been discussed in Percy's Reliques, vol. i., part 2; in Rimbault's Musical Illustrations of Percy's Reliques; and in Omerod's Cheshire, vol. iii. p. 333.
See also Notes and Queries, vol. ix. p. 305-573, and vol. x. p. 273.
"The Spanish Lady," and the man she "wooed," are just in the reverse
position of the "Turkish Lady" and her love, inasmuch as the "Spanish
Lady" had, with others of her sex, become captives to the English, and
the Englishman in question was her jailor :

"Garments gay and rich as may be,
　　Decked with jewels had she on.
Of a comely countenance and grace was she,
　　And by birth and parentage of high degree."

An order comes to release the lady prisoners, "with their jewels still
adornèd, none to do them injury." Our heroine, however, is loath to go :

"O! gallant captain, show some pity,
　　To a lady in distress;
Leave me not within this city,
　　For to die of heaviness:
Thou hast set this present day my body free,
But my heart in prison strong remains with thee."

The Englishman, although he was well aware that

"In his courteous company was all her joy,
　　To favour him in anything she was not coy,"

questions the sincerity of her love by reason of his being her country's foe. This she overrules. He tells her to "weep no more," as there are plenty of "fair lovers" in Spain. To this she replies:

> "Spaniards fraught with jealousie we often find;
> But Englishmen throughout the world are counted kind."

She implores him not to leave her to a Spaniard, "for you alone enjoy my heart." He says that English soldiers cannot "without offence" carry ladies about with them. She then offers to accompany him as his page. He declines that proposition on the score of economy:

> "I have neither gold nor silver,
> To maintain thee in this ease,
> And to travel is great charges,
> As you know, in every place."

Her answer is,

> "My chains and jewels, every one shall be thine own;
> And eke ten thousand pounds in gold, that lies unknown."

To this he pictures the many storms and dangers of the seas. She replies:
> "Well in troth, I could endure extremity;
> For I could find in heart to lose my life for thee."

All the lady's deep devotion, proposals of self-sacrifice, offer of gold and jewels prove of no avail; for the Englishman has forcible reasons for refusing her request, and he sees that the only course left for him is to disclose them:
> "Courteous lady, be contented;
> Here comes all that breeds the strife:
> I, in England, have already
> A sweet woman to my wife."

Thus baffled, the lady signifies it to be her intention to retire to a nunnery, to spend her days in prayer, and "to defie love and all her laws," courteously adding:

> "Commend me to thy loving lady;
> Bear to her this chain of gold,
> And these bracelets for a token;
> Grieving that I was so bold:
> All my jewels, in like sort, bear thou with thee;
> For these are fitting for thy wife, and not for me."

The tune of "The Spanish Lady" is to be found in the "Quaker's Opera," 1728—in the "Jovial Crew," 1731, &c.

There is an old ballad, of which there are many different versions, and which has from time to time appeared under different titles, more closely resembling "The Turkish Lady." In the argument, all the versions agree that a lord or squire "of high degree" went to Turkey to observe the manners and customs of the natives. That not conforming with their forms of worship, he was made to "draw carts and wains." He was then cast into a dungeon, and chained to a tree which grew in the middle of this prison. The Moor who had condemned him had a daughter, who, in her walks, in passing the prison, had heard him lamenting his fate. She bribed the jailor with gold and "white monie" to admit her to see the prisoner, whose liberation she effected, and gave him money to carry him to "his ain countrie." Before he went,

> "She took him frae her father's prison,
> And gied to him the best o' wine."
>   [Albeit the old gentleman was a Mahometan.]

At the same time expressing a fervent wish, while pledging his health, that "ye were mine!" She proceeded to propose that, if he would not wed with any other woman within seven years, she would wait for him. Ere the ship sailed, he, bowing low and reverentially, said:

> "Ere seven long years come to an end,
> I'll take ye to mine ain countrie!"

Time goes on, and the lady, who "could get no rest; nor day nor nicht could happy be," proceeds to this country, and immediately on her arrival ascertains the fact that the man she loved was formally betrothed to another that very day. She gains admittance to his house or castle, sends a message to him by the porter, which causes him to rise with such impetuosity, that he "made the table flee." The mother of the bride, when informed who his mysterious visitor is, implores him not to forsake her "ae dochter." To this he replies:

> "Tak hame, tak hame your dochter, madam,
> For she is ne'er the waur o' me;
> She cam to me on horseback riding,
> And she shall gang back in her coach and three."

The result is, that there being no courts in those days for hearing actions for breach of promise, where alleged wounded feelings are nicely weighed against gold, matters were satisfactorily arranged for all parties. The bride, who all the while had loved somebody else, got the man of her

heart, and the squire "of high degree" entered seriously into the bonds
of holy matrimony with the foreign lady, who had taken care to bring
over with her a handsome dowry. All and each lived happily in their respective spheres for many a long day afterwards, and had large families.
In addition to the broadsides, which characterize this ballad as "Lord
Bateman," Jamieson, in his "Popular Ballads and Songs from traditions,
manuscripts, and scarce editions," Edin. 1806, 8vo, vol. i., p. 117 and 127,
has two versions, one titled, "Young Beichan and Susie Pye," the other,
"Young Bekie," in which the heroine is called "Burd Isbel." Kinloch, in
his "Ancient Scottish Ballads, recovered from tradition, and never before
published," London, 1827, 8vo, has another version bearing the title of
"Lord Beichan and Susie Pye," and Mr. J. H. Dixon communicated
in 1842 to Richardson's Historians' Table Book, "Lord Beichan, a
Border Ballad." This last, Mr. Dixon reprinted in "Ancient Poems,
Ballads, and Songs of the Peasantry of England," which he edited for
the Percy Society in 1845. Among these he included "Lord Bateman." He had printed another version, which is called "Young Bondwell," in "Scotish Traditional Versions of Ancient Ballads," which he
had edited the preceding year for the same Society from a manuscript
of Mr. Peter Buchan of Peterhead. In this the name of the "foreign
land," where young Bondwell was "cast in prison strong," is not par-
ticularized. It is merely designated as "that countrie." On his return
from slavery his residence is "in the bonny towers o' Linne," wherever
that may be, the lady who follows him with "a maiden in every
hand," bears the name of "Dame Lessels," and she obtains her information as to the "weddin" from "a bonny little boy," who was water-
ing his horses at "the Water o' Tay." Mr. Dixon believes the original
locale of the ballad to be Northumberland. In Mr. Kinloch's ballad,
Lord Beichan returns to "Glasgow town." The name of the heroine
of the "Lord Beichan" in Dixon's Ancient Poems, above referred to, is
Saphia.

Mr. Dixon in the same collection next proceeds to print "Lord Bateman," prefacing it by these remarks : "This is a ludicrously corrupt
abridgement of the preceding ballad, being the same version which was
published a few years ago by Tilt, London, and also, according to the
title page, by Mustapha Syried, Constantinople, under the title of 'the
Loving Ballad of Lord Bateman.' It is, however, the only ancient
form in which the ballad has existed in print, and is one of the publications mentioned in Thackeray's Catalogues, preserved in the British
Museum." "Thackeray's imprint is found attached to broadsides published between 1672 and 1678." How Mr. Dixon arrives at the conclusion that this is an abridgement at all (setting aside his phrase, "ludicrously corrupt") is not very clear. His traditional "Lord Beichan,"
which did not appear in print until 1842, is by his own acknowledgment
"formed from a collation of *several* broadsheets, with the two ballads in

Jamieson's Book," none of which claim to date so far back as this abridgment. The heroine in this "Lord Bateman" is called "Sophia," which has been conjectured to have been suggested by the Mosque of Santa Sophia at Constantinople. On referring to a stall copy of this same version (circa 1817), which, by the way, is titled "Lord Bechin," the lady's name is there given as Susy Pye. All these differences of locality and name only indicate the local feelings of the *pro tempore* reciter.

We have several chap copies of the romance before us, all varying in the text. One is entitled, "Susan Py; or, Young Bichen's Garland Shewing how he went to a far country, and was taken by a savage Moor, and cast into prison, and delivered by the Moor's daughter, on promise of marriage; and how he came to England, and was going to be wedded to another bride; with the happy arrival of Susan Pye on the wedding day. Falkirk, printed by T. Johnstone, 1815." Another is called "An excellent Song, entitled Young Beighan and Susie Pye," of apparently the same date. And a third is simply called "Lord Bechin." The ballad called "Bateman's Tragedy" bears no affinity to "Lord Bateman." The full title of the old copy is enough to shew this. It runs thus:—"A Godly Warning to all Maidens by the example of God's Judgment shewed on Jerman's Wife of Clifton, in the county of Nottingham, who, lying in child-bed, was borne away, and never heard of after." The tragedy called "The Vow-breaker," by William Sampson, 1636, is founded on this. See Ritson's "English Songs. London, 1783," vol. ii.

Mr. Jamieson, with the utmost simplicity, conceives that the name of the hero was "Buchan," while Mr. Dixon boldly asserts, that the ballad, being a romance of Northumberland, his name, according to tradition (a tradition of yesterday) was Bertram or Bartram, to which family at one time "half of Northumberland belonged." He goes on in his Notes to his Scotish ballads in sober earnest to say: "To one unacquainted with the peculiarity of Northumbrian accent, it may seem strange how such a word as 'Bartram' could get corrupted to 'Bateman.' In the word 'Bartram' the letter *r* occurs twice, a letter which the Northumbrian peasantry have great difficulty to pronounce in common conversation, but which they have still greater difficulty to articulate when singing. Ask a Northumbrian peasant to pronounce 'Bartram,' and he will say 'Bwaatam.' The Editor speaks from experience." These observations are worthy of the earlier commentators on Shakespeare. As a counterpart, some have as gravely asserted that the ballad depicts an episode in the life of the father of Thomas à-Beckett, the title "Bekie" leading them, without much "stretch of labouring thought," to this conclusion. We have heard in Scotland a version of this same ballad, wherein the hero has been called "Lord Bangol." We are content to accept him under any name, as the story in which he figures is a good one, and under the firm conviction that his real name has not as yet been revealed to his posterity.   After all it is not a matter of much moment.   Mr. George Cruickshank has, in his usual clever style, illustrated the common version of Lord Bateman, and there was a burlesque drama on the subject, played successfully at the Strand theatre upwards of twenty years ago, in which were introduced *Tableaux Vivans*, embodying Cruickshanks' illustrations.   The ballad—"Lord Bateman" —has been recently revived by Mr. Sothern (Lord Dundreary), and partially sung by him in a sensation drama, played at the Haymarket, called "The Wild Goose."

The Turkish Lady.

Young virgins all I pray draw near,
A pretty story you shall hear ;
It's of a Turkish lady brave,
Who fell in love with an English slave.

A merchant ship at Bristol lay.
As we were sailing over the sea ;
By a Turkish rover took were we,
And all of us made slaves to be.

They bound us down in irons strong,
They whipped and slashed us all along;
No tongue can tell I'm certain sure,
What we poor sailors do endure.

[One of the seamen that were there,
An Englishman both fresh and fair,
Comely in stature, straight, and tall,
He went to Turkey amongst them all.]*

Come sit ye down, and listen a while,
And see how fortune on him did smile.
It was his fortune for to be
A slave unto a rich lady;

* This stanza is from a subsequent edition of the ballad.

She drest herself in rich array,
And went to view her slaves one day;
Hearing the moan this young man made,
She went to him and thus she said:—

" What countryman, young man, are you?"
" I am an Englishman, that's true."
" I wish you was a Turk," said she,
" I'd ease you of your misery.

" I'd ease you of your slavish work,
If you'll consent to turn a Turk.
I'd own myself to be your wife,
For I do love you as my life."

"O no, no no, no no," said he,
" Your constant slave I choose to be.
I'd sooner be burnt there at a stake,
Before that I'll my God forsake."

This lady to her chamber went,
And spent that night in discontent;
Sly Cupid with his piercing dart,
Did deeply wound this lady's heart.

She was resolvèd the next day,
To ease him of his slavery,
And own herself to be his wife,
For she did love him as her life.

She drest herself in rich array,
And with this young man sailed away,
Until they came to Bristol shore,
With jewels, diamonds, and gold great store.

Houses and lands she left behind,
And all her slaves are close confined;

B

Unto her parents she bade adieu,
By this you see what love can do.

Now she is turned a Christian brave,
And married is to her own slave,
That was in chains and bondage too,
By this you see what love can do.

THE EARL OF ESSEX.

THIS ballad, which we do not find in any other collection, is from a
broadside of some fifty years' existence. That it is of much older date in
itself seems evident. The subject carries us back to the times of Elizabeth
and of James the First, although the details are by no means historically
accurate. The spouse of the Earl of Essex was Frances, daughter of Sir
Francis Walsingham, and widow of Sir Philip Sidney. The Earl was
beheaded on the 25th February, 1601. The Countess was two years a
widow, and it is possible that during that time some "noble knight" may
have been paying court to her. But assuredly she did not again commit
matrimony until "she found," according to Devereux' Lives and Letters
of the Earls of Essex (before referred to), "a third husband in the person
of that Richard de Burgh, Earl of Clanrickarde, who was said to bear
some resemblance to her late husband. This marriage took place about
the time of the Queen's death." The Earl is no doubt the Irish lord
mentioned in the ballad, who "looked much like the Earl of Essex,"—
an accidental circumstance, which formed a feasible apology to the
general public (if any were required) for the Countess marrying for the
third time, but which failed to convince those "that wished her well."
The ballad states that she subsequently came to England, her "own two
sons to see." It is questionable whether the poet is not again at variance
with fact. As Countess of Essex, she had three sons and two daughters.
The two younger sons died young. The daughters were both married,
and ultimately became co-heiresses to their brother. The Earl of Clanrickarde was, in 4 Charles I., created Earl of St. Albans. He died in
1636. His son was, 21 Charles I., created Marquis of Clanrickarde,
which title, as well as that of St. Albans, became extinct on his death.
The former was subsequently revived.

In connection with the present subject, the following ballad may not
be an inappropriate introduction here. It is from "Reliquiæ Hearnianæ,"

vol. i., Oxon 1857, 8vo., and forms an entry in Hearne's Diary, on 13th March, 1707-8, but of course it is of much older date.

A NEW BALLAD.

(*To the tune of* "Chevy Chase.")

When good Queen Bess did rule this land,
    A lady of great fame;
There lived a man of great command,
    And Essex was his name.

This Essex did some wondrous things:
    By sea and land he fought;
He serv'd the French, drubb'd Spanish kings;
    But did not this for nought.

Places and pensions, grants good store,
    The queen did give unto him;
The more he had, he crav'd the more,
    Which did at last undo him.

This Earl grew proud, and not content
    With his too happy case;
His power made him insolent,
    Which did the queen amaze.

The general thought, 'twixt hopes and fears,
    High words would gain upon her!
The queen took courage, box't his ears,
    And bid him learn more manners.

He puff'd and blow'd, complain'd of fate,
    And his hard usage too;
Swore she should move some min'sters of state,
    But that she would not doe.

He treason hatch'd, and often spread;
    When, to prevent this evil,
The queen, enrag'd, lopt off his head,
    And then he was more civil.*

* Others read it:
        "And then he went to the devil."

Thus reign'd Queen Bess; thus, blest by God,
  Her subjects' hearts she won;
She bid her gen'rals talk big abroad,
  But here she'd rule alone.

The death of the Earl of Essex was a grievous blow to the Queen, and she many a time and oft repented of having signed his death warrant. When Sir John Harrington, Elizabeth's godson, came to Court in October 1601, he remarked that "the Queen was reduced to a skeleton; altered in her features; her taste for dress gone. Nothing pleased her; she stamped and swore violently at the ladies of the court, whom she tormented beyond measure." A letter to a Scotch nobleman from his correspondent in England, 1602, preserved in the Advocates' Library at Edinburgh says: "Our Queen is troubled with a rheum in her arm, which vexeth her very much, besides the grief which she hath conceived for the death of my Lord of Essex. She sleepeth not so much by day as she used, neither taketh rest by night. Her delight is to sit in the dark, and sometimes with shedding tears to bewail Essex."

The Earl of Essex.

THE very first time that married I was,
  It was to a noble lord ;
The Earl of Essex was his name,
  And his fame it was spread abroad.

For he was the Earl of three counties,
  And he made me the lady of all ;
And for one small fault to the queen he paid
  With his life which she could not recal.

The very next time that married I was,
  It was to a noble Knight ;
Sir John Littleton was his name.
  And he's gone to the wars to fight,

In France or in Flanders he lost his life,
  He was shot with bullets three.

Was there ever a lady in all the land,
    That had two nobler men then me?

I could not enjoy my widow's estate,
    Alas! and well-a-day ;
Until there came an Irish Lord,
    And he came a courting to me.

For he looked much like the Earl of Essex,
    In person, birth, and fame.
Soon I forsook my own native land,
    And to Ireland with him I came.

I had not been in Ireland a month,
    A month but scarcely three ;
Till there was I and my Irish Lord,
    We could never agree .

He called me a saucy English jade,
    And his words I could never abide ;
He told me he was as good a Lord,
    As ever lay by my side.

" O hold your tongue, dear lord," said I,
    And leave the dead alone.
" O hold your tongue, dear lord," said I,
    " For they're in the silent tomb.

" If the Earl of Essex were yet alive,
    In the field for to fight 'gainst thee,
He would scorn, I'm sure, to turn his back,
    Against nobler lords than thee."

Then to England soon I came,
    My own two sons to see ;
They asked me whether my Irish lord,
    And I did well agree.

" O cursed be the hour," I said,
" I saw him the eyes between.
And the very first time that married I was,
I wish that dead I'd been."

THE LOWLANDS OF HOLLAND.

ALTHOUGH "the Lowlands of Holland" as here given is of modern date, it may be fair to conjecture that its original source emanated from some incident connected with the Earl of Leicester's investment of the " Low Countries," or the wars of the Palatinate during the time of James the First, and the subsequent progresses there of people from England and Scotland. Whether the ballad is of English or Scotch construction is very uncertain. The Scotch, however, seem to have laid claim to it.

Another version of this song, said to be older, occurs in Herd's "Ancient and Modern Scottish Songs, Heroic Ballads," &c. Edin. 1776, 12mo. vol. ii., p. 2. It is of four stanzas, partly in Scotch. The locale of the lady is Galloway. She does not appear to have been married as in the present ballad. In Stenhouse's "Illustrations of the Lyric Poetry and Music of Scotland," Edin. 1853, 8vo, in a note respecting the music of the song "I love my Jean," he remarks:—"This air was partly composed by Mr. William Marshall, butler to the Duke of Gordon, by adding a second strain to the old air, called ' The Lowlands of Holland has twin'd my love and me,' and was by him named ' Miss Admiral Gordon's Strathspey.' Burns in the Reliques, speaking of the song "I love my Jean," which commences:—" Of a' the airts the wind can blaw," says, "I composed it out of compliment to Mrs. Burns. N.B.—It was during our honeymoon." Thus we gather that the air of "the Lowlands of Holland" was the first · strain of Burns' popular song, " Of a' the airts."

Herd's version is reprinted in Aytoun's "Ballads of Scotland." Edin., 12mo, 2 vols., 1858. A more lengthened version of the same ballad in the Scotch dialect, will be found in book 1st of "a Selection of Scots Songs. Harmonized, improved with simple and adapted graces. By Peter Urbani, Professor of Music." Edin., circa 1794. The air, which is in the key of F, is given in score, and is composed of both the first and second strains. The first strain is as nearly as possible that of M'Leod's "Oh ! why left I my hame?" The second strain is identical with the relative strain of " Of a' the airts."

Another and hitherto unknown version, extracted from a Scotch Newspaper of October 1859, is worth reprinting here, as being possessed of merit and differing very materially from all the other ballads of the same name. It is evidently of more recent date than any of the others now before us.

The contributor (J. B. G.), while observing that he is not competent to
judge "whether it deserves to be considered a genuine old fragment,"
remarks: "One thing is certain; whether ancient or not, it is by
no means a Scotish ballad, but seems to belong to the other side of
the border. An old female relative of mine, now deceased, used to
chaunt it to me long ago, and it is here given from memory, which may
account for a certain appearance of incompleteness, some verses perhaps
having escaped my recollection."

The Lowlands of Holland.
RECENT VERSION.

First when I was married and laid in marriage bed,
There came a young sea captain, and stood at my bed head;
Saying, " Rise up ! young Riley, and go along with me
To the Lowlands of Holland to fight and never flee."

" 'Tis but a day and half a night since I have wedded been,
How shall I go along with you and this my bridal e'en ?
How can I leave my bonny bride a hagbut-man to be
On the Lowlands of Holland to fight and never flee ?"

" The maids of Germanie are kind and lavish of their love ;
Their lips are like the rose in May ; their eyes are of the
    dove ;
And well they love young Englishmen who roam along with me,
On the Lowlands of Holland to fight and never flee."

" Oh tell me not of other maids, and this my bridal night ;
'Twould break my heart to leave my love, my joy, my soul's
    delight ;
Then kind and courteous captain, take some single man with
    thee,
On the Lowlands of Holland to fight and never flee."

" My ship is in the harbour, with her anchor at the prow,
And down the Humber comes the gale, I hear it piping now.
I may not go for other men to sail along with me,
On the Lowlands of Holland to fight and never flee."

Then up and spake the bonny bride, in the bed where that
    she lay;
"Oh kind and courteous captain, do not press my love away;
Five hundred crowns to thee I'll give in gold and white monie,
From the wearie wars in Holland to set my husband free."

" It may not be, it cannot be," the cruel captain said;
"Were I to take a bribe from thee, 'tis I would lose my head;
Our King must have brave warriors to send beyond the sea,
On the Lowlands of Holland to fight and never flee."

Then up and spake the bride's brother, "I have nor kith
    nor kin,
Save yonder new made wife that liggs her bridal bed within;
Then I will go along with you, sith better may not be,
On the Lowlands of Holland to fight and never flee."

" It may not be, it cannot be," the cruel captain cried;
"Full long I wooed sweet Marjorie, who still my suit denied;
I swore that she should rue the day she gave the scorn to me,
When the wearie wars in Holland took her lover o'er the sea."

"Now draw thy sword, thou coward loon, and dearly thou
    shalt rue."
" Upon them, lads!" the Captain cried, "and bind the
    gallants two;
The play is played; our bonny bark shall bear them o'er the sea,
On the Lowlands of Holland to fight and never flee."

BROADSIDE VERSION.

The night that I was married and laid in my marriage bed,
There came a bold sea captain and stood at my bed head;
Saying, " Arouse, arouse you, married man, and come along
    with me
To the lowlands of Holland to face your enemy."

For Holland is a pretty place for nobles to dwell in,
There is no place of harbour for seamen to remain ;
The sugar cane is plenty and the tea grows on its trees,
And the Lowlands of Holland's between my love and me.

I'll build my love a gallant ship a ship with noble sails,
Twenty-four bold mariners to roll her on the main ;
Come all you ranting roving heroes! come now, boys, pull
    away!
I wish I was with my true love although he's far away.

One evening as I walked down by a river side,
There came a bold sea captain and asked me to be his bride ;
" Your bride, your bride, young man," she says, " your bride
    I cannot be,
I had in the world but one true love and pressed he was
    from me.

" No scarf shall go o'er my shoulder nor comb go in my hair,
Neither moonlight nor candlelight shall view my beauty fair ;
Nor no man will I marry until the day I die,
Since the raging seas and stormy winds have parted my love
    and me."

Says the mother to the daughter, " why do you thus lament ?
Is there not men enough in this world to please your discon-
    tent,"
"There's not a man in all this world this night shall serve for me,
May woe attend the captain that pressed my love away."

ADMIRAL LOCKHART.

THE hero of this ballad was born on 11th Nov., 1721. At fourteen
years of age he entered the Navy. Having distinguished himself as first
Lieutenant to Sir Peter Warren and Lord Anson, he obtained in
1747 the command of the Vulcan fire-ship. In 1755, on the appearance of a rupture with France, Captain Lockhart was appointed to

the Savage sloop of war; and in March of the year following to the Tartar frigate. The bold actions he performed with this little ship were proverbial in the Navy for upwards of half-a-century, but are now, like all other meritorious services, unremembered. In Nov. 1758 he was transferred to the Chatham of fifty guns, under the orders of Admiral Hawke; he commanded the Shrewsbury of seventy-four guns in the action between the British and French fleets, in July 1778, which led to his promotion in 1779 to the rank of Rear-Admiral of the Blue; and having hoisted his flag on board the Royal George, sailed under the orders of Admiral Rodney, whose fleet fell in with eleven Spanish ships of the line. An engagement ensued, in which one vessel was blown up, and the Spanish Admiral, with other six of his ships, were captured. Admiral Lockhart afterwards superintended, under a tremendous fire, the landing of the stores for the relief of Gibraltar. In April 1782, he was appointed to the command of a squadron in the North Seas. Declining health compelled him to return to England; and the subsequent conclusion of hostilities rendered his re-appointment unnecessary.

In 1768 he became member of parliament for the boroughs of Selkirk, Peebles, Lanark, and Linlithgow, and also for the county of Lanark. He made his election for the county, and a new writ was ordered for the boroughs, 29th Nov., 1768. In 1780 he succeeded to a Baronetcy by the death of his elder brother, from whom he also inherited the estate of Carstairs, having previously succeeded to the estate of Balnagowan on the decease of General Ross, in consequence of which he had added the surname of Ross to that of Lockhart.

Sir John Lockhart Ross died on 9th June, 1790:—that event, however, is noted in the European Magazine to have occurred on 14th June, 1790.

A portrait of "Brave Admiral Lockhart," while commander of his Majesty's ship Tartar, in 1757, will be found in Hervey's Naval History.

ON THE BRAVE ADMIRAL LOCKART,

WHO COMMANDED THE "TARTAR" LAST WAR.

Tune—"Hearts of Oak."

YE sons of old Ocean, who're strangers to fear,
On board of the Shrewsbury quickly repair;

Brave Lockart commands her, rejoice every tar!
For Lockart commanded the Tartar last war.
    Hearts of oak are our ships, jolly tars are our men ;
        We always are ready,
        Steady, boys, steady ;
    We 'll fight and we 'll conquer again and again.

His conduct and valour we all must confess,
And Britains exult in the hopes of success ;
The ensigns of Louis great Lockart shall mar,
For Lockart, we know, was a Tartar last war.
    Hearts of oak, &c.

May kindness and friendship each bosom refine,
Nor civil dissension defeat our design :
The dread name of Drake makes the French quake with fear,
Joined with Lockart, who fought in the Tartar last war.
    Hearts of oak, &c.

Steel your breasts with revenge ere the battle 's begun!
We 'll trim the *soup-maigres*, tho' fifteen to one ;
Then shall the Carnatics, rich fraught from afar,
Each hero reward for the troubles of war.
    Hearts of oak, &c.

Haste, haste, all on board ! see the wind now is fair ;
Hoist the flag of Britannia aloft in the air ;
May the spirit of Lockart inspire ev'ry tar,—
Great Lockart, who fought in the Tartar last war.
    Hearts of oak are our ships, jolly tars are our men ;
        We always are ready,
        Steady, boys, steady ;
    We 'll fight and we 'll conquer again and again.

THE DISAPPOINTED SAILOR.

THE mention of Carthagena in this ballad naturally leads us to the period of Admiral Vernon's expedition "to destroy the Spanish settlements in the West Indies," which he had boasted in Parliament he could easily do. This was in 1739. Porto Bello having, after a fierce conflict, capitulated to Vernon, he proceeded against Carthagena early in the following year, and began to bombard the town ; but the force being totally inadequate to the reduction of so strong a place, he returned to Porto Bello. Reinforcements having arrived in January 1741, he was enabled to number under his command thirty-one sail of the line, while the land forces, under the command of Lord Cathcart, amounted to upwards of ten thousand men. Lord Cathcart having died soon after his arrival in the West Indies, the command of the troops devolved upon General Wentworth. They proceeded against Carthagena, but the two commanders having differed most decidedly respecting the mode of attack, the enterprise was a failure, and they were compelled to retire to Jamaica with great loss. It was then resolved to attack Cuba ; and they were so far successful, that the port of Walthenham was taken,—but there their success and conquest terminated. An expedition against Panama was next determined on ; but in this third enterprise the admiral was again subjected to disappointment and repulse. He all along had insisted that if the sole command had been placed in his hands, success was certain. He continued on the Jamaica station till the middle of October 1742, when both he and the general were recalled home. Intelligence of the reduction of Porto Bello had been received with much rejoicing in England, and at once had rendered Admiral Vernon so popular, that he was chosen member for Portsmouth ; and in the New Parliament in May 1741, he was elected for no fewer than three places, Ipswich, Rochester, and Penryn. He was also proposed for Westminster, and polled 3,290 votes, which was not very far short of the successful candidates, Sir Charles Wager and Lord Sundon. When he took his seat in the house, he made his election for Ipswich.

Admiral Vernon is said to have been the first naval commander who mixed water with the spirits allowed to the seamen, and to have given to this mixture the name of "grog." He died rather suddenly at his seat at Nacton, in Suffolk, on the 30th Oct. 1757. An account of the expedition against Carthagena will be found in Smollett's "Roderick Random."

The heroine of the following ballad had evidently anticipated the failure of the expedition, otherwise she would not have provided herself with a helpmate during Jack's absence. The idea of no prize-money being forthcoming had no doubt instigated her to break her word in favour of the more ready money.

The Disappointed Sailor.

EARLY one morning in the spring,
I went board ship to serve the king,
Leaving my dearest dear behind,
Who swore to me her heart inclined.

Oft did I fold her in my arms;
I doated on her thousand charms;
Our troth we plight, 'mid kisses sweet,
And vow we 'll wed when next we meet.

While I was sailing on the sea,
I found an opportunity
To forward letters to my dear,
But, oh! from her I ne'er did hear.

When before Carthagena town,
Where cannon balls flew up and down,
While in the midst of dangers there,
My thoughts dwelt always on my dear.

And when arrived on Britain's shore,
I hastened where I did adore,
Her father said, " What do you mean?
D'ye really love my daughter, Jean?"

Surprised, he made me this reply—
" My daughter does your love deny;
She 's married now, sir, for her life;
So, young man, seek another wife."

I cursed the gold, and silver, too,
And all false women that prove untrue,
Who first make vows, then such vows break,
And all for cursed riches' sake.

I would rather be on yonder shore,
Where thundering cannon loudly roar,—
I would rather be where bullets fly,
Than in false woman's company.

So I'll bid adieu to all womankind;
I'll sail the ocean round and round—
I'll sail the sea until I die,
Although the waves run mountains high.

Now from a window-lattice high,
The lady she made this reply—
"I pray, let reason take its place,
Before you do our sex disgrace.

"Do hold your tongue, you cruel man,
For of your letters I ne'er got one!
If the fault be great, love, 'tis none of mine,
So don't speak so harshly of womankind."

CAPTAIN DEATH.

Perhaps history does not afford a more remarkable instance of desperate courage than that shewn by the officers and crew of an English Privateer called "The Terrible," of 26 guns and 200 men, under the command of Captain Death. On the 23d December 1757, he engaged and made prize of a large French ship, the Grand Alexander, from St. Maloes, after an obstinate battle, in which his brother and sixteen seamen were killed. He directed his course for England with his prize and forty men; but in a few days fell in, off St. Domingo, with the Vengeance, a Privateer of 36 guns and 360 men, the Commander of which ordered an attack on the prize, which was easily retaken. The two ships then bore down upon the Terrible, the mainmast of which was shot away by the first broadside. Notwithstanding this disaster, the Terrible maintained such a furious engagement against both, as can hardly be paralleled in the annals of the British Navy. The French Commander (Mons. Bourdas) and his second Lieutenant were killed, with two-thirds of the existing crew ; but the gallant Captain Death, with the greater part of his officers and nearly his entire crew, having met with the same fate, his ship was boarded by the enemy, who found no more than twenty-six persons alive, sixteen of whom were mutilated by the loss of a leg or an arm, and the other ten grievously wounded. The ship itself lay a wreck upon the water, and presented a scene of horror and desolation. The victorious vessel was so shattered that it was scarcely able to tow the Terrible into St. Maloes.

This adventure was no sooner known in England than a subscription was raised for the support of Death's widow and the surviving portion of the crew.

There was a strange combination of names in connection with this privateer, the Terrible. It was equipped at Execution Dock, commanded by Captain Death. The appellation of his Lieutenant was Devil, and the surgeon's name was Ghost. Ritson, in the second volume of "a Select Collection of English Songs," in three volumes, Lond. 1783, in a footnote to a version of Captain Death, observes, that "this strange circumstance, mentioned by some writers, seems entirely void of founda-tion," but he gives no authority for contradicting the received impression. He states that the ballad was "written, as 'tis said, by one of the sur-viving crew." There are some slight differences between his version and the present. We also find a copy in "Early Naval Ballads," con-tributed to the Percy Society by J. O. Halliwell, in which there are some variations, evidently modern.

Captain Death.

THE muse with the hero's brave deeds being fired,—
For similar views had their bosoms inspired ;—
For freedom they fought and for glory contend.
The muse o'er the hero still mourns as a friend ;
Then oh! let the muse this poor tribute bequeath
To a true British hero, the brave Captain Death.

His ship was the Terrible, dreadful to see,
Each man was as gallantly brave as was he ;
Two hundred and more were his good complement,
But sure braver fellows to sea never went :
Each man had determined to spend his last breath
In fighting for Britain and brave Captain Death.

A prize they had taken diminished their force,
But soon this good prize was lost on her course ;
When the French man-of-war and the Terrible met,
A battle began with all horror beset.
No man was dismayed,—each as bold as Macbeth ;—
In fighting for Britain and brave Captain Death.

Grenades, fire, and bullets were soon heard and felt,
A fight that the heart of Bellona would melt,
The rigging all torn, the decks filled with blood,
And scores of dead bodies were thrown in the flood ;—
The flood, from the time of old Noah and Seth,
Ne'er bore the fellow of brave Captain Death.

But at length the dread bullet came wingèd with fate,
Our brave Captain dropt, and soon after his mate ;
Each officer fell, and a carnage was seen,
That soon dyed the waves to crimson from green,
Then Neptune arose and pulled off his wreath,
Instructing a Triton to crown Captain Death.

Thus fell the strong Terrible, dreadfully bold,
But sixteen survivors the tale could unfold.
The French proved the victors, though much to their cost,
For many stout French were with Englishmen lost.
And thus said old Time, " since good Queen 'Lizabeth
We ne'er saw the fellow of bold Captain Death."

PAUL JONES.

PAUL JONES, the terror of our coasts, was born near Kirkcudbright
in 1747. His real name was John Paul. His father was head gar-
dener to Lord Selkirk, and he was for a while one of the under gar-
deners. Having been dismissed Lord Selkirk's service, he went to sea.

Ere long he was appointed mate, and after several voyages to the West
Indies, became master of a vessel. When the rupture between Great
Britain and America took place, he being at Piscataway in New England, enlisted under the Revolutionary flag, assuming the name of Paul
Jones. His daring disposition and his knowledge of the British coasts,
pointed him out as a fit leader in the marauding schemes then in agitation. Towards the termination of 1777 he was actively employed, as
Commander, in fitting out the Ranger privateer, mounting eighteen guns,
and manned with a crew of one hundred and fifty men. In the course of
the winter he made two captures on the European side of the Atlantic,
both of which prizes he sent into a French port. In the month of April
following, he made his first appearance in his new capacity in the neighbourhood of his native place, and proceeded to put in execution a plan
for burning and destroying the town and shipping of Whitehaven during
the night; which was frustrated by one of the crew deserting, and arous-
ing the sleeping inhabitants. The alarm soon spread, the people mus-
tered in numbers just in time to assist in saving several of the ships from
fire. Jones then made the best of his way across the Solway Frith, and
by the dawn of morning entered the river Dee, which forms the harbour
of Kirkcudbright. At a short distance from St. Mary's Isle, on which
stands the castle of Lord Selkirk, he dropped anchor. The Earl happened to be in London at the time, of which Paul Jones being informed,
he was preparing to depart again, his object having been to capture the
Earl and retain him as a hostage; but his men had set out with a different view—to retaliate on this country for the wrongs inflicted on America
by the English. A boat was sent ashore, and a body of armed men
landed and marched to the castle, which they surrounded. Lady Selkirk, who was, with her children, alone resident, was summoned before
the two officers commanding the party, and in the politest manner requested to yield up all her silver plate, with which they departed. This
family plate Paul Jones, some years afterwards, obtained by purchase
from the crew, and sent it from France to Lady Selkirk. Off the Irish
coast, Captain Burdon of the Drake, sloop-of-war of fourteen guns, having mistaken the privateer for a merchantman, sent to impress some of
the crew—a mistake which resulted in his own death, as well as in that
of his Lieutenant, and the capture of his vessel, which Jones conveyed to
Brest, deeming it prudent to be out of the way of danger from the alarm
his daring conduct had created. He sailed with a small squadron from
Port L'Orient in July 1779, and, after several successful captures off the
Eastern Coast of Scotland, with the intention of burning the shipping in
Leith harbour, and collecting tribute from the defenceless towns on the
coast of Fife, he cast anchor under the island of Inchkeith, nearly op-
posite to Kirkaldy, but next morning, in endeavouring to beat up for
Leith harbour, a violent storm from the westward which had arisen,

C

speedily sent him and his squadron out of the Frith of Forth into the German ocean.

The present ballad appears to have been written to record one of Paul Jones' most remarkable adventures, but of which the poet has given a very garbled account, leading us to imagine that it had been written at the time from flying rumours, and before authentic reports of the action had reached this country. The true details are as follow :— Cruising off Flamborough Head, Jones, on the 23d September, fell in with a British convoy from the Baltic, under escort of his Majesty's ship, the Serapis of forty-four guns, commanded by Captain Pearson, and the Countess of Scarborough of twenty-two guns, commanded by Captain Thomas Percy (a natural son of the Duke of Northumberland). Paul Jones' squadron consisted of "Old Richard" of forty guns, and three hundred and seventy-five men ; the "Alliance" of forty guns, and three hundred men ; the "Pallas" of thirty-two guns, and two hundred and seventy-five men ; and the "Vengeance," an armed brig of twelve guns and seventy men. The result was one of the most memorable naval actions on record. The convoy took refuge under the guns of Scarborough Castle, and the action commenced between the "Old Richard" and the "Serapis," and was continued from half-past seven o'clock till nearly midnight in a calm sea and by the light of the moon. The "Richard," being a comparatively weak vessel, grappled with the "Serapis," and Paul Jones, with his own hands, fastened the vessels to each other. In this position they were desperately engaged for upwards of two hours, during which time the "Serapis" was on fire not less than ten or twelve times in different parts. The other frigates kept sailing round, raking fore and aft, killing or wounding almost every man on the main and quarter decks of the "Serapis," which, becoming in a most disabled condition, was finally compelled to strike. After a short engagement the "Countess of Scarborough" had surrendered to the "Pallas." The "Old Richard" was abandoned, and she sunk next day with a great number of the wounded on board. Paul Jones then took command of the "Serapis" and sailed for the Texel, which he reached in ten days. The honour of knighthood was conferred upon Captain Pearson for his gallant conduct, and Captain Percy was elevated to the rank of Post Captain. The Royal Exchange Assurance Company, for the protection afforded the rich convoy under their care, presented the former with a piece of plate of the value of one hundred guineas, and the latter with a similar present, worth fifty guineas. Paul Jones' own narrative of the event gives this incident, which occurs in the ballad, "A bullet having destroyed one of the pumps, the carpenter was seized with a panic, and told the gunner and another petty officer that we were sinking. Some one observed at the same time that both I and the lieutenant were killed ; in consequence of which, the gunner, considering himself as commanding officer, ran instantly to the quarter-deck in order to haul down the American colours, which he would have actually hauled down, had not the flag-staff been carried away at the time the 'Richard' grappled with the 'Serapis.' "

During the early part of the year 1780 Paul Jones was in France, and was there presented by his Majesty with a sword, on which was this motto: "Vindicati maris Ludovicus XVI. remunerator strenuo vindici." The hilt was of gold, and the blade was emblazoned with the royal arms, the attributes of war, and an emblematical representation of the alliance between France and America. Towards the end of the year he went to America, where Congress recognized his eminent services, and shortly afterwards appointed him to the command of the "America," a seventy-four gun ship. While upon an expedition to Jamaica, peace was proclaimed, upon which he returned to Philadelphia. In 1783 he obtained from France a large sum as prize-money, apparently upwards of ten thousand pounds. In 1788 we find commodore Paul Jones in search of active employment, tendering his services at Copenhagen to the Empress of Russia, which were accepted, and it is understood that, as rear-admiral in the Russian service, he commanded a squadron in the Euxine or Black Sea against the Turks. After this he is said to have purchased a small estate at Kentucky in Russia, and living in great splendour for some time, died at Paris in the summer of 1801, at the age of 53. Some twenty years afterwards, a frigate was despatched to France to receive his remains, which were conveyed to America for re-interment. Other accounts have it, that from some unexplained cause he became disgusted with the service of her Imperial Majesty, and in 1790 was negotiating with Kosciuszko, but that they never came to terms; that he in vain solicited employment from France, and that he died in Paris in 1792 in great poverty, Colonel Blackden raising a subscription to defray the expenses of his funeral.

We entirely agree with the Americans in their opinion that Paul was one of the ablest naval commanders who have borne their flag. He was the virtual founder of the United States navy, and was the first sea captain who compelled the British flag to strike to the stars and stripes.

In the "North Countrie Garland," a very scarce collection of ballads, privately printed at Edinburgh in 1824, the impression having been strictly limited to thirty copies, there is one of nine stanzas "from Mr. Pitcairn's MS. collection," bearing the title of "Paul Jones," but not especially referable to him. The editor says, "it was written down from the recitation of an old lady, and was much sung in Edinburgh by the populace on the occasion of Paul Jones making his appearance in the Frith of Forth, also during the strenuous opposition to the Popish bill. It was subsequently revived during the threatened invasion of

Britain by Bonaparte." It consists of a gossip, in alarm, running to acquaint her cronies with the news :—

> "Little do we see, but muckle do we hear,
> The French and Americans are a' comin here ;
> An' we'll a' be murdered,
> An' we'll a' be murdered,
> An' we'll a' be murdered,
> Before the New Year !
>
> . . . . .
>
> " For dinna ye mind, on this very floor,
> How we a' reek'd out, an' a' to Shirramuir,
> Wi' stanes in our aprons,
> Wi' stanes in our aprons,
> Wi' stanes in our aprons,
> An' wrought skaith, I'm sure."

J. Fenimore Cooper has endeavoured, but not very successfully, to
introduce him into a novel called the Pilot ; and Allan Cunningham has
written a romance entitled Paul Jones, which has been dramatized by
Tom Dibdin, and frequently acted in minor theatres.

" We learn," says Charles Kirkpatrick Sharp, in his curious notes to
Stenhouse's Illustrations, " from the Gallovidian Encyclopedia, that the
song of Paul Jones, formerly so popular, was composed by one Hack-
ston, who petitioned King George the Third for the office of laureate,
subscribing himself poet and private English teacher, parish of Borgue.
Paul Jones hath of late times burst forth as an historical hero, and a
knight of romance."

Our attention has just been directed to a book in 2 vols., Lond. 1843,
12mo, entitled "Memoirs of Paul Jones, late Rear-Admiral in the
Russian Service, Chevalier of the Military Order of Merit, and of the
Russian Order of St. Anne, &c., &c. Now first compiled from his
original Journals and Correspondence : including an account of his
services under Prince Potemkin, prepared for publication by himself."
From the preface we learn that several years since a life of Paul Jones
appeared in America, compiled by Mr. Sherburne, Register of the Navy
of the United States. An abridgement of the same work was reprinted
in London by Mr. Murray. Mr. Sherburne is said to have possessed
no adequate materials for his work, as Paul Jones' papers, with his
other property, were left, " by his will, dated at Paris on the day of his
death, to his sisters in Scotland and their children." His papers by
inheritance became the property of his niece, Miss Taylor of Dumfries.
" They consist of several bound folio volumes of private and official

letters and documents, as well as writings of a miscellaneous kind."
"The Journal of the Campaign of 1788 against the Turks, forms of
itself a thick volume. This Journal was drawn up by Paul Jones for the
perusal of the Empress Catherine II.; and was intended for publication
if the Russian government failed to do him justice. He felt that it
totally failed; but death anticipated his long-contemplated purpose."

From these Memoirs it appears that Paul Jones died in 1792, but by
no means without property. It is stated that as a boy he did not run
away to sea, but went by the consent of his parents, and that altogether
he was a better man than the common records and reports give him
credit for.

Having been charged by the United States with a mission to the court
of Denmark, and having a letter to deliver personally to Louis XVI.,
he went to France in Nov. 1787. Recommended by Mr. Jefferson, the
ambassador at Paris of the United States, to the notice of the Russian
government, after visiting Denmark, he proceeded to St. Petersburg,
where he remained a fortnight, and was "feasted at court and in the
first society." "The Empress," he writes to La Fayette, "received me
with a distinction the most flattering that perhaps any stranger can boast
of on entering the Russian service. Her Majesty conferred on me immediately the grade of Rear-Admiral." He was sent to command the
fleet against the Turks in the Black Sea, and received the order of St
Anne in recognition of his gallantry. A dispute with the Prince of
Nassau, who had been allowed to hoist the flag of Vice-Admiral on the
taking of Oczakow, and who had usurped much of the merit due to
Jones, eventually led to the dismissal of Paul Jones before the campaign
was ended. "The Prince Marshall [Potemkin] wished to establish a
permanent line of blockade in the road, by placing frigates there." He
wrote to Jones rather peremptorily on the subject. To which Jones
replied, "A warrior is always ready, and I have not come here as an
apprentice." He finally lost the favour of the Empress by an accusa-
tion brought against him of a criminal assault on a girl of twelve years of
age. Although he finally established his innocence, the Empress, with
that ultra sense of moral rectitude for which she was so remarkable,
could not with propriety again countenance a man whom the breath of
calumny had tainted. So, after having made the acquaintance of Kos-
ciusko at Warsaw, after sojourning some months at Amsterdam, and
paying a flying visit to England, he returned to France once more. It
does not seem that he acquired any property in Russia.

Jones appears to have been a pretty general admirer of the fair sex,
and to have occasionally indulged in poetical epistles to those he courted
for the nonce, while the ladies, of Paris more especially, seem to have
been deeply enamoured of him. Among his papers are several "irresis-

tible love-letters" addressed to him by a lady who chose to shelter herself
under the appellation of Delia.   They date from about 1780.

There is a kitcat portrait of Paul Jones in mezzotinto, after C. J.
Nolle, "printed for R. Wilkinson, at 58 Cornhill." He appears amid
fire and smoke on the deck of a shattered vessel, with a cutlass in his
hand, and innumerable pistols in his belt. He wears a cocked hat, and a
tight-fitting jacket with lapells.

Paul Jones the Pirate.

A noble fine frigate called Percy by name,
Mounted guns forty-four, out of L'Orient they came
For to cruise in the channel of old England's fame,
With their brave commodore, Paul Jones was his name.

We had not cruisèd above days two or three,
Than a man from a mast-head a sail he did see ;
A sail he did see, being a large forty-four :
Her convoy stood in for the old Yorkshire shore.

At length the proud Richards came up along side,
With a long speaking trumpet "from whence come?" he cried,
" Come answer me quickly, I have hailed you before,
Or else a broadside I will in to you pour."

We received the broadside from the proud Englishmen,
But soon our brave Yankies returned it again,
Broadside for broadside,—five glasses we run
When the undaunted flag of the Richards came down.

Our gunner being frightened, to Paul Jones he came,
Saying, " our ship's making water, and is likewise in flame;"
Paul Jones, with a smile to the gunner replied,
" If we can do no better we will sink alongside."

Now, my brave boys, we have taken a prize,
A large forty-four, with a twenty likewise ;
With twenty-five merchantmen loaded with store,
So we'll alter our course to the American shore.

A NEW SONG ON THE FRENCH SQUADRON,

THAT APPEARED IN THE FRITH OF FORTH, ON FRIDAY THE 17TH OF SEPTEMBER 1779.

THIS song is from a chap book, entitled, "Three excellent New Songs; I. The Americans in Tears since Collier's Victory; 2. A New Song on a French Fleet having appeared in the Frith of Forth; 3. The Quaker's Courtship. Entered according to order." *Circa* 1782. It bears reference to Paul Jones' appearance in the Frith of Forth, just mentioned, and evidences the fact, that three years after the event, there was a question and doubt as to who had been the mysterious visitants that had purposed invading our shores.

The inhabitants of the "lang town of Kirkcaldy" were dreadfully alarmed at the prospect of an invasion, the more so, if the invaders numbered among them the redoubtable Paul Jones, who was looked upon as a species of sea monster, devouring or destroying everything that came in his way. The people all flocked to the shore to take their observations, dreading the worst consequences. There was an old Presbyterian minister in the place,—a very pious and simple-minded old man, but somewhat eccentric in his mode of preaching, and especially in his appeals to the Deity, whom he would address in most familiar terms. This reverend gentleman was soon seen making his way through the crowd, hugging an old black arm chair which, although the tide was flowing, he placed at low-water mark, and coolly seated himself. Almost out of breath and in an angry tone of voice, lifting his eyes heavenward he thus began: "Now, 'deed, Lord, dinna ye think it's a shame for ye to send this vile pireet to rub our folk o' Kirkcaldy? for ye ken they're a' puir enough already, an' hae naething to spare. They're a' gaily guid, an' it wad be a peety to serve them in sic a wey. The wey the wun' blaws, he'll be here in a crack, an' wha kens what he may do? He's no ower guid for onything. Muckle's the mischief he has dune already. Ony pecket gear they hae gathered thegither, he will gang wi' the hale o't; may burn their hoozes, tak' their verra claes, an' tirl them to the sark; an' waes me! wha kens but the bluidy villain mightna tak' their lives. The puir weemen are a' frichtened oot o' their wuts, an' the bairns skirlin' after them. I canna thole't! I canna thole't. I hae been lang a faithfu' servant to ye, Laird; but gin ye dinna turn the wun aboot, and blaw the scoonrel oot o' oor gait, I'll no stir a fit, but'll juist sit here till the tide comes an' droons me. Sae tak' yer wull o't." About the time of the honest clergyman's supplication, the wind changed about and the storm arose, which caused the suspicious looking fleet to be driven perforce into the German Ocean. In the minds of the common people he of course got credit for a successful intercession, and his female worshippers became fully assured that, through him, access to brighter regions was easily attainable. The old gentleman himself actually believed that his suicidal threat had not gone without its value.

The name of this worthy and much-respected old gentleman was Shirra. So terror-stricken were the inhabitants of the kingdom of Fife by the appearance of these strange vessels, that the men of Pathhead had fires lighted on the adjoining heights, and kept watch and ward by day and night for a considerable time after the alarm had died away. The "Sir John," to whom allusion is made in the sixth stanza, was probably Sir John Halket, Bart. of Pitferran, previously Sir John Wedderburn, who about this time was possessed of the estate of Gosford, which at a subsequent date he transferred to his younger brother. Gosford in East Lothian is on the frith, almost immediately opposite to Wemyss Castle.

The words of this "New Song" have doubtlessly been arranged to suit the tune of "Donald M'Craw."

The French Squadron.

The French in this war,
Designed for Dunbar,
To plunder the great Provost Faa, man.
The town was in steir,
They trembl'd with feir,
Old wives they were greeting an' a', man.

CHORUS.

So he ran and she ran,
And she ran and he ran,
They frighten'd both great and sma', man.
If the French they come o'er
To our unguarded shore,
They'll burn an' plunder us a', man.

Upon Berwick sands
Were thousands to land,
To plunder both great an' sma', man.

The people for fear,
Had packed up their gear,
Cry'd, the French dogs will worry us a', man.
So he ran, &c.

To Haddington bent,
For Dragoons they sent;
They mounted their horse and awa', man.
And when they came there
They loudly did swear,
They'd slaughter the French with their pa', man.
So he ran, &c.

But, in spite of their teeth,
They came to Inchkeith,
As the folk in Edinburgh saw, man;
They bred such a steer
Round about the Leith pier,
They thought they would burn them a', man.
So he ran, &c.

Some swore by their saul!
'Twas plundering Jack Paul;
The greatest rogue that ever you saw, man.
And on the Fife shore,
They heard the guns roar;
They were near to Wemyss Castle and a', man.
So he ran, &c.

Sir John sent to see
What ships they could be,
With a boat, a pilot, and a', man.
But instead of tea,
Some powder did gi'e;
And the pilot they took awa', man.
So he ran, &c.

Oh! such preparation
Was ne'er seen in our nation ;
The men they got broadswords, and a', man.
I laugh'd at the fun,
With their old rusty guns,
They look'd as they were to shoot craws, man.
        So he ran, &c.   .

Then from Edinburgh toun
The cannon came doun,
They placed them a' in a ra', man ;
Such battering before,
Placed on a shore,
In my life before I ne'er saw, man.
        So he ran, &c.

They'd great packs of woo,
Their cannon were few ;
But were to slaughter down a', man.
The French took a fright,
Got off in the night,
They hoisted their sails and awa', man.
        So he ran, &c.

Some say they were Dens,
Other folk say Frenchmen,
While many say Smugglers and a', man ;
But if I tell aright,
For a' our great fright,
Ne'er a Frenchman was e'er there at a', man.
        So he ran, &c.

THE GOULDEN VANITIE.

This song, with the music, occurs in Mrs. Gordon's Memoir of
Christopher North.—Cr. 8vo, 1862, vol. ii. p. 317 ;—and, as it was held

in much estimation by the accomplished professor, we do not think our readers will be displeased to find that we have given it a place in this Collection. It was sung some twenty years ago at a convivial meeting at Lord Robertson's by Mr. P. S. Fraser, a gentleman justly held in much esteem by his fellow citizens of Edinburgh. On this occasion, the late J. G. Lockhart and Professor Wilson were of the party, and it made such an impression on the latter, that it haunted him during the night, and to his surprise he awoke next morning singing it. Lord Robertson was equally fascinated, and on the conclusion of the song, turned to Lockhart and said, "You Spanish ballad-monger, if you could produce anything like that, you would soon ding them a'." For its antiquity we cannot say anything. All we do know is, that it was orally transmitted to the gentleman who sang it, and that, according to his belief, it is upwards of a century old.

THERE was a gallant ship,
And a gallant ship was she,
    Eck iddle dee, and the Lowlands low.
And she was called "The Goulden Vanitie,"
    As she sailed to the Lowlands low.

She had not sailed a league,
A league but only three,
    Eck, &c.,
When she came up with a French Gallee,
    As she sailed, &c.

Out spoke the little cabin-boy,
Out spoke he,
    Eck, &c.;
"What will you give me if I sink that French Gallee?
    As ye sail," &c.

Out spoke the Captain,
Out spoke he,
    Eck, &c.,
"We'll gi'e ye an estate in the north countrie,"
    As we sail, &c.

"Then row me up ticht
In a black bull's skin,
  Eck, &c.,
And throw me o'er deck-buird, sink I or swim,
  As ye sail," &c.

So they've rowed him up ticht
In a black bull's skin :
  Eck, &c.
And have thrown him o'er deck-buird, sink he or soom,
  As they sail, &c.

About and about,
And about went he,
  Eck, &c.
Until he came up with the French Gallee,
  As they sailed, &c.

Oh ! some were playing cards,
And some were playing dice :
  Eck, &c.
When he took out **an instrument,** bored thirty holes at
 twice !
  As they sailed, &c.

Then some they ran with cloaks,
And some they ran with caps,
  Eck, &c.,
To try if they could stap the saut-water draps,
  As they sailed, &c.

About and about,
And about went he,
  Eck, &c.
Until he cam back to the Goulden Vanitie,
  As they sailed, &c.

"Now throw me o'er a rope,
And pu' me up on buird ;
Eck, &c.
And prove unto me as guid as your word ;
As ye sail," &c.

"We'll no throw you o'er a rope,
Nor pu' you up on buird :
Eck, &c.
Nor prove unto you as guid as our word."
As we sail, &c.

Out spoke the little cabin-boy,
Out spoke he,
Eck, &c.
"Then hang me, I'll sink ye as I sunk the French Gallee,
As ye sail," &c.

But they've thrown him o'er a rope,
And have pu'd him up on buird,
Eck, &c.
And have proved unto him far better than their word :
As they sailed, &c.

Golden Vanity, or the Low Lands Low.

THE second version of this ballad, now given, is from the collection
which forms the text book of this our "Popular Minstrelsy." It bears
the imprint of "Pitts, Printer, Toy and Marble Warehouse, 6 Great St.
Andrew Street, 7 Dials." The precise locality of the Low Lands Low
may be assumed to be either in the river Elbe, somewhere between its
mouth and the city of Hamburgh, or off the coast of South Holland, at
some spot where the tide between the mainland and some opposite island
or sandbank subsides in the same manner as between Holy Island and
the coast of Northumberland, where, with exception of a rapid flowing
stream, called, by the way, The Low, the island is connected with the
mainland once in every twelve hours.

I HAVE a ship in the North Countrie,
And she goes by the name of the Golden Vanity;
I 'm afraid she will be taken by some Turkish gallee,
    As she sails on the Low Lands Low.

Then up starts our little cabin boy,
Saying, "Master, what will you give me if I do them destroy?"
" I will give you gold, I will give you store;
You shall have my daughter when I return on shore,
    If you sink them in the Low Lands Low."

The boy bent his breast, and away he jumpt in;
He swam till he came to this Turkish galleon,
    As she laid on the Low Lands Low.

The boy he had an auger to bore holes two at twice;
While some were playing cards, and some were playing dice,
He let the water in, and it dazzled in their eyes,
    And he sunk them in the Low Lands Low.

The boy he bent his breast, and away he swam back again,
Saying, " Master, take me up, or I shall be slain,
    For I have sunk them in the Low Lands Low."

" I 'll not take you up," the master he cried,—
" I 'll not take you up," the master replied;
" I will kill you, I will shoot you, I will send you with the
    tide;
    I will sink you in the Low Lands Low."

The boy he swam round all by the starboard side;
They laid him on the deck, and it 's there he soon died:
Then they sewed him up in an old cow's hide,
And they threw him overboard to go down with the tide,
    And they sunk him in the Low Lands Low.

CAPTAIN GLEN'S UNHAPPY VOYAGE TO NEW BARBARY.

THIS "unhappy voyage" has been reprinted from a broadside *circa* 1815, and collated with a copy bearing date 1794. A copy is among the Roxburghe Ballads, with a conjectured date. There is no reason to believe otherwise than that the story is a mere fiction. At all events, no trace has as yet been found of even the existence of a Captain Glen.

The ballad is illustrative of the superstitions of seamen, whose firm belief in the supernatural is pretty general. The late Mr. O. Smith, the eminent actor, who has never been rivalled in melodramatic ruffians and stage demons, was in his youth in the merchant service. On one occasion, some years ago, he related in my presence this story. When the vessel to which he belonged was lying off the coast of Africa, the mate went ashore to remain all night. Mr. Smith took possession of this man's cot, it being more comfortable than his own, and as the bright moonlight streamed down through the hatchway he felt little inclination to sleep. By and by a figure appeared between him and the light. He averred that he then distinctly saw at the hatchway what he supposed to be the mate returned. This gave him no concern, for the mate was a person he was in the habit of constantly seeing, so he turned on his side and fell asleep. Next morning news arrived that at the particular time the appearance or apparition had been seen by him, the mate had been murdered by the natives. Mr. Smith was seriously under the impression that he had seen the tenant of another world; and, like Sir Walter Scott, his belief in ghosts remained unshaken to the last.

The superstition of the elements being quieted by the captain being pitched overboard, is older than the days of Jonah.

It were needless here to particularize all the "authenticated" accounts of the appearance of apparitions to living persons. Those who are curious in such matters, are referred to Hogg's Wonderful Magazine, 5 vols. 8vo., 1793-4, and to the "Terrific Register," 2 vols. 8vo., 1824.

Captain Glen's Unhappy Voyage to New Barbary.

THERE was a ship, and a ship of fame,
Launched off the stocks, bound to the main,
With an hundred and fifty brisk young men,
Well picked and chosen every one.

William Glen was our captain's name ;
He was a brisk and tall young man,
As bold a sailor as e'er went to sea,
And he was bound for New Barbary.

The first of April we did set sail,
Blest with a sweet and pleasant gale,
For we were bound for New Barbary,
With all our whole ship's company.*

One night the captain he did dream,
There came a voice which said to him :
" Prepare you and your company,
To-morrow night you'll lodge with me."

This waked the captain in a fright,
Being the third watch of the night,
Then for his boatswain he did call,
And told to him his secrets all.

" When I in England did remain,
The holy Sabbath I did profane ;
In drunkenness I took delight,
Which doth my trembling soul affright.

" There's one thing more I've to rehearse,
Which I shall mention in this verse :

---

* In the edition of 1794 this stanza occurs here:

> We had not sailed a day but two,
> Till all our whole ship's jovial crew,
> They all fell sick but sixty-three,
> As we went to New Barbary.

The music of this ballad will be found in the appendix to Motherwell's Minstrelsy, where this stanza only is quoted, with the difference of "league" in the first line for "day." "This common stall ballad," he remarks, "is generally sung to the tune now given." Glasgow, 1827. 4to.

A squire I slew in Staffordshire,
All for the sake of a lady dear.

" Now, 'tis his ghost, I am afraid,
That hath to me such terror made ;
Although the king hath pardoned me,
He 's daily in my company."

" O worthy captain, since 'tis so,
No mortal of it e'er shall know ;
So keep your secret in your breast,
And pray to God to give you rest."

They had not sailed a league but three,
Till raging grew the roaring sea ;
There rose a tempest in the skies,
Which filled our hearts with great surprise.

Our main-mast sprung by break of day,
Which made our rigging all give way ;
This did our seamen sore affright.
The terrors of that fatal night !

Up then spoke our fore-mast man,
As he did by the fore-mast stand,—
He cried, " Have mercy on my soul !"
Then to the bottom he did fall.

The sea did wash both fore and aft,
Till scarce one sail on board was left ;
Our yards were split, and our rigging tore :
The like was never seen before.

The boatswain then he did declare
The captain was a murderer,
Which did enrage the whole ship's crew :
Our captain overboard we threw.

D

Our treacherous captain being gone,
Immediately there was a calm;
The winds did cease, and the raging sea,
As we went to New Barbary.

Now when we came to the Spanish shore,
Our goodly ship for to repair,
The people were amazed to see
Our dismal case and misery.

But when our ship we did repair,
To fair England our course did steer;
And when we came to London town,
Our dismal case was then made known.

Now many wives their husbands lost,
Which they lamented to their cost,
And caused them to weep bitterly,
These tidings from New Barbary.

A hundred and fifty brisk young men,
Did to our goodly ship belong;
Of all our whole ship's company,
Our number was but seventy-three.

Now seamen all, where'er you be,
I pray a warning take by me;
As you love your life, still have a care
That you never sail with a murderer.

'Tis never more I do intend
For to cross o'er the raging main;
But I'll live in peace in my own country,—
And so I end my Tragedy.

Go High, Go Low.

From the Dairymaid, or Vocal Miscellany. Being a Collection of Choice Songs, Scotch and English. Edin. 1784, 12mo.

In Dibdin's Comic Opera of the Seraglio, produced at Covent Garden theatre in 1776, there is a song of similar rhythm. It commences thus :—

"Blow high! blow low! let tempest tear
The mainmast by the board," &c.

It is said, by the editor of the collected edition of Dibdin's songs, to have been written at sea during an excursion in a yacht, which stress of weather had prevented from regaining its haven for thirteen hours. It is a matter of doubt which of the two songs was first written.

Go high, go low, in every state
    The sailor's heart is true ;
In adverse or in prosperous fate
    He joins the crew.
Then toiling early, watching late,
    Defends his king and country's cause,
    In hopes to be,
    When come from sea,
    Cheered with applause.—
At home, when shouts his welcome crown,
    His wife's the liveliest of the throng,
Or, when care sinks his spirits down,
    Her endearing smile
    Rewards his toil,
    And greets his favourite song.
So when the nuptial knot is tyed,
Each morn you'll hail my blooming bride,
And gladly share my heart's content ;
A boon that kindly Heaven has sent.
I'll grasp the hand that made her mine,
To social scenes the hours resign,
While all the wonted strain shall join.
Go high, go low, in every state,
    The sailor's heart is true ;
In adverse or in prosperous fate,
    What's right he'll do.

JACKY TAR.

THIS song may in all probability date some time between 1780 and
1790, cotemporaneously with the very popular Naval Lyrics of
Charles Dibdin. The air to which it has been sung is the well-known
dance tune known as the Sailor's Hornpipe, which, it is believed, was
danced long before the tune was rendered vocal. Hornpipes are of very
ancient date. They appear to have been the peasants' dance, not only in
many of the provincial towns of England, but in Holland, and were
usually danced in wooden shoes. The instrument which discoursed the
music was a rude pipe, as the name sufficiently indicates. In the time
of Queen Elizabeth they appear to have been danced with partners, and
not as a single dance. Spenser refers to this :

> "A lusty tabrere,
> That to thee many a hornpipe play'd,
> Whereto they dancen *each with his own maid.*"

Ben Jonson also refers to the hornpipe as a general dance :

> "Let all the quicksilver i' the mine
> Run to the feet veins, and refine
> Your firkum jerkum to a dance
> Shall fetch the fiddlers out of France,
> To wonder at the hornpipes here
> Of Nottingham and Derbyshire."

In the Tatler we find it spoken of as a single dance : "Florinda
danced the Derbyshire hornpipe in the presence of several friends."

There are two very ancient ballads in MS. in the Public Library of
the University of Cambridge—one entitled the "Tale of a Basyn," the
other "The Frere and the Boy," which were printed, in a limited impression, small 4to, by Mr. Pickering in 1836, under the able editorial care
of Mr. Thomas Wright. These ballads had previously attracted the attention of Ritson and of the Rev. Mr. Hartshorne, the latter having introduced the Tale of a Basin into his Early Metrical Tales, while Ritson
has taken under his wing in his "Pieces of Ancient Popular Poetry"
the Friar and the Boy, which he had adopted from a copy printed by
Wynkyn de Worde. Mr. Wright is of opinion that the Tale of a Basin
was written in the earlier part of the fourteenth century, and the Friar
and the Boy during the reign of Henry VI. In both ballads, the heroes,
who are boys, use a pipe, such as shepherds use, with marvellous effect,
those who hear it being incapable of restraining themselves from dancing.

In the Friar and the Boy, the Friar is by this means compelled to dance a hornpipe solo:

" The ffreyre ynto the bosches went,
Up the berde ffor to hent
Hem thowt het was well doyn :
The boy cast awey hes bowe,
Wheytley anon, as I trowe,
And toke his pype anon.

As sone as the ffreyre the pype herde,
As a mad man he ferd,
He began to lepe and dans abowth.
Among the buschys smale and gret
The ffreyre ffast gan lepe.
* * * * * *
At the last the ffreyre leffyd op hys honde,
A seyd, y haffe dansed here all to lange.
I prey the holde the stell."

The story of a pipe possessed of similar qualities obtains among the peasantry of Germany, and has been noticed in the valuable collection of Kinder-und Haus-Marchen of the Grimms. It is also found in more northern climes under the title of " Herrauds ok Bosa Saga."

In none of the older treatises of dancing or of music does any description or even mention of the hornpipe occur. The only dance chronicled which at all seems to resemble it, is the "Musette" referred to by Monsieur Noverre in his works, 3 vols., 8vo, 1782. It is danced by the country people on the Continent at their merry meetings to the music of an instrument so named, bearing some affinity to the bagpipe. There is the music of "a new Hornpipe," in a small oblong quarto book, "sold by Henry Playford, near the Temple Church, 1688," called "the Division-Violin: containing a collection of Divisions upon several grounds for the Treble-Violin. Being the first music of this kind made publick."

Nancy Dawson, the friend of Ned Shuter, obtained much celebrity as a hornpipe dancer. She died at Hampstead 27th May 1767.

Jacky Tar.

WHEN Jack had pull'd the oar, and the boat was gone,
And the lassie on the shore with her head hanging down ;

The tears stood in her eyes, and her bosom heaving sighs,
Farewell, my dear, she cries, with your trousers on.
Farewell, said he, I go to sea, and you must stay behind;
But do not grieve, for while I live I ever will be kind,
And when I come to land, you will meet me on the strand,
And welcome Jacky Tar with his trousers on.

Now peace is proclaim'd, and the wars are all o'er,
The fleets they are moor'd, and the sailors come ashore;
Now you may see her stand, with her glass into her hand,
To welcome Jack to land with his trousers on.
While up on high she caught his eye, with all her lovely charms,
Her face he knew, and straight he flew, and caught her in
his arms;
Her hand he kindly press'd, as he held her round the waist,
And he kiss'd the bonnie lassie with his trousers on.

"O Jack! where have you been since you went from me?
And what have you seen upon the raging sea?
I mourned for your sake, while my heart was like to break,
For I thought I'd ne'er see Jack with his trousers on.
And while you stay'd, I sighed and pray'd to Neptune and
to Mars,
That they'd prove kind, and safely send you home from the
wars;
And now to my request they have been pleased to list,
And sent you to my breast with your trousers on."

"I've sailed the seas for you to the Torrid Zone,
From the confines of Peru to Van Dieman's Land,
From the Bay of Baltimore to the coast of Labrador,
But now I'm safe on shore with my trousers on.
I've beat the storms in many forms upon the raging main,
I've fought the foes with deadly blows, and many a hero
slain:
I've heard the cannons roar, I've rolled in blood and gore,
But now I'm safe on shore with my trousers on.

" I have been aloft when the winds have blown,
And I 've been aloft when the bombs were thrown ;
But like a sailor bold, I am now come from the hold,
With my pockets full of gold, and my trousers on.
And now no more from shore to shore I'll plough the raging
seas,
But free from strife, as man and wife, we'll live in peace and
ease."
To the church this couple hied, and the priest the knot has
tied,
And the sailor kiss'd the bride with his trousers on.

The Forecastle Sailor;

OR, THE GUARDIAN FRIGATE.

THIS "new song" is from a broadside of apparently 1788. It bears
no imprint.

THE wind blew a blast from the northward,
When we steered from the Cape of Good Hope,
The skies looked quite pitchy and wayward,
And the sea o'er our weather-bow broke ;
The boatswain piped all hands to bale her,
And I came down the backstay so glib,
For I am a forecastle sailor,
You may see by the cut of my jib.

" Start my timbers !" cries Ned Junk of Dover,
Plump to me as I landed on deck,
" With us it will soon be all over,
For the Guardian must quick go to wreck."
" Well ! well, we sha'n't live to bewail her,"
Cried I, and I pelted his rib,
" Come, work like a forecastle sailor,—
An' I don't, the gale shiver my jib."

We were running at nine knots an hour,
When but two leagues to leeward we spied
An island of ice like a tower,
And on it our ship swiftly hied.
But now 'twas no use for to bail her,
The water gained on her so glib ;
So each, like a true-hearted sailor,
Waited fate for to shiver his jib.

Some took to the boat, d'ye mind me,
Whilst some on the vessel's deck stood ;
Cried I, " May ' Old Davy Jones ' take me,
If I sail from my captain so good."
Now providence help'd us to bale her,
And we managed to patch up her rib :
Safe arrived is each true-hearted sailor,
To rig up his weather-beat jib.

Lament for the Loss of the Ship Union.

IN another copy of this piece which we have stumbled upon, the title
is "J. G.'s Lament for the Loss of the Ship Union." Who J. G. was
must, we fear, remain a matter of question, unless his "charming lovely
Ann," to whom he betook himself, be still alive, and will disclose the
secret. Instead of J. G. *lamenting*, he appears to have rather rejoiced
that the expedition to America was prevented in favour of more halcyon
days down "by the river Bann."
There is no imprint attached to either of the copies.

WHEN I was young and in my prime,
    The seas I had to rove ;
My friends together did combine
    To part me from my love.

To Belfast town they me conveyed,
    And without more delay

In the Union my passage paid,
  Bound for America.

'Twas on 14th day of May,
  From Belfast we did set sail ;
And down the Loch we bore away,
  With a sweet and pleasant gale.

Now farewell to the shamrock shore,
  And bonny banks of Bann,
And the sweet girl I do adore—
  My charming lovely Ann.

For St. Andrews we were bound
  Our course now for to steer ;
From Erin's shore away we bore,
  Thinking no danger near.

At ten o'clock on the third night
  We got a dreadful shock :
Our ship she dashed with all her might
  Against an unknown rock.

Then our hard fate for to lament
  It 's now we did begin ;
In discontent some hours we spent
  At South-east of Rathlane.

It 's overboard our stores we threw,
  Our cargo to the waves ;
Numbers to the shrouds then flew,
  Their precious lives to save.

The raging sea ran mountains high,
  And dismal were the skies ;
No light or land could we espy,
  And horrid were the cries.

It's there we lay till break of day,—
Describe our state who can?
Then to myself these words did say,
" Adieu, sweet lovely Ann."

Soon as we got a glimpse of light,
Our boats we did employ;
Towards the shore we took our flight,
Our hearts did leap with joy.

Providence to us proved kind,—
His name we do adore;
There's not a soul was left behind,
We all got safe to shore.

Now, farewell to America,
And the rocks of Rathlane;
No more I'll from my country stray,
To cross the raging main.

I'll go and see my bonny lass,
Down by the river Bann;
And all my days with her I'll pass,
My charming lovely Ann.

DEATH OF PARKER.

THIS ballad is contemporaneous with the event which it records. It bears the imprint of Oxlade, Printer, Portsea. Richard Parker, the subject of it, was a prominent personage at the mutiny at the Nore.

On the 15th April 1797, when Admiral Bridport, commanding the line-of-battle ships at Portsmouth and Spithead, ordered the signal for the fleet to prepare for sea, to the astonishment of all the officers, the men, by a previously concerted agreement, refused to lift an anchor until they obtained a redress of their grievances, petitions from all the ships having two months before been sent to Lord Howe, and no reply having been elicited. Two men from the crew of each ship were named as dele-

gates, and they selected Lord Howe's cabin as a place for their delibera-
tions. Every man in the fleet having been sworn to support the cause
in which he had embarked, all those officers who had given offence to
any of them were turned out of the fleet. The Lords of the Admiralty
endeavoured for some days, but ineffectually, to reduce the men to obedi-
ence, but the delegates informed them that nothing could be agreed to
unless under the sanction of Parliament and guaranteed by the King's
proclamation. The grievances complained of ought in justice to have
been earlier investigated and redressed, but real grievances were then as
now passed over, while imaginary ones are ever seized upon by weak
ministers as affording them the means of retaining their places. By the
aid of Lord Bridport, whom the men styled their "Father" and
"Friend," redress was obtained as well as his Majesty's pardon for the
offenders. What the men chiefly complained of was, that the wages
they were paid were at the rate settled by an act passed in the reign of
King Charles II., "when the necessaries of life, and slops of every denomination were at least thirty per cent. cheaper," and they wished such
amendments made as would enable them "and their families to live in
the same comfortable manner as seamen and mariners did at that time."
Their provisions also they wished to be of better quality and weight, and
they grievously complained of the want of vegetables on board, while
these could be procured at the several ports at which they touched.
They called attention to the manner in which the sick were attended,
and requested "that they may have the use of such necessaries as are
allowed for them in time of their sickness, and that these necessaries be
not on any account embezzled." They farther desired to be "granted
an opportunity to taste the sweets of liberty on shore, when in any harbour ; and when we have completed the duty of our ships after our return
from sea." This liberty to be limited. Their next request was, "that
if any man is wounded in action, his pay be continued until he is cured
and discharged." And finally they asked for a small augmentation of
the pensions from Greenwich College.

From the concessions made it was now thought that order would
ensue, but in the beginning of May the sailors at Portsmouth, thinking
that Government did not intend to keep faith with them, came ashore and
committed every kind of excess. Shortly afterwards the fleet at Sheerness
began to exhibit symptoms of discontent, and the ships then there were
taken possession of by the mutineers, and compelled to drop down to
the Great Nore. Sheerness was visited every day by the delegates, who,
after holding a conference, paraded the streets and ramparts of the
garrison. At the head of these men marched Richard Parker, who was
regarded as the admiral of their fleet, no officer having any command or
authority whatever. Parker was descended from a respectable family in
Exeter, Devon. He received a good education, was bred in the navy,

and about the conclusion of the American war, was an acting lieutenant in one of his Majesty's ships. Coming into possession of a considerable sum of money, he married the daughter of a farmer in Aberdeenshire, and with her obtained some property. Being for a while out of employment, he not only spent his money, but became involved in debt, which caused his incarceration in the jail of Edinburgh. The counties were raising seamen for the navy, and Parker volunteered for Perthshire. Upon paying a portion of his bounty to the incarcerating creditor, he was released from prison, and being put on board the tender then in Leith Roads was conveyed, with many others, to the Nore. Captain Watson, who commanded the tender, took notice of Parker for his activity and polite address.

Lords Spencer, Arden, and others, members of the Board of Admiralty, met the delegates and told them the seamen at Sheerness should have every indulgence that had been granted to the men at Portsmouth. The seamen, through Parker, said they had other grounds of complaint, and presented a list of eight items, the first and principal of which was the unequal distribution of prize money. The Lords Commissioners informed the delegates that they of themselves could do nothing, and on their return to London to report at head-quarters, the mutineers committed acts of plunder and piracy. The delegates then intimated that in order to bring matters to a crisis, they intended to block up the Thames, which they proceeded to do. A fresh president of the delegates was chosen daily, one day being the term of office. An Act of Parliament was passed in the beginning of June for the prevention and punishment of all traitorous attempts to excite sedition and mutiny. On the 7th of that month the Earl of Northesk, who had been held captive, arrived in town, charged with several propositions, in a letter addressed to the King, from the Mutineer Committee on board the "Sandwich." To this application no reply was returned, and shortly after divisions took place in the rebel councils. This led to the desertion and dispersion of several of the vessels, in which some men were killed and many wounded. Discord universally prevailed, and finally the delegates resolved to allow every ship to do the best for itself. The crew of the "Sandwich" were particularly desirous of submitting, provided a general pardon was granted, and this Parker did not oppose. They resolved to submit to the King's mercy, and the vessel proceeded to Sheerness, whence a boat was despatched for Parker, who quietly surrendered himself. On landing he was hissed by the populace, at which he said, "Do not hoot me. It is not my fault. I will clear myself." He was thence conducted to Maidstone gaol, under an escort of the West York militia.

The trial of Parker lasted three days, commencing on the 22d June. He, having no advocate, was heard in his own defence. He endeavoured to show from reliable exculpatory evidence that all he had done "was in

compliance with orders, for the purpose of rendering matters less disastrous than would otherwise have been." That he had never shown disre-
spect to the Admiral or any of the other officers, and that in Captain
Wood's case especially he had not only not been a party to, but had not
been cognizant of, his dismissal from his ship. That the mutiny origi-
nated in the "Inflexible," "and there it was always the most violent,"
and that the "Sandwich" had been threatened by the "Inflexible" with
summary destruction if the crew acted otherwise than they set down. All
was of no avail. The charges against him were found fully proved, and
he was sentenced to death; but the Court thought proper not to fix the
time of his punishment. On Friday the 29th of June, the prisoner, who
had been placed in the gun-room of the "Sandwich," was awakened
shortly after six o'clock by the Provost Marshall. After breakfasting,
he spoke of a will he had written, in which he had bequeathed to his wife
a little estate he said he was heir to. At half-past eight, the chaplain of
the ship was ready to attend him to prayers on the quarter-deck. At nine
the preparatory gun was fired, and prayers soon after concluded. On
ascending the scaffold he said, "I wish to declare the justice of the sentence under which I suffer; and I hope my death may be deemed a sufficient atonement, and save the lives of others." After his execution,
his body was taken ashore, and interred in the naval burying ground at
Sheerness.

On the morning of his execution, his wife had made several efforts to
get on board to take leave of him, but was prevented. She went to the
churchyard where he was buried, and, with the assistance of two women,
got his coffin away during the night, and had it conveyed in a fish-cart
out of the garrison, and taken first to Rochester, thence to a room which
she had hired for the purpose at the "Hoop and Horse-Shoe," Queen
Street, Little Tower-Hill. The circumstance of Parker's body being deposited there, caused the assemblage of a concourse of visitors, which
increased to such a number on the Sunday and Monday as to cause the
interference of the magistrates. Mrs. Parker was desired to attend the
Police Office in Lambert Street, where she was interrogated respecting
her intentions in removing the body of her husband. She replied, "To
take him down either to his own family at Exeter, or to mine in Scotland, to bury him like a Christian." She was then asked whether it
was true she had suffered the body to be shewn for money. She burst
into tears, and said, "Do I appear like a monster so unnatural?" It
was afterwards proved that there was not the smallest foundation for
such a report. The body was by order of the magistrates next moved
to the workhouse in Nightingale Lane, and from thence taken and buried
at Whitechapel Church.

Parker was a remarkably fine looking man. The brilliancy and expression of his eyes were of such a nature as to cause one of the witnesses

while under examination at his trial to quail beneath his glance, and
shrink abashed, and so become incapacitated from giving further testi-
mony. Another instance of this extraordinary expression of the eye was
in the person of Moffat, *alias* MacCoul, who was tried capitally at Edinburgh in 1820 for robbing the Paisley bank. A gentleman who was
present at Moffat's trial has informed us that "a glance of his eye went
completely through you. It was really quite oppressive." Burns, the
poet, has also been noticed by Sir Walter Scott for the peculiar brilliancy of his eye.

Parker appears from the evidence to have obtained scant justice; and
there can be no doubt that, being an educated man, and rather ambitious
of being an orator, he was made the mouthpiece and the tool of men of
harsher natures, whom even in death he did not betray.

Among our memoranda we find the following :—At the Exeter Assizes
in 1828, John C. Parker, son of the celebrated Richard Parker, who
commanded the mutineers at the Nore, obtained a verdict against his
aunts for the possession of an estate called Shute, which had belonged to
the elder brother of his father. The question turned upon the legitimacy
of the plaintiff, which was proved by his mother, a woman who exhibited
the remains of uncommon beauty, and who was married to Richard Parker at Edinburgh in 1793.

Douglas Jerrold founded a drama upon the subject of the "Mutiny at
the Nore." Parker is the hero; and to give some colour to his conduct,
an episode is introduced. On board the ship in which he served a watch
is stolen, and he is suspected as the thief. He denies the charge. His
testimonials of character are of no avail. He is found guilty, and punished. Subsequently he deserts, is recaptured, tried, and condemned to
death; but the sentence is commuted to a flogging through the fleet.
This is done after the real culprit has been discovered. The mover of
this vindictive sentence is Captain Arlington, whom Parker had supplanted
in the affections of the female whom he married. Parker then joins the
mutineers, is betrayed while visiting his wife in the Isle of Grain; but
on being captured, he shoots Captain Arlington. He is then hanged at
the yard-arm of the "Sandwich," not for mutiny, but for murder.

Death of Parker.

YE gods above, protect a widow!
And with pity look on me.
Help, O help me out of trouble;
Out of sad calamity!

It was, by the death of Parker,
Fortune prov'd to me unkind ;
And though hung for mutiny,
Worse than he were left behind.

Parker was my lawful husband,
My bosom friend, whom I loved dear ;
Yet at the time he was to suffer,
Alas ! I could not him get near !
Again I ask'd, again I tried them,—
Three times o'er and o'er, in vain ;
They still that one request denied me,
And ordered me on shore again.

The YELLOW FLAG I thought was flying,
A signal for my love to die ;
The gun they fired, as was required,
To hang him on the yards' arm high.
The boatswain did his best endeavour,
And I on shore was sent straightway,
Where I stood watching, like a mermaid,
To take my husband's corpse away.

At dead of night, when all was silent,
And many thousands fast asleep,
I, by two female friends attended,
Into the burying ground did creep.
Our trembling hands did serve as shovels,
With which the mould we moved away,
And then the body of my husband
Carried off without delay.

A mourning coach for him was waiting :
We drove to London with all speed,
Where decently I had him buried,
And a sermon o'er him said.

And now his sorrows are all over,
And he 's free from guilt and pain ;
I hope in heaven his soul is shining,
Where I shall meet with him again.

Farewell, Parker, thou bright angel
Once thou wert the navy's pride ;
Since we did not die together,
Separate we must abide.
I must wait awhile with patience ;
On earth I hope not long to stay,
When we shall meet once more in glory,
And all our sins be wash'd away.

SAILOR TAKING LEAVE OF HIS MISTRESS.

IT is not very easy to assign a date to this song. It can hardly advance a claim to have been co-existent with the expedition of Lord Peterborough. The probability is, however, that it is referable either to the hostilities commenced by France and Spain against England in 1779, on an alleged violation of the Treaty of Peace of 1763, with regard to the Spanish colonies in South America and to the French subjects in the island of Grenada; or to the war which was declared between Spain and England in 1800, and which culminated in the glorious victory of the British fleet at Trafalgar, on 21st October 1805, over the combined fleets of France and Spain. During the former, great apprehension of an invasion prevailed throughout the British Isles. The Channel fleet, under the command of Admiral Sir Charles Hardy, was powerful enough at all events to prevent the enemy from attempting such a thing. Several naval engagements took place and many captures were made, and it was not till the termination of the siege of Gibraltar, early in 1783, that peace was again restored. This siege lasted nearly two years. Much havoc was made among the combined fleets of France and Spain by the discharge of red-hot shot from the garrison. The total loss to the British during the siege was 1228 men. The memorable battle of Trafalgar lasted four hours. In the moment of victory, Lord Viscount Nelson, the gallant Admiral of the British fleet, was unhappily shot. The British lost fifteen hundred and eighty-seven men in all; the enemy, it is said, lost as many thousands. Nineteen sail of the line were taken. A storm having arisen after the action, part of the prizes were wrecked, and others destroyed. The Spanish Vice-Admiral, Alava, died of his wounds. Villeneuve, the French Commander, was sent to England, but was afterwards permitted to return to France. The French government reported that, dreading the consequences of a court martial, he had destroyed himself on his way to Paris; and it is supposed that Napoleon, who never acknowledged the loss of the battle of Trafalgar, did not much regret the fate of his admiral. Honours were heaped upon the memory of Nelson. A public funeral was decreed, and a public monument. Statues and monuments were also voted by most of the principal cities of his country. His brother was made an Earl, with a grant of £6000 a-year. £10,000 were voted to each of his sisters, and £100,000 for the purchase of an estate.

Sailor taking Leave of his Mistress.

" Now I'm coming to take my leave,
My charming Molly do not grieve,
For I'm going to the Spanish shore,
To leave my charmer, to leave my charmer,
To leave my charmer whom I do adore."

" My dearest Jamie, hearken to me :
How many ships there are lost at sea ;
You're safer in your true love's arms,
Free from all dangers, free from all dangers,
Free from all dangers and cold bitter storms."

" No storms or dangers, love, I fear ;
I will go to sea in a privateer ;
If it pleaseth fortune to spare my life,
When I return, love, when I return, love,
When I return, love, I'll make thee my wife."

" There's one thing more that disturbs my mind :
Some other girl I'm afraid you'll find,
And when you're on the Spanish shore,
Then you'll ne'er think on, then you'll ne'er think on,
Then you'll ne'er think on your Molly more."

E

"Though thousands of fine girls I see,
None shall enjoy my love but thee.
Then, says Molly, since you are so true,
I'll ne'er love any, I'll ne'er love any,
I'll ne'er love any, my jewel, but you."

Now these young lovers they did part—
Few know the grief of true love's smart—
For he took shipping, and away he went,
And left his Molly, and left his Molly,
And left his Molly in tears for to lament.

Then to old Spain his course did steer,
A British tar devoid of fear,
.   And soon returned with store of treasure,
To crown his true love, to crown his true love,
To crown his true love with joy and pleasure.

Now he his Molly leaves no more,
To mourn alone upon the shore,
But stays at home from the raging seas
To spend his treasures, to spend his treasures,
To spend his treasures and his Molly please.

A Relish for Old Nick.

Song on the threatened Invasion.   Written by "a Loyal Subject."
Tune, Vicar and Moses.
" Printed for J. Wallis, Ludgate Hill, price 1d., or 8d per dozen, by
J. Crowder and E. Hempsted, Warwick Square."

ARM! neighbours at length,
And put forth your strength,
Perfidious bold France to resist;

Ten Frenchmen will fly,
To shun a black eye,
If one Englishman doubles his fist.

But if they feel stout,
Why, let them turn out,
With their maws stuff'd with frogs, soup, and jellies,
Brave Nelson's thunder
Shall strike them with wonder,
And make the frogs leap in their bellies.

Their impudent boast
Of invading our coast,
Neptune swears they had better decline;
For the rogues may be sure,
That their frenzy he'll cure,
And he'll pickle them all in his brine.

And when they've been soak'd,
Long enough to be smok'd,
To the regions below they'll be taken;
And there hung up to dry,
Fit to boil or to fry,
When Old Nick wants a rasher of bacon.

Nelson's Glorious Victory at Trafalgar.

ARISE, arise, brave Britons!
    Perform your loudest lays;
And join me in a chorus,
    To sing Britannia's praise.
Once more the hero of the Nile
Did seek to make Britannia smile
With another victory on the file—
    O brave Nelson!

October, on the twenty-first,
   It being a glorious day,
The combined fleets of France and Spain
   Were just off Cadiz Bay ;
Their ships, in number thirty-three—
And Nelson, when he did them see,
Said, " Twenty then there is for me."
   O brave Nelson !

The signal made for fighting,
   Cannon began to roar ;
Our ships, in number twenty-seven,
   We shook the Spanish shore ;
And Nelson on the deck so high,
Aloud unto his men did cry,
" We'll conquer them, my lads, or die."
   O brave Nelson !

He broke their line of battle,
   And struck the fatal blow ;
He blew some up into the air,
   And some he sent below.
But, when with victory on his side,
A fatal ball his life destroyed,
He in the midst of glory died.
   O brave Nelson !

When the hero brave was dying,
   And with his parting breath,
He pray'd for England's glory,
   Till the moment of his death.
" Farewell, my lads, my glass is run,
This day must be my setting sun ;
But Providence, thy will be done,"
   O brave Nelson !

The battle it being over,
Which was a bloody fray ;
We twenty of their finest ships,
From them did take away.
Now Bonaparte ! boast no more,
To land upon our native shore,
Lest you in pieces should be tore,
Through brave Nelson.

May Collingwood's and Hardy's,
Like Nelson's fame resound,
And all our force by land and sea,
With good success be crown'd ;
May Britain's trade and wealth increase,
All wars and tumults ever cease,
And may we have a lasting peace,
Through brave Nelson.

CHESAPEAKE AND SHANNON.

THIS notable engagement took place on 1st June 1813. Early in
1812 war was declared by the United States of America against this
country, the great object of the American government being the conquest
of Canada. On the frontiers of Canada the Americans were defeated
with great loss, but their loss by land was compensated by their success
at sea for upwards of a twelvemonth. Very many English vessels were
either captured or sunk by the American frigates. It fell to the lot of
Captain Philip B. V. Broke of the Shannon to alter this sad state of
matters. The station of the Shannon was off the port of Boston, in
which harbour lay the United States frigate Chesapeake, Captain Law-
rence,—a fine ship of forty-nine guns—eighteen and thirty-two pounders,
—with a complement of four hundred and forty men. On the first of
June, Broke stood in with the Boston lighthouse, presenting himself as a
challenger to single combat. The Chesapeake sailed out of the harbour,

and came down upon the Shannon, and after exchanging two or three broadsides, came to closer quarters. Captain Broke gave immediate orders to board, and the Americans, after a desperate but disorderly resistance, were driven, sword in hand, from every post. The American flag was hauled down, and the proud old British Union floated triumphantly over it. The whole action was achieved in fifteen minutes. One young midshipman, Smith, particularly distinguished himself. Captain Broke in his dispatches made honourable mention of him, and recommended him among others for promotion. Mr. James in his Naval History says, "The Chesapeake's main-top was stormed by midshipman William Smith and his top-men—about five in number—who either destroyed or drove on deck all the Americans there stationed. This gallant young man had deliberately passed along the Shannon's foreyard, which was braced up to the Chesapeake's main-yard, and thence into her top." William Smith had entered the navy on board the Shannon in July 1806 as first-class volunteer, and had seen some service previous to the memorable exploit just recorded, for which, on 14th July 1813, he was promoted to the rank of lieutenant. He subsequently served on several stations, and in 1825 was in the East Indies, actively employed during the war in Ava, in which he particularly distinguished himself. In 1826 he was advanced for his services to the rank of commander, was employed in that capacity and in the Coast Guard Service until 1838. He was again in the East Indies until the close of 1844. He attained the rank of captain in 1846. Having prior to his first expedition to India married Miss Wilson, sister of one of the partners of Batson, Berry, and Co., Bankers, Berwick-on-Tweed, his domicile had from that time been in Berwick, and thither he returned in 1845. There he resided during the remainder of his life, very much respected by all who had the pleasure of his acquaintance. He was very popular as a magistrate for his impartial justice. He died in 1862, and was buried in the cemetery at Berwick-on-Tweed. His coffin was appropriately of oak, and his funeral was attended by the magistrates, town council, and a large number of the inhabitants of the borough. His coffin was borne by a detachment of the Coast Guard.

So certain had the Americans assured themselves of the capture of the Shannon, that a large crowd had been assembled on shore to welcome the victorious Chesapeake, and they could scarcely believe their eyes when they saw that vessel strike its colours and sail away out to sea in the company of the Shannon.

Captain Philip-Bowes-Vere Broke, said to be descended from an ancient family in the County Palatine of Chester, was created a baronet on 2d Nov. 1813.

The song which follows was at one time very popular, and used to be sung to the air of "Yankee doodle."

Chesapeake and Shannon.

THE Chesapeake so bold,　·
Out of Boston, I 've been told,
Came to take a British frigate,
　　　Neat and handy, O !
While the people all in port
Came out to see the sport,
With their music playing
　　　Yankee doodle dandy, O !

Now the British frigate's name,
Which for the purpose came
Of cooling Yankee's courage
　　　Neat and handy, O !
Was the Shannon—Captain Broke—
Whose crew were hearts of oak,
And for fighting were allowed to be
　　　The dandies, O !

The engagement scarce begun,
Ere they flinched from their guns,
Which at first they thought of working
　　　Neat and handy, O !
Then brave Broke he drew his sword,
Crying, " Now, my lads, we 'll board,
And we 'll stop their playing
　　　Yankee doodle dandy, O !"

They no sooner heard the word,
Ere they quickly jumped on board,
And haul'd down the Yankee ensign
　　　Neat and handy, O !

Notwithstanding all their brag,
Now the glorious British flag
At the Yankee's mizen peak
    Was quite the dandy, O !

Here 's a health, " Brave Broke," to you,
To your officers and crew,
Who on board the Shannon frigate
    Fought so handy, O !
And may it ever prove
That for fighting, as in love,
The true British tars
    Are the dandies, O !

LOSS OF THE ABEONA TRANSPORT.

THE Abeona Transport of 328 tons, under the charge of Lieutenant Mudge, R.N. sailed from Greenock in October 1820 with settlers for the Cape of Good Hope. On the 25th November following, about noon, while in latitude 4 deg., 30 min., North, and longitude 25 deg., 30 min., West, a fire broke out in the after store-room, while the chief mate was occupied there, and the flames made such rapid progress, that during the time three small boats were being got over-board, the tackles, &c., necessary for hoisting out the long-boat were consumed.—In these three small boats forty-nine persons were stowed with so scanty a supply of provisions that their fate must have been nearly as dreadful as that of their fellow-passengers left on board, had not a Portuguese ship from Bahia bound to Lisbon fallen in with them next morning at daylight, and received them on board. After having unsuccessfully cruised about the fatal spot till noon, in hopes of descrying some of the miserable sufferers, who might have clung to part of the wreck, they were safely and hospitably conveyed to Lisbon. Out of a crew consisting of twenty-one persons fourteen were saved. Among these were Lieutenant Mudge; Mr Fisher, the Surgeon; the Master of the ship; and the second mate;—the first mate in a most heroic manner, having refused to go into the boats, saying he would abide the fate of those left on board. Of the emigrants, consisting in all of thirty-one men, twenty-four women, fifty-five boys,

and thirty girls, there were only saved ten men, three women, sixteen
boys, and six girls, making a total of forty-nine persons saved out of one
hundred and sixty-one.

Burning of the Abeona.

FAREWELL, dear auld Scotland, the home of our fathers,
  Thy fair verdant vallies and rivers, adieu ;
Our acquaintances, friends, yea ! our sisters and brothers,
  We leave ye for ever for scenes that are new.

The ship is now riding engaged to convey us
  In peace and in safety across a rude sea,
Till we land at the Cape, where we hope to repay us,
  For our sorrow, auld Scotland, in parting from thee.

The ship she cleared out in the month of October,
  Well favoured by weather, by wind, and by tide,
And every advantage seemed round us to hover,
  As through the wide ocean we swiftly did glide.

But ah ! cruel fate, how deceiving thy projects,
  How soon are they clouded when brightest they shine,
And bear us for ever from all those dear objects,
  Which we hoped to enjoy in a far distant clime.

The transport, whose fate many friends are deploring,
  Was sea-tight and every way worthy to view,
But while all around a fierce ocean was roaring,
  A sight more terrific alarmed the whole crew.

The transport on fire, and no place for retreating,
  The emigrants' hearts were struck with dismay,
Then all for the boats kept so anxiously waiting ;
  But these soon were filled, and were floated away.

I he rest they were left to the fire or the ocean,
   Fond husbands and wives their dear children embrace,
And while they are joining in solemn devotion,
   The ship breaks in pieces and leaves not a trace.

The sight so appalling must strike all with pity,
   To think of the cries of the children on deck,
Of the fathers and mothers who left their own city,
   And perished in midst of the fast burning wreck.

The friends of the crew of the famed Abeona,
   May let a tear fall, when the story goes forth,
But the poor orphans left will sadly bemoan a'
   Their loss as they gaze on their desolate hearth.

These children no more to their mothers shall prattle,
   Who hopefully wait for good news from the sea,
And while relatives mourn o'er the lost Abeona,
   They fondly, auld Scotland, cling closer to thee.

Though poverty forces the Scotchman to journey,
   In quest of that lucre which worldly ones prize,
He leaves his loved country in hopes to return aye,
   For no other land is so dear to his eyes.

The following broadside tells its own story.   It is entitled

A MOST SERIOUS AND MELANCHOLY ACCOUNT OF THE
DEATH OF 20 YOUNG PEOPLE ;

Who were drowned off New Ferry on the 2nd of July 1821.

"IN this you have a most awful account of the vanity of human pursuits. These unfortunate persons had met to celebrate the wedding of
two of the party ; and, after the wedding ceremony was performed, they

went by water to Runcorn. On their return the boat upset ; when, melancholy to relate, the bride and nineteen others met their death."

Drowning of Twenty Young People.

At Liverpool a wedding was,
  On Wednesday last, they say,
In Eighteen hundred and twenty-one,
  It proved a woeful day.

Twenty-five fond youths united
  To join a marriage feast,
And all seemed quite delighted,
  Each was a merry guest.

Arm and arm, as free they walked,
  Unto the church to go,
And all on love they talked,
  But mark their overthrow.

The couple joined together,
  Homeward they quick did haste,
And all things being ready
  Upon the table placed

The bridegroom with a smile,
  " You're welcome all," said he;
The bride now urged the same,
  " Come, let's all merry be."

The dinner being over,
  Said one, both young and gay,
" 'Tis fine and pleasant weather,
  Let's take a trip to sea."

So all agreed together ;
  To sea those couples went,
And unto Runcorn steered,
  In love and sweet content.

They landed safe on shore,
  And to an inn they went ;
And sat and joked awhile,
  But mark the sad event.

The wind blew off the shore,
  A gentle breeze set in ;
Each man his lass did take,
  To sea they went again.

At half a league or more,
  They from the shore were seen,
A sudden squall came on,
  Their sorrows did begin.

A young man lost his hat,
  They turned to catch the same ;
The boat upset—they fell
  Into the wat'ry main.

The people on the shore,
  Who saw this awful scene,
Straight launched their boats to sea,
  To take their bodies in.

Twenty-five there were in all,
  They only five could save ;
The boatman, also all the maids,
  Sunk in a wat'ry grave.

The men they took on shore,
Their vital powers near spent :
When strength they felt restored,
Their sweethearts they lament.

Six girls were taken up,
The surgeons tried their skill ;
Their art was all in vain,
For nothing could prevail.

The bridegroom viewed his bride,
And kissed her lips sae sweet,
Her wedding clothes were turned
Into a winding sheet.

To Liverpool their bodies brought,
Their friends all wept aloud,
And deep and dismal were their groans,
Among the numerous crowd.

And you who view this sight
A warning take by this,
Prepare to take your flight
To everlasting bliss.

LAMENTATION FOR THE LOSS OF THE STEAMBOAT COMET.

THE Comet steamboat on her passage from Inverness to Glasgow, on
21st October 1825, when off the western point of Gourock (three miles
below Greenock) about two o'clock in the morning, was met by the steamboat, Ayr, Maclelland, Ayr, en route from Greenock for that port.
The two boats were going at great speed, (the Comet showing no light)

and, coming in violent contact with each other, the Comet was so seriously injured that she filled with water and sank almost immediately. The vessel was about a quarter of a mile distant from the shore when the accident occurred. About half an hour before, several of the passengers had been dancing on the deck, but at the time they had almost all gone below. On the shock being felt, everybody ran on deck. The water rushed in so rapidly that the engineman was wading up to the knees ere he reached the deck. Endeavours were made to keep the engine going, under the idea that the vessel might be driven on shore, but the influx of water was so strong as to stop it. During the short period which elapsed between the collision and the sinking of the vessel, about thirty people crowded into the yawl before it was cut loose, and so hastily was this done, that the one end of the boat was some time under water before the other end could be lowered, by which means the boat was upset, and they were all thrown into the flood. There were about sixty or seventy passengers on board, all of whom, with exception of nine and the master and pilot, were drowned. The captain of the Ayr did not attempt to render any assistance, but, amidst the screams and shouts of the drowning, put about and made instantly for Greenock. Those who were saved were chiefly rescued by wherries, which had put off from Gourock, on the first alarm being given. Among those drowned were Captain Sutherland, of the 33d foot, and his wife, to whom he had been united only six weeks previously. He was on his way to Glasgow, to join the Depot of his Regiment. Although he was a good swimmer, and might by little exertion have saved his own life, still as he could not save that of his wife, he preferred remaining with her, and they went down together locked in each other's arms.

Mr Graham of Corpach, Mr Hugh James Rollo, W.S., Mr Charles M'Allister, W.S., and his nephew Mr M'Allister were also among the drowned. The bodies of the two latter were conveyed to the Isle of Skye for interment. Mr Charles M'Allister was proprietor of an estate in Argyleshire. He was greatly esteemed by all who knew him, and his sad fate caused anguish to many hearts.

There were lost also six servants of Sir J. Radcliff, and a poor woman from Inverness with her family of six children.

Miss Jane Munro, aged 16, from Tain, proceeding to visit an aunt at Glasgow, whom she had never seen, was for a few days believed to have been among those drowned, but, by the assistance of a dog, (supposed to have belonged to Mr M'Allister) she had reached Gourock, where she had been carefully seen to by the pilot's wife. Mrs Martin, a poor woman with her baby in her arms, clung to a box, as the vessel was sinking, and succeeded in keeping the head of her baby above water; but a man and a couple of dogs, who were struggling near her, pushed the box from her grasp, and for two or three seconds she was unsuccoured. Another boat then floated within her reach, but in seizing it, she had wrested it from the grasp of a gentleman, who, to her horror, sank. She kept herself afloat till assistance came from Gourock, but she had been too much exhausted to preserve her child ; although still warm in her arms, it was no longer in life.

Popular indignation having been excited against the master of the Comet, M'Lelland, he, along with the pilot, M'Bride, was tried at Glasgow, when the latter was acquitted, but M'Lelland was found guilty of culpable homicide, and sentenced to three months' imprisonment.

Lamentation for the Loss of the Steamboat Comet.

O ! HEARD ye the sound
Of wailing and sadness,
On the shores of the north,
Where there lately was gladness ?
The steamboats were seen,
O'er the foaming waves bounding,
While with them was joy,
As yon point they were rounding,

On Thursday the Comet
Set sail in the morning,
From Fort William's shore,
She was swiftly returning
To the Clyde, where alas !
She was struck by another,
And sunk in the ocean,
To rise again never.

Ah ! many will pity
The sorrowing mother,
And sigh for yon beauty,
Who mourns for her lover.

Many tears may be shed,
But never, ah ! never,
Will their sobs wake the dead,
Who are sleeping for ever.

These, a moment before,
Of joy might be dreaming,
And thinking on home,
And a mother's eye beaming
Wi' joy on the son
She so tenderly cherished !
These dreams are all fled,
And full seventy perished.

From a grave in the deep,
There are few that were sav'd,
Amongst them a mother
Of her child was bereaved,
The hardened rocks rung
Wi' her heart's rending wailing,
" My child ! ah ! my child !"
She cried sad and despairing.

Ah ! who can foresee
What may happen to-morrow ?
This moment in joy,
And the next fu' o' sorrow,
And when we least think,
There is danger surrounding,
Too oft we have found,
There was sorrow abounding,

Let's prepare for our change now,
For time is uncertain.
Ah ! we know not the hour,
Nor the moment of parting.

Those true loving hearts
   Which so fondly we cherish,
We seldom take heed
   May speedily perish,—

And that in one moment,
   Without any warning,
Like those who were summoned
   On that fatal morning ;
And the homes they had left,
   In the hope of returning,
Became scenes of wo,
   Lamentation and mourning.

THE BATTLE OF ALMANZA.

ALMANZA or Almanca is a small town of Spain, in the district of Villena on the north east of Murcia.

The engagement, which the following Ballad commemorates, took place in its vicinity, on the 25th April, 1707, N.S. when the French and Spaniards, under the command of the Duke of Berwick, completely defeated the confederates, commanded by the Marquis das Minas and the Earl of Galway. At the first charge, the Portuguese cavalry abandoned the infantry, and the entire body were cut to pieces or made prisoners, but the cavalry, with their two generals, made a timely retreat to Catalonia, leaving the kingdoms of Valencia and Arragon to the mercy of the enemy.

The general appearance of the Broadside from which this has been printed would indicate the date of its issue to have been somewhere about 1760.

The Battle of Almanza.

Down by a chrystal river side,
　I fell a weeping ;
To see my brother soldier dear,
　Upon the ground lie bleeding.

It was from the Castle of Vino,
　We marched on Easter Sunday ;
And the battle of Almanza,
　Was fought on Easter Monday.

Full twenty miles we marched that day,
　Without one drop of water ;
Till we poor souls were almost spent,
　Before the bloody slaughter.

Over the plain we marched along,
　All in the line of battle ;
To the beat of drums and colours flying,
　And thundering cannons' rattle.

Brave Gallaway, our General,
    Cry'd, " Fight on ! while you may ;
Fight on ! brave-hearted Englishmen,
    You're one to five this day.

" Hold back ! nor make the first attack,
    'Tis what they do desire :
But when you see my sword I draw,
    Let each platoon give fire."

We had not marched some paces three,
    Before the small shot flew like thunder ;
Hoping that we should get the day,
    And likewise all the plunder.

But the Dutch fell on with sword in hand,
    And that was their desire ;
Thirty-five squadrons of Portuguese,
    They ran and ne'er gave fire.

The Duke of Berwick, as I have been told,
    He gave it out in orders,
That if the army should be broke,
    To give the English quarters.

" Be kind unto my countrymen,
    For that is my desire ;
With the Portuguese do as you please,
    For they will soon retire."

Now to conclude and make an end
    Of this my dismal story,
One hundred thousand fighting men
    Have died for England's glory.

Let no brave soldier be dismayed
    For losing of a battle ;

We have more forces coming on
Will make Jack Frenchman rattle.

THE RUNAWAY BRIDE.

WHETHER this ballad has been written to record an actual occurrence in "the North Countrie," we have failed to trace.   In Herd's Ancient and Modern Ballads, Vol. II., there is a Scots song of five stanzas, bearing the same title, but treating of

" A laddie and a lassie" who
" Dwelt in the South Countrie,"

and having resolved to be married,

" The bridal day was set
On Tiseday for to be ;
Then hey play up the rinawa' bride,
For she has taen the gie."

Her father and mother pursue her "unto the water of Tweed," and make inquiries after her in " Kelso toun."   The reply is by no means satisfactory :—

" Now wally fu' fa' the silly bridegroom,
He was as saft as butter ;
For had she play'd the like to me,
I had nae sae easily quat her.
I'd gien her a tune o' my hoboy,
And set my fancy free ;
And syne played up the runaway bride,
And lutten her tak the gie."

The Runaway Bride.

IF you'll go to the North Countrie,
If that you be but ready,
You'll hear how the Bride from the blacksmith ran
To be a liggar lady.

She ran away, she ran away,
    At home she would not tarry ;
And she is with the sergeant gone,
    His halbert for to carry.

The Lassies in the North Countrie
    They long to be a bride, man :
But when the wedding day is come
    With the bridegroom they will not bide, man.
      She ran away, &c.

In the toun of Keith, to lie I'm loth,
    The wedding day was set, man ;
But when the people gathered were,
    The bride they could not get, man.
      She ran away, &c.

Its wo be to the Low Countrie,
    And a' your men in Banff, man ;
Let the laddies frae the Highlands come
    And play you such a jamph, man.
      She ran away, &c.

They wrote a letter with great speed,
    To the bridegroom sent for fun, man ;
And when the tidings he did hear,
    Distracted he did run, man.
      She ran away, &c.

When the bridegroom heard, he cried, "alas !
    For ever I'll away, man ;
For this day I am ruined quite,
    My bride she's run away, man."
      She ran away, &c.

His young men and his maidens all
    Unto him did resort, man,

With laughter like to split their sides
    When they heard of such sport, man.
        She ran away, &c.

"All young men, if you please to stay,
    Your dinner it is ready;
But I'll go to the toun of Keith,
    And see to find my lady."
        She ran away, &c.

His maiden at his right side stands,
    And laughing thus did say, man,
" I think myself a happy maid
    Since she has run away, man."
        She ran away, &c.

His maiden at his right side stands,
    And laughing thus did say, man,
" If I live to another year
    We'll have our wedding day, man.
Since she's away, away is gone,
    At home she would not tarry;
I'll be a bride to the self-same man,
    And with him I will marry."

All you young men I pray beware,
    If ever you are to marry,
Take care your bride don't run away
    The halbert for to carry.
        She'll run away, &c.

All you young men I pray beware,
    If you be to wed, man,
Take care none of the Highland lads
    Come down to steal your bride, man.
For they'll away, they'll run away,
    At home they will not bide, man;

For the laddies from the Highlands come
And steal away our bride, man.

The Sodger's Return.

A new Song to the tune of "Push about the Jorum," 1777.

THE tither morn
When I, forlorn,
Aneath an aik sat moaning,
I did na trow
I'd see my jo
Beside me 'gain the gloaming,
But he fu trig
Lap ower the rig,
An' dawtingly did cheer me,
When I—what reck !
Did least expec
To see my laddie near me.

His bonnet he,
A thocht ajee
Cock'd sprush when first he clasp'd me ;
An' I, I wat,
Wi' fainness grat,
While in his grips he press'd me ;
Deil tak the war,
I, late an' air, .
Hae wished since Jock departed ;
But now as glad
I'm wi' my lad
As shortsyne broken-hearted.

Fu' aft at e'en,
Wi' dancing keen,
When a' were blythe an' merry,

I car'd na by,
Sae sad was I
In absence o' my deary.
But, praise be blest,
My mind's at rest,
I'm happy wi' my Johnny !
At kirk an' fair
I'se aye be there,
An' be as canty's ony.

Valiant M'Craws.

THE Mac-Raes or Mac-Raws were originally a powerful clan in Ross-shire, but ultimately became subject to the Mackenzies of Seaforth, whom they always followed. They were present at Glenshee, Glenfruin, &c. In 1793, when Sir John Sinclair published his Statistical Account of Scotland, all the inhabitants of Kintail were Mac-Raws.

"Seaforth's Regiment," which is so prominently brought forward in this ballad, was the old 78th Highlanders. It was raised in 1777 by Kenneth Mackenzie, who was appointed Colonel. He was the only son of Lord Fortrose, and grandson of the attainted Earl of 1715. He was born at Edinburgh 15th January 1744, was created an Irish Peer by the title of Baron Ardelve, and Viscount Fortrose in 1766, and was advanced to the Earldom of Seaforth, also in Ireland, in 1771. He died in August 1781, on his passage to India with his Regiment. He had married, 7th Oct. 1765, Lady Caroline Stanhope, eldest daughter of William, second Earl of Harrington. Her death occurred on 9th February 1767, at the early age of twenty. She left one daughter, Caroline, born 7th July 1766, who married Lewis Francis Drummond (Count Melfort), and lived beyond the advanced age of eighty. On the death of Lord Seaforth, in 1781, the title became extinct, but it was revived in 1797 in the person of Francis Humberstone Mackenzie, who died at Edinburgh in 1815. Although deaf and dumb, his lordship was a Fellow of several Learned Societies, had attained the rank of Lieutenant-General in the army, and was for many years Governor of Barbadoes.

The 78th Regiment, while at Edinburgh in Sept. 1778, had mutinied ; but by the kind treatment and prudence of General Skene, they were reclaimed to their duty.

The particulars are as follows :

The regiment, which had been quartered at Edinburgh for some time, was ordered for Guernsey, but a difference having subsisted between the officers and men, the latter alleging non-payment of bounty money, arrears of pay, and general ill-usage, they refused to go aboard the transports. About 500 men were, upon promises of redress, finally prevailed on to embark ; while the disaffected, of a like number, betook themselves to Arthur Seat, a high hill adjoining Holyrood, where they, being favoured by many of the people of Edinburgh, were plentifully supplied with provisions, and visited by persons of all ranks, General Skene (second in command in Scotland) and other noblemen and gentlemen who sought to reclaim them, being among the number. In consequence of it having been reported that the mutineers would march through the city, and that the troops who had been called there were prepared to oppose them, this bill was issued by the authorities, "Thursday, Sept. 24, 1778. All the inhabitants are to retire to their houses on the first toll of the fire-bell." Everything, however, remained quiet ; and happily a compromise was two days afterwards effected, the terms being a pardon for past offences, arrears to be paid before embarkation, and that the regiment should not be sent to the East Indies. The officers, conceiving that the terms granted were inconsistent with the future discipline of the regiment, and injurious to their professional character, declared, through the medium of the *Edinburgh Advertiser*, that the compromise was gone into without their advice and against their conviction. A Court of Inquiry was held, and the result was, the Court were unanimously of opinion : "That there is not the smallest degree of foundation for complaints against any officer in the regiment in regard to their pay and arrears ; and it further appears that the cause of the retiring to Arthur's Hill was from an idle and ill-founded report that the regiment was sold to the East India Company, and that the officers were to leave them upon their being embarked on board the transports." The mutineers went aboard the transports at Leith on the following Monday, "with the greatest cordiality and chearfulness," Lord Seaforth and General Skene "on their head." See Scots Magazine, vol. 40.

The present 78th (Highland) Regiment of Foot, or Ross-shire Buffs, was raised by letter of service, dated 7th March 1793. It ranks high in the annals of fame.

The expedition of the Prince of Nassau against Jersey was in 1779, but the writer of the following ballad has anticipated the month, as it was not till the 1st of May that the Prince appeared off St Ouen's Bay with his fleet, numbering from five to six thousand men. Here he attempted to disembark with his army, but the Jersey men by a forced march of the 78th Regiment, and the assistance of a corps of militia, supported by artillery, repulsed him. Thus frustrated, the Prince proceeded with his squadron to St Brelade's Bay ; but finding a similar

opposition there, he abandoned the enterprize. Dissension and recrimi-
nation among the French officers in consequence prevailed, and a second
attack was planned ; but before it could be effected the fleet, prepared
to cover the invasion, was attacked by a British squadron, under Sir
James Wallace, and nearly annihilated. In "Chroniques, des Iles de
Jersey, Guernesey, Auregny, et Serk par George S. Syvret. *Guernesey*,
8vo. 1832," will be found a French ballad, "Sur la retraite des
François hors de Jersey," wherein the Scotch Regiment, (*i.e.*, the 78th) is
particularly noticed :—

> "Etant accompagnés dans le même instant,
>   De cinq cents Ecossais—ce noble regiment—
>   Renommés pour la guerre dans les siècles passés
>   La gloire de l'Angleterre et celle de ses armées.
>
> •   •   •   •   •
>
>   L'on conclut aussitôt de marcher au rivage,
>   Où l'on pourrait plutôt defendre l'atterage ;
>   Le Capitaine Frazer, avec ses braves soldats,
>   Y marchant le premier d'un intrépide pas !"

In the despatches of Lieutenant-Governor Corbet, mention was made
of the gallantry of the 78th, and, in general orders given out at Jersey
on the 8th May 1779, they were highly complimented. They also received the thanks of the States of Jersey for their essential services,
through the medium of the Chief Magistrate of the Island.

Towards the end of the next year Jersey was again invaded by the French.
During the night of the 25th December, 1780, a signal fire appeared between Rosel and La Coupe, which was answered from the coast of
France. This was indicative of the absence of British ships of war from the
station. On the morning following, French troops were embarked at Gran-
ville under the command of the Baron de Rullecourt, who expected to capture the island during the festive season of Christmas when the inhabitants
were indulging in revelry. Baron de Rullecourt had been second in
command during the former expedition. He was a man of shattered fortunes, who hoped, by a successful adventure, to enrich himself and gain
high favour with the French king.

Rullecourt quitted France in very tempestuous weather ; many of the
transports were in consequence dispersed, and the rest obliged to seek
shelter at the rocky Island of Chauzey. This checked his progress,
and reduced his little army to 1200 men. With this force, however, he
reached Jersey on the night of the 5th January 1781, and being accompanied by a Jersey pilot, who having committed a murder, had sometime
before fled from the island. By this man's assistance he effected a land-

ing of 700 men, at a very rocky and dangerous point. Having seized on a small battery of four guns, which he manned, and leaving a company to protect the boats, and, if need be, to secure his retreat, he marched with his men unobserved into the town, where at the market place they killed the sentinel and surprised the guard. One man, however, escaped, and ran immediately to the general hospital, in which the Regiment of Highlanders was quartered.

At break of day the inhabitants were much astonished to see the market-place filled with French soldiers. The Lieutenant-Governor, Major Moses Corbet, was in bed when the intelligence was first brought him. His house was surrounded, and he with some others was taken prisoner. He was conveyed to the court-house, where the French General represented to him that resistance was useless ; that 4000 men had been landed in different parts of the island ; that the British troops stationed near La Roque were prisoners, and that two battalions were in the vicinity of the town. He then issued a proclamation in the name of the French king, promising protection to those who would submit quietly.

Having produced articles of capitulation for the island, he required Major Corbet to sign them under a menace, that, in default of compliance, he had orders to burn the town, with the shipping, and to put every inhabitant to the sword. The Major as he was then a prisoner refused, but on Rullecourt laying his watch upon the table and saying he would carry his threat into execution unless the articles were signed within half an hour, Major Corbet, as well as Major Hogg signed the capitulation. The Baron thus conceiving himself to be master of the island, produced a commission from the King of France appointing him a general in his army, and Governor of Jersey.

During these events, the militia had assembled in different places. Every regiment moved towards the town ; the greater part joined the Highlanders who were encamped in *le Mont Patibulaire* or *Gallowshill*, under the command of Captain Lumsdale : and a company marched to Elizabeth Castle. Corbet had despatched an order for the troops on the heights to bring their arms to the court-house, and sent notice of capitulation to the castle, to take possession of which the French army shortly afterwards left St. Heliers. Rullecourt marched at the head of the column, holding Major Corbet by the arm ; but they were no sooner on the beach than a couple of effective shots from the castle caused them to halt. An officer was despatched with a written order from Corbet to surrender. This, Captain Ailwards the officer in command, refused, and Rullecourt, denouncing vengeance, was compelled to retire. In the meantime the regular troops and militia were assembled on the heights, under the orders of Major Pierson of the 95th Regiment, the next in command to the Lieutenant-Governor. Advancing towards St Heliers, the Major was requested by Rullecourt to conform to the capitulation so as to prevent bloodshed and save the town from ruin. This being met by a refusal, and the British and Island troops pressing onwards towards the market-place, a fierce encounter resulted, during which Major Pierson was killed. Surprised and discouraged for an instant, the troops gave way ; but they soon rallied, and renewed the conflict, which terminated in the total defeat of the French and the death of Rullecourt by a projectile from the 78th Regiment. Major Corbet resumed the command, and such of Rullecourt's army, as were not either killed or captured, escaped to their vessels. The loss on the British side was fifty of the regulars killed or wounded, and about thirty of the militia. Major Pierson was interred in the Church of St Helier, and a monument erected to commemorate his bravery. This officer had scarcely attained his twenty-fourth year. Major Corbet was tried and superseded ; but is said to have received a pension. Although Jersey has since been frequently menaced and alarmed, it has not again experienced any further attack. Bonaparte, in his threatened invasion of England, called these islands " stepping-stones" to that kingdom, yet he never deemed it advisable to visit them.

There is an admirable line engraving of "the death of Major Pierson," which has now become very rare.

Our ballad is from a stall copy, *circa* 1782, of " Five Excellent New Songs, 1. The Valiant M'Craws; 2. The Spend Thrift clapt into Limbo; 3. The Garb of Old Gaul ; 4. The North Highland Volunteers; 5. I cannot love thee more." "Entered according to order."

A NEW SONG ON

The Valiant M'Craws of Seaforth's Regiment,

WHO DEFEATED THE FRENCH INVASION ON THE

ISLAND OF JERSEY, April 1779,

Tune.—" Arthur's Seat.

AT Arthur's Seat both early and late,
　　Our camp was secured by us a', man ;
And by capitulation for the good of our nation,
　　We shipped from Leith, and awa', man.
With a loud cheer to the ships we did steer,
　　Set sail, and to Jersey run o'er, man ;
We got a salute from the garrison stout,
　　By cannons which loudly did roar, man.

We were welcom'd by all, both by great and by small,
  They wondered to see our bold dress, man;
No breeks on our knee, our tartans so hie,
  And our language they could not express, man.
But we soon let them know, if ever a foe
  Came near to this island to plunder, man,
With her claymore, at sea or on shore,
  She would strike him as dead as a flounder, man.

Not long was it hence, when Nassau's Prince,
  With his fleet and his troops to invade us, man,
Sailed from the French shore, our island to gore,
  And briskly to cannonade us, man.
As for a long while, peace had guarded our Isle,
  They thought it had little defence, man,
But when they came near, we saw them so clear,
  And gave them to know our presence, man.

They took the alarm, but not without harm,
  We stick'd and shot hundreds and more, man;
We made them to flee from land to the sea,
  The Nassauites loudly did roar, man.
They damned us in French, we curs'd them in Earse,
  We crackéd their pows wi' claymore, man;
Then off they took flight, i' the dead of the night,
  Their wounded they left on the shore, man.

The French got such claws by the valiant M'Craws,
  They thought they were devils indeed, man;
And they lustily swore, they never no more,
  Wished to see a manjack of that breed, man.
May our brave Highland clans be honoured with fame,
  Wherever their leaders command them;
And all who won't join in this notable rhyme,
  May ill fortune for ever attend them.

WOUNDED NANCY'S RETURN.

THERE are numerous ballads on the subject of a girl assuming male
attire, and following her lover to the wars, either with his knowledge
or without it. Among them we may mention two presently before us,
stall copies of 1796, somewhat rough. One is called "Polly Oliver,"
wherein the heroine, in love with a captain, proceeds to Stafford, where
his regiment is, and enlisting as a full private, in the end discloses herself, and he marries her. The music of Polly Oliver, will be found in
Mr Chappell's "National English Airs," marked No. 10, London 1838,
4to. The other is titled "The frolicsome Maid, who went to
Gibraltar, and from a single soldier turned Captain, and yet chaste."
The argument is, a girl of fifteen is promised marriage by a soldier who
"loves and rides away," as sometimes will happen in such cases. She
enlists in his regiment, and "chooses" him for her comrade. Although
almost constantly with him, he never discovers her. He is "draughted"
to Gibraltar, where the girl insists on going also, and, after some hesitation by the Captain, the "Press-master" allows her.

" Then in Gibraltar stood guard o'er that tower,
Where every man there stood his own hour,
Our General then told me preferred was I,
From a soldier to an Ensign my colours to fly."

Our Ensign one day makes inquiry after his former comrade :—

" I called for Donald, 'where's Donald?' I said,
The answer they made me, 'he's gone to be wed.'"

The Ensign sends an "ingenious" man in search of Donald, who is
apparently not far off :—

" Then to the barracks, I ordered him home,
The guard house or land port shall be his doom."

The damsel, our Ensign's rival, is, during Donald's incarceration, thus
disposed of :—

" I conducted this damsel out of the town,
I gave her a guinea to buy a new gown ;
The very next quarters that ever we came,
I married the girl on one of our drums,
I finding the girl both loyal and true,
I gave her my linens to wash and to do."

The Ensign's sex all along remains undiscovered, and in the end she resolves to make serious proposals to Donald, as a reward of course for his having slighted her in early youth :—

" Seven years and better, a Captain I've been,
You may all know that while what a fortune I've win ;
But now my commission I intend to bestow
Upon my faithless comrade who a private does go. "

It is possible that these ballads, as well as " Wounded Nancy," may have been founded on real circumstances, although there is no record of the names of the persons who figure in them.   There are several well-known cases of females who have assumed male attire and served as soldiers and seamen.   Foremost among these is that of Hannah Snell, born in 1723.   When twenty years of age she became the wife of a Dutch sailor, James Summs, who shortly afterwards deserted her.   Assuming male attire, and under the name of James Gray, she set out in quest of her husband, and, having reached Coventry without getting any intelligence of him, enlisted.   At Carlisle, after a march of three weeks, she, with seventeen other recruits, joined her regiment.   Her serjeant, Davis, having formed a design against a young girl there, asked Hannah's aid in furthering his views.   Instead of doing so, she put the girl upon her guard, and, having obtained her esteem and confidence, was frequently in her company, which aroused Davis' jealousy.   Davis accordingly took the first occasion to charge his supposed rival with neglect of duty, for which she received five hundred lashes.   Fearful at length of her sex being discovered, she deserted, and in about a month, after many adventures, reached Portsmouth, where she enlisted as a marine.   In many sieges, in various parts of the world, she took part, and acquired the commendation of her officers.   Before Pondicherry, which after eleven weeks the army was compelled to abandon, Hannah was in the first party of English foot who forded the river breast high, under the incessant fire of a French battery.   She also on picket duty continued seven nights successively, and laboured very hard for a fortnight at the trenches.   She received several wounds, and, in order still to conceal her sex, extracted one bullet with her finger and thumb.   Subsequently as a sailor she encountered many adventures.   While at Lisbon, she ascertained that her long-lost husband had been confined at Genoa for the murder of a gentleman of some distinction there, and had finally expiated his crime by being put into a sack with some heavy stones and cast headlong into the sea.   Arriving in London, and being there recognised by a married sister, her story became known, and she acquired such a degree of popularity as to obtain an engagement as a singer at the Royalty Theatre, Well-close Square, where she appeared in the character of Bill Bobstay, a sailor, and in that of Firelock, a soldier, in which she went through the manual and platoon exercises in a masterly style. Government having conferred on her a pension of £20, in consideration of the hardships she had endured in the service of her country, she took a public house in the neighbourhood of Wapping, which, being well frequented, rendered her more prosperous in her latter days. She preferred the male attire, which she never laid aside during the rest of her life.

Another equally interesting case is that of Christian Davies, who followed her first husband to the wars in the guise of a soldier, and, to his disquietude, finding him attached to a Dutchwoman, she insisted upon remaining a soldier, enjoining his secrecy under pain of something horrible, and stipulating that they should pass as brothers. Being wounded at the battle of Ramilies (1705), her sex was discovered, and she was compelled to leave the service. Her husband's death made her free to marry again, and in about three months after his decease she gave her hand to Serjeant Jones, who received a mortal wound in the attack of St. Venant. At Dublin, her native city, she was married for a third time to a soldier named Davies. She found means to get her husband into Chelsea College with the rank of serjeant; and from the Queen, who had formerly ordered her a bounty of fifty pounds, she obtained an order for a shilling a-day for life. As Daniel Defoe was the biographer of mother Davies, it is uncertain to what extent he may have improved upon fact.

Mary Read, an Englishwoman, was another instance of a female serving as a soldier, and afterwards as a sailor. As she finally turned pirate, the details of her career will be found in Johnson's History of Highwaymen.

In Kirby's Wonderful and Scientific Museum there is a narrative of the adventures of Mary Anne Talbot, alias John Taylor, commonly called the female sailor, although she had also figured as a soldier.

The following romantic account from the obituary notices in the Scots Magazine of April 1779, adds one more lady to the list of those who followed the drum :—

"At Hammersmith, Mrs Ross, celebrated for her beauty and her constancy. Having met with opposition in her engagement with Captain Charles Ross, she followed him in men's clothes to America ; where, after such a research and fatigue as scarce any of her sex could have undergone, she found him in the wood lying for dead, with a poisoned wound, after a skirmish with the Indians ; when, having previously studied surgery in England, she saved his life by sucking his wound, and nursing him with scarce a covering for the space of six weeks, during which time she remained unsuspected by him, having dyed her skin with lime and bark. The Captain recovering, they removed into Philadelphia ; where, as soon as she had found a clergyman to join her to him for ever, she appeared as herself, the priest accompanying her. They lived for four years in a fondness that could only be interrupted by her declining health, the fatigue she had undergone, and the poison not properly expelled, which she had imbibed from his wound, undermining her constitution. The knowledge he had of it, and piercing regret of having been the occasion, affecting him still more sensibly, he died with a broken heart last spring at John's Town. She lived to return and implore forgiveness of her family, whom she had distressed so long by their ignorance of her destiny. She died, in consequence of her grief and affection, at the age of twenty-six."

" Wounded Nancy's Return " was printed and sold by J. Davenport, 3 Compass Court, Cow-Cross, West Smithfield, London, *circa* 1780.

Among other apparently contemporaneous ballads on a similar subject we have "The Female Drum-major," "The Lancashire Heroes," and "Jack Munro."

And there will be found in " Songs Compleat," otherwise " Durfey's Pills to Purge Melancholy," 12mo, London, 1719, vol. V. " The woman warrior, who lived in Cow-Cross, near West Smithfield, who, changing her apparrel, entered herself on board in quality of a soldier, and sailed to Ireland, where she valiantly behaved herself, particularly at the siege of Cork, where she lost her toes and received a mortal wound in her body, of which she since died on her return to London."

Wounded Nancy's Return.

'Twas after a long and tedious voyage
Young Nancy came from the cruel wars,
Where, in the cause of king and country,
She gloried in her wounds and scars.
All side by side with her own true love,
This brave young lass fought valiantly ;
And, with a courage most undaunted,
Followed up the enemy.

All clad in male attire, sweet Nancy
With her lover had set sail ;
She said that only death should part them ;
Dissuasions were of no avail.
No sooner landed than came orders
For our regiment to go
On the sudden forward boldly
To repel the haughty foe.

G

A sorrowing smile gave Nancy's true love
   As we into the field did ride,
With courage and strong resolution
   To subdue the foeman's pride.
All on a coal-black gelding mounted,
   With a glittering sword in hand,
Young Nancy looked so smart and noble,
   Waiting our officers' command.

And, drawn up in line of battle,
   Eager for the coming fray,
No sooner did the cannons rattle,
   Than Nancy trembled in dismay.
But ere long her nerves grew stronger,
   And " Forward !" was the battle-cry ;
Said she aloud, " Why should we falter ?
   We'll be conquerors or die !"

Then onward with our troopers rushing,
   Sword in hand she cleared the way :
For many hours in equal balance
   Hung the fortunes of the day.
Her true love was a handsome serjeant,
   Who so manfully did ride ;
Shielding her from all the dangers
   Which came thick on every side.

Still in the very heat of action
   Young Nancy she received a wound,
Which drove her lover to distraction,
   As down she fell upon the ground.
He dared not stay to yield her succour,
   As charging foremost in the fight ;
One anxious look he cast behind him,
   But the smoke obscured his sight.

In reckless manner plunging onward,
  The frightened foe turned right about ;
And following up our great advantage,
  We put them utterly to rout.
Our serjeant, who ne'er shirked his duty,
  From pursuit returning late ;
Fatigued, he hastened quite downhearted,
  To ascertain young Nancy's fate.

There amid the dead and dying,
  Some kindly hand a couch had made ;
And patiently was Nancy lying,
  Cheering those around her laid.
While her wound was being tended,
  Said she, " Frail mortals that we are—
There's small occasion to be daunted,
  'Tis but the accident of war."

When she saw her true love bending
  O'er her couch with streaming eyes,
She said, " Don't weep—still let us trust in
  God who rules our destinies."
From the field he gently bore her,
  And by her side watched night and day ;
Till returning health came o'er her,
  And safely she could come away.

Then to England home returning
  With such joyous hearts and light,
For their valour both rewarded
  Were with glory's stars bedight.
Doffing then her manly garments,
  Nancy sought a happy life ;
In presence of her former comrades,
  She became the serjeant's wife.

Now all you young lads, likewise maidens,
You plainly see what love will do ;
' For the honest heart and constant
What will woman not go through ?
Nancy braved all storms and dangers,
Boldly venturing life and limb,
To cheer her true love by her presence,
And shed her influence over him.

THE DISAPPOINTED LADY.

SIR Walter Scott has observed that "women are like turkeys, they always draw to the red rag." Whether arising from the attractive nature of the colour itself, or the presumed personal worth of the occupant of the scarlet jacket, it is an acknowledged fact that the "Bould Sodger Boy" possesses a fascination which few ladies of any susceptibility can withstand—a fascination only rivalled by that of the rattlesnake and the Priesthood. Strange to say, the "Jolly Tar" is never looked on with such favour,—although it is a noticeable circumstance that the British sailor holds a much higher post in the estimation of the Muses than the soldier does, his actions being more frequently chronicled in song than those of the landsman. Be that as it may, in affaires de cœur the true blue must haul down his colours, and "pale his ineffectual fire" before the red coat and the black. It has not been ascertained whether the following ballad was written to record any particular case of "scarlet fever." The story is common enough. "The disappointed lady," however, must surely have been generally accredited as "over hopeless hill" (to use a familiar term) ere she could have thought of making overtures to a com-mon soldier, and as her proposal does not appear to have been enter-tained, it is probable that, although styled by the Poet as "both charm-ing and young," either her age or the absence of personal attractions or both were too palpable to the meanest capacity to render her fortune a matter of any consequence to a young man who prized his liberty.

An instance occurred some years ago, not a hundred miles from the modern Athens, where a young lady of station and considerable fortune courted a "bold dragoon with his long sword, saddle, bridle, whack row de dow," and ultimately her good looks and cash secured that question-able bliss which the heroine of this ballad failed to obtain.

The version printed here emanated, towards the close of last century, from the press of "J. Kendrew, Printer, Colliergate, York."

The Disappointed Lady.

YE blooming young damsels give ear to my song,
'Tis of a gay lady both charming and young ;
She fancied a soldier so gallant and free,
And vowed in her heart that his bride she would be.

When she saw this young man on his way to parade,
She called him aside and to him she said—
" I am a young lady, if you fancy me
Your discharge I will purchase; and that speedily.

" For you are the man that I feel I adore—
'Tis for you that young Cupid has wounded me sore ;
A lady I am and my fortune is great,
I'll make you the master of all my estate."

" Dear honoured lady," this young man did say,
" I know not how soon we'll be marching away,
For we must obey when the rout, love, does come,
By the sound of a fife and the beat of a drum."

I'll away to my halls and there will I mourn,
Yet, hoping that soon the dear lad will return,
Neither noble nor squire my favour shall gain ;
For my soldier that's absent a maid I'll remain.

BONNET O' BLUE.

THE "blue bonnet" appears to have been a distinguishing badge of
the Highlanders, more particularly of those attached to the family of the
Stuarts. The "Bonnets of blue" appear to have been a terror to the
Covenanters. In "Lesley's March," a song of the time, believed by Sir

Walter Scott to be genuine, General Leslie is depicted as evincing a dread of being overtaken by the Scotish Royalists ere he can reach Newcastle, and in urging his army forward, is made to exclaim,—

> "March, march ! dogs of redemption,
> Ere the blue bonnets come over the Border."

See Hogg's Jacobite Relics, 8vo., 1819, Vol I.

To the spirit-stirring air, which was wedded to this song, and which was Lesley's favourite march, Sir Walter Scott has written a lyric equally popular. It is an address to the "Sons of the Mountain Glen," wherein they are called on thus :—

> "Stand to your arms then, and march in good order,
> England shall many a day
> Tell of the bloody fray,
> When the blue bonnets come over the Border."

See Monastery, Vol. II., Edition, 12mo., 1830.

Sir Walter Scott, has remarked in his notes on "The Battle of Both-well Bridge," (Minstrelsy of the Scottish Border, Part I), that "Blue was the favourite colour of the Covenanters, hence the vulgar phrase of a true blue whig," and, as his authority for this, he quotes a passage from the first edition of Spalding's History, a book most imperfectly edited. On referring to the Bannatyne Club edition of Spalding, which was printed in two volumes 4to, in 1828, under the superintendence of James Skene of Rubislaw, Esq., from a collation of two manuscripts, we find the passage in question thus given :—"But the countrie round about was pitiefully plundered, the meall girnells broken up, eaten and consumed ; no foul cock, or hen, left onkilled. The haill house dogs, messens and whelps, within Aberdein, killed and slaine upon the gate, so that neither hound nor messen, or other dog was left alive, that they could see. The reason was, when the first army came here, ilk captain, commander, servand and souldier had ane blew ribbin about his craig, in despyte and derision whereof, when they removed from Aberdein, some women of Aberdein (as was alleadged) knitt blew ribbins about their messens' craigs, whereat their souldiers took offence, and killed all their dogs for this very cause." May 1639.

At the present day "true blue," forms the livery, as indicating the earnest zeal and true patriotism of the Tory party. Substantially, the present Tories are Revolution Whigs, and have been so ever since the later reprehensible habits of Prince Charles Edward precluded every chance of a future rising in favour of the Stuarts. The following from "a collection of Loyal Songs, Poems &c., printed in the year 1750," appears with some differences in Hogg's Relics, first series, he having procured it from some other source, and mistakingly suggests that it may have been a Whig production. This "collection" was privately printed and is of extreme rarity.

TRUE BLUE.

I hope there's no soul met over this Bowl,
  But means honest ends to pursue ;
With the voice go the Heart, and let's never depart
  From the faith of an honest true Blue, true Blue,
  From the faith of an honest true Blue.

For our country and friends, we'll damn private ends,
  And keep old British virtue in view ;
Stand clear of the Tribe that address with a Bribe :
  Be honest and ever true Blue, &c.

On the politic Knave who strives to enslave,
  Whose schemes the whole nation may rue ;
On Pension and Place, that curse and disgrace,
  Turn your backs and be staunch to true Blue, &c.

As with Hound and with Horn we rise in the morn,
  With vigour the chase to pursue ;
Corruption's our cry, which we'll chase till it die.
  'Tis worthy a British true Blue, &c.

Here's a health to all those, who Slav'ry oppose.
  And our Trade both defend and renew ;
To each honest voice that concurs in the choice
  And support of an honest true Blue, true Blue,
  And support of an honest true Blue.

The popularity and potency of the Blue Bonnets has also been chronicled in other songs, such as "Lewis Gordon" and "Turn the Blue Bonnet wha can" :—

  "Now up wi' Donald, my ain brave Donald,
    It's up wi' Donald and a' his clan ;
  He's aff right early, away wi' Charlie,
    Now turn the blue bonnet wha can, wha can."
              Hogg's Jacobite Relics, 2d Series.

In the appendix to the same volume, "Part II. *Whig* Songs," there is a song about "a perjured fause loon, and his name it is Mar," who wishes

"To change a black hat for a bonnet that's blue,
Which nobody can deny, deny; which nobody can deny."

The most recent songs on the subject are, "Hurrah! for the Bonnets o' Blue," and "The Bonny Blue Caps."

From the celebrity achieved by the Blue Bonnets, the Blue Bonnet itself, as an article of wearing apparel, would seem to have been regarded as particularly *distingué* and in consequence to have been highly prized by Scotchmen generally ;—

"Oh! whar got ye that bonny blue bonnet?
Silly blind body canna ye see?
I gat it frae a braw Scotch callan
Between St Johnston and bonny Dundee."

The fascination of the Bonnet of Blue in the eyes of the fair sex has been forcibly illustrated not only in the following ballad, but forms one of the attractions of the original Highland Laddie :—

If I were free at will to chuse
To be the wealthiest Lawland Lady,
I'd take young Donald without trews,
With bonnet blue and belted plaidy.
O my bonny Highland laddie, &c,

See Thomson's Orpheus Caledonius, 8vo., London, 1733, vol. i. p. 28.
The importance of the Bonnet of Blue has been recognized even so far from the Scotish Borders as on the banks of "the Coaly Tyne."—the popular Newcastle song of "the Keel Row" alluding most pointedly to that portion of attire, regardless of all other :—

O weel may the keel row, the keel row, the keel row,
O weel may the keel row that my lad's in!
He wears a blue bonnet, blue bonnet, blue bonnet,
He wears a blue bonnet and a dimple in his chin."

Bonnet o' Blue.

AT Kingston-upon-Waldy, a town in Yorkshire,
I lived in great splendour and free from all care,
I rolled quite in riches, had sweethearts not a few,
I was wounded by a bonny lad and his bonnet o' blue.

There came a troop of soldiers as you now shall hear,
From Scotland to Waldy abroad for to steer;
There is one among them I wish I ne'er knew;
He's a bonny Scotch laddie wi' bonnet o' blue.

I cannot find rest, contentment has fled,
The form of my true love will run in my head,
The form of my true love still keeps in my view,
He's a bonny Scotch lad in his bonnet o' blue.

Early in the morning arising from bed,
I called upon Sally my own waiting maid
To dress me as fine as her two hands could do;
To seek out the lad and his bonnet o' blue.

So quickly she dressed me and quickly I came
To mingle with persons to hear my love's name,
Charles Stewart they called him, I felt it was true;
Once a prince of that name wore a bonnet o' blue.

My love he marched by with a gun in his hand,
I strove to speak to him but all was in vain,
I strove to speak to him away then he flew—
My heart it was with him and his bonnet o' blue.

She says, " My dear laddie, I'll buy your discharge,
I'll free you from soldiers, I'll let you at large,
I'll free you from soldiers if your heart will prove true,
And I'll ne'er cast a stain on your bonnet o' blue."

He says, " My dear lassie, you'll buy my discharge,
You'll free me from soldiers and let me at large?
For your very kind offer, I bow ma'am to you,
But I'll ne'er wear a stain in my bonnet o' blue.

" I have a sweet girl in my own country town,
Who I ne'er would forsake though poverty frown,

I ne'er will forsake the girl that proves true,
And I'll ne'er wear a stain in my bonnet o' blue."

I will send for a limner from London to Hull,
To draw my love's picture out in the full,
I'll set it in my chamber all close in my view,
And I'll think on the lad whose heart proved so true.

Battle of Waterloo.

This ballad, upon one of the most memorable themes of modern date, is evidently contemporaneous with the battle, in which the British were declared victors on 18th June 1815. For the most graphic account of the victory at Waterloo see Napier's History of the Peninsular War.

So uncertain in the minds of the people of this country was the anticipated result of the coming conflict, that the *Morning Chronicle* (a newspaper of great popularity and acknowledged sagacity at the time) gave vent to these croakings :—

On the 14th June, just four days before the grand result, it said,—"We believe that the allied Powers now inwardly regret the *rash* and *unwise* course they have taken. It will be seen that the French armies are *most formidable*, that they have no fewer than 200,000 veterans on the frontier, making part of an army of not less than 600,000 men.

" As to the attack of the English and Prussians on the *iron* frontier, as that of Flanders is called, Bonaparte trusts to the obstacles raised against it by *nature* and *art*. There are fourteen fortresses fully equipped and provisioned, which must be *taken* or *masked;* and from thence to Paris every military point is put in a state *of defence ! !*"

The same paper on 19th June, the day after Wellington's victory, the ·news of which (there being no electric nerve-distressing telegrams in those days) had not then reached this country.   " We see no prospect of avoiding the *fatal* extremity of war. The allies have *rashly* committed themselves, and everything that occurs in France appears to serve as a new pretext for their *infatuated* career ! ! "

The following anecdote may not inappropriately be introduced here: A Frenchman meeting an English soldier with a Waterloo medal, began to sneer at our Government for bestowing such a trifle, which at the most could not cost above three francs.   " That is true," said the other, " It did not cost the English Government quite three francs, but it cost the French a Napoleon."

On the 16th day of June my boys, in Flanders where we lay,
The bugle did the alarm sound before the break of day ;
The British, Belgians, Brunswickers, and Hanoverians too,
They Brussels left that morning for the plains of Waterloo.

By a forced march we did advance, till three in the after-
noon,
Each British heart with ardour burned to pull the tyrant
down,
Near Quatre-Bras we met the French, their shape to us seemed
new,
For in steel armour they were clad, for the plains of
Waterloo.*

Napoleon to his soldiers said, before that they began,
" My heroes, if we lose the day, our nation is undone ;
The Prussians we've already beat, so we'll beat the British too,
And display victorious eagles on the plains of Waterloo."

Our immortal leader Wellington no speech to us did make,
We were Peninsula heroes, and oft had made them shake,—
At Vittoria, Salamanca, Toulouse, and Burgos too ;—
They beheld their former conquerors on the plains of
Waterloo.

In bright array Britannia stood, and viewed her sons that day,
Then to her much loved hero went, and thus to him did
say,—
" If you the wreath of laurel twist from your opponent's brow,
Through ages all you shall be called the Prince of Waterloo."

The bloody fight it then began, and the cannons they did
roar,
We being short of cavalry, they pressèd us full sore,

---

* Referring of course to Bonaparte's " Invincibles,"—his Cuirassiers,
—who could not withstand the onslaught of the Scots Greys, that
gallant regiment having discovered the vulnerable part wherein these
Invincibles were assailable, viz.—in the groin, immediately below the
cuirass.

Three British cheers we gave them, with volleys not a few,
Which made them wish themselves in France, and far from
    Waterloo.

For full four hours or longer we sustained this bloody fray,
And during a long darksome night upon our arms we lay;
The orders of our General, next day we did pursue,
We retired in files, for near six miles, to the plains,of
    Waterloo.

This day both armies kept their ground, when scarce a shot
    was fired,
The French did boast a victory gained, because we had re-
    tired ;
This noble act of generalship them from their strongholds
    drew,
Where we got some share, by fighting fair, on the plains of
    Waterloo.

On the 18th, in the morning, both armies did advance,
On this side stood brave Albion's sons, on that the pride of
    France ;
The fate of Europe in our hands, each man his sabre drew,
And " Death or Victory ! " was the word on the plains of
    Waterloo.

Upon our right they did begin, Prince Jerome led the van,
With Imperial Guards and Cuirassiers, thought nothing
    could withstand :
But British steel soon made them yield, though our numbers
    were but few,
We prisoners made, but more lay dead, on the plains of
    Waterloo.

Then to our left they bent their course, in disappointed rage,
The Belgian line fought for a time, but could not stand the
    charge !

Then Caledon took up her drone, and loud her chanter blew,
Played Marshal Ney a new strathspey to the tune of Waterloo.

Here's a health to George our Royal King, and long may he
govern,
Likewise the Duke of Wellington, that noble son of Erin !
Two years they added to our time for pay and pension too,
And now we are recorded as men of Waterloo.

THE BRITISH GRENADIERS.

This once popular ballad has been inserted more for the purpose
of introducing the clever parody on it which follows, than for itself, although possessing much excellence.   Its author is unknown, and the
melody, according to Chappell, "is to be found in such different shapes
at different periods," as to render its date a matter of uncertainty.   The
copy which he republishes in " A Collection of National English Airs,
consisting of Ancient Song, Ballad, and Dance Tunes," &c. 2 vols. 4to.
Lond. 1838, is, he observes, "about eighty years old," but as regards
other two tunes, which are also there, and to which he refers as "evidently from the same source," he fixes the one at "two hundred, and
the other probably three hundred years old."   "The words of this song,"
says the same authority, "cannot be older than 1678, when the Gren-
adier Company was first formed, or later than the reign of Queen Anne,
when Grenadiers ceased to carry hand-grenades."—*Popular Music of
the Olden Time*, 152, 772.   Thomas Campbell, author of the "Pleasures
of Hope," wrote other words to the air, for which see the several collected editions of his Poems.
    The parody has been ascribed to the late Patrick Fraser Tytler, the
Scotish Historian,—a gentleman who occasionally indulged in poetic
aspirations of a like nature ; and who at the annual Symposia of the
Bannatyne Club was wont to enliven the assembled members with
effusions appropriate to the occasion.   The latter have been privately
printed, and are very scarce.
    During the War in the Crimea, in "a letter from the Camp," signed
" W. C." (Nov. 1855), which appeared in one of the public prints, the
following occurs :—

"The singing of old songs, catches, glees, and choruses, forms a principal feature in the amusements of the Camp.   During the long evenings of the past summer our men used to sit in some old redoubt or abandoned trench, and there the song and toast went round, and once or twice I heard some original and extemporaneous verses, *apropos* to the time and place, to our Government at home, to our Generals at headquarters, to the Czar in his palace, and to Johnny Russ in front, which were not only witty and satirical, but highly indicative of poetic genius. I took a note one evening of an encore verse to the "British Grenadiers," which was received with wonderful enthusiasm by a large number of red-coats, who were watching the infernal fire of the Redan upon our advanced trenches.   It was getting dark, but the Redan dropped shells every few seconds into our works, producing the effects of the most brilliant fireworks.   Unfortunately, when morning dawned, a terrible list of killed and wounded proved the accuracy of Russian artillery practice.   The verse was as follows :—

'And soon a song of victory shall cheer the hearts of all,
And triumph float from every breeze, borne from Sebastopol ;
Where Frenchmen brave, and black Zouaves,—the men who know no
    fears,
Have side by side like brothers fought with British Grenadiers ;
The great Redan shall thunder find, and we will find the cheers,—
With a row-dow-dow, and a row-dow-dow, for the British Grena-
    diers !'"

In Mr Chappell's version of this song there are several variations, the principal of which are noted below.   Upon the whole, we prefer our own.

The British Grenadiers.

SOME talk of Alexander,
And some of Hercules ;
Of Hector and Lysander,
And such great men* as these ;
But all the world acknowledges,
True valour best appears,—
    With a row-row-row, row-row-row
    Brave British Grenadiers.†

* Names.

† But of all the world's brave heroes,
    There's none that can compare

These ancients* of antiquity
Ne'er saw a cannon ball,
Nor knew the force of powder,
To slay their foes withall ;
But our brave boys have known it,
And banished all their fears,—
　　With a row-row-row, row-row-row,
　　Brave British Grenadiers.

When we receive the orders,†
To storm their pallisadoes,
Our leaders march with fuzees
And we with hand grenadoes,
We toss them from the glacis,
Amongst our enemies' ears,—‡
　　With a row-row-row, row-row-row,
　　The British Grenadiers.

Then Jove the god of thunder,
And Mars the god of war,
Rough Neptune with his trident,
Apollo in his car;
And all the gods celestial,
Descending from their spheres,
　　Do behold with admiration
　　Brave British Grenadiers.

But be you Whig or Tory,
Or any other thing,

　　With a tow, row-row-row, row-row-row,
　　　To the British Grenadiers.
　　　　Chorus.—But of all the world's, &c.

* Those heroes.　　　† Whene'er we are commanded.

　　‡ We throw them from the glacis
　　　Amongst the Frenchmen's ears.

I'd have you still remember,
To obey great George our king,
For if you prove rebellious,
We'll thunder in your ears,—
　　With a row-row-row, row-row-row,
　　Brave British Grenadiers.*

And when the siege is over,
We to the town repairs,
The citizens† cry "huzza, boys!
Here come the Grenadiers."
Here come the Grenadiers, boys,
Without e'er dread or fear,—
　　With a row-row-row, row-row-row,
　　Brave British Grenadiers.

Come fill us up a bumper,
And let us drink to those,
Who carry caps and pouches,
And wear the lacèd‡ clothes,
May they and their commanders,
Live happy many years,—
　　With a row-row-row, row-row-row,
　　Brave British Grenadiers.

Aitcheson's Carabineers.

From "Songs of the Edinburgh Squadron," a privately printed brochure of excessive rarity, pp. 36. This ballad is dated at Edinburgh "July 1821," and was sung to the air of the preceding ballad, "The

* This stanza is omitted in Mr Chappell's version.
† Townsmen.　　　　　　　　　‡ Loopèd.

British Grenadiers."   " Aitcheson " was—Aitcheson of Dromore, " The
Edinburgh Squadron " means the Royal Mid-Lothian Yeomanry Cavalry,
the members of which are composed of local gentlemen.

LET others talk of Elcho,*
  Or brave Lieutenant Hay,†
Of good M'Lean‡ our Cornet,
  Or our Staff-serjeant gay :§
Much as I love these heroes,
  Their fame a speck appears,
To the row-row, row-row-row,
  Of Aitcheson's Car'bineers.

Our troop contains some spoonies,
  That shame their bonny nags ;
They bump upon their saddles
  Like to a miller's bags.
But these our pride and glory,
  Sit firm upon their rears,
'Mid the row-row, row-row-row,
  Of Aitcheson's Car'bineers.

Sir John‖ himself doth wonder,
  When they recover ranks,
They come like claps of thunder,
  Descending on our flanks.
In fact they're more like Centaurs
  Than common cavaliers,—
In the row-row, row-row-row,
  Of Aitcheson's Car'bineers.

* Lord Elcho, now Earl of Wemyss.
† The late Sir Adam Hay.
‡ M'Lean of Ardgour in the County of Argyle.
§ The late Robert Whigham, Esq., Advocate.
‖ The late Sir John Hope of Pinkie, Bart., formerly M.P. for
Edinburgh.—An excellent horseman.

Then sure to Serjeant Aitcheson
A bumper now is due ;
He drilled our noble skirmishers,
He brought their worth to view.
May we all ride together
For many happy years,
To the row-row, row-row-row,
Of Aitcheson's Car'bineers.

DICK TURPIN.

RICHARD or (as he was more familiarly termed) "Dick Turpin," who, for a number of years about the beginning of last century, struck terror all over the kingdom by a series of daring highway robberies, was the son of a small farmer at Hampstead in Essex, and having received a common school education, was apprenticed to a butcher in Whitechapel. "His early youth," says Caulfield, "was distinguished by the impropriety of his behaviour and the brutality of his manners." He married a young woman of East Ham in Essex of the name of Palmer, and shortly afterwards commenced stealing his neighbours' cattle, which he cut up and sold. This was discovered, and he made a narrow escape from justice. He joined a gang of smugglers in Essex, then a gang of deer-stealers in Epping Forest, who eventually became housebreakers. Detailed accounts of Turpin's exploits, as well as his portrait, are given in Caulfield's "Remarkable Persons," Vol. IV. London, 8vo, 1820. See also "Newgate Calendar."

In Ainsworth's admirable romance of Rookwood—the most original work of the kind, with exception of "The Five Nights of St. Albans," which has appeared since Maturin's "Fatal Revenge"—Turpin is one of the principal actors, and has been so depicted by the author as necessarily to render him a favourite with the reader ; but, alas ! the character in fiction and that in reality is essentially different, and we seek in vain through Dick Turpin's actual history for any of those traits of generosity and good feeling with which the imaginary Turpin has been so plentifully endowed.

The description of Dick Turpin's ride from London to York within twelve hours, at a time when it took four days to perform the distance by coach, is most graphic, and the reader is forced to regret that the circumstance did not actually occur in the case of Dick Turpin, whom by this alleged act the romancist has rendered so interesting. The ride to York is, however, founded on a real incident which took place in 1676. The hero was one Nevison or Nicks, who plundered a traveller at four o'clock in the morning on the slope at Gadshill, and was in the bowling-green at York among the gay company there at a quarter before eight in the evening. The Lord Mayor happening to be there, Nicks sauntered up to him and enquired the hour, and when tried for the Gadshill robbery, and the prosecutor had sworn to the man, the place, and the hour, Nicks brought forward the Lord Mayor of York to prove an alibi.

During the early part of 1735 the cases of daring housebreaking in which Turpin and his accomplices were concerned became so numerous that rewards were repeatedly offered for the apprehension of the offenders. After a short time, one of the fraternity was thus tempted to betray two of his comrades, who were convicted and hung in chains. According to the account in the *Gentleman's Magazine*, "several of the villains being taken, *the country is in less fear.*" The gang being dispersed, Turpin went on the highway. Journeying towards Cambridge, he met a man genteelly dressed and well mounted, whom he instantly called upon to "Stand and deliver." The person he stopped happened to be King, a celebrated highwayman, who, bursting into a fit of laughter, exclaimed, "What! dog eat dog? Come, come, brother Turpin; if you don't know me, I know you, and shall be glad of your company." They struck a bargain, and, having committed numerous robberies, eventually became so well known that no public house would receive them as guests. Thus situated they made a cave at Epping Forest large enough to contain themselves and their horses, so artfully concealed that they could see passengers on the road while they themselves remained unobserved. Turpin's wife used to supply them with provisions.

In the beginning of 1737 many unsuccessful attempts were made to capture Turpin, and one man who endeavoured to take him in Epping Forest lost his life in the attempt. Immediately afterwards, on the night of Sunday the 22d May, he robbed several gentlemen in their coaches and chaises at Holloway, and the back lanes at Islington, and took from them several sums of money. One of the gentlemen signified to him that he had reigned a long time, to which Turpin replied, "'Tis no matter for that. I am not afraid of being taken by you; therefore don't stand hesitating, but give me the cole."

In the month following a pardon was promised to any of his accomplices who should cause his apprehension: "As likewise a reward of £200 to any person or persons who shall discover the said criminal, so that he may be apprehended and convicted of the murder or any of the robberies he has committed, over and above all other rewards to which they may be entitled."

It would seem that after the murder in Epping Forest Turpin went in search of King, whom he found; and King subsequently falling into the hands of the Philistines, called upon Turpin, who was close by, to fire upon one of them. This Turpin did, but by mistake shot King himself. Some vain attempts were made to capture Turpin, and even bloodhounds were called into requisition. He proceeded to Long-Sutton in Lincolnshire. There he stole some horses, for which he was taken into custody, but, contriving to escape from the constable, he made his way to Welton in Yorkshire, where he assumed the name of John Palmer, and lived as a private gentleman. The circumstance which led to his capture and subsequent execution is remarkable, as being of so trivial a nature that it appears somewhat strange any magistrate would have granted a warrant for his apprehension. Happening, whether by accident or design, to shoot a cock (supposed to have been a game-cock) belonging to his land-

lord, Mr. Hall (a neighbour) told him he was doing wrong, whereat
Turpin said, " I will shoot you, too, if you wait while I load my gun."
The officious neighbour went and informed Turpin's landlord of what
had passed. He was taken before the bench of justices then assembled
at Beverley, and, being unable to give security for his good behaviour,
was committed to Bridewell. On his examination he having stated that
he was well known in Spalding, inquiry respecting him was made there
by the Clerk of the Peace without effect, and, during his confinement
having been charged with horse-stealing by two persons who came from
Lincolnshire, he was removed from Beverley to York Castle. While
there, he wrote a letter to his brother-in-law in Essex, which was returned unopened to the post office, his brother-in-law having refused to
pay the postage. This letter being accidentally seen by Mr. Smith, the
schoolmaster who had taught Turpin to write, he recognised the handwriting, and the postmaster carried it to a magistrate, who arbitrarily
broke it open.

Thus was John Palmer, the prisoner in York jail, suspected to be
Dick Turpin; and Smith having been sent to York to identify him,
selected him from among all the other prisoners. On the 22d March
1739, John Palmer, *alias* Richard Turpin, was tried and convicted upon
two several indictments for horse-stealing. The evidence was clear and
full and the prisoner had little or nothing to say in his defence. He
acknowledged that his name was Richard Turpin, not the Richard
Turpin he was taken for, but another person of the same name. "Since
he was suspected to be Turpin," say the newspaper accounts of the
period, "the whole county have flocked here to see him, and have been
very liberal to him, insomuch that he has had wine constantly before
him till his trial, and 'tis said the jailor has made £100 by selling liquors
to him and his visitors." Many bets had been taken as to whether he
was the real person or not.

After conviction, his father tried in vain to get his sentence remitted
in favour of transportation. He assumed the most gay and thoughtless
manner and affected to make a jest of the dreadful fate that awaited
him. Not many days before his execution he purchased a new fustian
frock and a pair of pumps to wear on that occasion, and hired five
poor men, at ten shillings each, to follow the cart as mourners. He
gave hatbands and gloves to several other persons.

On the way to execution he bowed from the cart to the spectators with
the utmost nonchalance. He was executed on the 6th April 1739 along
with John Stead, who had been convicted for a similar offence. Stead
was very penitent, but Turpin behaved with the greatest boldness and
assurance to the very last. It was remarked that, as he mounted the
ladder, his right leg trembled, on which he stamped it down with an air
of assumed courage, and looked round about him; "then, after speak-

ing a few words to the topsman, he threw himself off the ladder, and expired in about five minutes."

Caulfield says, "Turpin suffered at York on the 10th April 1739," whereas the contemporary newspapers of 10th April say, " Last Saturday Richard Turpin and John Stead were executed at Tyburn."

The actual scene of his execution was about half a mile from the city of York. His grave was dug exceedingly deep, and every care was taken by his hired mourners to prevent the body from falling into the hands of the surgeons, but to no purpose. The very next night the body was gone. The mob, exasperated, searched for it in all the houses of surgeons and physicians in the city, and at last found it in a shop laid out for dissection. After having made sad havoc among the stock-in-trade of the doctor, they carried the body in triumph through the streets, and, replacing it in its coffin, procured some unslacked lime, and watched until they felt assured it was in a state of decomposition.

In 1836 the late Mr. Charles Kirkpatrick Sharp mentioned this curious fact to Mr. Maidment, that about forty years previously, while on a visit to Lord Le de Spencer, he had been introduced to a niece of Turpin. Her name was Piercy, and she either was, or had been, the wife of an opulent and respectable farmer. He called upon her at her own house, in company with one of the Le de Spencer family, and was most graciously received. She was then somewhere about fifty, and may be described as a comely, buxom dame. In early years, he remarked, she must have been very good-looking. He afterwards met her at a county ball, where she appeared splendidly attired, with a large gold watch, chain, and seals at her side. This, the neighbours maliciously hinted, was a legacy bequeathed by her uncle, who had obtained it in some of his marauding expeditions. Great attention was paid to her, as she was much respected by her neighbours. It may be proper to mention that she was possessed of considerable wealth.

The following ballad has been collated with a copy which appears in a chap-book of songs, circa 1796, where it is styled, "The Dung-hill Cock ; or Turpin's Valiant Exploits," and is therein set down " to be sung to its own proper tune." It is evidently contemporaneous with the circumstances which it narrates.

Turpin's Valour.

On Hounslow Heath, as I rode o'er,
I spied a lawyer riding before ;

" Kind sir," said I, " are you not afraid,
Of Turpin that mischievous blade ?"
   O rare Turpin, hero,
   O rare Turpin, O,

Says Turpin, " I have been most acute,
My gold I've hid in the heel of my boot ;"
"O," says the lawyer, "there's none can find
My gold, for it lies in my cap behind."

As they rode down by the Poulter mill,
Turpin demands him to stand still ;
Says he, "your cap I must cut off,
For my mare she wants a saddle cloth."

This caused the lawyer sore to fret,
To think he was so fairly bit ;
For soon was he rifled of his store,
Because he knew how to lye for more.

As Turpin rode in search of prey,
He met an exciseman on the way ;
He boldly bid him for to stand,
" Your gold," said he, " I do demand."

With that the exciseman he replied,
" Your proud demands must be denied ;
Before my money you receive,
One of us two must cease to live."

Turpin then without remorse,
He knocked him quite from off his horse ;
And left him on the ground to sprawl,
As off he rode with his gold and all.

As he rode over Salisbury plain,
He met Lord Judge with all his train :

Then hero-like he did approach,
And robbed the Judge as he sat in his coach.

An usurer as I am told,
Who had in change a sum of gold ;
With a cloak clouted from side to side,
Just like a palmer he did ride.

And as he jogged along the way,
He met with Turpin that same day ;
With hat in hand, most courteously,
He asked him for charity.

" If that be true thou tells to me,
I'll freely give thee charity ;
But I made a vow and it I'll keep,
To search all palmers that I meet."

He searched his bags, wherein he found
Upwards of eight hundred pound ;
In ready gold and white money,
Which made him to laugh heartily.

"This begging is a curious trade,
For on thy way thou hast well sped ;
This prize I count is found mony,
Because thou made an arrant lye."
        O rare Turpin, hero, &c.

For shooting of a dunghill cock,
Poor Turpin he at last was took ;
And carried straight into a jail,
Where his misfortune he does bewail.
        O poor Turpin, hero, &c.

Now some do say that he will hang,
Turpin the last of all the gang ;

I wish this cock had ne'er been hatched,
For like a fish in the net he's catched.
    O poor Turpin, hero, &c.

But if I had my liberty,
And were upon yon mountains high ;
There's not a man in old England,
Durst bid bold Turpin for to stand.
    O poor Turpin, hero, &c.

I ventured bold at young and old,
And fairly fought them for their gold :
Of no man kind I was afraid,
But now alas ! I am betrayed.
    O poor Turpin, hero, &c.

Now Turpin he's condemned to die,
To hang upon yon gallows high ;
Whose legacy is a strong rope,
For stealing of a dung-hill cock.
    O poor Turpin, hero, &c.

EVERYONE TO HIS OWN TRADE,

OR THE CHAPLAIN OUTWITTED BY THE HIGHWAYMAN.

THE date of this ballad is 1735, and it used to be sung to the tune of
" The King and the Miller of Mansfield."

The " Craftsman," alluded to in the second stanza, was a periodical of
the day, edited by " Caleb D'Anvers " of Gray's Inn. It was afterwards
re-published in fourteen volumes 12mo., London, 1731-37.

" Caleb D'Anvers " was the pseudonym of Nicholas Amherst. The
principal contributors to the "Craftsman" were Amherst, Lord Bolin-
broke, and William Pulteney, afterwards Earl of Bath.

The date of Amherst's birth is uncertain, but his death took place on
27th April, 1742. He was a poet as well as a political writer. He
published a thin volume of poems of exceeding merit. He also wrote
the "Terræ filius," a very curious satire on Oxford. It first appeared

during the year 1721, and was printed in fifty numbers. Subsequently
it was published in a collected form in 2 vols. 12mo, London, 1726. He
was a staunch Hanoverian, and naturally expected that his adherence to
that cause would have been recognised by those in power, and would have
led to his advancement.   But as is usual under such circumstances, his
claims were disregarded, and the loaves and fishes were distributed, according to custom, among the brainless kinsmen of political adventurers,
of whose votes the government might be doubtful.   Political patronage
is too often, even now, directed in favour of the most undeserving, because being unscrupulous, they are not otherwise to be depended on by
the party to whom they have sworn allegiance.   Pulteney, though possessing immense wealth and consequent influence, rendered Amherst no
assistance.   The extent of his generosity was a cask of Claret.   It is
believed that Amherst died of a broken heart, and was buried at the
expense of his printer, Richard Francklin.

The allusion to Haynes has not been ascertained.

Everyone to his own Trade.

OR THE CHAPLAIN OUTWITTED BY THE HIGHWAYMAN.

How happy a state does the Parson possess,
Who strives, by his preaching, all vice to suppress ;
On his pulpit and tythes he depends for support,
And for dispensations ne'er troubles the Court !
Though seldom he's dusty, or powder'd does go ;
The blacker his outside the more he's a beau,
His dress still's no rule that he's honester far
Than a Knight of St George in blue garter and star.
Than a Knight, &c.

If thus had the doctor, who travel'd along,
Thought more of a sermon than of an old song ;
His cash he'd have saved, and his credit likewise
And by his grave garb might have pass'd in disguise,
But nature prevails, tho' close fetter'd in chains ;
The *Craftsman* will write, tho' he's punished in Haynes.
The Parson most slily will hark to a joke,
Then says, " If not meant ill, it's never ill spoke."
Then says, &c.

Since therefore in life ev'ry one has his trade,
And each to serve t'other by nature was made;
Yet Highway collectors of all are most odd,
They spare neither lawyer nor good man of God.
But lately the case has quite otherwise happ'd,
When the reverend Chaplain was cunningly trapp'd;
Tho' his money he lost yet he still got his due,
A draw-back for tythe and an old song for new.
   A draw-back, &c.

The case then was thus :—as he rode the highway,
He saw a man travel quite sober, yet gay;
Who sung what the doctor seemed much to admire,
And often repeated it at his desire;
Till come to a fit place his prey for to catch,
He took from the doctor his money and watch;
But out of ten guineas he gave him one back,
That the doctor mayn't say that his tythe he did lack.
   That the Doctor, &c.

Now 'twixt these two traders, pray who's in the wrong?
One took for his tythe, and the other his song;
But as for the watch, as a body may say,
The Doctor gave that, as the time o' the day.
He'll curse King and Miller of Mansfield so famed,
And think of a robber whenever they're named.
Then let that dear song thus his reverence teach;
"Tis t'other's to rob and 'tis his trade to preach.
T'other sings e'er he robs, when this sings he should preach.
   T'other sings, &c.

THE FEMALE ROBBER.

From a copy bearing date 1796, " Entered according to order."
The following analogous story is from the *Caledonian Mercury* of 2d

December, 1735, (See also the Gentleman's Magazine, for November
1735) :—
  "On Monday last, 24 November, a wholesale butcher was robbed in
a very gallant manner, near Rumford, in Essex. He was attacked
by a woman on horseback, who presented a pistol, and demanded his
money.   He was amazed at such behaviour in one of her sex, and told
her he did not understand what she meant.   By this time a gentleman of
her acquaintance came up, and told him he was a brute to make any
hesitation in granting what a lady requested of him ; and damned his
blood if he did not immediately gratify her desire he would shoot him
through the head.   At the sight of the gentleman's pistol, the butcher
thought proper to grant the lady six guineas, some silver, and his watch,
which done, they parted in the most complaisant manner imaginable.'

The Female Robber.

Ye females of every station,
    Give ear to my frolicksome song ;
The like was ne'er known in the nation,
    'Twas done by a female so young.

She bought her a horse and a bridle,
    With saddle and pistols also ;
Resolving not to remain idle,
    But on the highway she would go.

She clothed herself in great splendour,
    Her breeches and sword she had on ;
Her body appeared mighty slender,
    'Twas dressed like a pretty young man.

And thus like a robber so pretty,
    She mounted with speed on her mare ;
She left all her friends in the city,
    And steered her course towards Ware.

The first that she met was a grocer,
    Walking with a cane in his hand ;

She soon to the spark rode up closer,
And boldly she made him to stand.

She took from him only one guinea.
The next was a taylor and shears ;
Because the poor rogue had no money,
She nimbly cut off both his ears.

There was too a pinching old tanner,
For the loss of his money he cried,
Because the poor rogue bawl'd out loudly,
She bravely tanned his hide.

The next was an honest exciseman,
She told him she must have the prize ;
She robbed him of eighty gold guineas,
Which he had received for excise.

The next was a cheating quack doctor,
Whose clothes were all daubed o'er with lace ;
She took both his coat and his money,
It was a most pitiful case.

The next was an honest old lawyer,
At Assizes he pleaded the laws,
She took both his watch and his money,
And this was the truth of the cause.

The next was a greasy fat landlord,
Whose paunch held a hogshead of beer ;
She ransacked him of forty gold guineas,
While he shook in his doublet for fear.

The next that came up were four robbers,
Well mounted on brave prancing nags ;
She desired them to stand and deliver,
And told them she wanted their bags.

The highwaymen all drew their rapiers,
   She bid them to stand on their guard ;
Then away this fair maid did caper,
   The highwaymen followed her hard.

They followed and soon overtook her,
   And gathered so fiercely around;
But as they made search for the lucre,
   By jakers! a woman they found.

The highwaymen all stood amazed,
   But she had no cause to complain ;
Though with her they did as they pleased,
   They gave her her money again.

THE CRAFTY FARMER.

THIS ballad is from a chap book, "Entered according to order, 1796," entitled "The Crafty Farmer, to which is added Bright Belinda, The Faithful Swain, Young Daphne." That it was first produced at a much earlier date seems evident, as we learn from tradition that the story on which it is founded was wont to be considered by the common people as applicable to Turpin, who, they affirmed, had once been foiled in a similar manner.

In "Early Ballads," edited with notes by Robert Bell, and published by Griffin and Co. (a small volume made up from other men's books), Mr Bell states that this ballad was "Printed for the first time in the collection of Ancient Poems, &c., published by the Percy Society." On referring to these Ancient Poems, edited by Mr James Henry Dixon in 1846, we find this account of it, which, by the way, is there called "Saddle to Rags:" "No ballad is better known in the dales of Yorkshire than *Saddle to Rags*. It has long enjoyed an extensive popularity. The present version was taken down by the Editor in October, 1845." Mr Dixon adds : "We have not been able to discover any broadside copy of the ballad, nor can we trace it in any collection, although we have met with *The Crafty Ploughboy*, or *The Highwayman Out-witted*, and some others of a like description, and having nearly the same plot, but they are all very inferior to *Saddle to Rags ;* the tune is, *Give ear to a frolicksome Lass, or, The Rant*, being the air better known as *How happy could I be with either ;* it may be found in Chappell's National English Airs."

In our version (the more ancient) there is no refrain to the stanzas, as in Mr Dixon's, from which we infer that the air he mentions was not the original air to which the words were sung. The refrain goes thus :—

> " With a till da dill, till a dill, dill,
> Till a dill, dill a dill, dee,
> Sing fal de dill, dill de dill, dill,
> Fal de dill, dill de dill, dee."

There are some slight verbal differences between the two versions, and there are two additional interpolated stanzas, in Mr Dixon's Copy. In the ninth stanza, in place of " The old man was thinking no ill," Mr Dixon has it :—" And riding a down a ghyll," explaining in a note that " ghyll," means, "a rocky valley branching out of one of the larger dales or passes." The fifteenth stanza as given by Mr Dixon is :—

> " The old man gallop'd and rode,
> Untill he was almost spent ;
> Till he came to his landlord's house,
> And he paid him his whole year's rent.

Then follows the stanza :—" He opened this rogues portmantle," but in place of " three hundred " the sum stated is :—

> " Five hundred pound in money,
> And other five hundred in gold."

Then :—

> " His landlord it made him to stare,
> When he did the sight behold,
> Where did ye get the white money,
> And where get the yellow gold ?"

And after the stanza, " I met a fond fool," comes in this :—

> " ' But now you're grown cramped and old,
> Not fit for to travel about ;
> ' O, never mind,' says the old man,
> ' I can give these old bones a root.'"

The same ballad under the title of " The Crafty Miller," has been printed in Maidment's "Scotish Ballads and Songs." 12mo. Edin. (Stevenson) 1859. The Editor remarks in introducing it :—" There are

numerous ballads, based on incidents of a similar description, among the
Editor's collections ; but they are English.   The following one, from a
Glasgow Stall copy, is clever.   It is not improbable, however, that it
may be a Southern composition."

The Crafty Farmer.

THE song that I'm going to sing,
   I hope it will give you content ;
Concerning a silly old man,
   That was going to pay his rent.

As he was riding along,
   Along all on the Highway ;
A gentleman thief overtook him,
   And thus to him did say.

" Well overtaken," said the thief,
   "Well overtaken said he ;"
And " well overtaken," said the old man,
   " If thou be good company."

" How far are you going this way ?"
   Which made the old man for to smile ;
" By my faith," said the old man.
   " I'm just going two mile."

" I am a poor farmer," he said,
   " And I farm a piece of ground ;
" And my half year's rent, kind sir,
   Just comes to forty pound.

" And my landlord has not been at home,
   I've not seen him this twelvemonth or more ;
Which makes my rent be large,
   I've to pay him just fourscore."

" Thou shouldst not have told any body,
　　For thieves there's ganging many,
If any should light on thee,
　　They'll rob thee of thy money."

" O never mind," said the old man,
　　" Thieves I fear on no side,
For the money is safe in my bags,
　　On the saddle on which I ride."

As they were riding along,
　　The old man was thinking no ill ;
The thief he pulled out a pistol,
　　And bid the old man stand still.

But the old man prov'd crafty,
　　As in the world there's many,
He threw his saddle o'er the hedge,
　　Saying, " Fetch it, if thou'lt have any."

The thief got off his horse,
　　With courage stout and bold,
To search for the old man's bag ;
　　And gave him his horse to hold.

The old man put's foot i' the stirrup,
　　And he got on astride ;
To its side he clapt his spur up,
　　You need not bid the old man ride.

" O stay !" said the thief, " O stay !
　　And half the share thou shalt have."
" Nay, by my faith !" said the old man,
　　" For once I have bitten a knave."

This thief he was not content,
　　But he thought there must be bags ;

I

He out with his rusty old sword,
   And chopt the old saddle in rags.

When he came to the landlord's house,
   This old man he was almost spent ;
Saying, " Come ! show me a private room,
   And I'll pay you a whole year's rent.

" I've met a fond fool by the way,
   I swapt horses and gave him no boot ;
But never mind," said the old man,
   " For I got the fond fool by the foot."

He open'd this rogue's portmantle.
   It was glorious to behold ;
There were three hundred pounds in silver,
   And three hundred pounds in gold.

And as he was riding home,
   And down a narrow lane ;
He espied his mare tied to a hedge,
   Saying, " Prithee, Tib, wilt thou gang hame ?"

When he got home to his wife,
   And told her what he had done ;
Up she rose and put on her clothes,
   And about the house did run.

She sung, and she sung, and she sung,
   She sung with a merry devotion ;
Saying, " If ever our daughter gets wed,
   It will help to enlarge her portion."

THE YORKSHIRE BITE.

This Ditty forms an appropriate sequel to the "Crafty Farmer,"
immediately preceding. In all probability it is the ballad to which Mr
Dixon makes reference under the title of "The Crafty Ploughboy, or the
Highwayman outwitted." It is from a collection of ballads, *circa* 1782,
"Entered according to order," being "Four excellent New Songs; 1.
The Yorkshire Bite; 2. The Golden Glove; 3. The Bold Hairy Cap;
4. The Laplander's Wish."

The term "Bite" is a cant phrase signifying "a cheat, a rogue, a
sharper." It is recorded of a criminal named Holloway, who figured
in the Newgate annals about the beginning of last century, that the very
day before his execution he gave a most remarkable "bite," which probably eclipses even the swindles of our own times. He sent for a
surgeon to whom he proposed to sell his corpse for dissection. The
surgeon, by no means unwilling to strike a bargain, offered him a certain
sum, with which, however, Holloway was not contented. "See here,"
said he, "is a vigorous and sound body! Here are limbs, here are
muscles!" and, stripping open his bosom, added, "here's a chest—so
plump, so white, as will rise to your knife and do credit to your art!
Don't this deserve ten shillings more than a common corpse?" Con-
vinced by his arguments, the doctor paid him the price demanded,
when, bursting into a loud laugh, he exclaimed, "A bite! a bite! by
Jingo! I am to be hanged in chains to-morrow," and so laughed the
astonished surgeon out of prison.

IF you please to draw near till the truth I declare,
I'll sing of a farmer who liv'd in Hartfordshire;
A pretty Yorkshire boy he had for his man,
For to do his business, his name it was John.
Derry down, &c.

One morning right early he called his man,
And when he came to him he thus began,
"Take this cow," he said, "this day to the fair,
She is in good order, and her I can spare."

This boy went away with the cow in a band,
And came to the fair, as we understand;

In a very short time he met with two men,
And sold them the cow for six pound ten.

They went to his master's host's house for to drink,
Where the farmer paid the boy down his clink:
The boy to the landlady then he did say,
"O what shall I do with my money, I pray?"

" I'll sew it in the lining of your coat," said she,
" For fear on the road you robbed should be ;"
Thus heard a Highwayman while drinking of wine,
Who thought to himself, the money is mine.

The boy took his leave and homeward did go,
The Highwayman he followed after also ;
And soon overtook him upon the highway,
"O well overtaken, young man," he did say.

"Will you get up behind me ?" the Highwayman said,
" But where are you going?" enquired the lad ;
" About four miles farther, for aught that I know,"
So he jump'd up behind, and away they did go.

They rode till they came to a dark, dark lane,
The Highwayman said, " I must tell you plain,
" Deliver your money, without any strife,
" Or else I will surely deprive you of life."

He found there was no time to dispute;
So jump'd up behind him without fear or doubt,
He tore from his linings the money throughout,
And among the long grass he strew'd it about.

The Highwayman instantly jumpt from his horse,
But little he dream'd it was for his loss ;
Before he could find where the money was sown,
The boy got on horseback and off he was gone.

The Highwayman flouted, and bid him to stay,
The boy would not hear him, but still rode away
Unto his own master, and to him did bring
Saddle and bridle and many fine thing.

When the maid servant saw Jack come riding home,
To acquaint her master ran into the room ;
The farmer he came to the door with a curse,
" What a plague! is my cow turn'd into a horse?"

The boy said, " good master, the cow I have sold,
But was robb'd on the road by a Highwayman bold ;
And, while he was putting it into his purse,
To make you amends I came home with his horse."

His master laugh'd till his sides he did hold,
And said, " For a boy thou hast been very bold ;
And as for the villain you served him right,
And has put upon him a true Yorkshire bite."

They opened the bags and quickly was told
Two hundred pounds in silver and gold,
With two brace of pistols. The boy said, " I vow !
I think, my good master, I've well sold your cow."

Now Jack, for his courage and valour so rare,
Three parts of the money he got for his share,
And since the Highwayman has lost all his store,
Let him go a robbing until he get more.

MAID OF RYGATE.

The chief incident in this ballad is similar to that of the two preceding. It appears to have been exceedingly popular throughout England
long after the time when the school of romantic Highwaymen had ceased

to exist. While on the subject, it may be observed that probably the best drawn portraiture of a Highwayman of that class which has been depicted, either in Play or Romance, will be found in the character called Colonel Lutwych, in G. P. R. James' excellent novel of Sir Theodore Broughton.

The Maid of Rygate.

NEAR Rygate there lived a farmer,
  Whose daughter to market would go,
Not fearing that any would harm her,
  For often she rode to and fro.

It fell one time amongst many,
  A great store of corn she sold,
She having received the penny
  In shillings, and guineas, and gold.

She rode a little way farther,
  But, dreading some danger to find,
She sewed it up in her saddle,
  Which was with the leather well lined.

She riding a little way farther,
  She met a thief on the highway,
A robber apparelled, well mounted,
  Who soon did oblige her to stay.

Three blows then he presently gave her,
  Load pistols he held to her breast,
Your money this moment deliver,
  Or else you shall die I protest.

This maiden was sorely affrighted,
  And so was poor Doby the steed,
When down off his back she alighted
  He quickly ran home with great speed.

Then this damsel he stripped nearly naked,
  And he gave her some sorrowful blows,
Says, "girl you must patiently take it ;
  I'll have both your money and clothes."

The thief up his bundle was making,
  His horse he obliged her to hold ;
The poor girl stood trembling and shaking,
  As though she would perish with cold.

The thief up his bundle was making
  And being rejoiced at his prize,
Says, "Yourself I shall shorly be taking,
  As part of my baggage likewise."

The girl while she held fast the bridle,
  Was beginning to grow more afraid.
Says she, " it's in vain to be idle,
  I'll show you the trick of a maid."

Then up on the saddle she mounted,
  Just as if she had been a young man,
As while on his money she counted,
  " Pray follow me, Sir, if you can."

The rogue in a passion he flew,
  He cursed her, he swears, and he blows,
At length his words were, " halloo !
  Stay girl! and I'll give you your clothes."

She says, " that's not so much matter,
  You may keep them, kind sir, if you please ;"
He runs but he could not get at her,
  His boots they so hampered his knees.

She rode over hedges and ditches,
  The way home she knew very well,

She left him a parcel of farthings,
   The sum of five shillings to tell.

This maiden was sorely benighted
   From seven till twelve of the clock,
Her father was sorely affrighted
   To see her come stripped to her smock.

"O daughter, the matter come tell me,
   And how you have tarried so long?"
She says, "some hard fortune befel me,
   But I have received no wrong."

They ended their sorrow with joy,
   When in his portmanteau was found,
In a bundle a great sum of money,
   In all about eight hundred pound.

O! was not this rare of a maiden,
   Who was in great danger of life?
With riches she's now overladen,
   No doubt she will make a good wife.

THE CANTERS' HOLIDAY.

Sung on the electing of a new Dimber Damber, *or* King *of the* Gypsies.

This and the ten succeeding lyrics are from "a collection of songs in the Canting Dialect" included in " Bacchus and Venus : or a select collection of near two hundred of the most witty and diverting Songs and Catches in Love and Gallantry, many whereof never appeared in print before," 12mo, London, 1737. An interpretation of the Cant terms will be found in the Appendix.

The preface to the reader of this book is so very curious that we cannot refrain from transcribing the greater portion of it here, forming as it does a suitable introduction to the subject of the Ballads which follow.

"It is observed by certain writers, that the *Emancipation of Slaves* was the *Original of Beggars* ; and that, by freeing from bondage the dregs of the people, who have not virtue and industry, without compulsion, to maintain themselves and families by Labour, the Publick has intail'd upon itself a perpetual Rent-charge, and at the same time given rise to the numerous bands of Pilferers and Robbers ; which, say they, nowhere abound so much as in the *Christian Countries* where *Slavery* is abolished : and as a farther proof of the justice of this observation, they add, That the Jews of old who allowed Slaves had no Beggars ; from whence they conclude, That there is no greater difference between the Slaves and the Beggars than between Fathers and their Heirs.

"Whatever truth there may be in this assertion, it is observable, with regard to our English Beggars, That the first Statute which makes provision for our Parish poor, is of no older date than Queen Elizabeth's reign ; which has given occasion for some witty people to remark, That the *dissolution* of the *Monasteries and Religious Houses* here in England had the same effect with us, as the *manumitting* of the *Slaves* had in other Countries, and made many people Beggars, who otherwise (free from the terrors of the rope and House of Correction) might have wallow'd out a stupid life in Ecclesiastic Idleness and Holy luxury : whereas now (say they, but 'tis to be hoped, with more wit than justice) all the numerous orders of Religious Locusts, or those Drones who were most likely to have been such, had it not been for the Dissolution, are become so many Beggars and Vagabonds ; by which means England sees only the numerous remains of one Popish Order, viz., *the Mendicants*, who have swallow'd up all the others.

"But, however this may be, it is certain that no country in the world has *within itself* better opportunities than England, to employ and make useful the Poor of all degrees, and of every age and sex, by means of our Woollen and other numerous manufactures. And that notwithstanding these native advantages, no country in this world abounds so much with Vagrants and Beggars ; insomuch that it is impossible to stir abroad in the streets, to step into any of the shops in London, or to take the .air within two or three miles of this great metropolis, but one must be attack'd with the clamorous and often insolent Petitions of Sturdy Beggars and Vagabonds, who by proper regulations, might be made equally useful to themselves and the Publick.

"In Holland, 'tis well known, though they have not near the oppor-tunities from their native manufactures to employ the poor, there is not a Beggar to be seen in the streets ; and if, by misfortunes, a person is reduced to want, and has strength to bear the fatigues of the Voyage, and to be useful to himself and the Publick when there, he is sent to their Settlements in the East Indies, and there well-provided for ; and if he has not strength, &c., he is taken care of in some one of the Hospitals provided for those purposes.

"The disorderly youth of both sexes, Night-Walkers and others, are disposed into Work-houses appropriated to each sex ;—the men into the *Raspelhuis*, where they are obliged to saw and rasp Brazil-wood and per-form other laborious works ; and those who, by Blows, are not to be brought to labour, are put into a large cistern, where the water is let in upon them and they are forced to pump hard to save themselves from drown-ing.   The women are put into the *Spinhuis*, where they are obliged to spin, sew, make lace, &c., for an honest livelihood ; and in one large room there have been eight hundred at a time, very well dress'd, and not only all of them neat, but many of them fine, by the fruits of their own in-dustry.   And nothing is more frequent than for Parents to put into these Houses of Correction disobedient or incorrigible children, who are kept there in apartments by themselves, if desired, (and either obliged to labour or not, as the Parents please) till they shew signs of penitence and amendment :   Whereas in these kingdoms, such refractory persons, for want of such early and gentle correction, too generally take to the highways, or to the committing such vile enormities as hurry them to an untimely end, and bring the gray hairs of their indulgent parents with sorrow to the grave.

"For orphans and children they have Hospitals in several towns, and particularly one at Amsterdam called *Weeshuis* which makes ample provision for six hundred of them.   Another called *Dolhuis*, nobly endowed for the sick.   One for old men, and such as are no longer able to support themselves by their work, called *Mannenhuis*.   And there is another very handsome Hospital for women of above sixty years of age, where four hundred of the Reformed Religion are maintained by the charity of those of that Persuasion, and with necessary attendants, &c.

"Besides all which, there are great sums of money collected for the poor; and upon all Assignations or Meetings at the Taverns or elsewhere, and upon many other occasions, whosoever fails to come at the exact time, forfeits more or less to the use of the poor ; and this seems to be enforced the more rigorously, in order to oblige persons to punctuality in their appointments, which, as the Soul of Business, is absolutely neces-sary to be observed in a Commercial state.

" Persons are also appointed to inspect the wants of the poor, and to oversee both their conduct and treatment they meet with ; and these are chosen by the Magistrates of each town from among the most eminent citizens of the place. These offices are generally a nursery for officers to serve the State in higher capacities, who are usually chosen from among such as have best behaved themselves to the poor under their care and inspection. To these the poor need but to apply, and their wants are readily supplied ; and in winter time Rugs, Turfs for firing, and at other times, Linen, Shirts, Sheets, Cloathes, and always Bread, are distributed among them. Nor is there the least distinction of Sect or Religion observed in these charitable distributions.

" By this brief account, let the Reader judge of the advantage which must thereby accrue to the Dutch Commonwealth in general, and to private persons in particular : How many poor Souls are almost daily reclaimed from their vicious courses by this means and saved from utter destruction, and render'd useful Members of the Commonwealth ; and how many robberies, murders, and invasions of private right, are hourly prevented.

" Upon the whole, it is submitted to the consideration of our Governors, whether something of this nature would not be proper to be followed in England, where, as I have said, we have such *native* opportunities of employing the poor to the greatest publick and private emolument ?

.   .   .   .

" The Canting dialect is a confused jargon, and not grounded on any rules ; and no wonder, since the practicers thereof are the chief Fathers and nourishers thereof. Yet even out of that irregularity many words seem to retain something of scholarship ; and it is observable that, even unknown to ourselves, we have insensibly adopted some of their terms into our vulgar tongue.

" The original of the Gypsies, Strowlers, and Fortune-tellers, who first gave rise to this peculiar dialect, as well as to all the species of Beggars and Canters that have been since in most nations, were from Bohemia: That the itinerants of that nation were very early noted all over Germany for their pretended skill in Palmistry, Physiognomy and other occult Arts, as well as for their private thefts and pilferings; that they affected to style themselves *Ægyptians* (whence the name of Gypsies) in order to give a reputation to their pretended skill : The people of Egypt as well as the Chaldeans being noted for Soothsaying, divers sorts of Augury, and an Hieroglyphical knowledge, which gained them no small esteem among the Vulgar of other Countries. That having in time spread themselves over Italy, Spain, and France in small gangs, and taking into their Society many of the profligate natives of the countries through which they passed, they imposed on the credulity of the women and ignorant vulgar by various arts, making themselves to be understood by means of those newly-admitted Interpreters, and so found to make themselves a peculiar dialect, which not a little further'd their designs in their double business of thieving and fortune-telling, and render'd difficult the detecting of them, and at the same time served to amuse the credulous.

" From Spain, in process of time, they found means to introduce themselves into Ireland, where, joining to their own villainous inclinations, the national barbarity and cruelty of the wild Irish, such was the influence of the climate upon them, that, from private Cheats and Thieves, as they had been in other countries, they threw off all disguises, and stuck not at the most execrable villainies, firing of houses, massacring whole families, and robbing and plundering in troops, till the name of *Ægyptians* was wholly lost in that of *Rapparees* or *Tories*, under which denomination there are several severe laws to this day in force against them.

" But now, being themselves terrify'd at the Barbarities of that savage people, they are said to have passed over to the Highlands of Scotland, and there, setting up for *Second sight* and *Prognostication*, they began to be adher'd to by some of the ignorant clans, and afterwards getting in with the itinerant Scotch Pedlars, they soon spread themselves beyond the Southern borders of Scotland, and found in England as fit and as credulous objects to work upon, as they had done in other countries. While others of them, pretending to reform and to detest their past wicked lives, set up for extraordinary purity; and, as one extreme is generally productive of another, they, suiting their humours to the genius of the Scottish nation, from itinerant Pedlars, became itinerant Preachers, and, in time, the venerable fathers of the Cameronian race, whose immediate descendants, by accustoming themselves to live hard, and to feed on sowre butter milk, and whipt cream, were thence, in process of time, denominated *Whigs*, and pursued the enthusiastic Cant of their forefathers. And thus 'tis observable, the names of the two factions into which this nation has been so long unhappily divided (as the most inveterate opposites are sometimes nearest akin) are owing, if my authority be good, to the same source, viz., the refuse and common Vagabonds of the three nations, that is to say, in other words, the pilfering Strowlers and Prognosticators of Germany, leaving their own country, became the Rapparees and Tories of Ireland; that by an easie and more natural transition than some persons are aware of, the Tories of Ireland, crossing the water, found themselves metamorphos'd, or rather converted, into the Whigs of Scotland; and finally that there opprobrious names were reciprocally communicated by party-rage to the two factions into which the three kingdoms have ever since been divided.

"The far greatest part of these Strowlers having thus passed into England, at first, divided themselves into five tribes or orders, which are called the Old Ranks of Canters, viz., 1. Cursitors; 2. Robberd's Men; or Outlaws; 3. Rogues; 4. Draw Latches; and 5. Sturdy Beggars. And notwithstanding several good laws were made against Vagabonds and Strowlers, &c., (which still remain in force) yet they, taking into their Society the Beggars of all denominations and all degrees of Villains and Profligates, more especially in Wales, the vulgar inhabitants whereof were always noted naturally for Petty-Larceny, Fortune-telling, and Genealogies, they became so very numerous that they were able to range themselves into sixty-four Bands or Tribes, including the above mentioned five, according to the several species of villainy, whereof each Order was most capable ; each Band having its Chief or Leader, who was usually the completest villain of the Tribe and distinguished by the title of the Dimber-Damber of such or such a Tribe."

Although the suggestion as to union workhouses has been fully carried out in England, still sturdy beggars, tramps, and thieves (both within and without the pale of the law) abound largely throughout the kingdom. —There seems, however, to be a dead-set against the gipsies. The progress of railways and the extension of suburban villas have operated against their retaining their free domicile at Norwood, and tribes have consequently taken to starring it through the country, and exhibiting their encampment to the curious, for a small fee payable at the entrance gate. —The rural Police have been the cause of the expulsion of numerous tribes from the inland districts of England, and these have sought a new home in Australia.

Yetholm, in Roxburghshire, which has always been a stronghold of the Scotish gypsies, has not yet been called upon to expatriate those of the dusky race, who form no inconsiderable portion of its constituency.

Canters' Holiday.

CAST your nabs and cares away,
This is Maunders' Holiday;
In the world, look out, and see,
Where's so happy a King as he?
(*Pointing to their newly elected Prince.*)

At the crowning of our King,
Thus we ever dance and sing;
Where's the nation lives so free,
And so merrily, as we?

Be it Peace, or be it War,
Here at liberty we are;
Hang all Harmanbecks, we cry.
We the Cuffin-queeres defy,

We enjoy our ease and rest,
To the field we are not press'd;
And when the taxes are increas'd,
We are not a penny cess'd.

Nor will any go to law
With a Maunder for a straw;
All which happiness, he brags,
Is only owing to his rags.

The Thief=Catcher's Prophecy.

FREQUENTLY SUNG BY A LATE NOTED THIEF-TAKER.

[JONATHAN WILD.]

Good people, give ear, whilst a story I tell,
Of twenty black tradesmen were brought up in hell,
On purpose poor people to rob of their due;
There's none shall be nooz'd, if you find but one true.
The first was a Coiner, that stampt in a mould;
The second a Voucher to put off his gold.
 Tour you well, hark you well, see where they're rubb'd,
 Up to the nubbing-cheat, where they are nubb'd.

The third was a Padder, that fell to decay,
Who used to plunder upon the Highway;

The fourth was a Mill-Ken, to crack up a door,
He'd venture to rob both the rich and the poor,
The fifth was a Glazier, who when he creeps in,
To pinch all the lurry he thinks it no sin.
          Tour you well, &c.

The sixth is a File-cly, that not one cully spares,
The seventh a Budge, to track softly up stairs ;
The eighth is a Bulk, that can bulk any hick,
If the Master be napt, than the Bulk he is sick,
The ninth is an Angler, to lift up a grate,
If he sees but the lurry his hooks he will bait.
          Tour you well, &c.

The tenth is a Shoplift, that carries a Bob,
When he ranges the city, the shops for to rob.
The eleventh a Bubber, much used of late ;
Who goes to the ale-house, and steals all their plate.
The twelfth is a Beautrap, if a Cull he does meet,
He nips all his Cole, and turns him into the street.
          Tour you well, &c.

The thirteenth a Famble, false rings for to sell,
When a Mob he has bit his Cole he will tell ;
The fourteenth a Gamester, if he sees the Cull sweet,
He presently drops down a Cog in the street ;
The fifteenth, a Prancer, whose courage is small,
If they catch him Horse-coursing, he's noozed for all.
          Tour you well, &c.

The sixteenth, a Sheep-napper, whose trade is so deep,
If he's caught in the corn he's marked for a sheep;
The seventeenth a Dunaker, that stoutly makes vows,
To go in the country and steal all the cows ;
The eighteenth a Kid-napper, who spirits young men,
Tho' he tips them the pike, they oft nap him again.
          Tour you well, &c.

The nineteenth's a Priggar of Cacklers, who harms
The poor Country Higlers, and plunders the Farms;
He steals all their poultry and thinks it no sin,
When into the Henroost, in the night, he gets in,
The twentieth's a Thief-catcher, so we him call,
Who if he be nabb'd will be made pay for all.
            Tour you well, &c.

There's many more Craftsmen whom here I could name,
Who use such-like trades, abandon'd of shame;
To the number of more than threescore in the whole,
Who endanger their body, and hazard their soul;
And yet, tho' good workmen, are seldom made free,
Till they ride in a cart, and be nooz'd on a tree.
      Tour you well, hark you well, see where they're rubb'd,
      Up to the nubbing-cheat, where they are nubb'd.

The Life and Death of the Darkman's Budge.

        THE Budge it is a delicate trade,
            And a delicate trade of fame,
        For when that we have bit the blow,
            We carry away the game.
        But if the cully naps us,
            And the lurries from us takes;
        O then he rubs us to the whit,
            Tho' we're hardly worth two makes.

        And when that we come to the whit,
            Our darbies to behold;
        We're forced to do penance there,
            And booze the water cold.
        But when that we come out again,
            And the merry cull we meet;
        We'll surely file him of his cole,
            As he pikes along the street.

And when that we have filed him,
　Tho't be but half a job ;
Then ev'ry man to the boozing-ken,
　To fence his merry hog.
But if the cully naps us,
　For want of care or wit,
Tho' he cannot take away our cole,
　He rubbs us to the whit.

And when we come unto the whit,
　For garnish they do cry ;
We promise our lusty comrogues
　They shall have it by and bye.
Then ev'ry man, with his Mort in his hand,
　Is forc'd to kiss and part ;
And after, is divorced away,
　To the nubbing-cheat in a cart.

And we come to the Nubbing-cheat,
　For running on the budge ;
There stands Jack Ketch, that sneaking wretch,
　Who owes us all a grudge :
For when that he hath nubbed us,
　And our friends tip him no cole,
He takes his chive, and cuts us down,
　And tips us into the hole.

But if we have a friend stand by,
　Six and eightpence for to pay ;
Then they may have our bodies back,
　And carry us quite away :
For at St Giles's or St Martin's,
　A burying place is still ;
And there's an end of a Darkman's Budge,
　And the whoreson hath his will.

K

Clear Out—Look Sharp!

Song commonly sung at a general Rendezvous, before they divide into parties, to stroll about the country.

Bing out, been Morts, and tour and tour,
   Bing out, been Morts, and tour ;
For all your Duds are bing'd awast,
   The been Cove hath the Lour.

I met a Dell, I lik'd her well,
   She was benship to my Watch,
So she and I did stall and cly,
   Whatever we could catch.

This Doxy Dell can cut been whids,
   And drill well for a Win ;
And prig and cloy so benshiply,
   Each Deuseavile within.

The Booth being rais'd, we stept aside,
   Thro' mire, and frost and snow ;
When they did seek then did we creep,
   And plant in Ruffman's Row.

To strowling-ken, the Mort bings then,
   To fetch Lour for her cheats ;
Duds and Ruffpeck, maugre Harmanbeck,
   We won by Maunder's feats.

You Maunders all, stow what you stall,
   To Rum-Coves what so quire ;
And Bucksom Dell, that snilches well,
   And takes Lour for her hire.

A Jybe well jerk'd, tick Rome-confeck,
    For back by Glimmar, to maund ;
To mill each Ken, let Cove bing then,
    Thro' Ruffmans, Jague, or Laund.

Till Cramprings quire, tip Cove his Hire,
    And Quire-ken do them catch ;
Old Ruffler mill the Quire-cuffin,
    So quire to been Cove's watch.

Booze, Mort, and Ken, been Darkmans then,
    The poor Cove's bing'd awast ;
On Chats to trine, by Rum-Coves Dine,
    For his long Lib at last.

Bing out been morts, and tour, and tour,
    Bing out of the Romevile fine ;
Now tour the cove that cly'd your duds,
    Upon the chats to trine.

The Strowling Mort's Praise of her Clapper=dogeon.

Now my Kinchin Cove is gone,
By the Rum-Pad maunded none
In Quarrons, both for Stamps and Bone,
Like my Clapperdogeon.

Dimber-Damber, fare-thee-well,
Palliards all thou didst excell ;
And thy Jockey bore the Bell,
Glymmer on it never fell.

Thou the Cramprings ne'er didst scour,
Harmans had on thee no Power ;

Harmanbecks did never toure
For thee; for why? thou still didst Loure.

Duds and Cheats thou oft hast won,
Yet the Cuffin quire didst shun;
And thy Deuseavile didst run,
Else the Chats had thee undone.

Cank and Dommerar thou couldst play,
Or Rum-maunder in one day;
And like an Abram-cove couldst pray,
Yet pass with Jybes well jerk'd away.

When the Darkmans hath been wet,
Thou the Crackmans down didst beat
For Glymmar; whilst a Quacking cheat,
Or Tib o' th' Buttery was our meat.

Redshanks then I could not lack,
And Ruffpeck still hung at my back;
Grannam ever fill'd my sack,
With Lap and Poplars held I tack.

To thy bughar and thy skew,
Filch and Jybes, I bid adieu;
Tho' thy Togeman was not new,
Yet the Palliard in't was true.

The Beggar's Curse.

IT is usual among the common people in Scotland when they intend to express the utter worthlessness of anything to say "it is not worth a beggar's (or tinkler's) curse."

The Ruffin cly the Nab of the Harmanbeck,
If we maund Pannam, Lap, or Ruff-Peck,

Of Poplars of Yarum, he cuts bing to the Ruffmans,
Or else he with cruelty swears by the Lightmans,
He'll seize us, and put our stamps fast in the Harmans,
The Ruffin cly the Ghost of the Harmanbeck
If we heave a Booth we straight cly the Jerk :
If we niggle or mill but a poor Boozing-Ken,
Or nip a poor Bung with one single Win,
Or dup but the Gigger of a Country-Cove's Ken,
Straight we're to the Cuffin Queer forced to bing;
And 'cause we are poor made to scour the Cramp-ring,
From thence at the Chats we trine in the Lightmans,
Plague take the Harmanbeck : Ruffin the Harmans. .

The Canter's Serenade.

SUNG early in the morning, at the Barn doors where their Doxies
have reposed during the night.

Ye Morts and ye Dells,
Come out of your Cells,
And charm all the Palliards about ye ;
Here birds of all feathers,
Through deep roads and all weathers,
Are gather'd together to toute ye.

With faces of Wallnut,
And Bladder and Smallgut,
We're come scraping and singing to rouze ye ;
Rise, shake off your straw,
And prepare you each maw
To kiss, eat, and drink till you're bowzy.

Retoure, my dear Dell.

EACH Darkmans I pass in an old shady Grove,
And live not the Lightmans, I toute not my love,
I surtoute every walk, which we used to pass,
And couch me down weeping and kiss the cold grass :
     I cry out on my Mort to pity my pain,
     And all our vagaries remember again.

Didst thou know, my dear Doxy, but half of the smart
Which has seiz'd on my panter since thou didst depart;
Didst thou hear but my sighs, my complainings and groans,
Thou'dst surely retoure and pity my moans :
     Thou'dst give me new pleasure for all my past pain,
     And I should rejoice in thy glaziers again.

But alas ! 'tis my fear that the false *Patri-coe*
Is reaping those transports are only my due :
Retoure my dear Doxy, Oh, once more retoure,
And I'll do all to please thee that lies in my pow'r ;
     Then be kind, my dear Dell, and pity my pain,
     And let me once more toute the glaziers again.

On Redshanks and Tibs thou shalt every day dine,
And if it should e'er be my hard fate to trine,
I never will whiddle, I never will squeek,
Nor to save my Colquarron endanger thy neck.
     Then once more, my Doxy, be kind and retoure,
     And thou shalt want nothing that lies in my pow'r.

All Men are Beggars.

Tune—*Greensleeves.*

THAT all men are beggars we plainly may see,
For beggars there are of ev'ry degree ;
Tho' none are so blest and so happy as we,
     Which nobody can deny, deny, which nobody can deny.

The tradesman he begs that his wares you would buy,
Then trusts you'd believe the price is not high ;
And swears ('tis his trade) when he tells you a lye,
     Which nobody can deny, &c.

The lawyer he begs you would give him a fee,
Tho' he reads not your brief, nor regardeth your plea,
But advises your foe how to get a decree,
     Which no body can deny, &c.

The courtier he begs for a pension or place,
A ribbon, a title, or smile from his Grace,
'Tis due to his merit, 'tis writ in his face,
     Which nobody can deny, &c.

But if by mishap he should chance to get none,
He begs you'd believe that the nation's undone;
There's but one honest man, and he is that one,
     Which nobody dare deny, &c.

The fair one she labours whole mornings at home,
New charms to create, and much paint to consume,
Yet begs you'd believe 'tis her natural bloom,
     Which nobody should deny, &c.

The lover he begs the dear nymph to comply,
She begs he'd begone, yet, with languishing eye,
She begs he would stay, for a maid she can't die,
     Which none but a fool would deny, &c.

Jack Shephard.

THE several preceding songs in the Canting Dialect are acknowledged lyrics of the Fraternity, "wherewith," according to the Preface previously referred to, "these Varlets generally divert themselves at their merry-makings. Those lately published on occasion of the late famous Shepherd, Blueskin, &c., though made by another sort of authors, may in time perhaps be adapted by the Canters to their own particular use, seeing the genius of the writers have so well hit upon the Language and Humours of their Brother Vagabonds."

The career of Jack Shephard was rendered remarkable by reason of his most surprising escapes from Newgate. Bereft of his father at an early age, his mother worked very hard in order to acquire the means to give him a decent education, and when of proper age he was apprenticed to a cane chairmaker in Houndsditch ; but after a short time, his master dying, he was put to another master in the same trade, who used him so cruelly that he ran away. His mother, through the influence of Mr. Kneebone, a woollen draper, then got him bound apprentice to a carpenter in Wych Street. There Jack served about four years very creditably, when he unfortunately made the acquaintance of the landlord of the Black Lion alehouse in Drury Lane, at that time the haunt of the most notorious vagabonds in London. He began to spend his evenings there, and to fall a victim to female blandishments, which, creating expense that his slender means could not compass, he resorted to the appropriation of other men's goods, and gradually becoming bolder, advanced with rapid strides from petty larceny to house-breaking, so that at the early age of twenty-two he was condemned to death for burglary, and was executed at Tyburn on the 16th November 1724. Mr. Kneebone, who had befriended Jack, was among the victims on whom he had levied involuntary contributions.

The Editor of "Bacchus and Venus" thus introduces the two following songs from Harlequin Sheppard, "a night scene, in grotesque characters, by John Thurmond. Acted at Drury Lane. 8vo, 1724."
—*See Biographia Dramatica.*

"The notable exploits and escapes of the late notorious John Shepherd became for the time so much the talk and entertainment of the town that the polite gentlemen of a certain Theatre thought it worth their while to lay aside Heroicks and learn the Canting Dialect, and, from being the awful representatives of ancient Heroes and Monarchs, thought fit, for the diversion of their audiences, and to show the universality of their genius and that no station of life misbecame their capacity and profession, to suffer themselves to dwindle into the characters of *Sharpers* and *Pickpockets* ; and accordingly the town was presented with a *night scene* in *grotesque characters*, wherein that unhappy Felon's misfortunes were re-acted under the title of *Harlequin Shepherd* for the public amuse-ment ; which was pompously embellished with the expense of new scenes painted from the real places of action.   To some of these celebrated wits it seems the whole *Canting Fraternity* are obliged for the following song, sung on the stage, as they tell us, by FRISKY MOLL, the supposed repre-sentative mistress of Shephard on occasion of his being retaken the second time."

Besides the Pantomime of Harlequin Sheppard, there was also a play on the subject of his exploits acted and printed shortly after his death.   His memory has been of late years revived by the publication of the Novel, bearing his name, written by Wm. Harrison Ainsworth and illustrated by George Cruickshanks, the popularity of which was such that it was dramatized and performed, with pecuniary advantage, in almost every Theatre throughout the kingdom.   The Lord Chamberlain after awhile however thought fit to step in and prevent its further repre-sentation as it was found that, from the sympathy in place of the indigna-tion entertained for the hero, the play was conducive to the demoralization of youth.   For the same reason " Oliver Twist " has been interdicted, although Mr Toole will occasionally revel in the character of the Artful Dodger during some of his provincial excursions to the delectation of an overflowing gallery of impressionable yet half informed members of the rising generation.   It would be well if the Lord Chamberlain put his veto upon all dramas of that class, for it cannot be otherwise than that evil to the community must result from the representation of such pieces as "the Golden Farmer," "The Ticket of leave man," The Ticket of leave woman," *et hoc genus omne.*   The object of dramatic representations should be to elevate the mind, not to lower and degrade it.

There was a very smartly written burlesque (and pantomime) satirizing the dramas manufactured from Ainsworth's Novel, entitled "Harlequin Jack Shepherd, or, the Blossom of Tyburn Tree"—produced at Covent Garden Theatre during Mr W. J. Hammond's management in 1839.

From Priggs that snabble the Prancers strong,
   To you of the Peter-Lay,
I pray now listen awhile to my song,
   How my Bowman he kick'd away.

He broke through all the Rubbs in the whit,
   And chiv'd his Darbies in twain ;

But filing of a Rumbo-Ken,
My Bowman is snabbled again.

I, Frisky Moll, with my Rum Cull,
Would suck in a Boozing Ken ;
But e'er for the Scran he had tipt the Cole,
The Harman he came in.

A Famble, a Tattle, and two Pops,
Had my Bowman when he was ta'en ;
But had we not booz'd in the Diddle Shops,
He'd still been in Drury Lane.

Blueskin.

A new Song sung at the Old Theatre in the famous Night
Scene, *call'd* Harlequin Shepherd.

"Nor ought it to be omitted that, to the same gentlemen, and the
same piece we owe the following song on occasion of the attempt of a
companion of Shephard, vulgarly called Blueskin, to cut the throat of
the famous *Jonathan Wilde* (a fatal omen of what after befel that noted
Thief-taker !) which we the rather insert as it contains some reflections
that may inform posterity what manner of persons some of their ancestors were ; and to what sort of transactions many of them will stand
indebted to History for a name, according to the opinion of our retailers
of Tragedy and Farce ; who at the same time are generally allowed to
understand the world."

In reflecting on this concluding observation it is somewhat curious
to observe that the reputed descendant of Jonathan Wild should in our
time have allied himself to Royalty and attained the dignity of a Peer of
the Realm.

"Blueskin" just mentioned, and who prominently figures in Ainsworth's novel, was a thief from his infancy. His real name was Joseph
Blake. At an early age he joined himself to Jonathan Wild's gang, and
after "a short life and a merry one" he came to the gallows, for having,

in company with Jack Shepherd and one Field, another of the gang, broken into the shop of Mr Kneebone, a Woollen-Draper, and stolen cloth to the value of thirty-six pounds. Mr Kneebone gave notice to Jonathan Wild, who with two more went to Blake's lodgings, and being denied admittance broke open the door.—When Blake saw Jonathan he surrendered, exclaiming "I know I am a dead man," but Jonathan told him not to be afraid, for although he could not save him any longer he would send him some good books to read in Newgate, and if he behaved well he would buy him a coffin. Blake was committed to Newgate, and on Field turning king's evidence, he was sentenced to be hanged. It was Jonathan Wild's intention to have been a witness at the trial, but having previously paid Blake a visit, Blake took occasion to spring suddenly upon him and with a clasp knife to wound him in the throat.—The knife happening to be rather blunt, the wound though dangerous did not prove mortal, but it incapacitated Wild from appearing to give his evidence.

While under sentence of death Blake spent most of his time in drinking, and having lax notions on the subject of religion thought that by a regular attendance at prayers in the Chapel during the short interval, he could not fail to make peace with heaven.—He was executed at Tyburn 11th November 1724, after having formed several ineffectual schemes for escape. On the occasion of his execution he was in a state of intoxication.

In reference to "Wood and his brass," in the sixth or concluding stanza, it happened that in 1723 there being a deficiency of copper coin in Ireland, the king, through the influence of his mistress, the Duchess of Kendal, who had been promised a share of the profits, granted to one William Wood, upon certain conditions, the patent right of coining halfpence and farthings, to the extent of £108,000, to be current in that kingdom. The patent was passed without consulting the Lord-Lieutenant or Privy-Council of Ireland, and the Irish Parliament felt insulted that the crown should thus have devolved upon an obscure individual, an iron-monger, one of its highest privileges. The family of Broderick, then almost the chief of the Whig interest, from conviction or from dislike to the Lord-Lieutenant, or from a mixture of these motives, threw their weight into the scale of opposition, and so secured those who made it from the charge of disaffection. While the struggle was impending, Dean Swift wrote his celebrated Drapier's letters, although it can scarcely be supposed that he actually considered Wood's project dangerous. Wood's halfpence were proved by experiments at the Mint, under the direction of Sir Isaac Newton, to equal in weight and purity those of England. But the danger and dishonour of the measure lay in its application to Ireland in its existing state, for although that ancient kingdom still retained the outward insignia of national legislation and

sovereignty, repeated and oppressive steps had been taken to reduce it
into the condition of a conquered province, it having no representative
in the British Parliament. Wood's privilege was therefore regarded as
involving the grand question of the servitude or independence of Ireland.
Both the Irish Houses of Parliament joined in addressing the Crown
against Wood's scheme. Parties of all denominations, whether religious
or political, united in expressing their abhorrence of the halfpence. The
tradesmen to whom the coin were consigned refused to receive them,
endeavouring, by public advertisement, to remove the scandal of being
concerned in the matter, and associations were formed for refusing
their currency. The mob, having thus taken up the cudgels, made
riotous processions, and burned the unhappy schemer in effigy. Dean
Swift, in addition to the Drapier's Letters, not only supplied the
hawkers with a variety of pungent ballads, and prose satires, fomenting
the popular indignation, and redolent of inuendoes against Wood's
patrons and abettors in England, but he also preached against the
obnoxious coinage. The Duke of Grafton, then Lord-Lieutenant,
finding that any proposition, however libellous and treasonable, was
now unhesitatingly published and eagerly perused provided Wood and
his halfpence could be dragged into the text, it became evident that
the scheme if enforced would occasion a civil war.

Sir Robert Walpole endeavoured to appease the general ferment by a
proclamation which limited the issue of half pence to £40,000 instead of
£108,000, thinking thereby to let the scheme drop gradually. This fail-
ing, he recalled Lord Grafton, and sent in his stead, as Lord-Lieutenant,
Lord Cateret, Secretary of State, who Walpole knew had been intrigu-
ing against him in the interior of the cabinet, and had greatly encouraged
the discontent in Ireland, by caballing with the Brodericks. He was
enjoined to carry on Wood's project if it were possible; if not, to drop
it, by the surrender or suspension of the patent. The publication of the
Drapier's fourth Letter, in which Swift boldly treats of injustice to
Ireland, and tells the people that the remedy is wholly in their hands,
alarmed the English government, and Cateret issued a proclamation
offering a reward of £300 for the discovery of the author of that "wicked
and malicious pamphlet, containing several seditious and scandalous
passages, highly reflecting upon his Majesty and his Ministers, and
tending to alienate the affections of his good subjects in England and
Ireland from each other." Harding, the printer of the Drapier's Letters,
was thrown into prison, but he resolutely refused to reveal the author.
A prosecution was directed against him at the instance of the Crown,
and the grand jury, conscious of what the country expected, brought into
court a verdict of *ignoramus* upon the bill, to the utter amazement and
resentment of Lord Chief-Justice Whitshed. Other three letters of the
Drapier were published by Swift, which had the effect of keeping the

popular indignation alive. Meantime Cateret yielded to the storm,—
Wood's patent was surrendered—and the patentee indemnified by a grant
of £3000 a-year, for twelve years. All eyes were now turned upon the
man whose fortitude and abilities had thus victoriously terminated the
first grand struggle for the independence of Ireland. The Drapier's
head became a sign, his portrait was engraved, was wrought upon
handkerchiefs, struck upon medals, and · displayed in every possible
manner, as the liberator of Ireland. A club too was formed in honour
of the patriot,—and, contrary to the usual course of public favour in
such cases, "the sun of Swift's popularity," as Sir Walter Scott happily
expresses it, "shone unclouded even after he was incapable of distinguishing its radiance."

Mr. Wood's son, Charles, became assay master at Jamaica, and was
the first to introduce platina into Europe. Mary Howitt, the literary
quakeress, was Charles' grand-daughter. See Redfern's History of
Uttoxeter, 1865. 12mo.

YE Fellows of Newgate, whose fingers are nice,
At diving in pockets or cogging of dice;
Ye Sharpers so rich, who can buy off the noose;
Ye honest poor rogues who die in your shoes,
　　Attend, and draw near
　　Good news you shall hear,
How Jonathan's throat was cut from ear to ear ;
　How Blueskin's sharp Penknife hath set you at ease,
　And ev'ry man round me may rob if he please.

When to the Old Bailey this Blueskin was led,
He held up his hand ; his indictment was read ;
Loud rattled his chains ; near him Jonathan stood,
And full forty pounds was the price of his blood ;
　　Then hopeless of life,
　　He drew his penknife,
To make a sad widow of Jonathan's wife,
　But forty pounds paid her, her grief shall appease,
　And ev'ry man round me may rob if he please.

Knaves of old to hide guilt by their cunning inventions,
Call'd briberies *grants*, and plain robberies *pensions*,

Physicians and lawyers who take their degrees,
To be learned in rogu'ry call pilfering *fees*,
    Since this happy day,
    Now every man may
Rob as safe (as in office) upon the Highway :
    For Blueskin's sharp penknife, &c.

Some cheat in the Customs, some rob the excise,
But he who robs *both* is esteemed most wise :
Churchwardens, who always have dreaded the halter,
As yet only venture to steal from the Altar,
    But now to get gold,
    They may be more bold,
And rob on the Highway now Jonathan's cold,
    For Blueskin's sharp penknife, &c.

Some by Publick Revenues, which pass through their hands,
Have purchased clean houses and bought dirty lands ;
Some to steal from a charity think it no sin,
Which *at home* (says the Proverb) *does always begin* ;
    But if ever you be
    Assign'd a Trustee,
Treat not orphans like masters of the Chancery,
    But take the highway and *more honestly seize*,
    For every man round me may rob if he please.

What a pother has here been with *Wood* and his *brass*,
Who would modestly make a few halfpennies pass ;
The patent is good and the precedent's old,
For Diomede changed his paper for gold.
    But let Ireland despise
    The new halfpennies,
With more safety to rob on the road I advise ;
    For Blueskin's sharp penknife has set you at ease,
    And ev'ry man round me may rob if he please.

𝔜e 𝔖camps, 𝔜e 𝔓ads, 𝔜e 𝔇ivers.

THIS is the song of the keeper of Bridewell in "the Choice of Harlequin, or the Indian Chief," a Pantomime composed by Mr Messink, of which the Editors of the Biographia Dramatica say:—"In probability of fable and in point of moral this piece, which was acted with great success at Covent-Garden 1781-2, was superior to nineteen-twentieths of its tribe." John Edwin, the Comedian, who performed the keeper of Bridewell, rendered the song exceedingly popular by introducing it in several other characters.

Ye Scamps, ye Pads, ye Divers, and all upon the lay,
In Tothil-fields' gay sheepwalk, like lambs ye sport and play;
Rattling up your darbies, come hither at my call,
I'm Jigger Dubber here, and you are welcome to Mill Doll.
    With my tow row, &c.

At your Insurance office the flats you've taken in,
The game they've play'd, my kiddy, you're always sure to win;
First you touch the shiners—the number up—you break,
With your insuring-policy I'd not insure your neck.
    With my tow row, &c.

The French, with trotters nimble, could fly from English blows,
And they've got nimble daddles, as monsieur plainly shows;
Be thus the foes of Britain bang'd, ay, thump away, monsieur,
The hemp you're beating now will make your solitaire.
    With my tow row &c.

My peepers! who've we here now? why, this is sure Black-moll:
My ma'am, you're of the fair sex, so welcome to Mill Doll;
The Cull with you who'd venture into a snoozing-Ken,
Like Blackamore Othello, should "put out the light—and then."
    With my tow row, &.

I think my flashy coachman, that you'll take better care,
Nor for a little bub come the slang upon your fare;

Your jazy pays the garnish, unless the fees you tip,   [whip.
Though you're a flashy coachman, here the gagger holds the
            With my tow row &c.

We're Scamps, we're Pads, we're Divers, we're all upon the lay,
In Tothil-fields' gay sheepwalk, like lambs we sport and play;
Rattling up our darbies, we're hither at your call,
You're Jigger Dubber here, and we're forc'd for to Mill Doll.
            With my tow row, &c.

Beggar's Lassies.

From "The Triumphs of Bacchus, or, the Delights of the Bottle."
London, 1719, 16mo.

        How blest are beggars' lassies,
            Who never toil for treasure;
        We know no care, but how to share
            Each day's successive pleasure.
        Drink away, let's be gay,
            Beggars still with bliss abound;
        Mirth and joy, ne'er can cloy,
            Whilst the sparkling glass goes round.

        A fig for gaudy fashions,
            No want of clothes oppresses;
        We live at ease with rags and fleas,
            We value not our dresses.
                Drink away, &c.

        We scorn all ladies washes,
            With which they spoil each feature;
        No patch or paint our Beauties taint,
            We live in simple nature.
                Drink away, &c.

No Cholick, Spleen, or Vapours,
    At morn or ev'ning teaze us ;
We drink not tea, or ratifie,
    When sick, a dram can ease us.
        Drink away, &c.

With ladies we are even,
    In Cupid's toils who caught are ;
For who so free with love can be,
    As any Beggar's daughter ?
        Drink away, &c.

We know no shame or scandal,
    The Beggars' laws befriend us ;
We all agree in liberty,
    And Poverty defends us.
        Drink away, &c.

Like jolly Beggar-wenches,
    Thus, thus we drown all sorrow,
We live to-day, and ne'er delay
    Our pleasure till to-morrow.
Drink away, let's be gay,
    Beggars still with bliss abound ;
Mirth and joy ne'er can cloy,
    Whilst the sparkling glass goes round.

The Merchant's Son, and the Beggar Wench of Hull.

From a chap copy, "Four New Excellent Songs; 1. Peace with America, a new Scotch song ; 2. The Merchant's Son ; 3. The Swain design'd for love and me; 4. O'er the Moor to Maggy. Entered according to order." *Circa*, 1782.

This ballad also occurs, with some verbal differences, in the second

L

volume of "a Collection of Old Ballads," Lond. 1723, 12mo., and has
been reprinted in Evans' Old Ballads, Lond., 1784, 12mo.

You gallants all, I pray draw near,
And you a pleasant jest shall hear;
How a poor beggar-wench of Hull
A Merchant's son of York did gull.
    Fa, &c.

One morning on a certain day,
He cloth'd himself in rich array;
And took with him, as it was told,
The sum of sixty pounds in gold.

So, mounting on a prancing steed,
He towards Hull did ride with speed;
Where in his way he chanc'd to see
A beggar-wench of mean degree.

She asked him for some relief,
And said, with seeming tears of grief,
That she had neither house nor home,
But for her living was forc'd to roam.

He seemed to lament her case,
And said, "Thou hast a pretty face;
If thou wilt lodge with me," he cried,
"With gold thou shalt be satisfy'd."

Her silence seemed to give consent,
So to a little house they went;
The landlord laugh'd to see him kiss
The beggar-wench and ragged miss.

He needs must have a supper dress'd,
And call'd for liquor of the best;
And then they toss'd off bumpers free,
The jolly beggar-wench and he.

A dose she gave him, as 'tis thought,
Which by the landlady was brought;
And quietly tuck'd him up in bed,
Secure, as if he had been dead.

Then did she put on all his clothes,
His hat, his breeches, and his hose;
His coat, his periwig likewise,
And seized upon the golden prize.

Her greasy petticoat and gown,
In which she rambl'd up and down,
She left the merchant's son in lieu,
Her bag of bread and bacon too.

Down stairs, like any spark, she goes,
Five guineas to the host she throws;
And smiling then she went away,
And ne'er was heard of to this day.

When he had ta'en his long repose,
He look'd about and miss'd his clothes,
And saw her rags lie in the room,
How he did storm, nay, fret and fume.

Yet wanting clothes and friends in town,
Her greasy petticoat and gown
He did put on, and mounted straight,
Bemoaning his unhappy fate.

You would have laughed to see the dress
Which he was in; yet, ne'ertheless,
He homeward rid, and often swore
He'd never kiss a beggar more.

𝕿𝖍𝖊 𝕵𝖔𝖇𝖎𝖆𝖑 𝕭𝖊𝖌𝖌𝖆𝖗, 𝖆-𝖇𝖊𝖌𝖌𝖎𝖓𝖌 𝖜𝖊 𝖜𝖎𝖑𝖑 𝖌𝖔.

From a broadside, circa 1700, bearing the title "Be Valiant Still, &c. A new song much in request, being the advice of an experienced lady in martial affairs to her lover, a young soldier. To the tune of *The old carle to daunton me.* Together with the Jovial Beggar."

The Jovial Beggar, with the tune, has been printed in the third volume of Durfey's Pills to purge melancholy, with a few verbal differences, and the omission of stanzas 4, 8, and 9.

There was a Jovial Beggar,
  With a wooden leg,
Lame from his cradle,
  And born for to beg.
And a-begging we will go,
  We'll go, we'll go, we'll go.
And a-begging we will go.

A bag for my oat-meal,
  Another for my rye ;
A little bottle by my side,
  To drink when I am dry.
    And a-begging we will go, &c.

A bag for my wheat,
  Another for my salt,
A little pair of crutches,
  To see how I can halt.
    And a-begging, &c.

A bag for my bread,
  Another for my cheese,
A little dog to follow me,
  To take up what I leese.
    And a-begging, &c.

To Pimlico we'll go,
  Where we will merry be,
With ev'ry man in's hand a can,
  And a wench upon his knee.
    And a-begging, &c.

And when we are disposed
  To tumble on the green,
We've got a long patch'd coat,
  To keep our trousers clean.
    And a-begging, &c.

Seven years I begg'd
  For my old master, *Wild,*
He taught me how to beg
  When I was but a child.
    And a-begging, &c.

I had a pretty knack on't,
  To wheedle and to cry;
And by young and old
  Much pitied was I.
    And a-begging, &c.

Fatherless and motherless
  Still was my complaint ;
And none e'er saw me
  But took me for a saint.
    And a-begging, &c.

I begged for my master,
  And got him store of pelf;
The stars now be praised,
  I beg for myself ;
    And a-begging, &c.

In a hollow tree
I live and pay no rent,
Providence provides for me,
And I am well content.
And a-begging, &c.

Of all the occupations,
The Beggar's is the best,
For when he is weary
He lays him down to rest.
And a-begging, &c.

I fear no plots against me,
I live in open cell :
Then who'd be a king,
When a Beggar lives so well?
And a-begging we will go,
We'll go, we'll go, we'll go,
And a-begging we will go.

AULD EDDIE OCHILTREE.

The following picture of a Blue-Gown Beggar, or "Gaberlunzie,"
issued from the press of David Webster, Printer, Horse Wynd, Edinburgh, shortly after the appearance of Sir Walter Scott's admirable
novel of "The Antiquary," in which, it will be remembered, there is a
blue-gown beggar of the same name, an exquisitely drawn character,
who figures very prominently. Prior to the publication of the novel,
hat class of Scotch mendicants had long ceased to be known. Some of
them, as well as many of the beggars who more immediately succeeded
them, confined their rounds to particular districts, and were in the habit
of paying periodical visits to most of the families resident in the several
ocalities. They always found a welcome in the Farmer's Ha,' the
Cottar's bield, and in the kitchen of "the big hoose up by." They were
accorded a lodging in some out-house, and even the poorest cottager

never refused them their usual *awmous*, invariably a *goupen* of meal, *i.e.*, as much as can be lifted in both hands conjoined.

Martin, author of "Reliquiæ Divi Sanctæ Andreæ," 1683, believes them to have been descended from the ancient bards, and thus proceeds : "They are called by others, and by themselves, Jockies, who go about begging ; and use still to recite the Sloggorne (gathering-words or war-cries) of most of the true ancient surnames of Scotland, from old experience and observation. Some of them I have discoursed, and find to have reason and discretion. One of them told me there were not now above twelve of them in the whole isle ; but he remembered when they abounded, so as at one time he was one of five that usually met at St Andrews."

In one of the Memorandum Books of the Scotish Antiquary, George Paton, (circa 1780) this note occurs :—

"A set of beggars travelled up and down the south and western parts of Scotland, and were never denied alms by any one. They always carried alongst with them a horn, and were styled Jocky with the Horn, or Jocky who travels broad Scotland." See Appendix to "Letters from Thomas Percy, &c., to George Paton," Edited by J. Maidment, Edin., 1830, cr. 8vo.

The Blue-gown Beggar, or King's Bedesman, was regarded, in virtue of the aristocracy of his order, as an important personage. "These Bedesmen," observes Sir Walter Scott in his advertisement to the Antiquary, "are an order of paupers to whom the Kings of Scotland were in the custom of distributing a certain alms in conformity with the ordinances of the Catholic Church, and who were expected in return to pray for the royal welfare, and that of the state. This order is still kept up. Their number is equal to the number of years which his majesty has lived ; and one Blue-Gown additional is put on the roll for every returning royal birth-day. On the same auspicious era, each Bedesman receives a new cloak, or gown of coarse cloth, the colour light blue, with a pewter badge, which confers on them the general privilege of asking alms through all Scotland, all laws against sorning, masterful beggary, and every other species of mendicity, being suspended in favour of this privileged class. With his cloak each receives a leathern purse, containing as many shillings Scots (pennies sterling) as the Sovereign is years old ; the zeal of their intercession for the King's long life receiving, it is to be supposed, a great stimulus from their own present and increasing interest in the object of their prayers. On the same occasion one of the Royal Chaplains preaches a sermon to the Bedesmen," and the royal birth-day, in so far as they are concerned, "ends in a hearty breakfast of bread and ale."

No notice of the Bedesmen occurs during Cromwell's time, but they again appear after the Restoration, and are particularly mentioned in an account of the rejoicings at Edinburgh, on the occasion of the

anniversary of the King's birth-day, 29th May 1665, quoted in a notice
of "Colonel Munro, a well-known Blue-gown Beggar," in Kay's
Portraits, Edin. 1842 :—"My Lord Commissioner, in his state, accompanied with his life-guards on horseback, and Sir Andrew Ramsay, Lord
Provost of Edinburgh, Bailies and Council in their robes, accompanied
with all the trained bands in arms, went to church, and heard the Bishop
of Edinburgh upon a text as fit as well applied to the work of the day.
Thereafter, thirty-five aged men, in blue gowns, each having got thirty-
five shillings in a purse, came up from the Abbey to the great church,
praying all along for his majesty."

Ferguson the Poet makes reference to one of the annual gatherings,
during his time, of the fraternity of Blue-gowns from all parts of the
country, to receive their allowance of bread and beer, their new gowns,
and leathern purses :—

> "Sing, likewise, muse ! how blue-gown buddies,
> Like scarecrows new ta'en doon frae woodies,
> Come here to cast their clouted duddies,
>   An' get their pay :
> Than them what magistrate mair proud is
>   On King's birth-day ?"

At the conclusion of the reign of King George III., the number of
Blue Gowns was eighty-two, corresponding with his advanced age.
When the Whigs came into power after the passing of the Reform Bill
in 1832, this ancient aristocratic order of Pensioners fell a prey to their
cheeseparing propensities; but with a praiseworthy consideration, they
allowed the annual bounty to be continued during the lifetime of the
then existing recipients.   One alleged reason for discontinuance of the
charity was, that the provision of Chelsea Hospital superseded the
original object of the privileges granted to them.

A nearly similar ceremony to that which took place at the distribution
of alms to the Scotish Blue-Gowns used to be observed in London on
Maundy Thursday, the day preceding Good Friday.   It was observed at
the Chapel Royal Whitehall, as a day "on which," according to
Archdeacon Nares' Glossary, "the King distributes alms to a certain
number of poor persons at Whitehall, and is so named from the maunds
in which the gifts were contained."   Maund, derived from the Saxon,
is used by Shakespeare, by Drayton, and by Hall in his Satires, to
signify "a basket."   It is also used by Herrick in the same sense, but
he also speaks of "maundie" as denoting "alms."   The Canting
Dictionary gives us "Maunders, Beggars : Maunding, To beg, Begging."
In Hone's Every-day Book, vol. i., p. 401, particulars are given of the
ceremony of this distribution, and how, on Maundy Thursday in 1814,

there were "distributed to seventy-five poor women and seventy-five poor men, being as many as the King was years old, a quantity of salt fish, consisting of salmon, cod, and herrings, pieces of very fine beef, five loaves of bread, and some ale to drink the King's health." After church evening service "silver pennies were distributed, and woollen cloth, linen, shoes and stockings to the men and women, and a cup of wine to drink the King's health."

" Anciently, on Maundy Thursday, the Kings and Queens of England washed and kissed the feet of as many poor men and women as they were years old, besides bestowing their *Maundy* on each. This was in imitation of Christ washing his disciples' feet. James II. is said to have been the last of our monarchs who performed this ceremony in person."

There is a ballad in Thomson's Orpheus Caledonius, also in Herd's Scots Songs, vol. ii. p. 61, called "John Ochiltree," which however bears no affinity to our present Ballad.

Auld Eddie Ochiltree.

Air "Duncan Gray."

O heard you o' the bauld blue-gown,
Auld Eddie Ochiltree ?
Weel kent in ilka country town,
Auld Eddie Ochiltree ;
When beggars o' the gangrell corps,
Are driven frae the hallen door,
The gudewife cries " Come ye in ower
Auld Eddie Ochiltree."

The bairns are a' fu' glad to see
Auld Eddie Ochiltree.
" Fling by your pocks !" they cry wi' glee,
" Auld Eddie Ochiltree."
The gudewife says " ye'll a' hinch roun',
An' let auld Eddie lean him doun.
Sit neist the fire, my braw blue-gown,
Auld Eddie Ochiltree."

Syne Eddie taks his wallets aff,
　　　　Auld Eddie Ochiltree,
Sets in the nook his long pike-staff,
　　　　Auld Eddie Ochiltree;
The lassies a' they look fu' fain,
To see auld Eddie come again,
The maiden brings a gude rough bane
　　　　To Auld Eddie Ochiltree.

The news are gi'en fu' waggishlie
　　　　By auld Eddie Ochiltree;
An' jokes, " for mony a joke had he,"
　　　　Auld Eddie Ochiltree.
He tells wha's bridal's to be neist,
And wha hae little time to waste,
An' wha's to stand afore the priest,
　　　　Auld Eddie Ochiltree.

The uncos are by him rehearsed,
　　　　Auld Eddie Ochiltree.
In births and bridals he's weel versed,
　　　　Auld Eddie Ochiltree.
He kens what's dune at kirk or fair,
At mill or smithy far and near,
An' hoo some wives their gudemen queer—
　　　　Auld Eddie Ochiltree.

Nae ferlie though the lassies grin,
　　　　Auld Eddie Ochiltree,
To hear his cracks an' jokes ilk ane,
　　　　Auld Eddie Ochiltree;
The weans the Gaberlunzie hail,
The ploughmen chiels lay by the flail,
The collie barks an' wags his tail
　　　　At auld Eddie Ochiltree.

The time it comes when man an' beast,
    An' auld Eddie Ochiltree,
Maun gang an' tak the needfu' rest,
    Auld Eddie Ochiltree ;
The auld gudeman the spence comes frae,
Cries " Jock ! ye'll tae the barn gae,
An' mak a bed o' gude clean strae
    For auld Eddie Ochiltree."

TOM A BEDLAM.

MAD Songs have from time to time engaged the attention of lyric
writers in this country, and not a few of these have been composed as
for mad beggars, or " Tom o' Bedlam," as such worthies have been
styled.   The earliest printed copy of the celebrated song of " Mad
Tom," which we now give under another title, is to be found in Playford's *English Dancing Master*, 1650-51.   It is there otherwise styled
"New Mad Tom of Bedlam," which would lead us to surmise that it
was not the first of the name.   Before Playford's time, songs, ballads,
and dance tunes or lessons for the Virginals were chiefly current in MS.
The Black-letter copies of the ballad in the Pepysian Library and in the
British Museum, are entitled "New Mad Tom of Bedlam ; or

> The man in the moon drinks Claret,
> With powder'd beef, turnips, and carrot,
> But a cup of old Malaga Sack,
> Will fire the bush at his back."   .
> "The tune is ' Gray's Inn Maske.' "

The selection of the tune of "Gray's Inn Maske" for a mad song is
curious, and by analogy some may consider it not inappropriate, as it
was the custom of the gentlemen of the Inns of Court to hold revels
four times a year, and represent masks and plays at these revels, and,
"that nothing might be wanting for their encouragement in this excellent study (the law)," they were obliged to dance.   "It is not many
years," adds Sir John Hawkins in his History of Music, Vol. ii. p.
137, "since the judges, in compliance with ancient custom, danced
annually on Candlemas Day."   These were "by special order of the
Society as appeareth in 9th Henry VI."   "Nor were these exercises
of dancing merely permitted, but thought very necessary, as it seems,
and much conducing to the making of gentlemen more fit for their books
at other times ; for, by an order made 6th Feb., 7 Jac., it appears that
the under-barristers were by decimation put out of Commons for
example's sake, because the whole bar offended by not dancing on the
Candlemas-day preceding, according to the ancient order of the Society
when the judges were present ; with this, that if the like fault were afterwards committed, they should be fined or disbarred."

The song of "Mad Tom " is mentioned in Walton's Angler, the first
edition of which appeared in 1653.   Sir John Hawkins observes, "this
song beginning ' Forth from my dark and dismal cell,' with the music
to it, set by Henry Lawes, is printed in a book entitled *Choice Ayres,
Songs, and Dialogues to sing to the Theorbo-Lute and Bass Viol*, fol. 1675 ;
and in Playford's *Antidote against Melancholy*, 8vo, 1669."   "The
music," Mr Chappell remarks, "has long passed as the composition of

Henry Purcell, and is still published with his name. Walsh paved the way to this error (in which Ritson and many others have followed him) by including it in a collection of Mr Henry Purcell's Favourite Songs out of his most celebrated Orpheus Britannicus and the rest of his Works." It is *not* contained in the Orpheus Britannicus, and both words and music may still be seen as *printed* eight years before Purcell's birth." Mr Chappell further remarks, " The words of the latter half of this song are not now sung. Another song set by George Hayden, also called ' Mad Tom,' the words of which commence ' In my triumphant chariot hurled,' has been 'stitched' upon it." George Hayden's song, and his duet " As I saw fair Clora," are to be found in a collection published by Pearson, entitled " The merry Mountebank, or, the Humourous Quack Doctor," 1732.

The elder D'Israeli, in his paper on " Tom a Bedlams " in Curiosities of Literature, observes: " An itinerant lunatic, chaunting wild ditties, fancifully attired, gay with the simplicity of childhood, yet often moan-ing with the sorrows of a troubled man, a mixture of character at once grotesque and plaintive, became an interesting object to poetical minds. It is probable that the character of Edgar, in the Lear of Shakespeare, first introduced the hazardous conception into the poetical world. Poems composed in the character of a Tom-o'-Bedlam appear to have formed a fashionable class of poetry among the wits ; they seem to have held together their poetical contests, and some of these writers became celebrated for their successful efforts ; for old Izaak Walton mentions ' Mr William Basse as one who has made the songs of the *Hunter in his Career*, and of *Tom-o'-Bedlam*, and many others of note.' Bishop Percy, in his *Reliques of Ancient English Poetry*, has preserved six of what he calls ' Mad Songs,' expressing his surprise that the English should have ' more songs and ballads on the subject of madness than any of their neighbours,' for such are not found in the collection of songs of the French, Italian, &c., and nearly insinuates, for their cause, that we are perhaps more liable to the calamity of madness than other nations. This superfluous criticism had been spared had that elegant collector been aware of the circumstance which had'produced this class of poems, and recollected the more ancient original in the Edgar of Shakespeare."

Dr Rimbault in " a little Book of Songs and Ballads, gathered from ancient music books, MS. and printed," Lond. 1851, cr. 8vo, mentions that " Aubrey in his *Natural History of Wiltshire* (MS.) says, ' Till the breaking out of the Civil Wars, Tom-o'-Bedlams did travel about the country. They had been once distracted men that had been put into Bedlam, where recovering to some soberness they were licentiated to go a-begging. They had on their left arm an armilla of tin about four inches long ; they could not get it off. They wore about their necks a great horn of an ox in a string or bawdrick, which when they came to a house for alms they did wind; and they did put the drink given them into this horn, whereto they did put a stopple. Since the wars I do not remember to have seen any of them." The learned Doctor adds, "Edgar, in Shakespear's King Lear, it will be remembered, carries a horn."

The following Songs of madness will be found in D'Urfey's "Songs Compleat, Pleasant and Divertive," 1719:

"A Mad Song—by a lady distracted with love. Sung in one of my (*i.e.* D'Urfey's) Comedies of Don Quixote: The Notes to it, done by the late famous Mr Henry Purcell; which, by reason of their great length are not printed in this Book, but may be found at the Musick Booksellers singly, or in his Orpheus Britannicus; performing in the tune all the degrees of madness."

In this song the lady is at the beginning "sullenly mad," then she turns "mirthfully mad—a swift movement"—next there is "melancholly madness," from which she becomes "fantastically mad," and ends by being "stark mad," and tearing her clothes and hair. Vol. i. p. 1.

In the same volume at p. 73, occurs "A Mad Dialogue, sung in my Play called the Richmond Heiress, by Mr Leveridge and Mrs Lynsey. Set to Musick by Mr Henry Purcell. In Orph. Britan." It terminates with a chorus of both :—

"Then mad, very mad let us be,
Very mad, very mad let us be,
For Europe does now with our frenzy agree,
And all things in nature are mad too as we."

Immediately following is "A song by a Mad Lady in Don Quixote." Set by Mr John Eccles."

In Vol. 5, page 32, there is another called "The Mad-man's Song," with the music, the chorus of which is—

"Then be thou mad, mad, mad let's be,
Nor shall the foul fiend be madder than we."

Of the six mad songs which Mr D'Israeli has mentioned as embodied by Bishop Percy in his Reliques, the others, in addition to Tom a Bedlam, are :—

"The distracted Puritan—mad song the second, was written about the beginning of the seventeenth century by the witty Bishop Corbet, and is printed from the third edition of his poems, 12mo, 1672, compared with a more ancient copy in the editor's folio MS." It commences thus :—

"Am I mad, O noble Festus,
When zeal and godly knowledge
Have put me in hope
To deal with the Pope,
As well as the best in the college?

Boldly I preach, hate a cross, hate a surplice,
Mitres, copes, and rochets ;
Come hear me pray nine times a day,
And fill your heads with crotchets."

" The Lunatic Lover,—mad song the third, is given from an old printed copy in the British Museum, compared with another in the Pepys collection ; both in black letter." It runs thus :—

"Grim King of the ghosts, make haste,
And bring hither all your train ;
See how the pale moon does waste,
And just now is in the wane.
Come, ye night hags, with all your charms,
And revelling witches away,
And hug me close in your arms ;
To you my respects I pay," &c.

" The Lady distracted with love,—mad song the fourth, was originally sung in one of Tom D'Urfey's comedies of Don Quixote, acted in 1694 and 1696 ; and probably composed by himself." This song has been already referred to as existing in D'Urfey's Songs compleat, &c.

" The Distracted Lover, mad song the fifth, was written by Henry Carey, a celebrated composer of music at the beginning of this [i.e., the eighteenth] century, and author of several little Theatrical Entertainments, which the reader may find enumerated in the 'Companion to the Play-House,' &c. The sprightliness of this songster's fancy could not preserve him from a very melancholy catastrophe, which was effected by his own hand. In his Poems, 4to, London 1729, may be seen another mad song of this author's beginning thus :—

" Gods ! I can never this endure,
Death alone must be my cure."

" The Frantic Lady,—mad song the sixth. This, like the fourth song, was originally sung in one of D'Urfey's comedies of Don Quixote, first acted about the year 1694, and was probably composed by that popular songster, who died Feb. 26th 1723. This is printed from the 'Hive, a Collection of Songs,' 4 vols. 1721, 12mo, where may be found two or three other mad songs not admitted into these volumes." See Percy's Reliques, 1767, vol. 2, p. 348 et seq.

In addition to these, mention is made in Playford's "Dancing Master," edition 1686, of an air styled "Mad Robin," which has been introduced in "the Lover's Opera," 1730.

And there are one or two Madmen's Songs in Fletcher's Play of "The Nice Valour ; or, the Passionate Madman" (circa 1624). Among these we may refer to the very poetic song of "Melancholy," which the Passionate Lord sings—a song to which Milton has laid himself under obligation for a portion of the imagery and sentiment with which his "Il Penseroso" abounds, and which Hazlitt has characterized as the "perfection of this kind of writing."

The well-known song of "My lodging it is in the cold ground," falls within our category.   The first account of the air we have is in Playford's "Musick's delight on the Cithern," 1666.   This, Mr Chappell discovered after long investigation, as it had always been believed that the air was coeval with the words which appear in Davenant's Comedy of "The Rivals," 1668.   Downes, in his Roscius Anglicanus, states that King Charles II. was so pleased on hearing Mrs Davis sing this song in the character of Celania, (a shepherdess mad for love) that he took her off the stage.   A daughter by her was named Mary Tudor, and was married to Francis Lord Ratcliffe, afterwards Earl of Derwentwater.   Mrs or Moll Davis was one of the female actresses who boarded with Sir William Davenant.   This Song is included in our present Collection under the title of "The Mad Shepherdess," from the version to be found in Evans' Old Ballads, 1784, vol. 3.

Mr T. Mozeen, author of the "Young Scarron," is also author of a Song entitled "The Bedlamite," which appeared in "A Collection of Miscellaneous Essays, London, Printed for the Author, 1762," 8vo.

The most recent mad song which has appeared, and which enjoyed popularity for awhile, was written by Charles Mackay, to the music of Henry Russell, who used to sing it at his entertainments.   It is called "The Maniac."

We print this song of Tom a Bedlam from the text of D'Urfey in "Songs Compleat, Pleasante, and Divertive ; set to musick by Dr John Blow, Mr Henry Purcell, and other excellent masters of the Town," otherwise known as D'Urfey's "Pills to purge melancholy," vol. 3d, London 1719, 12mo.

This is the first of the six songs referred to by Mr D'Israeli, which Bishop Percy has preserved in his Reliques.   The Bishop considers that it was written about the beginning of the seventeenth century.   He goes on to say, "This is given from the Editor's folio MS., compared with two or three old printed copies."

Tom a Bedlam.

Forth from the dark and dismal cell,
And from the deep abyss of hell,
Mad Tom is come to the world again,
To see if he can cure his distemper'd brain.

Fears and cares oppress my soul,
Hark ! how the angry furies howl,
Pluto laughs, and'Proserpine is glad,
To see poor naked Tom a Bedlam mad.

Through the world I wander night and day,
   To find my straggling senses,
In an angry mood old Time,
   With his Pentateuch of tenses.

With me he spyes, away he flies,
   For Time will stay for no man ;
In vain with cries I rend the skies,
   For pity is not common.

Cold and comfortless I lie,
Help ! oh help ! or else I die ;
Hark ! I hear Apollo's team,
   The Carman 'gins to whistle,
Chaste Diana bends her bow,
   And the Boar begins to bristle.

Come Vulcan, with tooth and tackles,
And knock off my troublesome shackles ;
Bid Charles make ready his wain,
To find my lost senses again.

Last night I heard the Dog-star bark,
Mars met Venus in the dark :
Limping Vulcan heat an iron bar,
And furiously ran at the God of War.

Mars with his weapon laid about,
Limping Vulcan had the gout,
For his broad horns hung so in his light,
That he could not see to aim aright.

M

Mercury, the nimble Post of Heaven,
  Stay'd to see the quarrel,
Bacchus giantly bestrid
  A strong beer barrel.

To me he drank, I did him thank,
  But I could drink no cyder ;
He drank whole Butts till he burst his guts,
  But mine were ne'er the wider.

Poor Tom is very dry,
A little drink for charity :
Hark ! I hear Acteon's hounds !
  The Huntsman whoops and hollows,
Ringwood, Rockwood, Jowler, Bowman,
  All the chase doth follow.

The man in the moon drinks claret,
Eats powder'd beef, turnip, and carrot,
But a cup of old Malaga sack,
Will fire the bush at his back.

A Tom a Bedlam Song.

THIS has been reprinted by Dr Rimbault from " Wit and Drollery,"
1659. It is also to be found at the end of " Le Prince d'Amour, "1660.

From the hag and hungry goblin
  That into rags would rend ye,
    All the spirits that stand
    By the naked man,
  In the Book of moons defend ye !
That of your five sound senses
  You never be forsaken ;
    Nor never travel from
    Yourselves with Tom
  Abroad to beg your bacon.

CHORUS.

Nor never sing, any food and feeding,
Money, drink, or clothing ;
Come dame or maid
Be not afraid,
Poor Tom will injure nothing.

Of thirty bare years have I
Twice twenty been enraged ;
And of forty, been
Three times fifteen
In durance soundly caged.
In the lovely lofts of Bedlam,
In stubble soft and dainty,
Brave bracelets strong,
Sweet whips, ding dong,
And a wholesome hunger plenty.
Yet did I sing, &c.

With a thought I took for Maudlin,
And a cruise of cockle pottage,
And a thing thus—tall,
Sky bless you all,
I fell into this dotage.
I slept not since the conquest ;
Till then I never waked ;
Till the roguish boy
Of love, where I lay,
Me found, and stript me naked.
Yet do I sing, &c.

When short I have shorn my sow's face,
And swigg'd my horned barrel,
In an oaken Inn
Do I pawn my skin
As a suit of gilt apparel.

The moon's my constant mistress,
  And the lonely owl my marrow;
    The flaming drake
    And the night-crow, make
  Me music to my sorrow.
    Yet do I sing, &c.

The palsie plague these pounces,
  When I prig your pigs or pullen;
    Your calves take,
    Or mateless make
  Your chanticleer and sullen;
When I want provant, with Humphrey I sup,
  And when benighted,
    To repose in Paul's,
    With waking souls,
  I never am affrighted.
    Yet do I sing, &c.

I know more than Apollo,
  For, oft when he lies sleeping,   '
    I behold the stars
    At mortal wars,
  And the rounded welkin weeping;
The moon embraces her shepherd,
  And the queen of love her warrior;
    While the first doth horn
    The stars of the morn,
  And the next the heavenly farrier.
    And yet do I sing, &c.

With a host of furious fancies,
  Whereof I am commander;
    With a burning spear,
    And a horse of air,
  To the wilderness I wander;

With a knight of ghosts and shadows,
I summoned am to Tourney
Ten leagues beyond,
The wide world's end ;
Methinks it is no journey.
Yet do I sing, &c.

𝕸𝖆𝖉 𝕸𝖆𝖚𝖉𝖑𝖎𝖓.

To find out Tom of Bedlam.

From Durfey's "Pills to Purge Melancholy," Vol. iv., with the Music.

To find my Tom of Bedlam ten thousand years I'll travel,
Mad Maudlin goes with dirty toes to save her shoes from
gravel.
> *Yet will I sing bonny boys, bonny mad boys, Bedlam boys
> are bonny;*
> *They still go bare, and live by the air, and want no drink
> nor money.*

I now repent that ever poor Tom was so disdain'd,
My wits are lost since him I crost, which makes me go thus
chain'd:
> Yet will I sing, &c.

My staff hath murdered Gyants, my bag a long knife carries,
To cut mince-pyes from children's thighs, with which I feast
the Fairies :
> Yet will I sing, &c.

My horn is made of thunder, I stole it out of heaven,
The rainbow there is this I wear, for which I thence was
driven.
> Yet will I sing, &c.

I went to Pluto's kitchen, to buy some food one morning,
And there I got souls piping hot, with which the spits were
turning :
> Yet will I sing, &c.

Then took I up a Cauldron, where boyl'd ten thousand
'tornies,
'Twas full of flame, yet I drank the same, and wished them
happy journeys.
Yet will I, &c.

A spirit as hot as lightning did on my travels guide me,
The sun did shake and the pale moon quake, as soon as e'er
they spy'd me :
Yet will I, &c.

And now that I have gotten a lease than doomsday longer,
To live on earth with some in mirth, ten whales shall feed
my hunger :
Yet will I, &c.

No Gipsie, Slut, or Doxy shall win my mad Tom from me,
We'll weep all night, and with stars fight, the fray will well
become me :
Yet will I, &c.

And when that I have beaten the man i' th' moon to powder,
His dog I'll take, and him I'll make bark as no dæmon
louder :
Yet will I, &c.

A health to Tom of Bedlam, go fill the seas in barrel,
I'll drink it all, well brew'd with gall, and maudling-drunk
I'll quarrel :
Yet will I, &c.

𝔐𝔞𝔡 𝔗𝔬𝔪.

In Halliwell's "Notices of Fugitive Tracts and Chap-books," printed
for the Percy Society, July 1849, occur these :—

MAD TOM'S GARLAND, composed of six excellent songs, 12mo,
licensed and entered according to order.   N.D.

This Tract will call the play of *King Lear* and Poor Tom to the
reader's remembrance.   The annexed cut is reduced from a larger one

on the title page, and affords a good idea of the *Bedlam Beggar* thus
described by Holme, 1688 :

" The Bedlam is in the same garb, with a long staff, and a cow or ox-horn
by his side ; but his clothing is more fantastick and ridiculous, for being
a madman, he is madly decked, and dressed all over with ribbons,
Feathers, cuttings of cloth, and what not, to make him seem a madman,
or one distracted, when he is no other than a dissembling knave !"

A facsimile of the woodcut alluded to will be found as a tail-piece to
this our collection of Mad Songs. See page 189.

The following definition of " An Abraham Man " is given in " The
Fraternitie of Vacabondes ; as wel of ruflyng Vacabondes as of beggerly,
of Women as of Men, of Gyrles as of Boyes, with their proper names
and qualities. Lond., 1575, 12mo :"—" An Abraham Man is he that
walketh bare armed, and caryeth a packe of wool, or a stycke with
baken on it, or such lyke toy, and nameth himself poore Tom."

I am old mad Tom, behold me,
I am old mad Tom, behold me,
   And my wits are quite fled from me !
I am mad, I am sure, I am past all cure,
   Yet I hope to be reclaimed.

I apprentice was to Vulcan,
I apprentice was to Vulcan,
   And serv'd my master faithful,
Who makes all tools for such jovial souls,
   But the gods have been ungrateful.

I'll climb the lofty mountains,
I'll climb the lofty mountains,
   There will I fight the gypsies ;
I'll play at bowls with the sun and moon,
   And win them in the eclipses.

I'll climb the frosty mountains,
I'll climb the frosty mountains,
   I'll gather stars by clusters,
   And put them into my budget :
And if that I am not a roaring boy,
   Let all the nation judge it.

I'll climb the snowy mountains,
I'll climb the snowy mountains,
    And there will I skim the weather;
I'll pluck the rainbow from the skies,
    And splice both ends together.

BESS OF BEDLAM'S GARLAND, containing several excellent new songs,
12mo, N. D.

    See, see, poor Bess of Bedlam,
      In mournful plight and sadness;
    I shake my chains and rack my brains
      In all extremes of madness.

Bess of Bedlam.

From a Chap Copy, "Entered according to order, 1799."

See, see poor Bess of Bedlam,
    In mourning plight and sadness,
I shake my chains and wreck my brains,
    In all extremes of madness.

How sharp's the pointed arrow,
    Which flew at my poor breast!
In mischief dipp'd and venom steep'd,
    That broke my peaceful rest.

With love my soul is flaming,
    Nought my sorrows hinder;
My pulse beats high—I scorch and fry,
    My heart burns to a cinder.

My eye-balls roll and wander,
    Methinks I now behold him;
I'll stretch my arms to meet his charms,
    But alas! I can't enfold him.

Fly, all ye loves and graces,
To Jove with this petition,
To break my chain, and send my swain,
And heal my sad condition.

But ah ! if Jove refuse,
I'll set my cell on fire,
T' assuage my breast, I'll burn my nest,
And, Phœnix-like, expire.

A Mad Song.

From " The Session of the Critics : or, the Contention for the Nettle.
A Poem. To which is added, A Dialogue between a Player and a Poet.
With Notes Explanatory and Critical, after the manner of the learned
Dr. Bentley. With the following Miscellanies, viz. :—

London, folio. N. D. [Circa 1720.]

I'll bark against the Dog-star,
I'll crow away the morning,
I'll chase the moon till it be noon,
And I'll make her leave her horning,

But I will find bonny Maud, merry mad Maud,
  And look whate'er betides her,
For I do love her beneath or above
  The dirty earth that hides her.

I'll crack the Poles asunder,
  Strange things I will devise on,
I'll break my brain 'gainst Charles's wain,
  And I'll grasp the round horizon.
But I will find bonny Maud, &c.

I'll search the caves of slumber,
  I'll please her in a Night's Dream,
I'll tumble her in the Elysian fields,
  And I'll hang myself on a Sun-Beam.
But I will find bonny Maud, &c.

I'll sail upon a mill-stone,
  I'll make the Sea-Gods wonder,
I'll plumb the deep till I wake all asleep,
  And I'll tear the Rocks asunder.
But I will find bonny Maud, &c.

I'll dive as soon to the Damned,
  And rebellious laws I'll teach them,
Neither Sky, Earth, nor Sea, nor Hell shall go free,
  Nor the Gods, could I but reach them.
But I will find bonny Maud, &c.

I'll arm myself with Thunder,
  I'll rally all my Forces,
The Sun I'll dart, if he stirs, to the Heart,
  Or I'll remove his Horses.
But I will find bonny Maud, &c.

I'll mount the Skies with a vengeance,
  I'll charm the rainy weather,
The Rainbow I will drag from the Sky,
  And I'll tie both ends together.
But I will find bonny Maud, &c.

All the spheres shall play in Concert,
  And the Stars shall dance in a passion,
There's one in haste shall girdle my waist,
  And I'll wear it for a Fashion.
But I will find bonny Maud, &c.

Bedlam City, or The Maiden's Lamentation.

From a Broadside issued by "Pitts, Printer, Toy and Marble Warehouse, 6 Gt. St. Andrew Street, Seven Dials," and compared with another copy "printed for W. Armstrong, Banastre Street," (Liverpool).

Down by the side of Bedlam city,
  There I heard a maid complain ;
Making grievous lamentation,
  Lost my lov'd, my only swain.

CHORUS.

Billy is the lad that I do admire,
  He is the lad that I do adore ;
Now for him his love lies dying,
  For fear she should never see him more.

I wish I had wings, I would fly to him,
  And lock him close within these arms ;
Cruel parents to refuse him !
  Oh ! he had ten thousand charms.

Hark I hear the cannons rattle,
   How the drums and trumpets sound,
Now he lies in midst of battle,
   Dying with his bleeding wounds.

Oh don't you see my Billy coming,
   Don't you see him in the cloud;
With guardian angels standing round him,
   See about him how they crowd.

Down on a bed of straw she tumbled,
   Making her moan and this reply;
I've lost my only joy and comfort,
   How could my parents him deny?

The Mad Shepherdess.

My lodging is on the cold ground,
   And very hard is my fare;
But that which troubles me most is
   The unkindness of my dear.
Yet still I cry, O turn love,
   And I prithee love turn to me,
For thou art the man that I long for,
   And alack! what remedy?

I'll crown thee with a garland of straw then,
   And I'll marry thee with a rush ring;
My frozen hopes shall thaw then,
   And merrily we will sing;

Or turn to me my dear love,
   And I prithee love turn to me,

For thou art the man that alone canst
  Procure my liberty.

But if thou wilt harden thy heart still,
  And be deaf to my pitiful moan ;
Then I must endure the smart still,
  And tumble in straw all alone ;
Yet still I cry, O turn love,
  And I prithee love turn to me,
For thou art the man that alone art
  The cause of my misery.

A SOUTH SEA BALLAD, OR, MERRY REMARKS UPON EXCHANGE-ALLEY BUBBLES.

To a new Tune, call'd, "The Grand Elixir, or the Philosopher's Stone Discovered."

THIS song appeared in September 1720. It is characterized by Mr Thomas Wright, in his very curious volumes of "England under the House of Hanover," London 1848, 8vo., as "the celebrated South-Sea Ballad, which was sung about the streets of London for months together, and helped not a little to bring stock-jobbing into discredit."

For several years prior to the introduction of the South Sea scheme, a thirst for money speculations pervaded a large portion of the Western parts of Europe. The national finances of France had fallen into such a pitiable state, that the government was upon the verge of bankruptcy. John Law, of Lauriston, who in consequence of having killed a man in a duel, had retired to France, imparted a project to the Regent, whereby it was conceived this national calamity might be averted. The result was that Law got up the Mississippi Scheme, in 1717, under the Regent's sanction, who made him the principal Director. This Company was to have a monopoly of the trade to the country of the Mississippi, in North America, on condition that they should undertake the payment of the State bills. They went on for two years without any remarkable success, when, by a junction with the French India and China Companies, a sudden and immense rise took place in the value of the shares, or "actions," as they were then called. Mr Law and the Regent then resolved to extend the company still further, which caused a rapid rise in the price of the shares, till in a short time they attained the market value of eleven hundred per cent. premium. Law thence became to be regarded as a wonderful financier, even more so than "the Railway King" of our own times, and so precious was he deemed to the French nation that the mere report of his slight indisposition caused a fall in the funds. The success of Law's scheme was such as to relieve the government from its pecuniary difficulties, to enrich the nobility and courtiers, and to create an overflow of money throughout all Paris. Law was made a member of Privy-Council, and Comptroller-General of the finances of France.

In England the success of the French scheme was considered as worthy of imitation. A chartered trading company, called the South Sea Company, which had been established in 1711, was, through the medium of Sir John Blount, one of the Directors, brought before the notice of the Ministry as a means to relieve the country of the national debt, which had become unusually heavy by the long war,—and a Bill was introduced into the House of Commons for that purpose. After considerable opposition, especially from Sir Robert Walpole, who was not in the Ministry, the South Sea Bill was passed in April 1720. A few days after, Walpole published a pamphlet pointing out the mischief which might be expected from the project, but the thirst of the people for dealing in South Sea shares had already begun, so that in a short time the Stock commanded in the open market a premium of nine hundred per cent.

Stock jobbing now seemed to engross the attention of every one. The fever had set in, and it raged for some months with unabated violence.

Although a proclamation had been issued forbidding the formation of Joint Stock Companies without sanction of the government, a large number of these sprung up, and soon became known by the appellation of "Bubbles." Many of these, as is usual on like occasions, were mere swindling speculations. No matter whether the scheme propounded was practicable or not, the shares were eagerly subscribed without inquiry. The shares of a Company, which merely advertized as "an undertaking which will in due time be revealed," were in this manner taken up. In the "Political State of Britain" will be found a list of these bubbles in July 1720, in all one hundred and four, the projects principally being impossibilities. The shares in all the different schemes rose to enormous premiums, those in a Water Engine Company, for instance, on which four pounds were paid, rose to fifty pounds. Exchange-Alley was crowded from morning till night with persons of both sexes. Numerous individuals rose from indigence to profusion, and, as the motto of the beggar on horseback is "light come, light go," many of these expended their winnings in riotous living and profligacy. Most of them set up their carriages, and mingled with the more aristocratic of the land in driving in the park. The rabble however soon discovered them, and "stock jobbers'" carriages could not be seen abroad without a chance of their being mobbed.

But erelong a change came o'er the spirit of this dream. Law's financial plans in France had become embarrassed, and on Saturday the 20th July, in the midst of the mania in London, news came that on the previous Wednesday, Law had been assaulted by the populace, who broke his coach, beat his coachman and compelled him to fly to the Palais Royal for refuge. The timely arrival of the Swiss guards prevented them from perpetrating the further outrage of destroying his house. The public blamed the great projector for the misery in which they now found themselves involved, and by the pressure from without he was forced to resign his office of Comptroller of Finance. He was permitted to depart secretly from France. Under the assumed name of M. du Jardin he repaired to Brussels, and subsequently to

Venice.   In 1721 he came to England, and was a source of jealousy to
the anti-ministerial party.   His property, and that of his brother
William, Director-General of the India Company, (who was imprisoned
in the Bastile) had been seized upon and confiscated, under the pretext
that the two brothers were owing twenty millions of livres to the India
Company, whereas, instead of being indebted, there were some millions
of livres due to them.   So great had been his acquisition of wealth, that
Law had bought no less than fourteen estates with titles annexed to them ;
among which was the Marquisate of Rosny, which had belonged to the
Duke of Sully, the friend and minister of Henri Quatre.   So long as the
Regent lived he kept up the hope of the restitution of his property and of
his recall to France.   He corresponded constantly with the Regent, who
continued to remit his official salary of 20,000 livres per annum.   The
sudden death of the Regent, however, which took place on 2d Dec.
1723, was a fatal blow to Law.   His expectation of recovering any
part of his property diminished, his pension ceased to be remitted, and
he became embarrassed on every side.   He finally quitted Britain in
1725, and took up his residence at Venice, where he died in very poor
circumstances on the 21st March 1729, at the age of fifty-eight.   See
Memoirs of the life of John Law of Lauriston.   By J. P. Wood, Edin.
1824.   12mo.

The South Sea Company, anticipating the extension of the panic to
London, determined to put down the other companies which had been
got up without legal authority, but alas ! this act hastened the catastrophe
of which they were so fearful.   The destruction of these opened the eyes
of the public to the fallacy of premiums upon Stock, and the result was
that the shares of the South Sea Company lost their buoyancy and sunk
from £850 to £175 per share.   Of those therefore who had bought at
the higher price, and had been estimating the value of their worldly gear
at the inflated quotations of the day, suddenly found that, in place of
their pound they could only realize four shillings, many died of broken
hearts, and others left the country never to return, while those wiley
"jobbers" who had bought the Stock in a rising market and had realized
before it took the downward turn, retired upon their ill-gotten fortune
and consequent respectability ; never troubling themselves to count the
number of tombstones of their too sanguine victims over which they had
vaulted.

Our copy of the "South Sea Ballad," has been taken from an 8vo.
pamphlet pp. 56, called "The Delights of the Bottle : or, the Compleat
Vintner.   With the humours of Bubble Upstarts, Stingy Wranglers,
Dinner Spunges, Jill Tiplers, Beef Beggars, Cook Teasers, Pan Soppers,
Plate Twirlers, Table Whitlers, Drawer Biters, Spoon Pinchers, and
other Tavern Tormentors.   A Merry Poem.   To which is added, a South
Sea Song upon the late Bubbles, by the author of the Cavalcade.

The Fair, 'tis true, yield wonderful delights,
But, when we're old, torment us with their slights ;
The bottle therefore is a faster friend,
Because that kindly soothes us to our end.

London, printed for Sam. Briscoe, at the Bell-Savage on Ludgate Hill, 1720."

Mr Wright has reprinted the ballad in his "England under the House of Hanover," with some trifling differences ; and James Hogg has it, with the music, in his "Jacobite Relics" 1st series page 138, but with the omission of the third stanza, the first half of the fourth, and the first half of the tenth stanzas. He has also this difference in stanza eighth :

> For me I follow reason's rules,
> Nor fat on South Sea diet.

And in stanza ninth he substitutes the word "bubble" for "Babel."

A South Sea Ballad.

In London stands a famous pile,
And near that pile an alley,
Where merry crowds for riches toil,
And Wisdom stoops to Folly.
Here, Sad and Joyful, High and Low,
Court Fortune for her graces,
And, as she smiles or frowns, they shew
Their gestures and grimaces.

Here, Stars and Garters do appear,
Among our Lords the rabble,
To buy and sell, to see and hear
The Jews and Gentiles squabble.
Here, crafty courtiers are too wise
For those who trust to fortune ;

N

They see the cheat with clearer eyes,
  Who peep behind the curtain.

Our greatest Ladies hither come,
  And ply in chariots daily;
Oft pawn their jewels for a sum,
  To venture't in the Alley.
Young Misses too from Drury-lane,
  Approach the 'Change in coaches,
To fool away the gold they gain
  By their impure debauches.

Long heads may thrive by sober rules,
  Because they think and drink not;
But Headlongs are our thriving fools,
  Who only drink and think not.
The lucky rogues, like Spanish dogs,
  Leap into South Sea water,
And there they fish for golden frogs,
  Not caring what comes a'ter.

'Tis said that Alchemists of old,
  Could turn a brazen kettle,
Or leaden cistern into gold,
  That noble tempting metal.
But if it here may be allow'd,
  To bring in great with small things,
Our cunning South Sea, like a god,
  Turns nothing into all things.

What need have we of Indian wealth,
  Or Commerce with our neighbours,
Our Constitution is in health,
  And Riches crown our labours.
Our South Sea ships have golden shrouds,
  They bring us wealth, 'tis granted,
But lodge their treasure in the clouds,
  To hide it till its wanted.

O Britain! bless thy present state,
    Thou only happy nation;
So oddly rich, so madly great,
    Since Bubbles came in fashion.
Successful rakes exert their pride,
    And count their airy millions,
Whilst homely drabs in coaches ride,
    Brought up to town on pillions.

Few men, who follow reason's rules,
    Grow fat with South Sea diet;
Young Rattles and unthinking fools,
    Are those that flourish by it.
Old musty Jades, and pushing Blades,
    Who've least consideration;
Grow rich apace, whilst wiser heads
    Are struck with consternation.

A race of men, who, t'other day
    Lay crush'd beneath disasters,
Are now by Stock brought into play,
    And made our Lords and Masters.
But should our South Sea Babel fall,
    What numbers would be frowning,
The losers then must ease their gall
    By hanging or by drowning.

Five hundred millions, notes and bonds,
    Our Stocks are worth in value;
But neither lie in goods or lands,
    Or money, let me tell you.
Yet tho' our Foreign trade is lost,
    Of mighty wealth we vapour,
When all the riches that we boast
    Consist in scraps of paper.

The Hubble Bubble.

To the tune of "O'er the Hills and far away."

FROM a Broadside contemporaneous with the South Sea Scheme. "Quincompoy" in the second stanza bears reference to Law's House, where all his business was transacted. It was situated in the Rue Quinquenpoix in Paris.

JEWS, Turks, and Christians, hear my song,
I'll make you rich before it's long ;
Sell Houses, Lands, and eke your Flocks,
And put your money in the stocks.
　For Hubble Bubble's now in play,
　Come, buy the Bubble whilst you may,
　There's Hubble Bubbles night and day,
　At Jonathan's and Garraway.

Ye Scotsmen who love Law so well,
Ye Irish who have Bulls to sell ;
Ye Dutch and Germans come and buy,
Leave off your trade in *Quincompoy.*
　Ye Hubble Bubbles high and low,
　Who with your Stocks do ebb and flow,
　Come o'er the hills and far away
　To Jonathan's and Garraway.

Now purchase in both Fools and Wise,
For Stocks will either fall or rise ;
For how can they be at a stay,
When Time and riches fly away ?
　Hubble Bubble come away,
　Let every Bubble have its day ;
　Here's brave new Bubbles for your pay,
　At Jonathan's and Garraway.

Come all, who would by fishing gain,
Venture like Gamesters on the main ;

Whate'er you lose Projectors get,
For you're the Gudgeons in the net.
   Hubble Bubble, &c.
        A. M.'s Fishery.

Come all who would large gains secure,
Or ships upon the sea insure ;
For those great gain must surely find,
Who trust the faithless sea and wind.
   Hubble Bubble, &c.
        Insurance on Ships.

Come all ye nymphs of gay desire,
Insure your House and Hoops from fire ;
A House insured brings better rent,
Come then insure your tenement.
   Hubble Bubble, &c,
        Insurance from Fire.

For tho' you should be all in flames,
Here's the New River and the Thames,
And gentlemen to raise your water,
To quench your fire, and smoke to scatter.
   Hubble Bubble, &c.
        Insurance on Water.

Come Ladies all, we let you know,
You shall be clean from top to toe ;
No Belle shall have a spot on her,
For here comes " clean your shoes, your honour !"
   Hubble Bubble ! great and small,
   Away to Chimney Sweepers' Hall ;
   They'll sweep your chimneys night and day,
   At Jonathan's or Garraway.
        For cleaning Shoes and Chimneys.

Ye cleanly night-men, next draw near,
To raise Estates you need not fear.

Where cent for cent's in money told,
Gold finders surely must find gold.
　　Hubble Bubble, &c.
　　　　　For cleaning Jakes.

Italian Songsters come away,
Our gentry will the *piper* pay,
Make haste in time, for ere it's long,
Your op'ras won't be worth a song.
　　Hubble Bubble, &c.
　　　　　Fiddle Faddle Projects.

A Bubble is blown up in air,
In which fine prospects do appear;
The Bubble breaks, the prospect's lost,
Yet must some Bubble pay the cost.
　　Hubble Bubble; all is smoke,
　　Hubble Bubble; all is broke,
　　Farewell your Houses, Lands, and Flocks,
　　For all you have is now in Stocks.

NAVIGATION; OR, THE CANAL FEVER.

Tune—Let us all be unhappy together !

The great apparent advantages to the commerce of this country, and
the remunerative nature of the speculation itself, caused the general
attention of the public to be drawn towards Canals, until in 1792 the
country was in a state of ferment on the subject, and every one was
eager to obtain shares in some such undertaking. The first Canal which
had been projected was the Bridgewater Canal between Worsley, Manchester, and Runcorn.—It had been carried through, amid many difficulties, by Francis, Duke of Bridgewater, at an ultimate cost of £220,000.
The Income derivable from it eventually reached £80,000 a-year, yet
James Brindley, the Engineer (at the beginning an humble Wheelwright),

with a praiseworthy conscientiousness, did not set such a high value
on his services as the aspiring Engineers of our time. The Canal was
planned and executed by him at a rate of pay considerably less than that
of our ordinary mechanics, 3s. 6d. per day being the highest wage he
received while in the Duke's employment. The Grand Trunk Canal,
from the Mersey to the Trent, a most formidable undertaking, had also
been completed under Brindley's care, and numerous others were projected and afterwards carried out under his inspection. These had been
gradually brought into working order over a period of nearly twenty
years, when the Canal fever broke out. "Notices of eighteen new Canals
were published in the 'Gazette' of the 18th August in that year [1792.]
The current premiums of single shares in those companies for which
acts had been obtained, were as follows :—Grand Trunk, £350 ; Birmingham and Fazeley, £1170 ; Coventry, £350 ; Leicester, £155, and
so on. There was a rush to secure shares in the new schemes, and the
requisite Capitals were at once eagerly subscribed. At the first meeting,
held in 1790, of the promoters of the Ellesmere Canal, 112 miles in
extent, to connect the Mersey, the Dee, and the Severn, applications
were made for four times the disposable number of shares. The movement extended to Scotland, where the Forth and Clyde Canal, and the
Crinan Canal, were projected ; and to Ireland, where the Grand Canal
and Royal Canal were undertaken. In the course of the four years
ending in 1794, not fewer than eighty-one Canal and Navigation Acts
were obtained ; of these, forty-five were passed in the two latter years,
authorizing the expenditure of not less than £5,300,000. As in the
case of the Railways at a subsequent period, works which might, without pressure upon the national resources, easily have been executed if
spread over a longer period, were undertaken all at once ; and the usual
consequences followed, of panic, depreciation, and loss."—See Lives of
the Engineers, by Samuel Smiles, 2 vols., London 8vo., 1862.

The present Song is from a small collection entitled "A Touch on the
Times, being a collection of New Songs to old tunes, including some
few which have appeared in former editions. By a Veteran in the class
of political Ballad Street Scribblers,

> Who, when good news is brought to Town,
> Immediately to work sits down,
> And business fairly to go through,
> Writes Songs, finds Tunes, and sings them too.

Birmingham, Printed for the author, at the office of the executors of T. A.
Pearson, and sold by Knott and Lloyd, 1803."—The author, in his address
"To the Public," says :—"Throwing aside his weak, yet willing, efforts
to please for the moment, and worn down by *thirty-six* years hard
service in the humble station of a publican, when in the best of his days

he was not by nature fit for the task, at the age of *seventy-two* he feels himself far more inclined, over his cheering cup, with a social companion, to handle his pipe than his pen." . . . . "With hearty thanks to all his friends, and as a well-wisher to the prosperity of his native town, and the kingdom in general, he concludes his very brief and formal address,

> With hopes to pleasing scenes renew,
> That after times may soon ensue.

> J. FREETH."

Prefixed to his book is a portrait of "John Freeth, Published April 22d., 1788, as the Act directs, by Pearson and Rollason, Birmingham."

Navigation; or, the Canal Fever.

Navigation's become such a trade,
  That thousands who ne'er saw the ocean,
When projects are artfully laid,
  Trip away at each favourite motion;
In person to fondly attend,
  What jockey would not mount his poney,
And ride to the very Land's end,
  When the object is making of money?

Some people cried up *Hampton Gay*,
  As prospects the greatest possessing,
The *Grand Junction*, 'tis clear, bears the sway,
  And the mania still is increasing ;
At *Ell'smere*, don't think I'm in jest,
  Regardless of lodging or weather,
Of *Land navigators* at least,
  Full a thousand assembled together.

To mortals who share common sense,
  'Tis clear from this strong *Canal Fever*,
Whatever divines may advance,
  Mankind are as sordid as ever;

Content e'en with those can't be had,
  Who riches immense have been saving,
For spite of philosophy's aid,
  The mind is continually craving.

From projects, no doubt, some there are
  Who get themselves into a hobble;
The *Glo'ster* at present bids fair,
  But the *Bristol* turned out a mere bubble;
The winners much artifice use,
  The losers without affectation,
Say Christians can outdo the Jews
  In matters of deep speculation.

So fast—for the rage what can stop —
  This keen *Influenza* is growing,
When piece-meal the earth is cut up,
  To keep speculation a-going;
Their plans will extend, I'll be bound
  (Whoe'er the assertion may rail at),
To the *moon*, soon as Herschel has found
  A half-way house just to regale at.

Whilst schemers their wishes to crown,
  For shares take a rapid excursion,
Our plan, when the sun has gone down,
  Is to *share* in the evening's diversion ;
Their nests, by the cast of a die,
  However so well some may feather,
True friendship of life to enjoy,
  Is to meet and be happy together.

Speculation on the Present Day.

From the same Collection as the preceding song.

In this busy wrangling age,
   Full of fraud and dissipation,
Gaming is the public rage,
   All seem fond of speculation.

In the funds we every day,
   See some kind of fluctuation;
Go as may the mind astray,
   There's no check to speculation.

Gambling's grown to such a pitch,
   In all quarters of the nation,
Some get poor, and others rich,
   By mere daily speculation.

Wheat and barley, oats and hops,
   Come in common circulation;
Small if should be found the crops,
   Greater then the speculation.

Many in this world of strife,
   Oft have made this observation,
" In the articles of life,
   That there's too much speculation."

Some for copper, some for brass,
   Coals and timber—but the fashion,
Which all others did surpass,
   Once was inland navigation.

Iron foundries many view
   With an eye of admiration;

Cotton spinning, England through,
Is a thriving speculation.

Now and then a sudden burst
Fills the mind with consternation ;
Often is DAME FORTUNE curst,
Thro' a misjudged speculation.

On the Stock Exchange, affairs
Sometimes cause extreme sensation ;
When the *Bulls* outwit the *Bears*,
That is called keen speculation.

London's much esteemed Lord Mayor,
Merchants and Administration,
Flagrantly imposed on were
By a spurious fabrication.

State Consols, how strange to say
(What surprising alteration),
Varied nine per cent. one day !
By this knavish operation.

From the daring mischief seen
(Mischief which *delays* occasion),
Frankly 'tis allowed there's been
Too much room for speculation.

More than two months in suspense,
Intermixed with joy and sorrow,
Nothing certain—all pretence—
Peace to-day and war to-morrow.

What a harvest for stock-jobbers,
Such an instance, people say,
Ne'er occurred for *licensed robbers*,
Till the present bustling day.

All mankind are fond of power,
Still there will be variation,
Prospects changing every hour—
There's no end to speculation.

THE POYAIS EMIGRANT.

THE following account of the Poyais Scheme is appended as a note to
a very clever song by Theodore Hook, in vol. ii. page 29, of that
agreeable book, "The Life and Remains of Theodore Edward Hook,
by the Rev. Mr. Barham," Lond. 1849, cr. 8vo. The refrain runs thus:

"Then a fig for King George, and his old fashioned way,
And hey for Macgregor, cacique of Poyais."

"In 1822, a year remarkable for its Stock-jobbing bubbles, it will be
remembered a person styling himself Sir Gregor MacGregor, and, in
virtue of a certain contract with his Majesty, Frederick Augustus, King
of the Musquito nation, Cacique of Poyais, contrived to open a loan
for the amount of £200,000, a large proportion of which was actually
subscribed. In pursuance of his scheme, he appointed various ministers
of State, officered several regiments, and bestowed a liberal allowance
of titles and orders. Green was, appropriately enough, selected by his
highness as the national colour; there were green hussars, green
knights, green commanders—and greenhorns in sufficient abundance to
furnish forth handsomely his new principality. In addition to this, two
or three shiploads of miserable creatures were sent out as emigrants, and
landed on the Musquito shore, in North America, where, on the western
side of the Black River, the present realm of Poyais was supposed to lie.
They found, indeed, an unwholesome tract of unreclaimed swamp, on
which, by the gracious permission of Frederich Augustus, who entirely
repudiated all connection with Sir Gregor, they were allowed to live,
as long as famine and fever would let them. Most of these poor wretches
perished miserably; some few, wasted with hunger and sickness, were
fortunately brought off. The Kingdom of Poyais is still we believe to
let."

This statement is not too highly coloured. His Highness—Sir Gregor
—took up his residence at the west-end of Edinburgh, besides having a
villa, a few miles out of town, to which he retired when fatigued with the
affairs of State. His wife (said to be a sister of Bolivar) was with him.
He held his Levees at certain periods; these were attended by various

competitors for his favour, who were anxious to obtain either civil or
military appointments in his service. Being anxious to assimilate
the administration of justice as much as possible to that of England, and
holding the opinion that the union of Law and Equity (as in Scotland)
was not suited to the climate of Poyais, he experienced considerable
difficulty in getting a Lord Chancellor. With some hesitation he
conferred the honour, with a Peerage, upon a gentleman of the name of
Pattison, who had some small practice as a Scotch writer or attorney.
When his arrangements were to a certain extent completed, he gave a
splendid Reception at his town house, where the principal members of
his Court were graciously received. The Poyaisian courtiers assembled
in an outer drawing-room, until the great man was ready to receive them.
At a given signal, the royal minstrels in attendance commenced a martial
strain, upon which the folding-doors which separated the back from the
front drawing-room were thrown open and his Highness was discovered
seated upon a throne on the dais, and the different officials were pre-
mitted to advance and kiss his hand. After this they retired and partook
of an elegant collation—the only substantial benefit they apparently ever
got. This information was given by a gentleman, who, although not
present himself, had the particulars from a friend who was.

Sir Gregor was successful in selling several lots in his dominions of
Poyais. It was said that upon arriving in this Country, Sir Gregor was
recommended to consult an eminent Judge, as to the initiatory steps to be
taken, who advised that the deed, to which a mark was appended as indicating the consent of the Musquito monarch, should be recorded in the
Books of Council and Session, as a probative writ. Whether this was
correct we cannot say, but such was the general belief at the time, and the
party consulted was said to be Lord Balgray. The consideration for
the grant also, it was rumoured, was alleged to be a quart bottle of rum,—
the seductive influence of which had induced the sable monarch to part
with a slice of his birth-right. When this was mentioned to an eminent
legal wit, he observed that "It must be true, as the Deed bore upon its
face unmistakeable symptoms of being a *rum* Contract."

The song now presented has been printed from a copy sent in the form
of a circular "to Miss Austin, South St. David Street," a lady nearly
related to the Cacique,—who had been at the expense of printing and
generally circulating the song, by way of advertising his project.—Miss
Austin was an elderly lady at the time, and died not very long since
considerably above ninety years of age. She was a daughter or grand-
daughter of Dr. Austin, by whom the song, "For lack of gold," is said
to have been written. She was also related to the noble family of
Semple.

The Cacique had presented this lady with a grant of land in this El
Dorado, which she, being a very prudent person, disposed of to a

tradesman in Edinburgh, who flattered himself that he would make a
fortune by cultivating coffee. When the Bubble burst, Miss Austin, without any solicitation, sent for the tradesman and cancelled the transaction,
returning the money, the amount of which was considerable. Having
direct knowledge of the verity of what is here stated, and as instances
of the kind are by no means common, we think it due to the memory of
this excellent old lady to put it upon record.

The songs issued by disinterested parties on the subject of the Poyais
scheme, formed a very striking contrast to "the smiling vales, and
citron groves" depicted by our poet. In one, entitled "The Poyais
Emigrant's Lamentation," several stanzas similar in sentiment to the
following occur:

> Oh! sad was the day,
>   When wi' braving emotion,
> Fair Freedom we sought,
>   O'er the dark stormy ocean;
> And we left far behind us
>   The friends we adored ;
> And for pleasure and wealth
>   Wild Americ' explored.
>
> Oh! where are the charms
>   They employed to bewitch us?
> And where is the wealth
>   That they said would enrich us?
> But many, the brave,
>   Whom their country did cherish,
> Have sailed o'er the wave,
>   In the deserts to perish.
>
> Dear Scotia, farewell!
>   And thy charms fondly reaving,
> We'll remember thee still,
>   Midst the strangers we're braving.
> Dear Britons bewail
>   Your American brothers,
> Oh! ne'er leave your vale,
>   Or the home of your fathers.

𝕿𝖍𝖊 𝕻𝖔𝖞𝖆𝖎𝖘 𝕰𝖒𝖎𝖌𝖗𝖆𝖓𝖙.

A NEW SONG.

Tune, "O'er the Muir among the heather."

My bonny lassie, will ye gang
To yon green land that blooms sae cheerie?
Yon fairy land, o' wealth and joy,
A hame o' rest to bless the wearie.

CHORUS.

We'll a' gang to Poyais thegither,
We'll a' gang ower the seas thegither,
To fairer lands and brighter skies,
Nor sigh again for Hieland heather.

Through smiling vales, 'neath lofty hills,
Through citron groves we'll stray thegither,
Our star o' life will sweetly set,
When blest wi' wealth and ane anither.
We'll a' gang to Poyais, &c.

Wi' jewels rare I'll busk your hair,
The fairest flowers for you I'll gather;
The rose's bloom, its rich perfume,
Are sweet as ony Hieland heather.
We'll a' gang to Poyais, &c.

The sugar cane for you I'll raise,
The orange tree shall bloom to cheer ye;
The stream, the hill, your board shall fill,
And want shall never mair come near ye.
We'll a' gang to Poyais, &c.

I'll gang wi' you, my bonny lad,
Across the seas I care na whither;

In fair Poyais, 'mang joys like these,
We needna sigh for Hieland heather.
We'll a' gang to Poyais, &c.

The fav'ring breezes softly blow,
The boat comes rowin' o'er the ferry;
Then come my lassie, let's awa,
For here we will nae longer tarry.
We'll a' gang to Poyais thegither,
We'll a' gang ower the seas thegither,
To fairer lands and brighter skies,
Nor sigh again for Hieland heather.

BUBBLES OF 1825.

THIS very clever song is from the pen of the accomplished Theodore
Hook, and appeared at the time in the John Bull Newspaper, of which he
was then the Editor.   Although a fair subject for satire, " The Bubbles
of 1825 " were not so devoid of practicability, generally, as those proposed
a hundred years previously.   Many of the projects, which were considered
wild and were abandoned during the great and consequent panic which
occurred in 1826, have since then been carried out, and one of the most
outré schemes brought forward in this song, in ridicule of projectors
generally, has recently been gravely discussed, and will in all probability, in these days of (so-called) "progress," be acted on at no very
distant date, viz. :—

" A tunnel underneath the sea from Calais Strait to Dover, sir."

Although it is not very clear what advantage there would be in making
such a passage, except to render an invasion of our tight little island
more facile, and the wooden walls of Old England nugatory.

The result of the speculative mania of 1825 was very disastrous.   It
was not confined entirely to London, but the " canny Scots," who had
been extensively affected, suffered in a corresponding degree.   In Edinburgh many schemes were started, being chiefly echoes of those propounded in London.   Among these was a company to supply Edinburgh
with pure and unadulterated milk, the capital for which was readily

subscribed, and large dividends were anticipated. A building was erected at St Margaret's, about a mile and a half eastward of Edinburgh, now in the possession of the North British Railway Company. There were apartments for the Manager of the Dairy, and the entire centre of the building was formed into an arena with a gallery round, and was lighted by a dome in the roof. So long as this "Cow Palace," as it was termed, existed, visitors were admitted to the gallery, on payment of one shilling, to see the cows paraded below and milked. The milk was conveyed in spring carts into town in long deep cans, securely padlocked, so as to ensure no tampering with it by the way.

However ruinous the majority of the speculations of 1825 eventually became, the Railway mania of 1845 exceeded them, inasmuch as speculation became more general, and in place of dabbling in shillings the British public gambled for pounds. The excitement raged for several months, and was quite as great during the time it lasted as the Parisian infatuation of 1720. Shares, on which a deposit of 50s. had been paid, changed hands at the market price of £40, and the moment it was whispered that George Hudson, the Railway King, had looked over a hedge at the ground which some projected Railway proposed to occupy, up went the shares like lightning to the most inconceivable premium. Hudson was looked upon as the greatest genius of the time, an alchemist who could by a touch transmute iron into gold. The shares of any Railway with which he was connected were not to be purchased except at an enormous, and consequently unremunerating, ransom. He was fêted, run after, worshipped. Ladies of quality, peers, peeresses, and all the nobles of the land vied with each other in every possible way to gain his favour, hoping to obtain a few of the golden atoms which fell from the "great man's" coffers. But "envy will merit as its shade pursue," and it was impossible for the Railway King to reign long and please every one. Some honest fellows to whom the game of speculation had not turned out to be a profitable one, began to find flaws in the man by whom they had thought to better their fortunes, and charges were unjustifiably brought against him of his having taken advantage of companies with which he had been connected. Hudson was therefore driven from his throne, and after having relinquished the bulk of his fortune to appease the clamour of his virtuously indignant enemies, he retired to Paris, where he has been sojourning for many years and preferring in a Court of Law his claims for a very large sum of money due to him by certain persons in Spain, a considerable portion of which was recently awarded him.

The Railway mania of 1845 was a source of much fun and satire to the writers of the then very spirited periodical " Punch." We quote a specimen, which, it is believed, came from Thackeray's pen :—

It is entitled " Railroad Speculators," and is headed by a clever woodcut of two seedy swells of the lower order.

The night was stormy and dark.   The town was shut up in sleep :
Only those were abroad who were out on a lark, Or those who'd no
beds to keep.

I pass'd through the lonely street.   The wind did sing and blow ; I
could hear the policeman's feet clapping to and fro.

There stood a potato-man In the midst of all the wet ; He stood with
his 'tato-can In the lonely Haymarket.

Two gents of dismal mein, And dank and greasy rags, Came out of a
shop for gin, Swaggering over the flags :

Swaggering over the stones, These shabby bucks did walk ; and I
went and followed those seedy ones, And listened to their talk.

Was I sober or awake ? Could I believe my ears ? Those dismal
beggars spake Of nothing but railroad shares.

I wondered more and more : Says one—" Good friend of mine, How
many shares have you wrote for In the Diddlesex Junction line ?"

" I wrote for twenty," says JIM, " But they wouldn't give me one ;"
His comrade straight rebukèd him For the folly he had done :

" O JIM, you are unawares Of the ways of this bad town ; *I* always
write for five hundred shares.   And *then* they put me down."

" And yet you get no shares," says JIM, " for all your boast ;" " I
would have wrote," says JACK, " but where was the penny to pay the
post ?"

" I lost, but I couldn't pay That first instalment up ; but here's taters
smoking hot—I say, Let's stop my boy and sup."

And at this simple feast The while they did regale, I drew each ragged
capitalist Down on my left thumb-nail.

Their talk did me perplex, All night I tumbled and tost, And thought
of railroad specs, And how money was won and lost.

" Bless railroads everywhere," I said, " and the world's advance ;
Bless every railroad share In Italy, Ireland, France ; For never a beggar
need now despair, And every rogue has a chance."

SPEC.

THE reference to " Judge Abbot " and " Eldon " in the third stanza of
the succeeding song is presumed to apply to the question of liability as
elucidated in the case of *Kearly v. Codd*, Dec. 23 1826.   In this case
Abbot, afterwards Lord Tenterden, observed " it is important that the
public should know if they connect themselves with a company of this
description, they are every one of them liable to pay the demands upon
it."   That is to say, each shareholder may be individually sued for the
entire liabilities. See Carrington and Payne, 2 p. 409.   And this was so
until changed by an Act passed in 1848 to facilitate the winding up
of Joint Stock Companies.   Abbot further ruled in "the King *v.* Mott,"
2 Carr. and Payne 541, that Directors or others issuing Scrip or Stock
beyond the fixed amount, were liable to a criminal prosecution.

𝕭𝖚𝖇𝖇𝖑𝖊𝖘 of 1825.

Tune—" Run neighbours run."

Run, neighbours, run ! you're just in time to get a share
   In all the famous projects that amuse John Bull ;
Run, take a peep on 'Change, for anxious crowds beset us
      there,
   Each trying which can make himself the greatest gull.
No sooner are they puff'd than a universal wish there is
For shares in mines, insurances, in foreign loans and
      fisheries.
No matter where the project *lies*, so violent the mania,
In Africa, New Providence, Peru, or Pennsylvania !
      Run, neighbours, run ! you're just in time to get a
         share
      In all the famous Bubbles that amuse John Bull.

Few folks for news very anxious at this crisis are,
   For marriages, and deaths, and births, no thirst exists ;
All take the papers in, to find out what the prices are
   Of shares in this or that, upon the brokers' lists.
The doctor leaves his patient, the pedagogue his Lexicon,
For mines of Real Monte, or for those of Anglo-Mexican ;
Even *Chili* bonds don't cool the rage, nor those still more
      romantic, sir,
For new canals to join the seas, Pacific and Atlantic, sir.
      Run, neighbours, run ! &c.

At home we have projects too for draining surplus capital,
   And honest master Johnny of his cash to chouse ;
Though t'other day, Judge Abbot gave a rather sharpish slap
      at all,
   And Eldon launched his thunder from the Upper House.
Investment banks to lend a lift to people who are undone,
Proposals for Assurance—there's no end of that in London

And one amongst the number, who in Parliament now press
  their bills,
For lending cash at eight per cent. on coats and inexpressibles.
    Run, neighbours, run ! &c.

No more with her bright pails the milkman's rosy daughter
  works,
A company must serve you now with milk and cream ;
Perhaps they've some connection with the advertizing *Water
  Works,*
  That promise to supply you from the limpid stream.
Another body corporate would fain some pence and shillings
  get,
By selling fish at Hungerford, and knocking up old Billings-
  gate ;
Another takes your linen, when its dirty, to the suds, sir,
And brings it home in carriages with four nice bits of blood,
  sir.
    Run neighbours, &c.

When Greenwich coaches go by steam on roads of iron rail-
  ing, sir,
  How pleasant it will be to see a dozen in a line ;
And ships of heavy burden over hills and valleys sailing, sir,
  Shall cross from Bristol Channel to the Tweed or Tyne.
And Dame Speculation, if she ever fully hath her ends,
Will give us docks at Bermondsey, St Saviour's, and St
  Catherine's ;
While sidelong bridges over mud shall fill the folks with wonder,
  sir,
And lamp-light tunnels all day long convey the Cockneys
  under, sir.
    Run, neighbours, run, &c.

A tunnel underneath the sea from Calais straight to Dover, sir,
  The qualmish folks may cross by land from shore to shore,

With sluices made to drown the French, if e'er they would
come over, sir,
Has long been talk'd of, till at length 'tis thought a *mon-
strous bore.*
Amongst the many scheming folks, I take it *he's* no ninny,
sir,
Who bargains with the Ashantees to fish the coast of Guinea,
sir,
For secretly, 'tis known, that another brilliant view he has,
Of lighting up the famous town of Timbuctoo with oil gas.
　　Run, neighbours, run ! &c.

Then a company is formed, though not yet advertizing,
　　To build, upon a splendid scale, a large balloon,
And send up tools and broken stones for fresh Mac-Adam-
izing
　　The new discover'd turnpike roads which cross the moon.
But the most inviting scheme of all, is one proposed for
carrying
Large furnaces to melt the ice which hems poor Captain
Parry in ;
They'll then have steamboats twice a-week to all the newly-
seen land,
And call for goods and passengers at Labrador and Green-
land.
　　Run, neighbours, run ! &c.

Come ! Come ! Come !

THIS drinking song has just been introduced to the select public through the medium of the Early English Text Society, who have printed, under the Editorial care of J. W. Hales, M.A., and F. J. Furnivall, M.A., and issued to subscribers a limited impression of "Bishop Percy's Folio Manuscript" in which it occurrs.   Percy on the margin has written :—"a curious old drinking song, supposed to be sung by an old gouty Bacchanal." We have for the most part adopted Percy's corrections of the more obscure passages, and in one or two instances have ventured to put forth our own.

The Percy Manuscript is now the property of the nation, having been acquired by the British Museum.   For upwards of a Century its very existence was questioned; and Ritson actually insinuated doubts as to the Bishop's truthfulness in his alleged quotations.   In the Biblio-graphical Decameron of Dr Dibdin will be found some specimens of the text from which we inferred that it had been compiled between the years 1650 and 1660.   This conjecture has been verified by the portion now printed.   In it popular poems by Carew, Withers, Cleveland, &c., are to be found.

Come! Come! Come!
Shall we mask or mum?
By my halidom,
   What a coil is here!
Some are born to sway,
While others must obey,
Ay, or else, I pray
   Who stands in fear?
What though this toe,
With gout I limp on so,
Does cause me mickle woe?
   Ah, welladay!
Yet, returning spring
Better things will bring,
Which will make us sing
   Fal lal lal lay.

Wherefore, fellow gods
Will you fall at odds?
What a fury mads
  Your mortal* brains?
For a little care
Of the world's affair
Will you fret and swear,
  And vex your veins?
No, gods, no!
Let your fury go,
And let mortals do
  Well as they may;
For the jocund spring
New vintages will bring,
Which will make ye sing
  Fal lal lal lay.

Merry mocking Moes†,
With thy toting nose,
And thy mouth that grows
  To thy lolling ear.
Stretch that carping mouth
Right from north to south,
And quench thy craving drouth
  In vinegar.‡
Though be large thy tongue,
Large and far too longe,
Ere thou sing this song
  Of fal lal lal la!

* Percy queries this "Immortal."
† "Mows—*i.e*, mocking, *sc*. Momus—*Percy*."
‡ Decker, in the Proem or introductory chapter of his "Gull's Horn-book, or fashions to please all sorts of Gulls," 1609, in urging his determination to satirize the Gulls or Bucks of his day, among others apostrophizes Momus thus:—"As for thee, Momus, chew nothing but hemlock; and spit nothing but the syrup of aloes upon my papers till thy very rotten lungs come forth for anger. I am snakeproof; and though, with Hannibal, you bring whole hogsheads of vinegar-railings it is impossible for you to quench or come over my Alpine resolution."

Join thou Momus' grace
Unto Vulcan's pace,
And with filthy face
    Cry " waw! waw! waw!"
O sweet brother mine,
That art god of wine,
Wilt taste thee of the vine
    To this blithe companie?
Jolly king of quaff,
Carouse awhile and doff
Thy bright liquor off,
    And then follow me
To the sweeter soil
Of fair Exus Isle,
Wherein it haps this coil
    Was every day,
For this refreshing spring,
And another thing,
Will make all gaily sing
    Fal lal lal lay.

Nimble Mercury,
Thou Olympian spy,
Wilt thou wash thine eye
    In this fountain clear?
Whensoe'er you go
To the world below,
You shall light on no
    Such liquor there.
What although you are
A swiftly wingèd star
That flyeth quite as far
    As shineth day?
Yet here's a subtle thing,
Your heart will nimbly wring,
And make you briskly sing
    Fal lal lal lay.

And you that reckoned are,
The mighty god of war,
And shine a cruel star,
　Perverse and froward,
Mars with speed prepare
Thine ancient warlike spear,
And target, too, for here
　'S a combat toward.
Then, if you will fox me,
Be sure I will fox thee,*
Then after let's agree
　And end this fray,
Since this sweet-breathèd spring,
And this other thing,
Can make us gaily sing
　Fal lal lal lay.

Venus, love's fair queen,
For rarest beauty seen
In youth so freshly green,
　And loved so young,
Thou, myrtle-wreathed that art,
My very own sweet heart,
Shalt have a gracious part
　In cup and song.
Though this foot of mine be wrong,
Fools will find my sword full long,
And my heart as fully strong ;
　Cast care away !
Since this sweet scented spring,
And this other thing,
Still causes us to sing
　Fal lal lal lay.

---

* " A Toping word."—*Percy.*　To render tipsy.　*He has caught a fox,*
he is very drunk.—See *Canting Dictionary,* 1737.

Great and bright Apollo,
Cloath'd in shining yellow,
Prithee leave thy fellow
    Muses dear.
See! here is choicest wine,
The Fates say must be thine,
Belike it will refine
    Thy music clear.
To the willing wire
Of this your own sweet lyre,
You must impart a fire
    Another day.
For this sweet breathing spring,
And this inspiring thing
Will eftsoons make you sing
    Fal lal lal lay.

Juno, so austere,
And my mother dear,
You come but in the rear
    Of a bowsing feast.
And as your grace I greet,
With this regard, I meet,
That the grape is still as sweet
    For the last is the best.
Let fall I prithee now
That anger from your brow
To your rebuke I bow,
    And weighty sway.
Come! 'tis a gracious thing,
And prone to please your King,
To join with us and sing
    Fal lal lal lay.

And thou—thou awful sire
And mighty King of Fire!
Let mantling wine aspire
    To thy great throne,

And in our chorus here,
Of merry voices clear,
Come thou thy part and bear
    Immortal drone ;
For then will grace descend,
And rage and fury end,
With Stygian fiends contend,
    And dwell for aye,
While nectar forth shall spring,
And the heavens with thunder ring,
When Jove himself shall sing
    Fal lal lal lay.

Come! Vulcan, Momus, speed ye,
Hermes and Bacchus, heed ye!
While Mars and Venus, lead ye!
    By two and two :
Phœbus brightest, fair,
Juno rightest, rare,
And the mightyest there
    Among the crew,
For Jove and one and all,
In their celestial hall,
Purpose high festival
    And holiday,
Since this enlivening spring,
Brings life to everything,
And forces you to sing
    Fal lal lal lay.

THE PRAISE OF ALE.

FROM a Broadside without date or printer's name, but believed to have been published about the middle of the, seventeenth century.—At this period, a jug of "good old ale" was generally acceptable and was patronized even by Ladies of the Court.   In an extract from the account Book of Colonel Robert Walpole, the grandfather of Horace Walpole, relating to his expenses during his annual visit to London, while fulfilling his Parliamentary duties, frequent entries occur for "Nottingham Ale" and "Lambeth Ale."—In addition to these we find that the Colonel on March 12th, 1691, " Paid for a Bottle of Uskybath—3s." but whether for his own drinking is not noted.—See Miller's Fly leaves 1st. series, 12mo, 1854.

In " Heylin's Cosmographie," 1652, we find ale and beer thus noticed; "The usuall and naturall drink of the country is beer, so called from the French word *boire* (for wines they have not of their own growing;) which, without controversie, is a most wholesome and nourishing beverage ; and being transported into France, Belgium, and Germany, by the working of the sea is so purged, that it is amongst them in highest estimation, and celebrated by the name of *la bonne Beere d'Angleterre*.   And as for the old drink of England, Ale, which cometh from the Danish word *oela*, it is questionless in itself, (and without that commixture which some are accustomed to use with it,) a very wholesome drink ; howsoever it pleased a poet, in the reign of Henry III. thus to descant on it :—

Nescio quid monstrum Stygiæ conforme paludi,
Cervisiam plerique vocant, nil spissius illa,
Dum bibitur, nil clarius est dum mingitur, ergo
Constat quod multas fæces in ventre relinquit.

in English thus :—

Of this strange drink, so like the Stygian Lake,
Which men call ale, I know not what to make,
Folk drink it thick and void it very thin,
Therefore much dregs must needs remain within."

There is a song entitled "Old English Ale," in Durfey's Pills, vol. iv, which treats of a "liquor that men call *Ipse*," the potency of which is thus described:

"The strongest wine in Flanders or Spain,
   Or yet in the Palsgrave's country ;
Is nothing like t'our English ale,
   That liquor of life, called *Ipse*.

The strongest soldier that ever did fight,
Or the bravest commander of a marshalsea,
To the ground may be brought, I hold him a groat,
If he swagger too long with *Ipse*.

.   .   .   .

The taylor that eats more bread at a meal,
Than any tradesman does at three,
A halfpenny loaf will serve him a week,
If his cap be fudled with *Ipse*.

The immense advantage which malt liquor derives from having under-gone a short sea voyage,—a fact which Heylin touches upon—is unquestionable, and it has of late years been found that Sherry is greatly enhanced by a voyage to the East Indies and back.

Ale does not now seem to be such a favourite beverage as it used to be, and we shrewdly suspect that this is owing to its degeneracy, for as time goes on a more inordinate desire for higher profits obtains, and in malt liquor and wine every device is tried to manufacture an article at a cheaper rate for which the old prices may be imposed on the general public.

As an addition to the several songs on the subject of Ale in this collection, an old friend, who has successfully contributed to our Ballad literature, has furnished us with the following :—

JOHN BARLEYCORN, MY JO, JOHN.

John Barleycorn, my jo, John,
  Now we will notes compare,
My hair was curly auburn ance,
  My brow was smooth and fair.
Now I am turning bald, John,
  I've got a withered hue,
And there's a little birdie sings
  A' this I owe to you.

John Barleycorn, my jo, John,
  You are a merry chiel,
And it will not deny, John,
  That I ha'e lo'ed you weel.
But friendship, may prove fause, John,
  The bright the sunny glow
That cherishes, may scorch the flower,
  John Barleycorn, my jo.

John Barleycorn, my jo, John,
    I didna think a trace
O' ony thing like care, John,
    Could shade your smiling face.
Yet whyles the fairest fruits, John,
    That summer day can show,
May hide a canker at the heart,
    John Barleycorn, my jo.

The Praise of Ale.

Come all you brave wights,
That are dubbed ale-knights ;
Now set out yourselves in fight :
And let them that crack
In the praises of *sack*,
Know *malt* is of mickle might.

Though sack they define,
To be holy, divine,
Yet is it but natural liquor ;
Ale hath for its part,
An addition of art,
To make it drink thinner or thicker.

Sack's fiery fume
Doth waste and consume
Men's *humidum radicale*,
It scaldeth their livers,
It breeds burning fevers,
Proves *vinum venenum reale*.

But history gathers,
From aged grandfathers,
That ale's the true liquor of life ;
Men lived long in health,
And preserved their wealth,
Whilst *Barley-broth* only was rife.

Sack quickly ascends,
And suddenly ends
What company came for at first ;
And that which yet worse is,
It empties men's purses,
Before it half quenches their thirst.

Ale is not so costly,
Altho' that the most lye
Too long by the oil of barley :
Yet may they part late,
At a reasonable rate,
Though they come in the morning early.

Sack makes men, from words,
Fall to drawing of swords,
And quarrelling endeth their quaffing;
Whils't Dogger-ale barrels
Bear off many quarrels,
And often turn chiding to laughing.

Sack's drink for our *masters* ;
All may be ale-tasters !
Good things the more common the better ;
Sack's but single broth ;
Ale's meat, drink, and cloth,
Say they that know never a letter !

But not to entangle
Old friends till they wrangle,
And quarrel for other men's pleasure—
Let *ale* keep his place,
And let *sack* have his grace,
So that neither exceed the due measure.

The Tankard of Ale.

IN a Collection of old ballads, 3 vols., Lond. 1725, vol. iii., is a
ballad, entitled, "The X-Ale-tation of Ale." It consists of forty-six
stanzas. From it the present ballad has evidently been adapted, the
prevailing sentiment being identical, and one or two stanzas nearly
similar.

From chap copy of "Three Excellent New Songs; 1. The Rock and
a wee pickle tow ; 2. The Tankard of Ale ; 3. Labour in vain," *circa*
1794.

NOT drunk nor yet sober, but brother to both,
 I met a young man upon Alesbury Vale ;
I saw by his face, that he was in good case
 To go and take share of a tankard of Ale.
  Laru la re, laru, &c., I saw by his face, &c.

There's the hedger that works in the ditches all day,
 And the bondman that handles the flail,
Will talk of great things, about princes and kings,
 When once they shake hands with a tankard of ale.
  Laru la re, laru, &c., He'll talk, &c.

There's the beggar that begs, without any legs,
 Who has scarce got a tatter to cover his tail ;
Is as merry in rags, as a miser with bags,
 When once he shakes hands with a tankard of ale.
  Laru la re, laru, &c., She's as, &c.

There's the widow who buried her husband of late,
 Has scarcely forgot how to weep and to wail ;
But thinks ev'ry day ten, till she's marry'd again,
 When once she shakes hands with a tankard of ale.
  Laru, &c.

There's the old parish Vicar, when he's in's liquor,
He merrily doth on's parishioners rail;
" Come pay up your tythes, or I'll kiss all your wives,"
When once he shakes hands with a pot of good ale.
Laru, &c.

There's the old Parson's Clerk, his eyes are so dark,
And the letters so small, he scarcely can tell;
But he can tell each letter, and sing the psalms better,
When once he shakes hands with a pot of good ale.
Laru, &c.

There's the blacksmith by trade, a jolly brisk blade,
Cries, "fill up the bumper, dear host, from the pail;"
So cheerful he'll sing, and make the house ring,
When once he shakes hands with a tankard of ale,
Laru, &c.

There's the tinker, ye ken, cries " old kettles to mend,"
With his budget and hammer to drive in the nail;
Will spend a whole crown, at one sitting down,
When once he shakes hands with a tankard of ale.
Laru, &c.

There's the mason, brave John, the carver of stone,
The Master's grand secret he'll never reveal;
Yet how merry is he with his lass on his knee,
When once he shakes hands with a tankard of ale.
Laru, &c.

You maids who feel shame, pray me do not blame,
Though your private ongoings in public I tell;
Young Bridget and Nell to kiss will not fail
When once they shake hands with a tankard of ale.
Laru, &c.
P

There's some jolly wives, love drink as their lives,
  Dear neighbours but mind the sad thread of my tale ;
Their husbands they'll scorn, as sure's they were born,
  If once they shake hands with a tankard of ale.
          Laru, &c.

From wrangling or jangling, and ev'ry such strife,
  Or anything else that may happen to fall ;
From words come to blows, and sharp bloody nose,
  But friends again over a tankard of ale.
          Laru, &c.

Come, Cheer up Your Hearts.

This and the four following Bacchanalian songs are from "Bacchus
and Venus," a select Collection of Songs, London, 12mo, 1737.

COME, cheer up your hearts,
  And call for your quarts,
And let there no liquor be lacking ;
  We have money in store,
  And intend for to roar,
Until we have sent it all packing ;
  Then, Drawer, make haste,
  And let no time waste,
But give every man his due ;
  To avoid all trouble,
  Go fill the pot double,
Since he that made one, made two.
Since he that made one, made two.

Come drink, my hearts, drink,
  And call for your wine,
'Tis that makes a man to speak truly ;
  What sot can refrain,
  Or daily complain,
That he in his drink is unruly ?

Then drink and be civil,
Intending no evil,
If that you'll be ruled by me.
For claret and sack,
We never shall lack,
Since he that made two, made three,
Since he, &c.

The old curmudgeon
Sits all the day drudging
At home, with brown bread and small beer;
With scraping damn'd pelf,
He starveth himself,
Scarce eats a good meal in the year.
But we'll not do so,
Howe'er the world go,
Since that we have money in store.
For claret and sack,
We never will lack,
Since he that made three, made four,
Since he, &c.

Come drink, my hearts, drink,
And call for your wine;
D'ye think I'll leave you i' th' lurch!
My reckoning I'll pay,
E'er I go away,
Or hang me as high as Paul's Church.
Tho' some men will say
This is not the way
For us in this world to thrive:
'Tis no matter for that,
Let's have t'other quart,
Since he that made four, made five,
Since he, &c.

A plague of old Charon,
His brains are all barren,

His liquor (like coffee) is dry ;
But we are for wine,
'Tis a drink more divine,
Without it we perish and die.
Then roll it about,
Until 'tis all out,
We'll affront him in spite of his Styx ;
If he grudges his ferry,
We'll drink and be merry,
Since he that made five, made six,
Since he, &c.

But now the time's come,
That we all must go home,
Our liquor's all gone that's for certain ;
Which makes me repine,
That a god so divine,
Won't give us one cup at our parting ;
But since all is paid,
Let's not be dismay'd,
But fly to great Bacchus in heaven ;
And chide him, because
He made no better laws,
Since he that made six, made seven,
Since he, &c.

Ye Commons and Peers.

FROM good liquor ne'er shrink,
In friendship we'll drink,
And drown all grim care and pale sorrow ;
Let us husband to-day,
For time flies swift away,
And no one's assur'd of to-morrow.

Of all the gay sages,
That grac'd the past ages,
Dad Noah the most did excel;
He first planted the vine,
First tasted the wine,
And got nobly drunk as they tell.
Say, why should not we,
Be as bosky as he,
Since here's liquor as well will inspire?
Then fill up my glass,
I'll see that it pass,
To the *manes* of that good old squire.

Love or Liquor?

RESPECTING this song, the editors of Stenhouse's "Illustrations of the Lyric Poetry and Music of Scotland" have this note, "*O steer her up, and haud her gaun.* Ramsay wrote a Bacchanalian song to this ancient tune, and printed it in his Tea-Table Miscellany, 1724. He very properly suppressed the old song, enough of which is still but too well known. The first four lines of the song in the Museum [Johnson's] were taken from Ramsay's, and the rest of it was written by Burns for that work."

Although the version of this song in the Tea-Table Miscellany, which is reprinted in the second volume of Herd's Scotish Songs, presents several of the phrases in the Scots dialect, it is questionable whether Ramsay was the author. With exception of the two first lines, which bear no reference whatever to the sentiment of the song, there is nothing to connect it with Scotland. Indeed, the mention of "the Drawer," (a personage unknown in Scotland), and the idiom throughout leads us to think that its origin was English. The chief difference in Ramsay's edition worth noticing is in the last line of the second stanza, which he thus renders, "And let wind and weather gowl."

O steer her up, and haud her gaun,
Her mother's at the mill, jo;
But since she will not take a man,
E'en let her take her will, jo.

Pray thee, lad, leave silly thinking,
  Cast the thoughts of love away;
Let's our sorrows drown in drinking,
  'Tis folly longer to delay.

See this glass of shining claret,
  How invitingly it looks!
Take it off, and never spare it,
  Plague on fighting, love, and books.
Let's have pleasure while we're able,
  Bring us in the mighty bowl;
Place't on the middle of this table,
  Till thou quench thy thirsty soul.

Call the drawer, let him fill it
  Full as ever it can hold;
O take care you do not spill it,
  'Tis more precious far than gold.
When you've drunk a dozen bumpers,
  Bacchus will begin to prove,
Spite of Venus and her Mumpers,
  Drinking better is than love.

I'll never get drunk any more.

ACCORDING to Thomas Croften Croker, in his "Popular Songs o.
Ireland," London, cr. 8vo., 1839, this song, as he had been informed,
"was sung with much effect by a man named Eagan at the early meetings of a Temperance Society in the south of Ireland, upon which
occasions the lines referring to the suicide proceeding of hard drinking :
    " For your own brains out you're dashing,
      Don't you feel your head quite sore?"
were always received with marked approbation."
   In turning over the leaves of a little Book called "The Triumphs of
Bacchus ; or, the Delights of the Bottle.—London : Printed for J.
Watson, over against Hungerford-market in the Strand, 1729," we find
a song numbered 73 commencing "Come, my hearts of gold, Let us
be merry and wise," of which the concluding line of each stanza (and
there are six of eight lines each) is " And we'll ne'er be drunk again."—
It goes on to say :—

A cup of old sack is good,
　To drive the cold winter away ;
'Twill cherish and comfort the blood
Most when a man's spirits decay ;
But he that doth drink too much,
　Of his head he will complain ;
Then let's have a gentle touch,
　And ne'er be drunk again.

Good Claret was made for man,
　But man was not made for it ;
Let's be merry as we can,
　So we drink not away our wit ;
Good fellowship is abus'd,
　And wine will infect the brain ;
But we'll have it better us'd,
　And ne'er be drunk again.

.　　　.　　.　　　.

Enough's as good as a feast
　If a man did but measure know ;
A Drunkard's worse than a beast,
　For he'll drink till he cannot go :
If a man could time recall
　In a Tavern that's spent in vain ;
We'd learn to be sober all,
　And never be drunk again.

　This song has apparently been transferred to the pages of the
"Triumphs of Bacchus and Venus" from "Durfey's Pills to purge
melancholy," in volume 4th of which both words and tune will be found.
It is there styled "The Reformed drinker."

Tune,—Malbrook.

ONE night when I got frisky
Over some potent whisky,
Like waves in the Bay of Biscay,
　I began to tumble and roar.
My face was red as a lobster,
I fell and I broke my nob, sir,
My watch was picked from my fob, sir—
　Oh ! I'll never get drunk any more.

Now, I'm resolved to try it,
I'll live upon moderate diet;
I'll not drink but will deny it,
    And shun each ale-house door;
For that's the place they tell us,
We meet with all jovial good fellows;
But, I swear by the poker and bellows,
    I'll never get drunk any more.

The landlady is unwilling
To credit you for a shilling,
She straightways sends her bill in,
    And asks you to pay your score.
And if with money your stockèd,
She'll not stop till she's emptied your pocket,
Then the cellar door is lockèd,
    And you cannot get drunk any more.

So by me now take caution,
Put drinking out of fashion,
For your own brains out you're dashing:
    Don't you feel your head quite sore?
For when all night you've tarried
Drinking of punch and claret,
In the morning home you're carried,
    (*Saying*) "I'll never get drunk any more."

A man that's fond of boozing,
His cash goes daily oozing;
His character he's losing,
    And its loss he will deplore.
His wife is unprotected,
His business is neglected,
Himself is *dis*-respected,
    So, do not get drunk any more.

A Catch on a liquor called Punch.

GLASGOW has long been celebrated for the excellence of its punch, and the true receipt for making it is contained in this couplet :—

> " Rum miscetur aqua, dulci miscetur acetum,
> Fiat ex tali fœdere nobile Punch."

You may talk of brisk claret, sing praises of sherry,
Speak well of old hock, mum, cyder, and perry,
But you must drink *Punch* if you mean to be merry.

A bowl of this liquor the gods being all at,
Thought good we should know it by way of new ballad,
As fit for both our and their highnesses' palate.

Then thanks to the gods, those tipplers above us,
They've taught us to love, and therefore they love us,
And to drink very hard is all they crave of us.

A Bacchanalian Song.

Sung by Mrs Atkins at Sadler's Wells.

FROM "a Collection of Miscellaneous Essays—by T. Mozeen, London, 1762."

Thomas Mozeen was bred to the Law, but cast it aside for the more honest calling of a Stage-Player. He was for awhile attached to the Theatre in Drury Lane, but finding that his merits were not appreciated, he retired into private life. "He gave some proofs," say the Editors of the Biographia Dramatica, "of genius and humour in the writing way, being reputed the author of a very diverting account of the adventures of a summer company of Comedians, detached from the Metropolitan Theatres, commencing capital heroes within the limits of a barn, and to the audience of a country town. The book is entitled 'Young Scarron.' He has also written some little poems which were published by subscription, together with a farce entitled ' The Heiress ; or the Antigallican.' He died 28th March, 1768." The "little Poems" form the Collection from which this song has been printed.—He also published in 1764, "The Lyrick Pacquet," a collection of songs written by him for Sadler's Wells Theatre and the use of the Public Gardens, and sung by Messrs Lowe and Vernon, 12mo. pp. 120. Mr Croker has reprinted three of the Songs in his " Popular Songs of Ireland."

COME booze, my Lads, booze; push the Bottle about,
　　Ye Ninnies, for whom would you save?
Your wife, with her fondness who makes such a rout,
　　She'll laugh ere you're cold in the grave.
Mankind are mere shams wear what vizors they please,
The only true friends are fair bumpers and ease.

Do you scrape for a son, whom, with cost and with care,
　　You have hitherto anxiously bred?
The first in the chamber shall be the young heir
　　To pluck pillow from under your head.
Nunc, nunc est bibendum, our motto you see,
Stick, stick to it close, and be happy as we.

For friend or for mistress art heaping up dirt?
　　Ah! trifler!—how little you know!
An ear-ring your fair Saint's true love will pervert,
　　Distress of your friend makes a foe.
What need of advice against hoarding of pelf?
A Bumper, a Bumper will speak for itself.

Haste, haste ye to us, but do as we do,
　　I warrant you ne'er will repent ;
The Tale of a Tub is both merry and true,
　　I ne'er knew what other Tales meant,
Let 'em preach, let 'em fight, let 'em cavil and brawl,
A Bumper and ease I prefer to 'em all.

The Pitcher.

FROM a MS. found with others (among which were some original MSS. of Burns) in the repositories of a very old but now decayed family in Dumfriesshire. Its date is evidently about 1770, and it has been conjectured to be a production of Riddell of Glenriddell—a patron of Burns, who is said to have been his assistant in the composition of the legendary poem entitled "The Bedesman of Nithsdale."

"The sneaking milksop, Jemmy Twitcher" referred to in the fourth stanza, was Lord Sandwich, an unpopular member of the administration, whose connection with Miss Reay was brought prominently before the public in consequence of her having been murdered in the Piazza, Covent-Garden, while stepping into her carriage on leaving the Theatre, by an insane Clergyman, the Rev. Mr. Hackman (at one time in the army), who had fallen desperately in love with her. For this murder Hackman was executed, there not having been in those days any absurd sympathy with mono-maniacs. A very graphic account of the whole transaction will be found in the Life and Correspondence of M. G. Lewis, 2 vols., 8vo. Lond., 1839.

The silver moon she shines so bright—
   She shines so bright, I swear, by nature,
That if my hour-glass goes but right,
   We've time to drink another pitcher—
For 'tis not day, 'tis not yet day,
   Then why should we forsake good liquor,
Until the sun beams round in play,
   We've time to call for t'other pitcher.

They say were I to work by day,
   And sleep at night, I'd grow much richer,
But what is all this world can give,
   Compared to mirth, my friend, and pitcher.
For 'tis not day, &c.

Though one may get a handsome wife,
   Yet strange vagaries may bewitch her,
Unvex'd I'd live a single life,
   And boldly call for t'other pitcher.
For 'tis not day, &c.

I dearly love a hearty man,
   No sneaking milksop, Jemmy Twitcher,

Who loves his friend, and loves his can,
   And boldly calls for t'other pitcher—
For 'tis not day, 'tis not yet day,
   For why should we forsake good liquor,
Until the sun beams round in play,
   We'll sit and push about the pitcher.

English Good Ale.

From a chap-book titled, "The two Sailors outwitted, or eggs and
bacon. To which are added, The Smart Robin Gray; The Martial
Invasion; The Jealous Husband. Well Paid; The Lover's Summons;
English Good Ale. Entered according to order," *circa* 1793.

THE truths that I sing none deny me,
   They're truths that must ever prevail;
Ye poor dogs of France, we defy ye,
   By the force of our English good ale.

The tricks ye attempt but in vain are,
   They are what we expected, and stale;
Your troops and your fleets our disdain are,
   By the force of our English good ale.

When Bess, that brave Queen, rul'd the nation,
   'Twas Spain's great Armada did fail;
She dealt to the Dons' tribulation,
   By the force of our English good ale.

And thus we shall serve them for ever,
   Tho' their loads on our necks they'd entail;
There's none like our people so clever,
   By the force of our English good ale.

Free-born, we support our Defender,
   To our sons we hand down to detail;
Defy the de'il, Pope, and Pretender,
   By the force of our English good ale.

Johnnie Dowie's Ale.

"Johnnie Dowie" was a vintner in Libberton's Wynd, in the old town of Edinburgh. His tavern was long celebrated for the excellence of its ale, which emanated from Younger's brewery at Croft-an-righ, and, in consequence, as well as for Johnnie's affability and attention, was much frequented towards the end of the last, and the beginning of the present century by many of the most distinguished citizens of Edinburgh, it being the custom of those times for every one to resort during a portion of the evening, for social converse and amusement, to some favourite "howf," or place of meeting. This Wynd, which led from the Lawnmarket to the Cowgate, was pulled down upwards of thirty years ago, to make way for George the Fourth's Bridge. Johnnie Dowie's Tavern was situated near the top of Libberton's Wynd, overlooking the spot devoted to the erection of the common gallows for the execution of criminals. It presented, both internally and externally, anything but a comfortable aspect. The principal room, which looked into the Wynd, was capable of containing about fourteen persons, but all the other rooms were so small they could hardly contain half that number, and they were so dingy, and dark, that, during the day, when in occupation, they required the aid of candle-light. During Burns's six months' sojourn in Edinburgh Johnnie Dowie's was his favourite haunt, and for a long time he was set down as the author of the following ballad, it having been printed on slips by Johnnie, and circulated among his customers as Burns's. It was afterwards printed as illustrative of a short biographical notice of John himself, in the Scots Magazine for 1806, and has been ascertained to have been the production of Mr Hunter of Blackness. John contrived to amass property to the extent of about £6000. He died in 1817. He was twice married, and had several children by his first wife. His son attained the rank of Captain in the army. Portraits of Johnnie Dowie will be found prefixed to the notice in the Scots Magazine, above mentioned, and in the collected edition of Kay's Etching's, vol. ii., Edin. 1842, 4to.

"Antiquarian Paton," referred to in the ballad, was a clerk in the customs, who, although in receipt of a salary of only £90 a-year, contrived to amass a large and very curious library.

A' ye wha wis', on e'enings lang,
To meet and crack and sing a sang,
And weet your pipes, for little wrang
　　　To purse or person,
To sere Johnnie Dowie's gang,
　　　There thrum a verse on.

O, Dowie's ale! thou art the thing,
That gars us crack, an' gars us sing,
Cast by our cares, our wants a' fling
   Frae us wi' anger;
Thou e'en mak'st passion tak' the wing,
   Or thou wilt bang 'er.

How blest is he wha has a groat
To spare upon the cheering pot;
He may look blythe as any Scot
   That e'er was born;
Gi'es a' the like, but wi' a coat,
   An' guide frae scorn.

But thinkna that strong ale alone,
Is a' that's kept by Dainty John;
Na, na, for in the place there's none,
   Frae end to end,
For meat can set ye better on
   Than can your friend.

Wi' looks as mild as mild can be,
An' smudgin' laugh, wi' winkin' e'e;
An' lowly bow down to his knee,
   He'll say fu' douce,
" Whe, gentlemen, stay till I see
   What's i' the hoose."

Anither bow, " Deed gif ye please,
Ye can get a bit toasted cheese;
A crum o' tripe, ham, dish o' pease,
   (The season fittin';)
An egg, or, caller frae the seas,
   A fleuk or whitin'.

" A nice beef-steak, or ye may get
A gude buff'd herring, reisted skate

An ingons, an' (though past its date)
A cut o' veal ;
Ha, ha, it's no that unco late,
I'll do it weel."

O, Geordie Robertson, dreigh loun,
An' Antiquarian Paton soun' ;
Wi' mony ithers i' the town,
What wad come o'er ye,
Gif Johnnie Dowie should stap down
To th' grave before ye ?

Ye sure wad brek your hearts wi' grief,
An' in strong ale find nae relief,
War ye to lose your Dowie—chief
O' bottle keepers ;
Three years at least now, to be brief,
Ye'd gang wi' weepers.

But gude forbid, for your sakes a',
That sic a usefu' man should fa' ;
For, friens o' mine, between us twa,
Right i' your lug,
You'd lose a howff, baith warm an' braw,
An' unco snug.

Then, pray for's health this mony a year,
Fresh three 'n-a-ha'penny, best of beer,
That can (tho' dull) you brawly cheer—
Recant you weel up ;
An' gar you a' forget your wear,
Your sorrows seal up.

"Another bottle, John."
"Gentlemen, 'tis past twelve, and time to go home."

THE FOUR DRUNKEN MAIDENS.

THIS Ballad has been printed from a Broadside bearing the imprint of "C. Crashaw, Printer, Coppergate, York," along with another entitled "Oh no, my Love, not I !" evidently dating about the beginning of the present century. The use of strong waters, at the time it was written, must not have prevailed to any noticeable extent among females, otherwise the doings of the four maidens from the Isle of Wight (whose names are happily now buried in oblivion) would not have been deemed as a remarkable subject to be chronicled by the Flying Stationers. The Isle of Wight was long the harbour of smugglers, and the facilities thus afforded to its denizens to procure liquor at a cheap rate, may have induced habits of private drinking among females. There is one peculiarity worth noticing, that Malaga, now a wine little used, must have been abundant and popular at the time.

In the earlier part of last century it appears to have been no disgrace for ladies as well as gentlemen in Scotland to become somewhat "elevated" at Entertainments where much excitement otherwise prevailed, but there is no authentic record of such wholesale bouts as that indicated in the outrageous conduct of the Four Maidens. At what was called "the Cummerfealls," which in genteel society was a merry meeting some few evenings prior to a christening, immediately after supper there was a scramble for sweatmeats, "wrestling and pulling at one another with the utmost violence. When all was quiet, they went to the stoups (for there was no bottles for wine) of which the women had a good share ; for, though it was a disgrace to be seen drunk, yet it was none to be a little intoxicated in good company." See Barclay's "view of the change of manners in Scotland," an interesting paper printed in the Edinburgh Magazine of August, 1817, (Constable's)—and subsequently included amongst the Caldwell Papers, the contribution of Colonel Mure to the Maitland Club.

Mr Barclay was a citizen of Edinburgh (of very good family) and was born towards the close of the seventeenth century. He was the grand-uncle of the late accomplished antiquary and very ill-used gentleman, W. B. D. D. Turnbull.

In a footnote the Editor remarks, "if we ought to yield any credit to a French author, the English ladies, during the reign of King Charles I. went a step beyond this in the use of wine"—and he makes this sweeping statement upon the very questionable authority of a French Romance of 1642, entitled "La Courtisanne Dechifrèe, dediée aux dames Vertueuses de ce temps."—

A writer in the "Press" newspaper of so recent a date as the month of April 1867, touching upon the baneful habit of "secret tippling,' which he treats of as a matter of common observation, makes the following bold assertions respecting London females of the middle and higher classes, assertions which at best can only be applicable to the select few. "The fair dames have secret recesses in their boudoirs, too frequently well supplied with cognac, or L. L. whisky, (wine, of course, they can take openly at table); not so hidden is the flushed face, the tremulous hand, and the unsteady gait. It is a sad photograph, which may be seen too often, sometimes in the salon, not infrequently *en passant* from the carriage door to the entrance to some fashionable West-end emporiums, some of the proprietors of which, we have more than heard it whispered, keep slight refreshments set for wearied and distressed Dames, their customers. As for home consumption, the supply for the boudoir,— which could hardly be furnished by a servant,—that is too frequently supplied by the fashionable *modiste*, who charges openly for it in the bill ;—perhaps a little jesuitically, for cognac or L.L. whisky is set down as 'small trimmings,'—'inside linings' would be equally as good a phrase. The females of the middle classes generally make a confidante of a particular servant, or discover a penchant for pastry, spend an occasional hour in one of those shops, whose proprietors emulate the doings of the aforesaid *modistes*. Again, medical men will tell you with what affectionate care some ladies hug nervous complaints, and how readily they take as medicine various 'strengthening tinctures,' less medicinal than alcoholic. It is, in many instances, to time-serving medical men that so many ladies are indebted for the first growth of the pernicious habit. In many instances the habit arises from the neglect of a husband, and the consequent solitary life ; this is evinced by the fact that those dames who have been morganatically married, and are thus left much to themselves, are more given to tippling than any other class, excepting, perhaps, the lowest order. Whatever the cause, the result is equally terrible amongst all classes. In the higher, by embittering the temper, and keeping up a constant irritability, it becomes a source of continued dissension and frequently separation ; in the middle, it is the ruin of the husband and children, by the downward road to a lower status ; in the lower class, the workhouse or the gaol."

The Four Drunken Maidens.

Four drunken Maidens came from the Isle of Wight,
Drunk from Monday morning till Saturday night ;
When Saturday night came they would not go out,
And the four drunken Maidens they pushed the jug about.

In came Bouncing Sally and her cheeks like any bloom,
"Sit about dear sister and give me some room,

Q

I will be worthy of my room before I do go out!"
And the four drunken Maidens they pushed the jug about.

There was wood-cock and pheasants, partridges and hare,
And all sorts of dainties ; no scarcity was there ;
There was forty quarts of Malaga, they fairly drank it out,
And the four drunken Maidens they pushed the jug about,

Down came the landlady to see what was to pay,
This is a forty pound bill to be drawn here this day ;
There is ten pounds apiece and they would not go out,
And the four drunken Maidens they pushed the jug about.

Sally was a walking along the highway,
And she meet with her mother and unto her did say ;
" Where is the head dress you had the other day?
And where is your mantle so gallant and so gay,"
" So gallant and so gay we had no more to do,
We left them in the alehouse; we had a randan row."

Cold Water.

THE following clever song is from a very interesting little volume
entitled "Journal of a Wanderer," which appeared at Edinburgh in 1844,
12mo.   The book was published anonymously, having for a Frontispiece
the "Portrait of the Author," which has been understood to represent
Mr John Reid, author of another volume entitled "A Manual of Scottish
Stocks and British Funds."   Mr Reid was at one time a very successful Stockbroker in Edinburgh, but on the approach of the Railway
Mania of 1845, foreseeing the very speculative character of transactions
in such wild Stocks, he wisely withdrew from business to enjoy his
"otium cum dignitate."

In Eden's green retreats,
    A water brook that play'd
Between soft mossy seats,
    Beneath a plane-tree's shade,

Whose rustling leaves
Danc'd o'er its brink,
Was Adam's drink,
And also Eve's.

Beside the parent spring
Of that young brook, the pair
Their morning chaunt would sing;
And Eve to dress her hair
Kneel on the grass
That fring'd its side,
And make its tide
Her looking-glass.

And when the man of God
From Egypt led his flock,
They thirsted, and his rod
Smote the Arabian rock,
And forth a rill
Of water gush'd,
And on they rush'd,
And drank their fill.

Would Eden thus have smil'd
Had *wine* to Eden come?
Would Horeb's parching wild
Have been refreshed with rum?
And had Eve's hair
Been dress'd in *gin*,
Would she have been
Reflected fair?

Had Moses built a still,
And dealt out to that host
To every man his gill,
And pledged him in a toast—

How large a band
Of Israel's Sons
Had laid their bones
In Canaan's land?

" Sweet fields beyond deaths' flood
Stand dress'd in living green,"
For, from the throne of God,
To freshen all the scene,
A river rolls,
Where all who will
May come and fill
Their crystal bowls.

If Eden's strength and bloom
Cold water thus hath given,
If e'en beyond the tomb
It is the drink of heav'n,
Are not *good wells*,
And *crystal springs*
The very things
For our *hotels* ?

CATAWBA.

In a letter from Cincinati, "the Queen City of the west," which
appeared in the *Illustrated News* early in 1858, the following curious
particulars as to wine in America are introduced :—"Another source of
wealth has been developed in Ohio, by Mr Nicholas Longworth of the
'Queen City,' to whom America owes the introduction of the grape
culture for the purposes of wine making, and to whom the whole world
ought to be grateful for the invention of such delicate luxuries as dry and
sparkling Catawba.   Dry Catawba is a finer wine of the hock species and
flavour than any hock that comes from the Rhine ; and sparkling Catawba
of the pure, unadulterated juice of the odoriferous Catawba grape, trans-

cends the Champagne of France (even if this be made of grape near Rheims, and not of rhubarb, turnips, and apples in the neighbourhood of Marseilles and London,) as much as a bright new sovereign transcends an old shilling. Mr Longworth in early life tried many experiments with the indigenous grape, but it was not until he reached old age that he was rewarded by success. Having resolved to concentrate his attention upon one grape with a rich muscadine flavour, he succeeded, about ten years ago, in producing out of it the sparkling Catawba, a wine which competent judges who have tasted all the wines of the world pronounce to be far superior to any sparkling wine which Europe can boast, whether they came from the Rhine or the Moselle, or from the Champagne districts of France. Perhaps this letter will be the first intimation that millions of people will receive of the existence of this bounty of nature ; but there is no risk of false prophecy in the prediction here hazarded, that not many years will elapse before the dry and the sparkling Catawba will be recognised in Europe as they are in America, as the best and purest of all wines, except Claret and Burgundy. . . . Thus much for Catawba in serious prose ; let its praises be now celebrated in equally serious verse :"—

Catawba.

Ohio's green hill-tops
　Grow bright in the sun,
And yield us more treasure
　Than Rhine or Garonne;
They give us Catawba,
　The pure and the true,
As radiant as sunlight,
　As soft as the dew,
And fragrant as gardens
　When summer is new.
Catawba that sparkles—
　Catawba at rest—
Catawba the nectar
　And balm of the West.

Champagne is too often
　A trickster malign,
That flows from the apple
　And not from the vine;

But thou, my Catawba,
  Art mild as a rose,
And sweet as the lips
  Of my love, when they close
To give back the kisses
  My passion bestows.
Thou'rt born of the vintage,
  And fed on its breast,
Catawba the nectar
  And balm of the West.

When pledging the lovely,
  This sparkler we'll kiss;
When drinking to true hearts,
  We'll toast them in this;
For Catawba is like them,
  Though tender yet strong,
As pleasant as morning,
  And soft as a song
Whose delicate beauty
  The echoes prolong.
Catawba ! Heart-warmer !
  Soul-cheerer ! Life-zest !
Catawba the nectar
  And balm of the West.

Red Wine.

Reprinted from a Periodical published at Glasgow in 1846.

Let Cynics and Priests rail as much as they will,
  This world is all joyous and bright ;
And I'll be its strenuous worshipper still,
  Nor tire in pursuit of delight.

There are things in this earth to make it divine,
  But one above others I prize—
'Tis the potent and mirth-giving juice of the Vine—
  The solace and joy of mine eyes.

Young flowers are lovely—their odour how sweet !
  But for me they may blossom and bear—
No jessamine Bower—no rose-shaded seat
  With the fragrance of Wine can compare.

And woman—the fairest—may sit by my side—
  May press her cheek gently to mine—
Yet the roses there mantling are ever denied
  The lustre and blush of red wine.

Then bring me the Wine, Boy !—Again and again
  I'll replenish and empty the bowl ;—
I feel as a God were in every vein—
  A rapture has seized on my soul.

Oh ! how the Earth totters—the sky becomes black—
  My vision grows dark as the sky—
Oh! help me, good Bacchus—oh! help me! Good lack !
  I'm falling—I'm fainting—I die.

Jolly Bacchus.

This jovial song, which has in some degree been superseded by the
more modern " For he's a jolly good fellow," was for a very long period
exceedingly popular, and even now it may occasionally be heard in the
social assemblies of those who desire to recal the pleasant associations of
their earlier years. It used to be sung at all social gatherings, but with
this difference,—instead of " Come sit you down !" it was " We'll all
rise up together ;" and at the conclusion of that stanza the action consisted in each man holding his glass full of liquid to his next neighbour's

mouth and causing him to drink, to ensure that each and all had his quantum of the contents of "the flowing bowl." The more waggish of the company, instead of holding the glass to their neighbour's mouth, held it either above or below, so that, in the attempts to drink, a considerable portion of the liquor frequently deluged the neckcloth and shirt of the unwary one. The last stanza then immediately followed, which went thus :—"See ! it runs down his gizzard !" &c.

It is called in Durfey's Pills, where it occurs with the music,

BACCHUS'S HEALTH,

and is there set down "to be sung by all the company together with directions to be observed."

First man stands up with a glass in's hand and sings.

Here's a health to jolly Bacchus,
Here's a health to jolly Bacchus,
Here's a health to jolly Bacchus,—I-ho, I-ho, I-ho ;
For he doth merry make us,
For he doth merry make us,
For he doth merry make us,—I-ho, I-ho, I-ho.

At the following star they all bow to each other and sit down.
At the dagger all the company beckon to the Drawer.

*Come sit ye down together,
Come sit ye down together,
Come sit ye down together, I-ho, I-ho, I-ho ;
And † bring more liquor hither,
And bring more liquor hither,
And bring more liquor hither, I-ho, I-ho, I-ho.

At the following Star the first man drinks his glass while all the others sing and point at him.
At the Dagger they all sit down, clapping their next man on the shoulder.

It goes into the * Cranium,
It goes into the Cranium,
It goes into the Cranium, I-ho, I-ho, I-ho ;

And † thou'rt a boon companion,
And thou'rt a boon companion,
And thou'rt a boon companion, I-ho, I-ho, I-ho.

*Then the second man takes his glass, all the company singing
" Here's a health," &c., so round.*

'TWAS MERRY IN THE HALL.

THE following used to be sung by W. II. Murray, who was for upwards of thirty years manager of the Old Theatre Royal, Edinburgh, and one of the cleverest comedians of a time when Liston, Mathews, Wrench, Power, Emery, Old Farren, and Keeley trode the boards. It was understood to be Mr. Murray's own composition, and he always introduced it in the character of Sir Mark Chase in Morton's "Roland for an Oliver." The burthen is paraphrased from an old proverb "'Tis merry in Hall when Beards wag all," the first record of which we find about the beginning of the fourteenth century in the Metrical Romance (attributed to Adam Davie) of "Alexander." Thus:

> "Merrie swithe it is in halle
> When the berdes waveth alle."

Heywood has it in his Epigrammes on Proverbes. It occurs in Epigram ii. under the phrase "wagging beards :"—

> "*It is mery in hall, when beards wagge all ;*
> Husband, for this, these woordes to-night I call :
> This is ment by men in their merie eating,
> Not to wag their beardes in brauling or threating :
> Wyfe, the meaning hereof differth not two pinnes,
> Between wagginge of men's beardes, and women's chins."

Again, it occurs in Shakespeare's Second Part of Henry IV., act 5, scene 3 :—

> "Be merry, be merry, my wife has all,
> For women are shrews, both short and tall :
> '*Tis merry in hall, when beards wag all,*
> And welcome merry shrove-tide."

William Stafforde, in his "Briefe Conceipte of English Policye," 1581, mentions it as "a common Proverbe," and a contemporaneous writer in describing a banquet refers to a song at that time embodying it, but which we have not yet met with : "The table taken up, the plate presently conveyed into the pantrie, the hall summons this consort of companions (upon payne to dyne with Duke Humphfrie, or to kiss the hare's foot) to appear at the first call ; where a song is to be sung, the under song or holding whereof is, *It is merrie in hall, where beardes wag all.*"—See "The Serving-man's Comfort," 1598.

The "black Jack" to which allusion is made in the last stanza, was a drinking jug made of leather. There is an old song in praise of, and titled, "the leather bottèl," of which there is a black-letter copy in the British Museum at least two hundred years old. It has been reprinted in Chappel's Collection of National English airs, No. 43. After showing the advantage of "the leather bottèl" over "cans of wood and glasses fine," the ballad goes on to say:

> Then what do you say to these black pots three ?
> If a man and his wife should not agree,
> Why they'll tug and pull till their liquor doth spill:
> In a leather bottèl they may tug their fill,
> And pull away till their hearts do ake,
> And yet their liquor no harm can take.
> So I wish in heaven his soul may dwell,
> That first found out the leather bottèl.

> Then what do you say to these flagons fine ?
> Oh, they shall have no praise of mine,
> For when a Lord is about to dine,
> And sends them to be filled with wine,
> The man with the flagon doth run away,
> Because it is silver most gallant and gay.
> So I wish, &c.

> A leather bottèl we know is good,
> Far better than glasses or cans of wood,
> For when a man 's at work in the field,
> Your glasses and pots no comfort will yield ;
> But a good leather bottèl standing by,
> Will raise his spirits whenever he's dry.
> So I wish, &c.

> .   .   .   .   .

> And when the bottèl at last grows old,
> And will good liquor no longer hold,
> Out of the side you may make a clout,
> To mend your shoes when they're worn out ;
> Or take and hang it up on a pin,
> To serve to put hinges and odd things in.
> So I wish, &c.

There is another version of "the Leathern Bottel," being Song 78 in "The Triumphs of Bacchus; or, the Delights of the Bottle," Lond. 1729, 16mo, which has been reprinted from Durfey's Pills to purge Melancholy, wherein it will be found, with the music, at page 247 of vol. iii.

The song which follows it in both collections is "the bonny Black Jack " to the same air, which we print *ad longum* immediately after this.

Now ancient English melody
    Is banish'd out of doors,
And nought is heard, in our day,
    But Signoras and Signors.
        Such airs I hate,
        Like a pig in a gate !
Oh ! give me the good old strain-ai-ain :
    " It was merry in the hall
    When their beards wagged all "—
We shall never see the like again-ai-ain,
We shall never see the like again.

On beds of down our dandies lay, [*Anglicé*, " lie."]
    And waste the cheerful morn,
While our Squires of old would rouse the day
    With the sound of the bugle horn ;
        And their wives took care
        The feast to prepare,
For when they left the plain—
    Oh ! " 'twas merry in the hall
    And their beards wagg'd all "—
We shall never see the like again.

'Twas then the Christmas tale was told
    Of goblin, ghost, or fairy ;
And they cheer'd the hearts of the tenants old
    With a cup of good canary.
        And they each took a smack
        Of the coal black Jack,
Till the fire burn'd in their brain.
        Oh ! 'twas merry in the hall
        And their beards wagg'd all—
May we soon see the like again.

The Bonny Black=Jack.

THE allusion in the eighth stanza of this song to the Pillars of Hercules leads us to suspect that the Black-Jack was derived from the usage of leathern bags, especially in Spain, for the conveyance of wine. The wine of Cyprus, which is much esteemed, is very much destroyed in flavour in consequence of the inner lining of the leathern bag being, to prevent leakage, commonly covered with pitch, or some other resinous substance. This disagreeable flavour, from similar causes, is not unfrequently imparted to the Spanish wine Val de penas—a wine otherwise very pleasant to drink.

The mention of Val de penas recals the story of Don Quixote and his ludicrous adventure at an Inn, where he makes fierce havoc among some unoffending skins filled with wine. Lest our readers may have forgotten it, we shall relate the leading incidents. During the reading of the novel of the "Impertinent Curiosity" by the Curate, "Sancho came running in in great confusion from the garret where his master, Don Quixote lay, bawling aloud: "Make haste to the assistance of my master, who is this precious minute engaged and grappled in the roughest battle that ever my eyes beheld! Egad! he has given that same giant, the enemy of my lady the Princess of Micomicona, such a back-stroke, as hath sliced off his head, as smooth and clean as the skin of a turnip!" That instant they heard a great noise in the apartment, and Don Quixote pronounced aloud, "Stay! villain, robber, caitiff, here I have thee, and thy scymitar shall not avail." "Go in," said Sancho, "and part the fray, or lend your assistance to my master; though I believe that will be needless by this time, for the giant is certainly dead; nay, I saw with my own eyes his blood running about the floor, and his head cut off, lying on one side as large as a wine bag." The innkeeper rushed into the apartment, with the whole company at his heels, and found the Knight in a very ludicrous situation. He appeared in his shirt, displaying a pair of long lank legs, not extremely clean; his head was covered with a little red, greasy nightcap, belonging to the landlord; round his left arm he had wrapped the blanket of his bed, to which Sancho, for good reasons known to himself, bore an inveterate grudge; and in his right, he wielded his drawn sword, with which he laid about him at a furious rate, talking as if he was actually at blows with the giant; but, what was very surprising, his eyes were shut all the time, and he was fast asleep, dreaming of this encounter; for his imagination was so much ingrossed by the adventure he had undertaken to achieve, as to make him dream that he was already arrived in the kingdom of Micomicon, and engaged in single combat with his gigantic adversary, instead of whom he hacked the wine-bags so furiously that the whole room was afloat with their contents." See Smollett's Don Quixote, vol. i., Lond. 1755, 4to.

The "black-jack" formed a portion of the theatrical properties required in the representation of Brome's comedy of " The Jovial Crew, or the Merry Beggars," 4to Lond. 1652. The Stage Directions are:—"Enter Randal and three or four servants with a great kettle, and black-Jacks, and a Baker's basket, all empty." *Actus Primus.* In Brome's comedy there are one or two canting songs.

'Tis a pitiful thing that now-a-days, sirs,
Our Poets turn leathern Bottle praisers;
But if a leathern theme they did lack,
They might better have chosen the bonny black Jack;
For when they are both now well worn and decay'd,
For the Jack, than the Bottle, much more may be said;
And I wish his soul much good may partake
That first devis'd the bonny Black Jack.

And now I will begin to declare,
What the conveniences of the Jack are;
First, when a gang of good fellows do meet,
As oft at a fair, or a wake, you shall see't;
They resolve to have some merry Carouses,
And yet to get home in good time to their houses;
Then the *Bottle* it runs as slow as my rhyme,
With *Jack* they might have all been drunk in good time;
And I wish his soul in peace may dwell,
That first devis'd that speedy vessel.

And therefore leave oft your twittle-twattle,
Praise the Jack, praise no more the leathern Bottle;
For a man at the Bottle may drink till he burst,
And yet not handsomely quench his thirst;
The master hereat he maketh great moan,
And doubts his Bottle has a spice of the stone;
But if it had been a generous Jack,
He might have currently what he did lack;

And I wish his soul in Paradise,
That first found out that happy device.

Be your liquor small or thick as mud,
The cheating Bottle that cries, "good! good!"
Then the master again begins to storm,
Because it said more than it could perform ;
But if it had been in an honest Black Jack,
It would have prov'd better to sight, smell, and smack ;
And I wish his soul in Heaven may rest,
That added a Jack to Bacchus's feast.

No Flaggon, Tankard, Bottle, or Jug,
Is half so fit, or so well can hold tug ;
For when a man and his wife play at thwacks,
There's nothing so good as a pair of *Black Jacks*,
Then to it they go, they swear, and they curse,
It makes them both better, the Jacks ne'er the worse ;
For they might have bang'd both till their hearts did ache,
And yet no hurt the Jacks could take ;
And I wish his heirs may have a pension,
That first produc'd that lucky invention.

Socrates and Aristotle,
Suck'd no wit from a leather Bottle ;
For surely I think a man as soon may
Find a needle in a Bottle of Hay ;
But if the Black-Jack a man oft toss over,
'Twill make him as drunk as any philosopher ;
When he that makes Jacks from a peck to a quart,
Conjures not, tho' he lives by the aid of black art ;
And I wish, &c.

Besides, my good friend, let me tell you that fellow
That fram'd the Bottle his brains were but shallow ;
The case is so clear I nothing need mention,
That Jack is a neater and deeper invention ;

When the Bottle is cleaned the dregs fly about,
As if the entrails and brains flew out ;
But if in a cannon-bore Jack it had been,
From the top to the bottom all might have been clean ;
And I wish his soul no comfort may lack,
That first devis'd the bouncing Black Jack.

Your leathern Bottle is us'd by no man,
That is a hair's-breadth above a plough man ;
Then let us gang to the *Hercules Pillars*,
And there visit those gallant Jack Swillers ;
In these small, strong, sour, mild and stale,
They drink Orange, Lemon, and Lambeth ale.
The chief of Heralds there allows
The Jack to be of an ancienter house.
And may his successors never want Sack,
That first devis'd the long *Leather Jack*.

Then for the Bottle you cannot well fill it
Without a tunnel, but that you must spill it,
'Tis as hard to get in, as it is to get out,
'Tis not so with a Jack for it runs like a spout,
Then burn your Bottèl, for what good is in it ?
One cannot well fill it, nor drink, nor clean it,
But if it had been in a bonny Black-Jack,
'Twould come a good pace, and hold you good tack.
And I wish, &c.

He that's drunk in a Jack looks as fierce as a spark,
That were just ready cock'd to shoot at a mark ;
When the other thing up to the mouth it goes,
Makes a man look with a great Bottle nose ;
All wise men conclude that a Jack new or old,
Tho' beginning to leak, is however worth gold ;
For when the poor man on the way does trudge it,
His worn-out Jack serves him for a Budget ;
And I wish his heirs may never want Sack,
That first contriv'd the leather Black-Jack.

When Bottle and Jack stand together, fie on't!
The Bottle looks just like a Dwarf to a Giant ;
Then have we not reason the Jack for to choose,
For they can make Boots, when the Bottle mends Shoes ?
For add but to every Jack a foot,
And every Jack becomes a boot ;
Then give me my Jack, there's a reason why,
They have kept us wet, and they'll keep us dry ;
I now shall cease, but as I'm an honest man,
The Jack deserves to be call'd *Sir John.*
And may they ne'er want for belly nor back,
That kept up the trade of the Bonny Black-Jack.

TOBACCO.

CHARLES KNIGHT, quoting from "Aubrey," in one of the volumes of his very entertaining Scrap-Book, "Half-Hours with the Best Authors," observes :— "Sir Walter Raleigh was the first that brought tobacco into England and into fashion. In our part of North Wilts—Malmesbury Hundred—it came first into fashion by Sir Walter Long. They had first silver pipes. The ordinary sort made use of a walnut-shell and a straw. I have heard my grandfather Lyte say, that one pipe was handed from man to man round the table. Sir W. R. standing in a stand at Sir Ro. Poyntz's Park at Acton, took a pipe of tobacco, which made the ladies quit it till he had done. Within these thirty-five years 'twas scandalous for a divine to take tobacco. It was sold then for its weight in silver. I have heard some of our yeoman neighbours say, that when they went to Malmesbury or Chippenham market, they culled out their biggest shillings to lay in the scales against the tobacco ; now, the customs of it are the greatest his majesty hath."

It is somewhat remarkable that, although almost every contemporary playwright and pamphleteer, and even royalty itself (see King James's "Counterblast to Tobacco,") had some reflection upon the use of tobacco, Shakespeare should never have noticed it. Dekker has satirized it in his "Gull's Hornbook," (1609) and in his "Wonderful Year," he fears

"Or some smok'd gallant, who at wit repines,
May dry tobacco with my wholesome lines."

R

Tobacco having been introduced into England in 1583, it was still a novelty when Dekker wrote, and its use was then an indication of puppyism. An inordinate use of perfumes also prevailed among the fops of fashion at the same period, and this formed a source of ridicule with most writers of that day.

Tobacco and feathers appear to have been extravagant luxuries when Dekker wrote. In the comedy of "The Sun's Darling," (a joint production with Ford) occurs mention of "a nimble rascal, some alderman's son, wonderous giddy and lightsome, one that blew his patrimony away in feathers and tobacco." Wine and tobacco were sold by Apothecaries. See Middleton and Dekker's "Roaring Girl," also Taylor's Life of "Thomas Parr," 4to, 1635.

In the "Merry Devil of Edmonton" reference is made to Cane-Tobacco, which may probably be something similar to the modern pigtail :—

"The nostrils of his chimnies are still stuff'd
With smoke more chargeable than cane-tobacco."

Ben Johnson, in the Induction to Cynthia's Revels, makes one of the characters say, "I have my three sorts of tobacco in my pocket, my light by me." &c. Those three sorts were probably what Dekker characterizes as "roll Trinidado, leaf, and pudding" tobacco.

Smoking tobacco prevailed in the Theatres, especially among those who paid their sixpence or shilling for a stool upon the stage, whither "your criticks, gallants, and such as would distinguish themselves sate." The play in Shakespeare's time began at one, almost immediately after dinner; in Dekker's time it began soon after three. The avocations or amusements of the audience previous to the commencement of a theatrical representation were various ; "Some read, some played at cards ; some drank ale, and smoked tobacco." See Malone's Shakespeare, vol. i. part 2, page 121.

There was a poem written in 1625 by Raphael Thorius, ("commonly called Thoris,") Physician, entitled "Hymnus Tabaci," which was "made English by Peter Hausted, Mr. of Arts Cambridge," and Curate of Uppingham in Rutland. It was printed at London "by T. N. for Humphrey Moseley, and are to be sold at his shop at the sign of the Princes Arms in St. Paul's Churchyard, 1651," 16mo. The title is "Hymnus Tabaci; a Poem in honour of Tabaco, heroically composed by Raphael Thorius." Touching upon the inspiriting influence produced by drinking (i.e. smoking) tobacco, the poet goes on to describe how tobacco was first discovered.

"Fill me a pipe (boy) of that lusty smoke,
That I may drink the god into my brain,
And so inabled write a buskind strain;

For nothing great or high can come from thence,
Where that blest plant denies his influence.
No mortal had the honour to descry
This noble herb first, but a Deity;
'Twas found by Bacchus, when the god wound up
To his true height, by his own charming cup,
Led th' Indian's forth under the warlike spear,
Whose glittering head an Ivy Twine did wear ;
And the all-sovereign weed being found out thus,
Too late (alas) hath been made known to us."

The North-American Indians entertain the belief that tobacco is of
sacred origin, although scarcely two tribes agree in the details of the
manner in which the boon was conferred on man. "In substance, however," says the writer of "Savage Life," in "the Boy's own Library,"
"the legend is the same with all. Ages ago, at the time when spirits
considered the world yet good enough for their occasional residence, a
very great and powerful spirit lay down by the side of his fire to sleep
in the forest. While so lying, his arch-enemy came that way and
thought it would be a good chance for mischief ; so, gently approaching
the sleeper, he rolled him over towards the fire, till his head rested
among the glowing embers, and his hair was set ablaze. The roaring
of the fire in his ears roused the good spirit, and, leaping to his feet, he
rushed in a fright through the forest, and as he did so, the wind caught
his singed hair as it flew off, and carrying it away, sowed it broadcast
over the earth, into which it sank and took root, and grew up tobacco."

Since its first introduction into this country, tobacco, in its various uses,
has been freely indulged in, oftentimes for its questionable efficacy in a
medicinal point of view, more frequently for its intoxicating and sooth-
ing qualities, but most of all for fashion's sake, and more so of late years
in the form of cigars, in which small boys just emerging from school are
wont to revel, under the mistaken belief that to be seen smoking, even
dried cabbage leaves, must elevate them in the eyes of the softer sex,
who might thus be favourably impressed with the idea of their manhood.
In a pamphlet titled "*The Perfuming of Tobacco, and the great abuse
committed in it*," 1611, the drinking of tobacco is thus described :—

"The smoke of tobacco (the which Dodoneus calls rightly henbane of
Peru) drunke and drawen by a pipe, filleth the membranes of the braine,
and astonisheth and filleth many persons with such joy and pleasure,
and sweet losse of senses, that they can by no means be without it."

So universally does smoking tobacco prevail in our times, that the
public streets of all our large towns are swarming with smokers of high
and low degree, polluting the atmosphere with their presence, and
depriving the more sober of a mouthful of fresh air.

In Boston (U. S.) and in Russia, a penalty is inflicted on those found smoking in the streets, and it would be well to follow that example in this country; we have not, however, the same excuse for doing so, as the object in these places is to prevent fire, wood being the prevailing agent in the construction of the houses.

Tobacco has been alleged by many to be most efficacious in the prevention and cure of diseases. Pepys, in his Diary, mentions tobacco as antidote for the plague, according to popular belief :—

"7th June 1665. . . . The hottest day that ever I felt in my life. This day, much against my will, I did in Drury Lane see two or three houses marked with a red cross upon the doors, and ' Lord, have mercy upon us!' writ there ; which was a sad sight to me, being the first of the kind that, to my remembrance, I ever saw. It put me into an ill conception of myself and my smell, so that I was forced to buy some roll-tobacco to smell and chaw, which took away the apprehension." See Lord Braybrooke's edition (the third) vol. iii., p. 23. Lond., 1848, 5 vols. cr. 8vo.

He also mentions the smoke of tobacco as beneficial to horses when affected with the staggers : "The coachman was fain to light, and hold him up, and cut his tongue to make him bleed, and his tail; then he blew some tobacco in his nose, upon which the horse sneezed, and, by and by, grew well, and drew us all the rest of our way as well as ever he did."—*Ibid.*, vol. iv. p. 160.

It is a strange fact that of all the European States, Great Britain should stand alone in prohibiting the growth of tobacco. In almost every other country, many of which have a climate similar to ours, the cultivation of the tobacco plant is not only a source of revenue, but a profitable occupation. Why this prohibition should endure in these days of (what they term) "free trade" seems odd. Notwithstanding this veto upon the cultivation of the tobacco plant in this country, it has been frequently attempted with profit. It is thus noticed in Pepys' Diary : "19th Sep. 1667.—Comes my cosen, Kate Joyce. . . She tells me how the Life-guard, which we thought a little while since was sent down into the country about some insurrection, was sent to Winchcombe [a market-town in Gloucestershire] to spoil the tobacco there, which, it seems, the people there do plant contrary to law, and have always done, and still been under force and danger of having it spoiled, as it hath been often-times, and yet they will continue to plant it. The place, she says, is a miserable poor place."—Pepys, vol. iv. p. 199.

The present version of a very popular song is from a broadside copy "printed by J. Catnach, 2 Monmouth Court, Seven Dials," bearing this additional information: "Shops supplied very cheap. Sold by W. Marshall, Bristol. Sold by Pierce, Southborough." A nearly similar version occurs, under the title of "The Indian Weed; or a true moral between a man's life and a pipe of tobacco," in "the New Academy of Compliments," Glasgow, 1789, 12mo. The order of the stanzas, and several of the phrases differ in a slight degree. The last stanza runs thus:

> "The ashes that are left behind
> Is for to put us all in mind,
> That we came from dust,
> And return we must,
> Think on this when you smoke tobacco."

An earlier version, with the music, will be found in Durfey's "Pills to Purge Melancholy," 1719, vol. iii. There are also some differences, the most noticeable of which is this stanza which Durfey places last:

> "The smoak that does so high ascend,
> Shows you man's life must have an end;
> The vapour's gone,
> Man's life is done,
> *Think of this and take tobacco.*"

The version which we print as follows is still earlier. It is from a MS. in the possession of Mr Collier. It bears the initials G. W. at the end, which the editor, in Miller's "Fly Leaves," first series, 1854, considers to be "George Withers," adding: "Like Milton, Withers indulged in the luxury of smoking; and many of his evenings in Newgate (during his long imprisonment), when weary of numbering his steps or telling the panes of glass, were solaced with 'meditations over a pipe,' not without a grateful acknowledgement of God's mercy in thus wrapping up 'a blessing in a weed.'"

Another version will be found in Rimbault's "Little Book of Songs and Ballads," Lond., 1851, "from a broadside with the music, printed at London, 1670." "It is also found," continues the Editor, in "Merry Drollery Compleat, 1670, and in 'two Broadsides against Tobacco,' the first given by King James of famous memory, his Counterblast to Tobacco; the second transcribed out of that learned Physician Dr Edward Maynewaring, his Treatise of the Scurvy, 4to, Lond., 1672." In the same "Little Book" will be found: 1st "the praise of Trinidado, from Weelkes' Ayres or Phantasticke Spirites, 1608;" 2d "Tobacco's a Musician, from a MS. set of Part-books in the handwriting of Thomas Weelkes, 1609," inserted in Holidays' Texnotamia, or the Marriage of the Arts, 1618. 3d "Ale and Tobacco, from Ravenscroft's Brief Discourse, 1614." 4th "The Triumph of Tobacco, from an old volume

of songs, with the music, temp. Charles II.," which, with some material
differences, will be found under the title of "The Triumph of Tobacco
over Sack and Ale," in the Musarum Deliciæ, vol. ii. Lond. 1817, 8vo,
reprinted from the third volume of Old Ballads, Lond. 1725, 12mo.
This, by the way.

Why should we so much despise,
So good and wholesome an exercise,
     As early and late
     To meditate ;
Thus think and drink tobacco.

The earthen pipe so lily white,
Shows that thou art a mortal wight,
     Even such,
     And gone with a small touch ;
Thus think and drink tobacco.

And when the smoke ascends on high,
Think on the worldly vanity
     Of worldly stuff,
     'Tis gone with a puff;
Thus think and drink tobacco.

And when the pipe is foul within,
Think how the soul's defiled with sin,
     To purge with fire,
     It doth require ;
Thus think and drink tobacco.

Lastly, the ashes left behind,
May slowly show to move the mind,
     That to ashes and dust
     Return we must ;
Thus think and drink tobacco.

It has been alleged that this song of "Tobacco" is the production of
Moses Brown, originally a pencutter, but who subsequently entered into
holy orders under the patronage of Hervey, author of the Meditations,
and became Vicar of Olney in Bucks, and Chaplain to Morden College.
He was the author of a tragedy called "Polidus," a farce called "All-be-
devilled," and a Poem called "Sunday Thoughts," &c., but as it is evident
from the preceding quotations that versions of this popular song were
current towards the end of the seventeenth century, it is utterly impos-

sible that Moses Brown could have been the author, he having been born
in 1703. Mr J. H. Dixon has introduced a version in his "Ancient
Poems, Ballads, and Songs," Edited for the Percy Society in 1846, with
this observation: "This song is a mere adaptation of a portion of the
Rev. Ebenezer [Ralph?] Erskine's poem, *Smoking Spiritualized*, which
we give at page 37 of the present work." "Ralph Erskine," as he
informs us, "was born at Monilaws, in the county of Northumberland,
on the 15th of March 1685."

Tobacco.

Tobacco is an Indian weed,
Grows green in the morn, cut down in eve,
　　It shows our decay,
　　We came from the clay;
Think of this when you're smoking tobacco.

The pipe that is so lily white,
In which most men take great delight,
　　It's broke with a touch,
　　Men's lives are such;
Think of this when you're smoking tobacco.

The pipe that is so foul within.
It shows men's souls are stain'd with sin,
　　For it doth require
　　To be cleansed by the fire;
Think of this when you're smoking tobacco.

The smoke that from the pipe doth fly,
It shows we are nothing but vanity,
　　For it's gone with a puff,
　　Like all earthly stuff;
Think of this when you're smoking tobacco.

The dust that from the pipe doth fall,
It shows we are nothing but dust at all,
　　For we came from the dust,
　　And return we must,
Think of this when you're smoking tobacco.

A Catch on Tobacco,

Sung by Four Men Smoking their Pipes.

"From Bacchus and Venus," 1737.

Good, good indeed ;
The herb's good weed;
Fill thy pipe, Will,
And I prithee, Sam, fill,
And yet sing still,
And yet sing still,
What say the learn'd?
What say the learn'd?
Vita fumus, vita fumus.
    'Tis what you and I,
    And he and I,
    You, and he, and I,
    And all of us *sumus.*
But then to the learned say we again,
If life's a smoke as they maintain;
If life's a vapour without doubt,
    When a man does die,
    He should not cry,
That his glass is run but his pipe is out.
But whether we smoke or whether we sing,
Let's be loyal and remember the King,
Let him live, and let his foes vanish thus, thus, thus,
Like, like a pipe, like a pipe of Spanish, thus, thus, thus,
    A pipe of Spanish !

THE PIPE OF TOBACCO.

THIS song bears the imprint of "W. J. Shelmerdine," and its date is about 1794. On the subject of the tobacco pipe a very clever song appeared in an Edinburgh newspaper some few years ago. It was called "The Cutty." It consisted of seventeen stanzas, of which the following are a specimen :—

> " When nobs come oot to walk aboot,
> And show their shapes to leddies ;
> They're ne'er withoot their grand cheroot,
> For that they think well bred is.
>
> And when they meet—no in the street,
> But aiblins ower a meal like—
> Then oot they draw a merschaum braw,
> An' that looks real genteel like.
>
> Weel ! there's nae ban on ony man,
> Let him be braw or sootie ;
> I'll no debar their grand cigar,
> But I'll haud to my cutty.
>
> . . . .
>
> The winter's blast, aft gey an fast,
> Blaws your genteel cigar oot ;
> My cutty's fire, wi' tap o' wire,
> Burns no a grain the waur o't.
>
> . . . .
>
> So now I'll ripe my cutty pipe,
> And bauldly face rude Boreas ;
> And, as I fill, ower ilka ill,
> I'll still haud on victorious."

Snuff-taking does not now prevail in any great degree—the more extended taste for smoking having superseded it. The following "Epigram on Snuff-taking," from a MS. collection of the middle of last century purchased some time ago at an auction in Leicester Square, is curious, and is worthy of preservation as recording the practice, now happily exploded, of those of the gentler sex indulging in snuff. It is a well-known fact that the spouse of George III. was addicted to this filthy habit—a circumstance which caused his majesty to speak of her by the elegant appellation of " Snuffy Charlotte."

> Whatever apes there are of Indian breed,
> In apish tricks some people them exceed ;
> Witness that odious and indecent fashion
> Of smutty snuffy noses in our nation.
> When Tonsor hath used all the art he knew,
> To smooth, to sweeten, and set out a beau ;
> Then straight out comes a box of stinking dust,
> 'Cause others do bedaub their face, he must.
> Cœlia, the fair, both paints and pulves her hair,
> And her unseemly parts all covered are ;

Yet open and exposed is one foul place,
Her nose besnuffed—the scandal of her face ;
Yet Cœlia like an angel is adorned—
What whim then cause her make herself deformed ?
Who would pretend a graceful look to prize,
And yet this nasty fashion idolize ?

The Pipe of Tobacco.

Why should life in sorrow be spent,
    When pleasure points out the road
Wherein each traveller with content
    May throw off the ponderous load ?

And instead, in ample measure,
    Gather fruits too long left ripe ;
What's this world without its pleasure ?
    What is pleasure bot a pipe ?

See the sailor's jovial state,
    Mark the soldier's noble soul ;
What does heroes renovate ?
    What refines the splendid bowl ?

Is it not tobacco dear,
    That from the brow fell grief can wipe ?
Yes ! like them with jolly cheer,
    I find pleasure in a pipe.

Some are who are fond of grief,
    Some take pleasure in sad strife,
Some pursue a false belief,
    Few there are that enjoy life.

Some delight in envy ever,
    Others avaricious gripe ;
Would you know our greatest pleasure ?
    'Tis a glowing social pipe.

𝔥unting 𝔖ong.

This Song is from "Cephalus and Procris."—A Dramatic Masque, with a Pantomime Interlude, called "Harlequin Grand Volgi," acted at Drury Lane, 8vo, 1733.
Reprinted in "Songs of the Chase," Lond. 1811, 12mo, with the omission of the second stanza.

Hark, away! tis the merry-ton'd horn,
Calls the hunters all up with the morn ;
To the hills and the woodlands we steer,
To unharbour the out-lying deer ;

CHORUS.

And all the day long, this, this is our song,
Still hollowing and following so frolick and free ;
Our joys know no bounds, while we're after the hounds,
No mortals on earth are so happy as we—

And when in the woodlands we are,
We'll follow then closely the deer,
Our hounds have a scent of the game,
The huntsman still winds for the same,
    CHORUS—And all the day long, &c.

Round the woods when we beat, how we glow !
While the hills they echo, hillo !
With a bounce from his cover he flies,
Then our shouts they go round to the skies.
    CHORUS—And all the day long, &c.

When we sweep over the vallies, or climb
Up the health-breathing mountain sublime,
What a joy from our labours we feel !
Which alone they who taste can reveal.
    CHORUS—And all the day long, &c.

At night when our labour is done,
Then we'll go hollowing home,
With hollo! hollo! and huzzay!
Resolving to meet the next day.
CHORUS—And all the day long &c.

The Fisherman's Song.

From "A new Academy of Compliments, or the Complete English
Secretary, with a collection of Playhouse Songs," Glasgow 1789, 16mo.
In the preface to the reader, the Editor in pointing out the several per-
fections of his book goes on to say: "To which are added, for the
better recreation of the reader, many curious new songs, greatly in request
at court, playhouses, and balls, and in general, graceful to the city and
country." This song has been reprinted in "Songs of the Chase," 12mo.
London, 1811. It is the production of Thomas Durfey, and will be found
in the first part of his play of Massaniello. He has also printed it with
the music, set by Mr Leveridge, in the first volume of his "Songs Complete, Pleasant, and Divertive," 1719.

Of all the world's enjoyments
    That ever valued were,
There's none of our employments
    With fishing can compare;
Some preach, some write,
Some swear, some fight,
    All golden lucre courting;
But fishing still bears off the bell,
    For profit or for sporting,
Then who a jolly fisherman, a fisherman would be,
    His throat must wet,
    Just like his net,
To keep out cold at sea.

The country squire loves running
    A pack of well mouthed hounds;
Another fancies gunning
    For wild ducks in his grounds;

This hunts, that fowls,
This hawks, Dick bowls,
  No greater pleasure wishing ;
But Tom that tells
What sport excels,
  Gives all the praise to fishing.
      Then who, &c.

A good Westphalia gammon,
  Is counted dainty fare,
But what is that to salmon,
  Just taken from the Ware?
Wheat ears and quails,
Cocks, snipes, and rayles,
  Are priz'd while season's lasting ;
But all must stoop
To crawfish soup,
  Or I've no skill in tasting.
      Then who, &c.

Keen hunters always take to
  Their prey with too much pains ;
Nay, often break a neck too,
  A penance for no brains :
They run, they leap,
Now high, now deep,
  Whilst he that fishing chooses
With ease may do't,
Nay, more to boot,
  May entertain the Muses,
      Then who, &c.

And tho' some envious wranglers,
  To jeer us will make bold,
And laugh at patient anglers,
  Who stand so long i' th' cold ;

They wait on Miss,
We wait on this,
   And think it easy labour ;
And if you'd know
Fish profits too,
   Consult our Holland neighbour.
      Then who, &c.

THE JOLLY ANGLERS.

FROM the press of "J. Pitts, Printer, 6 Great St. Andrew Street, 7
Dials."—A reprint, no doubt, of a Ballad of the last Century.   A copy,
with some differences, will be found in "Songs of the Chase," London
1811, 12mo.

   The following verses in the Praise of Angling, were, according to
Miller's Fly Leaves, 2d series, 1855, found in a copy of Colonel Venable's
Angler 1662, and signed "Nagrom Notpoh," *i.e.*, Morgan Hopton.
These may come in not inappropriately here :—

      Cards, dices, and tables pick thy purse,
      Drinking and drabing bring a curse,
      Hawking and hunting spends the chink,
      Bowling and shooting ends in drink.

      The fighting cock and the horse race,
      Will sink a good estate apace,
      Angling doth bodyes exercise,
      And maketh soules holy and wise.

      By blessed thoughts and meditation,
      This, this is angler's recreation ;
      Health, profit, pleasure, mixt together,
      All sport's to this not worth a feather.

The Jolly Anglers.

   Oh ! the jolly anglers' life
      Is the best of any ;

It is a fancy void of strife
And belov'd by many.
It is no crime at any time,
But an harmless pleasure;
It is a bliss
Of lawfulness,
It is a joy,
Not a toy,
It is a skill
That breeds no ill,
It is sweet
And compleat
Adoration to the mind,
It is witty, pretty, decent, pleasant pastime,
We shall sweetly find,
If the weather proves but kind,
We shall have our leisure.

In the morning up we start
Soon as daylight's peeping,
We take a cup to cheer our heart,
And leave the sluggard sleeping.
Forth we walk, in merry talk,
To some pleasant river
Near the Thames'
Silver streams;
With our hook,
Near the brook,
There we stand,
Rod in hand,
Fixing right
For a bite.
All the time the fish allure,
Come leaping, skipping, bobbing, biting,
Dangling at our hooks secure,
With this pastime, sweet and pure,
We could fish for ever.

As we walk the meadows green,
 Where the fragrant air is,
Where the object's to be seen
 Oh ! what pleasure there is.
Birds do sing and flowers spring
 Full of delectation,
  Whistling breeze
  Runs thro' the trees :
  There we meet
  Meadows sweet,
  Flowers find
  To our mind :
  It is a scene
  So serene
From the sweet refreshing bowers,
Living, giving, easing, pleasing vital powers,
 From those herbs and flowers
 Raised by those falling showers
 For man's recreation.

Through the shady forest
 Where the horn is sounding,
Hound and huntsman roving,
 There is sport abounding.
A hideous noise is all their joys
 Not to be admired :
  When we fish
  To gain a dish,
  With our hook
  In the brook,
  Watch our float !
  Spare our throat,
While they are sweltering to and fro,
Tantivee ! Tantivee !
 The horns loudly blow,
 Hounds and huntsmen all of a row,
 With their pastime fired.

We have gentles in our horns,
  We have worms and paste too ;
We have coats to stand a storm,
  We've baskets at our waists too.
We have line, choice of twine
  Fitting for our angle.
      If 'tis so,
      Away we go
      Seeking out
      For roach or trout,
      Eel or pike,
      Or the like,
      Dace or bleak
      There we leak,
    Barbell, jack, or many more,
Gudgeon, roaches, perches, tenches,
    Here's the jolly angler's store,
    We have choice of fish galore,
    We will have our angling.

If the sun's excessive heat,
  Should our bodies swelter,
To bush or hedgerow we'll retreat
  For a friendly shelter.
If we spy a shower nigh,
  Or the day uncertain ;
      Then we flee
      Beneath the tree,
      There we eat
      Victuals sweet,
      Take a coge,
      Smoke and foge.
    If we can no longer stay,
We go laughing, joking, quaffing, smoking,
    So delightful all the way,
    Thus we conclude the day
    With a cup at parting.

S

To Know each Fish's Haunt.

From "*The Secrets of Angling*, by J. D. (John Davors), augmented by W. Lauson. Printed for Frances Coles, 1652."

Now that the angler may the better know
    Where he may find each fish he may require ;
Since some delight in waters still and slow,
    And some do love the mud and slimy mire ;
Some others where the stream doth swiftly flow,
    Some stoney ground, and gravel some desire ;
        Here shall ye learn how every sort doth seeke
        To haunt the layre that doth his nature like.

Carp, Eele, and Tench do love a muddy ground,
    Eeles under stones or hollow roots do lie,
The Tench among thick weeds is soonest found,
    The fearful Carp into the deep doth flie,
Bream, Chub, and Pike, where clay and sand abound,
    Pike loves great pooles, and places full of frie :
        The Chub delights in stream or shady tree,
        And tender Bream in broadest lake to be !

The Salmon swift the rivers sweet doth like,
    Where largest streams into the sea are led,
And spotted Trout the smaller brooke doth seeke,
    And in the deepest hole there hides his head,
The prickled Perch in every hollow creek,
    Hard by the banke and sandy shore is fed,
        Perch, Trout, and Salmon love clean waters all,
        Green weedy-roots, and stoney gravel small.

So doth the Bullhead, Gudgion, and the Loch,
    Who most in shallow brooks delight to be ;
The Ruffe, the Dace, the Barbell, and the Roch,
    Gravell and sand do love in less degree,

But to the deep and shade do more approach,
   And over head some covert love to see
   Of spreading poplar, oake, or willow green,
   Where underneath they lurke for being seene.

The mighty Luce great waters haunts alway,
   And in the stillest place thereof doth lie,
Save when he rangeth forth to seek his prey,
   And swift among the fearful fish do flie ;
The dainty Humber loves the marley clay,
   And clearest streams of champion country nigh.
     And in the chiefest pooles thereof doth rest,
     Where he is soonest found, and taken best.

The Cavender amidst the waters faire,
   In swiftest streams doth most himself bestow,
The Shad and Tweat do rather like the laire
   Of brackish waves, where it doth ebb and flow,
And thither also doth the Fleck repaire,
   And flat upon the bottom lieth low.
     The Peele, the Mullet, and the Suants good
     Do like the same, and therein seek their food.

But here experience doth my skill exceed,
   Since divers countries divers rivers have,
And divers rivers change of waters breed,
   And change of waters sundry fish do crave,
And sundry fish in divers places feed,
   As best doth like them in the liquid wave.
     So that by use and practice may be known
     More than by art or skill can well be shown.

So then it shall be needless to declare
   What sundry kinds there lie in secret store,
And where they do resort, and what they are,
   That may be still discovered more and more ;

Let him that list no pain nor trouble spare
To seek them out as I have done before,
And then it shall not discontent his minde,
How choice of place and change of game to finde.

A Ballad of the Seventeenth Century.

THE following Ballad was communicated under the above title to a Scotch newspaper of date November 1823, by a correspondent subscribing himself O. F. It is stated to have been "found lately, written on the Fly-leaf of an old copy of 'The Whole Duty of Man.'" While entertaining grave doubts of its alleged antiquity, we insert the Ballad as being clever enough of its kind, and as a contribution towards the chronicles of the salmon—a fish which has formed the subject of more legal enactments for its preservation than even poor human nature itself.

Some very curious particulars of the habits of the salmon may be found in "The Art of Angling. London, 1743," 12mo., for which see Appendix.

In the Quarterly Review also several papers respecting the salmon have occasionally occurred. The statistical portion of these papers, on which their chief value rests, were the result of investigations made for a long series of years by the late Mr William Paulin, Manager of the Berwick Shipping Company (or more properly, Fishing Company) Berwick-on-Tweed. The death of this gentleman was very striking.—He had been undergoing an examination by a Committee of the House of Commons on one of the Tweed Fishery Bills, and upon leaving the Committee Room, he suddenly expired.

THE salmon fish is a lordly fish,
It lo'es the stream that's wide ;
But I wadna' be the proud salmon,
For a' the waves of Clyde.

For then when ta'en by the wiley fisher ;
I wad be sent to the Broomielaw,
And bought, and boiled, and ta'en to fill
A Glasgow Merchant's maw.

In a Glasgow Merchant's swollen paunch
Sae comfartley to swim,
Whilst the deepening seas o' cauld rum punch,
Rise to the very brim.*

But I wad be the little trout
That swims the narrow Gryffe,
And then to a gentle lover's haun
I might resign my life.

And he wad send me hame to the ane,
The ane that he lo'es weel,
And as I wad be a dainty fish
She wad eat me a' hersell.

And think na ye I wad be proud
When she fixed her sparkling e'e on me?
And think ye na it would be sweet,
When her lips sae red were pressed to me?

When I was served on her siller dish,
Oh, I wad speak to that lady bright;
" Oh, lady fair, beyond compare,
When my banes are picked they're not useless quite.

" My gude back bane, wi' a' its ribs,
Will mak a kame for your yellow hair ;
And my head will haud your sharp bodkins ;
And my teeth will mak a necklace rare.

" Ye may spangle a' your silken gown
Wi' the siller scales frae aff my skin ;
And my skin itsell will mak a purse,
To haud the siller pennies in."

---

* " This stanza must be interesting to the antiquary, from its showing
the antiquity of what it refers to."

The Angler's Life.

Tune—The Banks of Indermay.

This and the song which follows are from "The Art of Angling, Rock and Sea-Fishing: with the Natural History of River, Pond, and Sea Fish. Illustrated with 133 Cuts, London, 1743," 12mo. The author in his Preface introduces them thus: "As it is usual in books of Angling to insert Poetical Amusements, two of my friends, who are well known to the Publick on account of their ingenious performances, have been at the pains to compose the following lines for that purpose."—The first is subscribed M. B. the second J. D.

When vernal airs perfume the fields,
And pleasing views the landskip yields:
The limpid stream, the scaly breed,
Invite the angler's waving reed.
The musing swain what pleasures seize;
The talking brook, the sighing breeze,
The active insect's buzzing wing,
And birds that tuneful ditties sing.

At latest eve, at early dawn,
The angler seeks the scented lawn,
And roams, to snare the finny brood,
The margin of the flow'ry flood.
Now at some osier's wat'ry root
The Chub beguiles, or painted Trout;
No cares nor noise his senses drown,
His pastime, ease and silence crown.

Adieu, ye sports of noise of toil
That crowds in senseless strife embroil;
The Jockey's mirth, the Huntsman's train,
Debauch of health, and waste of gain.
More mild delights my life employ,
The angler's unexpensive joy.
Here I can sweeten fortune's frowns,
Nor envy kings the bliss of crowns.

The Pleasures of Angling.

Tune—All in the Downs, &c.

An altered version of this song to another tune occurs in "Songs of the Chase," 12mo, London, 1811.

ALL in the fragrant prime of day,
  Ere Phœbus spreads around her beams,
The early angler takes his way
  To verdant banks of crystal streams.
If health, content, and thoughtful musing charm,
What sport like angling can our cares disarm?

There ev'ry sense delight enjoys,
  Zephyr with odours loads his wing ;
Flora displays ten thousand dyes,
  And varied notes the warblers sing.
      If health, content, &c.

On the soft margin calmly plac'd,
  Pleas'd he beholds the finny brood
Thro' the transparent fluid haste,
  Darting along in quest of food.
      If health, content, &c.

The skilful angler opes his store,
  (Paste, worms, or flies his hook sustains,)
And quickly spreads the grassy shore
  With shining spoils that crown his pains.
      If health, content, &c.,

If some fierce show'r in floods descends,
  A gloomy grove's thick shade is near;
Whose grateful umbrage safe defends
  Till more inviting skies appear.
      If health, content, &c.

Those blissful thoughts his mind engage,
To crowded noisy scenes unknown ;
Wak'd by some Bard's instructive page,
Or calm reflexions all his own.
    If health, content, &c.

Thus, whether groves or meads he roams,
Or by the stream his angle tends ;
Pleasure in sweet succession comes,
And the sweet rapture never ends.
If health, content, and thoughtful musing charm,
What sport like angling can our cares disarm?

THE RURAL DANCE ABOUT THE MAY-POLE.

Tune—The First-figure Dance.

THIS spirited song is, with exception of the last stanza, from "Bacchus and Venus ; or a select collection of near 200 of the most witty and diverting Songs and Catches in Love and Gallantry," Lond. 12mo, 1737.

The last stanza we find in a copy of the Ballad in "Poems collected by the Right Honourable Lady Aston," which were preserved with other MSS. found in the library at Tixall, under the title of "The Tixall Poetry." This volume was printed at Edinburgh in quarto, 1813, and was edited by Arthur Clifford, the joint-editor with Sir Walter Scott of Sadler's State Papers. These "Poems," collected by Lady Aston, had been copied some time about the middle of the seventeenth century. The Astons had formerly been proprietors of Tixall, or "Tick's Hall," in Staffordshire, and at the time when "the Tixall Poetry" made its appearance, it was in possession of Mr Clifford's elder brother. Dr Rimbault prints the song with the last stanza in "a little Book of Songs and Ballads, gathered from ancient Musick Books, MS. and printed," Lond. 1851, cr. 8vo. He states that his copy "is given from a MS. collection of songs, with the music, written about the middle of the seventeenth century, and formerly in the library of Staunton Harold, Leicestershire, the seat of Earl Ferrers ;" adding, that "it differs materially from a copy printed in Westminster Drollery, the second part, 1672." He also takes occasion to correct Mr Dixon as to an assertion respecting the last stanza, by referring to the copy in the Tixall Poetry, and to the MS.

from which he prints. He characterises the version which Mr Dixon
has embodied in his "ancient Ballads and Songs of the Peasantry of
England" as a *corrupt modern* copy. This cannot be, as it is, with a
few slight verbal differences, similar to the text we now use. The remark which Mr Dixon makes, and which Dr Rimbault quotes as incor-
rect, is this : "The last verse in our copy is modern, and, we believe,
was written by a comic song writer, who, a few years ago, had the
impudence to palm the whole song off, on those who knew no better, as
his own composition." Before proceeding to call Mr Dixon to account,
the learned Doctor should have turned to the stanza in question, and, as
he would have found that it is altogether verbally different from that
which he himself has given, he would then have found no reason to
doubt Mr Dixon's assertion. The stanza adhibited to Mr Dixon's copy
is :—

> " Good night, says Harry,
> Good night, says Mary,
> Good night, says Dolly to John ;
> Good night, says Sue,
> Good night, says Hugh ;
> Good night, says every one.
> Some loitered on the way,
> And bound themselves with love-knots, love-knots,
> To meet the next holiday."

With reference to the mention of " Packington's Pound" and " Sellinger's Round," in the third stanza :—The music of "Sellinger's Round,"
i.e., St. Ledger's Round, or "the beginning of the world," is in Queen
Elizabeth's and Lady Neville's Virginal Books, and in some of the early
editions of the " Dancing Master." Sir John Hawkins refers to it as
" the oldest country-dance tune now extant." Several of the tunes in
Queen Elizabeth's Virginal Book appear to have been renamed from
countries or eminent men with whom they were in particular favour, as
had been the custom in her father's time.

Mr Chappell, while observing " it is difficult to say from which of the
ancient family of St Ledger it acquired its name," surmises with some
reason that "it was from Mr Anthony St Ledger, whom Henry the
Eighth appointed Lord-deputy of Ireland in 1540, and who was one of
the most active in the downfall of Cardinal Wolsey."

The figure employed in Sellinger's Round is thus described by Playford
in his " Dancing Master," 1686 :—

> " Round for as many as will.

Take hands, and go round twice, back again. All set, and turn S,
that again. Lead all in a D forward and back, that again. Two singles

and a D back, set and turn single, that again.   Sides all, that again.
Arms all, that again.   As before, as before."

Country dances were formerly as often danced in circles as in parallel
lines.

The tune of "Packington's or Pagginton's Pound" will also be found
in Queen Elizabeth's Virginal Book ; in "a new Book of Tablature,"
1596 ; in the "Collection of English Songs," printed at Amsterdam in
1634 ; in "Select Ayres," 1659 ; in "a choice collection of 180 Loyal
Songs," 1685 ; in Playford's "Pleasant Musical Companion," Part ii.,
1687 ; in "The Beggar's Opera," 1728 ; in "The Musical Miscellany,"
vol. v. ; and in many other collections.   Mr Chappell suggests that it
may have taken "its name from Sir John Packington, commonly called
'lusty Packington,' the same who wagered that he would swim from
Whitehall Stairs to Greenwich for the sum of £3000.   'But the good
Queen, who had particular tenderness for handsome fellows, would not
permit Sir John to run the hazard of the trial.'"

In Ben Jonson's "Bartholomew Fair," the song commencing, "My
masters and friends and good people draw near," is thus introduced :—
"Cokes. We shall find that in the matter ; pray thee, begin !
Night. To the tune of Pagginton's Pound, sir ?
Cokes. (Sings) Fa, la la la, la la la, fa, la la la ! Nay ! I'll put thee
in tune and all ! Mine own country dance ! Pray thee, begin."—
Act 3.

Referring to this, Mr Chappell suggests that "as Ben Jonson calls it
Pagginton's Pound, and as Thomas Pagginton was one of the musicians
retained in the service of the Protector Somerset on the death of Henry
VIII. (A.D. 1547), it was probably a country dance composed by him."
—See National English Airs, 4to, 1838.

To "jet it," in the same stanza, means to step or tread haughtily.
So in Shakespeare's Twelfth Night, Act 2, Scene 5—" Contemplation
makes a rare turkey-cock of him ; how he jets under his advanced
plumes."

Mr Dixon has remarked that the most correct copy of this song is the
one in the Westminster Drollery.   It is there called "The Rural dance
about the May-pole, the tune, the first figure-dance at Mr Young's ball,
May 1761."

This "rural song" was introduced some few years ago in one of the
very clever pantomimes annually produced at the Theatre Royal, Edinburgh, under Mrs Wyndham's superintendence.   It was sung by a party
of children attired as haymakers, and was followed by a characteristic
dance.   The effect was excellent, and the air, which will be found in
Chappell's National English Airs, became popular for a time.   The
air, with the words of the first, fourth, and sixth stanzas merely (occasionally verbally different) is also in Durfey's Pills, vol. iii., 1719.   We
give the Tixall differences below.

The Rural Dance about the May-pole.

1.   Come lasses and lads,
Take leave of your dads,
And away to the May-pole, hye ;
For every he
Has gotten a she,
With a minstrill standing by ;
For Will has gotten his Jill,
And Johnny has gotten his Joan,
To jigg it, jigg it, jigg it, jigg it,
Jigg it up and down.

2.   " Strike up," says Wat,
" Agreed," says Kate,*
" And I prithee, fiddler, play ;"
" Content," says Hodge,
" So," says Madge,
" For this is a holiday."
Then every man did put
His hat off to his lass,†
And every girl did curtsie,
Curtsie, curtsie on the grass.

3.   " Begin," says Hal,
" Ay, ay," says Mall,
We'll lead up Packington's pound ;
" No, no," says Noll,
" And so," says Doll,
" We'll first have Sellinger's round."
Then every man began to foot it round about ;
And every girl did jet it, jet it, jet it in and out.

4.   " You're out," says Dick ;
" 'Tis a lie !" says Nick,

---

* " Matt."   † Then every lad did doff
His hat unto his lass.

"The fiddler played it false ;"
"'Tis true," says Hugh,
And so says Sue,
And so says nimble Al'ce.*
The fiddler then began to play the tune again,
And every girl did trip it, trip it, trip it to the men.

5.   "Let's kiss," says Jane,
"Content," says Nan,
And so says every she ;
"How many?" says Batt,
"Why three," says Matt,
"For that's a maiden's fee ;"
But they instead of three did give them half a score,
And they in kindness gave 'em, gave 'em, gave 'em as
many more.†

6.   Then after an hour
They went to a bow'r,
And play'd for ale and cakes,
And kisses too,
Until they were due
The lasses kept the stakes.
The girls did then begin to quarrel with the men,
And bid them take their kisses back, and give 'em their
own again.

7.   Yet there they sat
Until it was late,
And tir'd the fiddler quite ;
With singing and playing,
Without any paying,
From morning until night.
They told the fiddler then they'd pay him for his play,
And each a twopence, twopence, twopence gave him,
and went away.

* Joyce.   † "Kindness," thrice—"gave 'em" only once.

" Good night," says Tom,
And so says John,
" Good night," says Dick to Will ;
" Good night," says Sis,
" Good night," says Pris,
" Good night," says Peg to Nell.
Some ran, some went, some stay'd, some dallied by the way,
And bound themselves by kisses twelve to meet next holiday.

The Country Man's Delight.

THIS will be found in "Pills to Purge Melancholy," vol. iv., with music.

Mr Chappell, in his "Collection of National English Airs," before referred to, remarks:—" *Under the Greenwood Tree* is to be found in the *Dancing Master*, generally in 6-4 time. Its popularity caused it to be introduced into *The Devil to Pay, The Village Opera, The Jovial Crew, The Cobbler's Opera*, &c. From the similarity of the title of this song to that of Shakespeare's, in *As You Like It*, we were, at first, led to suppose that the tune might be the same to which those words were sung, before Dr Arne composed the one now adopted; but a song in *Durfey's Pills to Purge Melancholy*, called the 'Countryman's Delight,' appears to be the original. In a collection in 1590, reprinted by Andro Hart in 1621, under the title of 'Ane Compendious Booke of Godly and Spiritual Songs,' &c., one of the songs, ot which the first lines are preserved, is ' Hay, trim goe trix, *under the greenwood tree.*'"

This "godly song" has been partially quoted by Sir Walter Scott in his historical novel, "The Abbot," and it will be found in its entirety in the reprint of the 1578 edition of this "Compendious Booke," admirably edited by David Laing, Esq., LL.D., 12mo., Edin. 1868— a work of the greatest interest to the admirers of old Scotish literature. The rhythm of the song resembles as nearly as possible that of "The Countryman's Delight," so that the music of the latter might, with a very slight variation, be adapted to it, while the rhythm of Shakespeare's song will not admit of such adaptation.

"The beginning of the world" alluded to in the third stanza is "Sellinger's round," of which we have just treated. The origin of this second title is thus accounted for in the comedy of Lingua, 1607:—

" *Anamnestes.* By the same token, the first time the planets played, I remember Venus the treble ran sweet division upon Saturn the bass. The first tune they played was *Sellenger's round*, in memory whereof, ever since, it hath been called *the beginning of the world*."

IN summer time, when flowers do spring,
  And birds sit on a tree;
Let Lords and Knights say what they will,
  There's none so merry as we :
    There's Will and Moll,
    Here's Harry and Doll,
  With Brian and bonny Betty ;
    Oh, how they did jerk it,
    Caper and ferk it,
  Under the greenwood tree.

Our musick in a little pipe,
  That can so sweetly play ;
Whom we do hire from whitsontide,
  Till latter Lammas-day :
    On Sabbath days,
    And Holy-days,
  After Evening-prayer comes he :
    And then, &c.

" Come play us Adam and Eve," says Dick,
  " What's that?" says little Pipe,
"It is the beginning o' th' world," quoth Dick,
  For we are Dancing-ripe :
    It's that ye call,
    There have at all,
  He plaid with a merry glee :
    O then, &c.

In comes our Gaffer Underwood,
  And sets him on the Bench ;
His wife and daughter ne'er-be-good,
  That pretty round-faced wench :

There's neighbour chuck,
And Habakkuk,
They all come here to see:
O how, &c.

From thence we go to Sir William's ground,
And a rich old Cub is he;
And there we dance around, around,
But the devil a penny we see :
From thence we get
To Sommerset,
Where men be frolick and free:
And there, &c.

THE SECOND PART.

My Lord's son must not be forgot,
So full of merry jest ;
He laughs to see the girls so hot,
And jumps in with the rest :
He doth them assail
With his Calves' tail,
And he thrusts it in to see
O how they do, &c.

A plague of all those shuffling knaves,
That do our sports despise :
We value not the sneaking slaves,
They're more precise than wise:
Bots on them all
Both great and small,
And such Hypocrisie ;
For we will, &c.

Tho' bonny Nell do bear the bell,
'Mongst gallants gay and brisk aye ;
Our Margery's as light as she,
And yet she is not frisky ;

When she with trusty Arthur meets,
　And Bob with Barnaby;
　　O how they do stump it,
　　Jigg it and jump it,
　Under the greenwood tree.

We fear no plots of Jews or Scots,
　For we are jolly swains;
With plow and cow and barley-mow
　We busie all our brains;
　　No city cares,
　　Nor merchant's fears,
　Of wreck or Piracy;
　　Therefore we can flaunt it,
　　Revel and rant it,
　Under the greenwood tree.

O'er Hills and Dales, and Whitson-ales,
　We dance a merry fit;
When Susan sweet with John doth meet,
　She gives him hit for hit;
　　From head to foot,
　　She holds him to't,
　And jumps as high as he;
　　O how they do spring it,
　　Flounce it and fling it,
　Under the greenwood tree.

With ribbond red in hat or head,
　Young Ralph to skip doth haste;
Joan has a new long scarf of blue,
　That reaches to her waist:
　　With Petticoats,
　　As light at motes,
　Which in the sun we see;
　　O! how they did skip it,
　　Trample and trip it,
　Under the greenwood tree.

No time is spent with more content,
  In City, Court, or Camp ;
We fear no Covent-Garden gout,
  Or Pickadilly cramp ;
    From scurvy we
    Are always free,
  And evermore shall be ;
    So long as we whisk it,
    Jigg it and frisk it,
  Under the greenwood tree.

On meads and lawns we trip like fawns,
  Like fillies, kids, or lambs ;
We have no twinge to make us cringe
  Or crinkle in the hams :
    When some disease
    Doth on us seize,
  With one consent go we;
    To jigg it and jerk it,
    Caper and ferk it,
  Under the greenwood tree.

When we're well fir'd, and almost tir'd,
  That night is drawing on ;
And that we must confess (as just)
  Our dancing day is done :
    The night is spent,
    In sweet content,
  Dreaming once more that we
    Merrily sport it,
    Kiss it and court it,
  Under the greenwood tree.

T

𝕿𝖍𝖊 𝕻𝖔𝖆𝖈𝖍𝖊𝖗.

From a Broadside " Printed by J. Catnach, 2 Monmouth Street, 7 Dials. Battledores, Lotteries, and Primers sold cheap. Sold by Marshall, Bristol, and Hook, Brighton."

Mr Chappell has this song, with some slight variations, in his National English Airs. It is there titled "The Lincolnshire Poacher," and Lincolnshire is the locality throughout. In the generally accepted version as usually sung, the locality is placed in a more southern county, thus :—

"When I was boon apprentice 'twas down in Zomersetshire," &c.

The air in Mr Chappell's book is styled " In the season of the year," and he remarks : "In the season of the year, sometimes called The Poacher's Song, the date or origin of which it is difficult to trace ; but so well known among the peasantry, that it has been sung by several hundred voices together at Windsor, at the harvest-homes of George the Fourth."

Mr W. T. Moncrieff, (now deceased,) the author of many successful dramatic pieces, introduced this song with additions into an operatic drama called "Van Dieman's Land," which was produced at the Surrey theatre under Elliston's management some forty years ago. In the printed edition (1831) this note occurs : "The author of this drama first heard the old part of this song sung at a small roadside house in the little village of Lillishul, Warwickshire ; and was so pleased with the humour and melody of it, that he was induced to add half a dozen new verses to it. This is the first time it has appeared in a complete state." The " moral," which forms the concluding stanza of Mr Moncrieff's version, is clever :—

"Vhat made me vond of powching vurst,
    If you vould vish to hear,
It was becase I vound that beef
    And mutton were so dear.
Vhile I get geam and venzon cheap,
    Which is a reazon clear ;
Oh ! 'twas ma delyght in a zhiny night,
    In the zeazon o' the year.
        Oh ! 'twas," &c.

Mr Moncrieff fixes his locale in Zomersetshire.

When I was bound apprentice in fam'd Northamptonshire,
I served my master truly for almost seven year,
Then I took up to poaching, as you shall quickly hear ;
Oh! it's my delight of a shiney night, in the season of the year.

THE FOX. 291

As me and my comrades were setting of a snare,
The game-keeper was awatching us—for him we did not care;
For we can wrestle,—fight, my boys,—jump over anywhere;
For it's my delight of a shiney night, in the season of the year.

As me and my companions were setting four or five,
And taking of them up again, we took the hare alive;
We popt him into the bag, my boys, and through the wood did steer; [year.
For it's my delight in a shiney night, in the season of the

We threw him over our shoulders and wandered through the town,
Called into a neighbour's house, and sold him for a crown;
We sold him for a crown, my boys, but did not tell you where;
For it's my delight in a shiney night, in the season of the year.

Well! here's success to poaching, for I do not think it fair,
Bad luck to every gamekeeper that would not sell his deer,
Good luck to every gamekeeper that wants to buy a hare;
For it's my delight in a shiney night, in the season of the year.

THE FOX.

THIS ballad is certainly upwards of forty years old. It appears to have
been rescued from its fugitive form, and embodied in a small collection
of songs printed at Edinburgh "for Joseph Skeafe, 3 South Hanover
Street, 1832," under the title of "The Opera, or Cabinet of Song," and
believed to have been edited by the Scotish poet, James Ballantyne, author
of "the Gaberlunzie's wallet." There is a version of "the Fox" printed
in the 10th volume of Notes and Queries, 4to, 1854, where it is given
as "an old Cornish song," and is titled "The Fox's nightly foraging
tour." Whether it is the original version is not very clear. The differ-

ences, which are chiefly verbal, are generally immaterial. The last
stanza has not the repeated line ; thus :—

> " The fox and his wife they had such strife,
> They never ate a better goose in all their life ;
> They tore it abroad without fork or knife,
> And the little ones pick'd the bones, O !"

The Fox.

The fox he went out one cold winter night,
And he pray'd to the moon to give him some light,
For he had a long way to travel that night
　Before he could reach the town, O !
　　Town, O ! town, O !
For he had a long way, &c.

At length he arrived at the farmer's yard,
For the ducks and the geese he was not afeard,
He swore that the best of them would grease his beard
　Before he would leave the town, O !
　　Town, O ! &c.

He seized the grey goose by the neck,
He threw him astride across his back,
Which made the grey goose cry quack ! quack !
　And the blood it came trickling down, O !
　　Down, O ! &c.

Old mother Slipperslopper jumped out of bed,
She opened the casement and popp'd out her head ;
" Get up, John, get up ! for the grey goose is dead,
　And the fox has been into the town, O !
　　Town, O !" &c.

So John he got up to the top of yon hill,
He sounded his bugle-horn both loud and shrill ;
" Blow on !" cried the fox, " that is better music still,
　For I'm glad I've got clear out of town, O !
　　Town, O !" &c.

When Reynard he had arrived on the plain,
He threw down his burden to ease a load of pain ;
He quickly took it up, and he travell'd on again,
    For he thought he heard the sound of the hounds, O !
        Hounds, O ! &c.

When Reynard he had arrived at his den,—
Of young ones he had nine or ten,—
" You're welcome, father fox, you must travel back again,
    For we think it's a lucky town, O !
        Town, O !" &c.

The fox and his wife they had some strife,
They tore up the grey goose without fork or knife ;
They tore up the grey goose without fork or knife,
    And the young ones picked the bones, O !
        Bones, O ! &c.

Drive the Cold Winter Away.

Reprinted from a Black Letter Copy in the Pepysian Collection ;
" Printed at London by H. G."—[Henry Gosson.]

The tune will be found in Playford's Dancing Master, also in Durfey's
Pills to Purge Melancholy, vol. iv., where the first five stanzas only are
given. These are reprinted in Chappell's National Airs.

It has also been reprinted in full in Dr Rimbault's Little Book of
Songs and Ballads, where it is titled "In Praise of Christmas." The
variations between this and Durfey's Copy, are given in footnotes.

ALL hail to the days that merit more praise
    Than all the rest of the year,
And welcome the nights that double* delights,
    As well for the poor as the peer !
Good Fortune attend each merry man's friend,
    That doth but the best that he may ;
Forgetting old wrongs, with carols and songs,†
    To drive the cold winter away.
        To drive, &c.

* Bring us.   † Forgetting old wrong with a cup and a song.

Let misery pack, with a whip at his back,
  To the deep Tantalian flood;*
In Lethe profound, let Envy be drown'd,
  That pines at another man's good ;
Let sorrow's expense be banded from hence,†
  All payments have greater delay,
We'll spend the long nights in cheerful delights,
  To drive the cold winter away.
          To drive, &c.

'Tis ill for a mind to anger‡ inclined,
  To think of small injuries now ;
If wrath be to seek, do not lend her thy cheek,
  Nor let her inhabit thy brow.
Cross out of thy books malevolent looks,
  Both beauty and youth's decay,§
And wholly consort, with mirth and with sport,
  To drive the cold winter away.
          To drive, &c.

The Court in her state, now opens her gate,‖
  And gives a free welcome to most ;¶
The city likewise, though somewhat precise,
  Doth willingly part with her roast ;**
But yet by report, from city and court,
  The country will e'er gain the day ;
More liquor is spent, and with better content,
  To drive the cold winter away.
          To drive, &c.

* Down to the Tartarian flood.
† Come a thousand years hence.   ‡ Envy.
§ All malcontent looks, though beauty and youth may decay.
‖ This and the succeeding stanza precede "'Tis ill for a mind," &c.
        " Now the Courtier in State sets open his gate."
    To all.   ** Will help both the great and the small.

Our good gentry there, for cost do not spare,
    The Yeomanry fast not till Lent;
The farmers and such, think nothing too much,
    If they keep but to pay for their rent.
The poorest of all now do merrily call,
    When at a fit place they can stay,
For a song or a tale or a cup of good ale,
    To drive the cold winter away.
            To drive, &c.

Thus none will allow of solitude now,
    But merrily greets the time,
To make it appear, of all the whole year,
    That this is accounted the prime;
December is seen, apparel'd in green,
    And January fresh as May
Comes dancing along, with a cup and a song,
    To drive the cold winter away.
            To drive, &c.

THE SECOND PART.

This time of the year is spent in good cheer,
    And neighbours together do meet,
To sit by the fire, with friendly desire,
    Each other in love to greet;
Old grudges forgot, are put in the pot,
    All sorrows aside they lay,
The old and the young doth carol this song,
    To drive the cold winter away.
            To drive, &c.

Sisley and Nanny, more jocund than any,
    As blithe as the month of June,
Do carol and sing, like birds of the spring,
    No Nightingale sweeter in tune,

To bring in content, when summer is spent,
   In pleasant delight and play,
With mirth and good cheer, to end the whole year,
   And drive the cold winter away.
            And drive, &c.

The shepherd, the swain, do highly disdain
   To waste out their time in care,
And Clim of the Clough* hath plenty enough,
   If he but a penny can spare
To spend at the night in joy and delight,
   Now after his labours all day,
For better than lands is the help of his hands,
   To drive the cold winter away.
            To drive, &c.

To mask and to mum kind neighbours will come,
   With wassels of nut-brown ale,
To drink and carouse, to all in the house,
   As merry as bucks in the dale ;
Where cake, bread and cheese, is brought for your fees,
   To make you the longer stay
At the fire to warm, will do you no harm,
   To drive the cold winter away.
            To drive, &c.

When Christmas's tide comes in like a bride,
   With holly and ivy clad,
Twelve days in the year, much mirth and good cheer,
   In every houschold is had ;
The country guise is then to devise,
   Some gambols of Christmas play,
Whereat the young men do the best that they can,
   To drive the cold winter away.
            To drive &c.

---

* Clim of the Clough, a once famous Archer in the North of England.
See the old ballad of Adam Bell, &c. in Percy.

When white bearded frost hath threatened his worst,
  And fallen from branch to briar,
Then time away calls from husbandry halls,
  And from the good countryman's fire,
Together to go to plow and to sow,
  To get us both food and array,
And thus with content the time we have spent,
  To drive the cold winter away.
      To drive &c.

He that will not Merry be.

FROM Ramsay's Tea-Table Miscellany, 1724.

He that will not merry, merry be,
  With a generous bowl and toast,
May he in Bridewell be shut up,
  And fast bound to a post:
Let him be merry, merry there,
  And we'll be merry, merry here;
For who can know where we shall go
  To be merry another year?

He that will not merry, merry be,
  And take his glass in course;
May he b' obliged to drink small beer,
  Ne'er a penny into his purse;
    Let him be merry, &c.

He that will not merry, merry be
  With a comp'ny of jolly boys,
May he be plagued with a scolding wife,
  To confound him with her noise;
    Let him be merry, &c.

He that will not merry, merry be
With a laughing bright-eyed maid,
Let him be bury'd in the churchyard,
And me put in his stead ;
Let him be merry, &c.

The Town Gallant's Song.

FROM "Bristol Drollery—Poems and Songs—London, Printed for Charles Allan, Bookseller in Bristol, 1674." The address, which is dedicated to "The Young Gallants," is subscribed N.C.—probably Nathaniel Crouch.

We are born, then cry,
We know not for why;
And all our lives long,
Still but the same song.

Our lives are but short,
We're made Fortune's sport.
We spend them in care,
In hunting the hare,

In tossing the pot,
In venturing our lot
At dice, when we play
To pass time away.

We dress our selves fine,
At noon we do dine ;
We walk then abroad,
Or ride on the road.

With women we dally,
Retreat and then rally ;
And then in our bed,
We lay down our head.

And all this and more,
We'll do o'er and o'er,
Till we're called on to die,
In the cold grave to lie.

Then let us be merry,
Send down to the ferry
A bottle for him,
Old Charon the grim,
A bribe for our stay,
Till we must away.

THE TOWN GALLANT.

FROM Durfey's Pills, Vol. 3., with the music. Reprinted in the Triumphs
of Bacchus. It also appears, with the music, in Ritson's "Ancient
Songs, from the Time of King Henry III. to the Revolution," Lond.
1790, 8vo. Ritson conjectures it "to be a production of the merry reign
of Charles the Second." "There is a copy of it," he adds, "with considerable variations, and some additional stanzas, in the valuable collection of Major Pearson."

The following "Bacchanalian Song," from a collection of Essays by
T. Mozeen, 1762, gives vent to the same thoughtless philosophic reflection :—

Come bind my brows, ye wood-nymphs fair,
  With ivy wreaths come bind my brows ;
Hence grief and woe, and pain and care,
  To Bacchus I devote my vows.
    Dull cynic rules
    Are fit for fools ;
Let those digest the food who can ;
    But love and wine
    Shall still be mine,
O let me laugh out all my span !

No wounds, O love, e'er let me feel,
  But such as spring from eyes and shapes ;
A curse on those that come by steel ;
  I hate all blood, but blood of grapes.

Then fill up high
The bowl, that I
May drink and laugh at fools of sense.
Why need we fear
To want next year?
'Twill be all one a hundred hence.

In Ramsay's Tea-Table Miscellany, vol. iv., a similar song will be found titled "A hundred years hence." It is founded on "the Town Gallant," several lines of which it contains. It treats of "the Butterfly Courtier," "the Beautiful Bride," "the Right-hearted Soldier," "the Merchant," "the Rich Bawling Lawyer," "the Plush-coated Quack," "the Meagre-chopp'd Usurer," "the Learned Divine," "the Poet himself," and "the True-hearted Mason."

And there is another song of the same sort to be found, with the music, in a curious cr. 8vo. volume, called "the Convivial Songster," "London, printed for John Fielding, No. 23 Paternoster Row," circa 1790, which commences thus :—

All you that are wise and think life worth enjoying,
    Or soldier, or sailor, by land or by sea,
In loving and laughing your time be employing,
    Your glass to your lip and your lass on your knee.
Come sing away, honeys, and cast off all sorrow !
Though we all die to-day, let's be merry to-morrow ;
A hundred years hence 'twill be too late to borrow
    A moment of time to be joyous and free !
        Chorus—Come sing away, honeys, &c.

Among the emanations from the press of Pitts, Seven Dials, we have a ballad called "Happy Tom," in which, as "this, that, and t'other," he calculates, "will do him no good a hundred years hence," he promulgates the doctrine that "*he* is to blame who will *slave* his poor carcase for pence." In short, he eschews hard work and frugality.

The Town Gallant.

Let us drink and be merry, dance, joke, and rejoice,
With claret and sherry, theorbo and voice.
The changeable world to our joy is unjust,
All treasure's uncertain, then down with your dust ;
In frolicks dispense your pounds, shillings, and pence,
For we shall be nothing a hundred years hence.

We'll kiss and be free with Moll, Nelly, and Betty,
Have oysters and lobsters with maids that are pretty ;
Fish dinners will make a lass jocund and free ;
Dame Venus (love's goddess) was born of the sea ;
With Bacchus and with her we'll make no pretence,
For we shall be done for a hundred years hence.

Your most beautiful girl, that hath all eyes upon her,
That barters herself for a hogo of honour ;
Whose lightness and brightness doth shine in such splendour,
That none but the stars are thought fit to attend her ;
Though now she be pleasant and sweet to the sense,
Will be damnably mouldy a hundred years hence.

Your chancery lawyer, who subtilly strives
To lengthen out suits the full term of three lives ;
Such suits which the clients do wear out in slavery,
Whilst the pleader cants on as a cloak for his knavery ;
May of subtilty boast, and with conscience dispense,
But *non est inventus* a hundred years hence.

Then why should we turmoil in cares and in fears,
Our tranquillity turn all to sighs and to tears ?
Enjoyment let's court till the worms do corrupt us,
'Tis certain *post mortem* there's *nulla Voluptas* ;
And may those who succeed us shew similar sense,
And make themselves happy a hundred years hence.

𝕿𝖍𝖊 𝕻𝖗𝖔𝖉𝖎𝖌𝖆𝖑'𝖘 𝕽𝖊𝖘𝖔𝖑𝖚𝖙𝖎𝖔𝖓;

Or, My Father was Born before me.

In Durfey's Pills to Purge Melancholy, vol. 3.
"The Prodigal's Resolution" has been reprinted in Ritson's "Ancient
Songs, from the time of King Henry the Third to the Revolution,"
Lond. 1790, 8vo. He thus prefaces it : "From Thomas Jordan's

London Triumphant, 1672, 4to. This Jordan was the professed pageant writer and poet laureate for the city, and, if author of the following
piece, seems to have possessed a greater share of poetical merit than
usually fell to the lot of his profession. The title is prefixed, and the
music added from Durfey's Pills to purge Melancholy, vol. 1, ed. 1712."

I am a lusty lively lad,
    Now come to one and twenty;
My father left me all he had,
    Both gold and silver plenty.
Now he's in grave, I will be brave,
    The ladies shall adore me ;
I'll court and kiss, what hurt's in this?
    My dad did so before me.

My father was a thrifty sir,
    Till soul and body sundred;
Some say he was a usurer,
    For thirty in the hundred.
He scraped and scratched, she pincht and patcht,
    The mother, sooth ! that bore me ;
But I'll let fly, there's good cause why,
    My father was born before me.

My daddy has his duty done,
    In getting so much treasure ;
I'll be as dutiful a son,
    For spending it in pleasure.
Five pound a quart shall cheer my heart,
    Such nectar will restore me ;
But I'll let fly, there's good cause why,
    My father was born before me.

My grannum lived at Washington,
    My grandsir delv'd in ditches ;
The son of old John Thrashington,
    Whose lantern leather breeches

Cry'd, " Whither go ye ? whither go ye ? "
Tho' men do now adore me,
They ne'er did see my pedigree,
    Nor who was born before me.

My grandsir striv'd, and wiv'd, and thriv'd,
    Till he did riches gather ;
And when he had much wealth achiev'd,
    Oh ! then he got my father.
Of happy memory, cry I,
    That e'er his mother bore him ;
I ne'er had been worth one penny
    Had I been born before him.

To Free-school, Cambridge, and Gray's Inn,
    My grey-coat grandsir put him,
Till to forget he did begin
    The leathern breech that got him.
One dealt in straw, the other in law,
    The one did ditch and delve it ;
My father store of satin wore,
    My grandsir beggar's velvet.

So I get wealth, what care I if
    My grandsir was a sawyer ;
My father prov'd to be a chief,
    And subtile, learned lawyer.
By Cook's Reports and tricks in courts,
    He did with treasure store me,
That I may say, " Heaven bless the day
    My father was born before me."

Some say of late a merchant that
    Had gotten store of riches,
In's dining-room hung up his hat,
    His staff, and leathern breeches ;

His stockings gartered up with straw,
    Ere Providence did store him ;
His son was Sheriff of London, 'cause
    His father was born before him.

So many blades now rant in silk,
    And put on scarlet cloathing,
At first did spring from butter-milk,
    Their ancestors worth nothing.
Old Adam and our grandam Eve,
    By digging and by spinning,
Did to all kings and princes give
    Their radical beginning.

The Spendthrift clapt into Limbo.

To its own Tune.

FROM a chap copy of " Five excellent new Songs.   1. The Valiant
M'Craws ; 2. The Spendthrift clapt into Limbo ; 3. The Garb of Old
Gaul ; 4. The North Highland Volunteers ; 5. I cannot love thee more.
Entered according to order," *circa* 1782.

On the fly-leaf of an old volume (1690) occurs this not inappropriate
admonition :—

> "Spend not, nor spare too much ; be this thy care,
> Spare but to spend, and only spend to spare ;
> He that spends more may want, and so complain,
> But he spends best that spares to spend again."

I once was great, full little I'm grown,
    A mimic of *multum in parvo ;*
I'm buried alive in a cluster of stone,
    Some say it is what I deserve, O !
In what they have said there is somewhat of truth,
I have been a wild and extravagant youth ;
Some hundreds have spent upon Rachel and Ruth,
    For which I am clapt up in limbo.

The song that I sing it is absolute true,
  Mark well my open confession ;
It is of myself, give the devil his due,
  I hope I will make an impression
On the harden'd hearts of prodigal beaux ;
Friends, let me tell you now, under the rose,
Those who love you the best will prove your worst foes
  If ever you get into limbo.

My father he left me five hundred a-year,
  My mother she left me her jointure ;
But little of that from mortgage was clear,
  Still I went to the bottle and pointer.
Still day after day to the tavern I went,
My land I sold off, all my money I spent,
My heart was so harden'd it would not relent
  Till once I was clapt up in limbo.

I once loved a brace of as delicate jades
  As ever brought ninepence to nothing ;
I kept them as long as my credit would hold
  Together with meat, drink, and cloathing ;
My creditors they for their debts would not stay,
But still hunted after me day after day,
And now into jail they have cast me, you'll say
  To drink the cold water in limbo.

I used to rant as if I could fly,
  And strut like a crow in a gutter ;
Most people did call out, whene'er I pass'd by,
  " There goes Master Fopling Flutter."
Like top and top-gallant I hoisted my sails,
With my fringed cravat, with wig and three tails ;
But now I am ready to gnaw my own nails,
  Confined in a chamber in limbo.

And as I was lying one day on the straw,
  Bewailing my woeful condition,

U

With hunger my fingers was ready to gnaw,
   I sigh'd and brought forth this expression :
" If I could but get the young queans to my hand
To argue the case, very long I'd not stand
To thrash the young vixens as small as the sand ;
   I'd teach them to leave me in limbo."

I had an old uncle who lived in the West,
   When he heard of my sad disaster—
Poor soul ! his heart was never at rest,
   His sorrows came faster and faster—
He came to the prison to see my sad case,
No sooner I saw him than I straight knew his face,
And on him stood gazing like one in amaze ;
   I wish'd then to be out of limbo.

Said he, " if I set thee once more on thy legs,
   And put thee in credit and fashion,
D'ye think you can leave off your Bridgets and Pegs,
   And can you now bridle your passion ?"
" Believe me, dear uncle, if ever they come
To tempt and beguile, as before they have done,
Odds wounds, I'll belabour their hides like a drum ;
   I'll teach them to leave me in limbo."

He threw me a purse of five hundred pounds,
   Which was all told me out to a penny ;
Receiving the same, I return'd him my thanks,
   Then I went to see Betty and Jenny.
Disguised in my rags, they knew nought of my gold,
They turn'd me right out in the rain and the cold ;
You'd laugh'd to have seen how the creatures did scold,
   And jeer'd at my lying in limbo.

They had no sooner got sight of my gold,
   Than my pockets they fell apicking ;

I beat them so long as my cane would hold,
And then fell to cuffing and kicking.
One called out murder, while the other did scold,
But I was not able my hands for to hold ;
I thrashed their bodies for the good of their souls,
And taught them to leave me in limbo.

Come all you young gallants, take heed what I say,
I'd have you take warning by me, boys.
That little you have don't you make it away,
For fear you be serv'd such as I was.
They'll kiss you and bless you with many fine tales ;
So soon as your money begins for to fail,
They'll be the first that will pack you to jail ;
Take care that you keep out of limbo.

THE ENJOYMENTS OF TOWN.

WITH reference to the several games mentioned in the second stanza:—
"Pell," or Pell-mell, whence comes the name of the locality contiguous
to St James's Park, London, where the game used to be played, is
understood to have been derived from *Pailée Maillé*, a game somewhat
resembling cricket, and imported from France in the reign of Charles
II. In Pepys' Diary is this entry : "2d April 1661. To St James's
Park, where I saw the Duke of York playing at Pelemele, the first time
that ever I saw the sport."
"Racket," or Tennis, "Cribbidge," and "Backgammon," are still
popular games and well known. "In" and "Hazard" are what used
to be termed "games without the tables," while Backgammon and Tick
are "games within the tables." We learn from "the Compleat Gamester, or instructions how to play at all manner of usual and most gentile
games,"—London, 16mo, 1710,—that "*Inn* and *Inn* is a game very much
used in an *ordinary*, and may be play'd by two or three, each having a
box in his hand. It is play'd with four dice." "Hazard :—*Hazard* is a
proper name for this game, for it speedily makes a man or undoes him ;
in the twinkling of an eye either a man or a mouse. This game is play'd

but with two dice, but there may play at it as many as can stand round the largest round table." This anecdote is worth noting:—

" For a gamester that would win without hazarding much his money, dice that will run very seldom otherwise but sixes, cinques, quatres, &c., are very necessary. If those instruments are not to be had, a taper-box will not be amiss, that as the dice are thrown in may stick by the way, and so thrown to advantage. I have heard of one who, having spent the major part of his patrimony in good fellowship, and such pastimes as the heat of the blood with vigorous youth most prosecute, at length consider'd how he should live hereafter; and finding but small encouragements at home, and lesser abroad, thought if he could contrive a way to win a considerable sum at play (having been a great loser himself), that should be the basis of his future settlement. After various consultations within himself, he at length contrived this stratagem : he caused a box to be made, not as they are usual screwed within, but smooth, and procured it to be so well painted and shadowed within that it lookt like a screw'd box ; now this box was but half board wide at top and narrow at bottom, that the dice as aforesaid might stick, and the box being smooth would come out without tumbling. With this box he went and play'd at *Inn and Inn*, by virtue whereof, and his art of taking up and throwing in his dice into the box, he got the first night a thousand pound, and the next night two hundred a-year, with a coach and six horses, which coach and six horses (being very valuable) he sold; but the estate he lives on to this day with great improvements, and never would handle a dye since, well knowing how many worthy families it hath ruined."

"Tick,"*i.e.*, "Tick-tack" is something similar to Backgammon. It is so called from "Touch and take," for if you touch a man you must play him through to your loss. The "Compleat Gamester," in describing this game, says, "All your men must stand on the ace-point, and from thence play forward, but have a care of being too forward, or so at least-wise that doublets reach you not." There is a game called "Tick" mentioned by Drayton, which, according to Halliwell, is still played in Warwickshire. He thus describes it·—" A boy, touched by one who is in the first instance fixed upon to commence the game, is in his turn obliged to overtake and touch another of the party, when he cries *tick!* and so the game proceeds." See Dictionary of Archaic and Provincial Words, London, 2 vols. 8vo, 1852. This game is very popular among the youth of both sexes in the lowlands of Scotland, where it goes by the name of "Tig."

The Enjoyments of Town.

From "Bristol Drollery," 1674.

The sports on the green we'll leave to the swains,
The rise of their loves, and reward of their pains;
At the tavern we'll dine, then close up the day,
At night, at a *Mask*, a *Ball*, or a *Play:*
　And when this is done we'll laugh and lie down,
　And our evening delights sweet slumbers shall crown.

At the *Pell* we will play, or a race we will run,
We'll sport with the *Racket*, and when that is done,
At *Cribbidge*, at *In*, or at *Hazard* a main,
From *Tick* or *Baggamon* we will not refrain :
　And when we have done, we'll laugh and lie down,
　And our passed delights sweet slumber shall crown.

Then we'll away to the gardens or park,
With lures for the ladies instead of the lark,
With graces attractive, are fetch'd from Love's mine,
And his darts shall secure us the prey we design :
　And when we have done, we'll laugh and lie down,
　And dreams of our loves, enjoyment shall crown.

LONDON IS A FINE TOWN.

Throughout many generations London, with its vices and its follies, has been repeatedly and not unjustly satirized.   Here is a

DESCRIPTION OF LONDON.

From "The Cabinet for Wit: or an infallible recipe to cure stupidity," by Timothy Sharpe, Esq.   London, 8vo., 1751.

Houses, churches, mix'd together,
Streets unpleasant in all weather,

Prisons, Palaces, contiguous,
Gates, a bridge, the Thames irriguous.
  Gaudy things enough to tempt ye,
Showy outsides, insides empty ;
Bubbles, trades, mechanic arts,
Coaches, wheelbarrows, and carts.
  Warrants, bailiffs, bills unpaid,
Lords of Laundresses afraid ;
Rogues that nightly rob and shoot men,
Hangmen, aldermen, and footmen.
  Lawyers, poets, priests, physicians,
Noble, simple, all conditions ;
Worth beneath a threadbare cover,
Villainy bedaub'd all over.
  Women, black, red, fair, and gray,
Prudes, and such as never pray ;
Handsome, ugly, noisy, still ;
Some that will not, some that will.
  Many a beau without a shilling,
Many a widow not unwilling ;
Many a bargain, if you strike it ;
This is London ! how d'ye like it ?

Looking at London in the present day, from a country point of view,
it is certainly a very fine place to enjoy oneself in for a fortnight, if one
goes in quest of pleasure—blessed with good health and a well-filled
purse.   Without money, or its bold counterfeit, brass, existence is
denied you in London, hence thieving under colour of the law and otherwise obtains many proselytes there, while the more conscientious get
beaten down and trampled on, and either find a refuge in the workhouse, or under the waters of the Thames.   The tone of several foreign
nations, whose word has never been their bond, has been gradually
of late years, diffused over London.   The influx of foreigners themselves—fellows who have no career in their own country, and whose
sole object is "your money," are by degrees elbowing out our native
merchants, and usurping the city.   It therefore becomes a matter of
question whether England was a gainer by the battle of Waterloo.   Since
that event, our tight little Island has been open to the foreign invader to
come and go unchallenged—he is freely allowed to sneak in amongst us
and to decamp with his pillage when occasion best suits him.
  The English people have ever been prone to encourage foreign fashions,
foreign manufactures, and foreign adventurers, while they leave their own
countrymen to starve.   This petting of foreigners is admirably brought
out in D'Israeli's very clever book, "the Adventures of Captain
Popanilla," Lond. 1828, 8vo.

Ever since the introduction of foreign singers and actors into this country, now some hundred and seventy years ago, the court paid to them, and the large sums heaped upon them has been a grievance which native performers have all along in vain exclaimed against. In most instances sprung from the lowest dregs of the people, foreign singers, when they honour this country with their presence, assume or command a professional position, higher than that ever accorded to English actors of greater intellectual and scholastic attainments. The facilities afforded the people in continental towns, by speculative teachers, for the acquirement of a musical education on easy terms, enables the merest cow-boy possessed of an improving voice to become eligible for the caresses of the English, and the consequent receipt of a fortune, with all its attendant luxuries. And yet in the northern portion more especially of our own country may be found as good voices as either Italy or Germany ever produced, but the absence of economical musical tuition, and above all the prejudice of the people, which has yet to be overcome, against having their children degrade themselves and their connections by becoming public performers, all of whom they regard as enlisted in the service of Satan, hinders in a great degree the development of musical as well as dramatic ability, and the advancement of music itself throughout this country.

Not only in the song we now introduce is the grievance we refer to noticed, but it is advanced in many others, of which the following, from a Ballad Opera, called "The Livery Rake," performed in 1733, is a specimen :—

The Italian nymphs and swains
    That adorn the opera stage,
        With their fal, lal, la, &c.,
How we die upon their strains !
    They so sweetly do engage,
        With their fal, lal, la, &c.,
Their ha, ha, ha, ha, ha, without a grain of sense,
Has mollified our brains, and we're fobb'd out of our pence,
        By their ha, ha, ha, &c.

But I hope the time will come,
    When their favourers will find,
        With their fal, la, la ! &c.,
They have paid too great a sum
    To Italian pipes for wind,
        With their fal, lal, la, &c.,
When English wit again, and merit too shall thrive,
And men of fortune to support that wit and merit strive,
        Without ha, ha, ha, &c.

Not content with taking nearly the entire control in London of Opera, to the ruin of all those who patriotically embark in any undertaking for the revival and encouragement of our English music and composers, foreigners have actually of late years been usurping the place of our native actors and actresses, and have been distorting the poetry of Shakespeare and our other dramatists to the delectation of the metropolitan votaries of fashion.   Some three or four years ago, nearly at one and the same time, we had Fechter at the Lyceum, Miss Bateman at the Adelphi, Mademoiselle Beatrice and Mademoiselle Stella Colas at the Haymarket, Madame Celeste at the Victoria, and Ada Isaacs Menkin at Astley's.   For a ballet dancer to come before the discriminating British public with any but a foreign appellation would be presumptuous in the extreme, and tantamount to a failure.   Even hair-dressers of native extraction must hide their diminished ,heads before the "artistes in hair" who come from foreign parts, and for whose exertions the brave Britons are cheerfully mulcted in at least double the charge they would hesitatingly bestow upon a native artificer.

Signor Farinelli, to whom allusion is so particularly made in our present song, was the son of a miller in the neighbourhood of Naples, and from this circumstance he derived his cognomen, his real name being Carlo Broschi.   He was born at Andrea in 1705.   Having studied singing under Porpora, at the age of seventeen he accompanied him to Rome, Porpora having been engaged to write an opera for one of the theatres there.   He was now brought suddenly into notice by the performance of the great vocal feat for which he became so celebrated. Hogarth, in "Memoirs of the Opera in Italy, France, Germany, and England," 2 vols. 12mo, 1851, thus describes this extraordinary vocal effort: "In an opera which was then performed, there was a song with an obligato accompaniment for the trumpet, sung by Farinelli, and accompanied by a great performer on that instrument.   Every night there was a contest between the singer and the trumpet player, which gradually became more and more earnest, as the audience began to take an interest in it, and to take different sides.   At length both parties seemed resolved to bring it to an issue.   After each of them had swelled out a note and tried to rival the other in brilliancy and force, they both had a swell and shake together, in the interval of a third, which was continued so long that both seemed to be exhausted, and the trumpeter at length gave it up, imagining probably that his antagonist was as much spent as himself; but Farinelli, with the greatest apparent ease, and with a smile on his face, as if to show that he had been all the while only sporting with his adversary, broke out all at once in the same breath with fresh vigour, and not only continued the swell and shake upon the note, but started off into a series of rapid and difficult divisions, till his voice was drowned by the acclamations of the audience."

In 1734 Farinelli came to England, to the theatre in Lincoln's Inn Fields, where the nobility's opera was carried on under the direction of Porpora, as opposed to Handel. The emolument derived from his salary, his benefit, and presents from people of distinction, was estimated at £5000 a-year. To admire Farinelli became the fashion and the infatuation of the hour. This, Hogarth has satirized in one of the series of his "Rake's Progress." He left London in 1737, with the intention of returning the year following. He had, in the summer of 1736, made a short excursion to Paris, where he was again most enthusiastically received, although there existed a strong prejudice against Italian music and Italian singing. His return to England was frustrated by his being invited to Madrid at the request of the Queen of Spain, whose husband Philip V. was labouring under a mental disorder, which caused him to fall into a state of apathy, neglecting everything. Having always evinced a sensibility to the power of music, the Queen contrived that a concert should take place in a room adjoining the King's apartment, and Farinelli having sung two of his most pathetic airs, the king sent for him, complimented him highly, and asked him how he could recompense him for the display of such talents. Farinelli, previously instructed, begged that his majesty would allow the attendants to shave and dress him, and that he would endeavour to appear in council as formerly. From this time the king's disease gave way to medical treatment. Farinelli was taken into the service of the court, and a pension of £3150 a-year was settled upon him, one of the conditions being that he was not to sing any longer in public. During the first ten years of his residence at the court of Spain, he sang to the king every night the same four airs, one of which was the famous "Pallido il Sole" of Hasse ; and he grew so much in royal favour as to be honoured with the order of St Jago.

Dr Busby has a very different and falacious account of this Spanish engagement of Farinelli, which we repeat, as showing how, even in such a case as this, there are always two ways of telling a story. "The celebrated Farinelli, whose delicious notes so highly charmed the English amateurs of the early part of last century, and whose powers extorted from a lady of quality this precious exclamation, 'One God, one Farinelli!' received at his retirement from this country a pension of two thousand a-year from the King of Spain, who was himself a vocalist. The Italian, however, deemed the pension too little when obliged to listen to the strains of his Catholic Majesty." See Concert-room and Orchestra Anecdotes, 3 vols. 12mo, 1825.

Farinelli continued in favour with Ferdinand VI., the successor of Philip, and at his hands was dignified with the order of Calatrava. He persuaded Ferdinand to establish an opera, and he introduced the best composers and singers of the time. On the death of his patron he was obliged to quit Spain, as Charles III., the brother and successor of

Ferdinand, had an absolute distaste to music.   His pension was however continued to him.

Dr Burney, who visited Farinelli at Bologna in 1770, describes him as having left off singing and amusing himself on the harpsichord and Viol d'Amour.   He had a number of harpsichords made in different countries, each of which he had named after some celebrated Italian painter.   He had his sister and her two children living with him.   Of the younger (an infant) he was doatingly fond, although it was peevish and unamiable.   He was most attentive to the English who visited him in his retirement.   He died at Bologna in 1782, in the seventy-seventh year of his age.

In addition to the pension of 1400 piastres, or £3150, per annum accorded him by Philip V., a coach and equipage were maintained for him, and his Majesty presented him with his portrait set in diamonds, valued at £1200 sterling; the Queen gave him a gold snuff-box, with two large diamonds in the lid; and the Prince of Asturias, a diamond button and loop.   While in England, Frederick, Prince of Wales, sent him a finely-wrought gold box, richly set with diamonds and rubies; in the box were enclosed a pair of brilliant diamond knee-buckles of great price.

The tall ungainly figure of Farinelli is well hit off in the cut which forms the tail-piece of the present song.   The other characters represent Signora Cuzzoni (a popular cantatrice), who was remarkably short, and Heidegger (manager of the King's theatre), who was repulsively ugly. The original of this caricature is a very fine etching, nine in. by eight in. Underneath are the following lines, presumed to be the passing thoughts of Heidegger, under whose management masquerades (cordially patron- ized by George the Second) had become the rage, but the evil effects of such mixed assemblies on the morals of the people, caused the Bishop of London, in 1726, to declaim against them, which frightened the Government into issuing a Proclamation for their suppression.   The only result of this was that thereafter they were carried on under the Italian title of Ridottos, or the English one of Balls.

> Thou tunefull scarecrow and thou warbling bird,
> No shelter for your notes these lands afford.
> This town protects no more the sing-song strain,
> Whilst balls and masquerades triumphant reign.
> Sooner than midnight revels ere should fail,
> And o'er Ridotto's harmony prevail,
> That cap (a refuge once) my head shall grace,
> And save from ruin this harmonious face.

The only original we have ever seen is in the collection of Mr Maidment

of Edinburgh; and it has been reckoned so rare, that the late Mr
Charles Kirkpatrick Sharpe, who was an excellent draughtsman, asked
permission to copy it. Mr Wright has inserted a woodcut of this
etching, similar to ours, in his "England under the house of Hanover," 2 vols, Lond. 1848, 8vo. He remarks that "the caricature
is said to have been designed by the Countess of Burlington, and
to have been etched by Goupy; at least so we learn from a manuscript
note on a copy in the possession of Mr Burke." Again, it has
been attributed to Hogarth, whose separate sketch of "Heidegger in
a rage" shows him sitting in precisely the same grotesque attitude as
that in which he appears in the caricature. For this sketch see
"Hogarth illustrated by John Ireland," 8vo, 1795, vol. 3. Hogarth
also depicted Farinelli, Cuzzoni, and Senesino in a scene from Handel's
Ptolemeo, in which Farinelli's awkwardness and unwieldy manner are
well designed.

London is a fine Town.

FROM "a New Academy of Compliments, or the complete English
Secretary, with a collection of Playhouse Songs." Glasgow 1789, 16mo.

O London is a dainty place,
    A great and gallant city!
For all the Streets are pav'd with gold,
    And all the folks are witty.
And there's your lords and ladies fine,
    That ride in coach and six;
That nothing drink but claret wine,
    And talk of politicks.

And there's your beaux with powder'd clothes,
    Bedaub'd from head to chin;
Their pocket-holes adorned with gold,
    But not one sous within.
And there the English actor goes
    With many a hungry belly;
While heaps of gold are forc'd, God wot,
    On Signor Farinelli.

And there's your dames with dainty frames,
  With skins as white as milk ;
Dressed every day in garments gay,
  Of satin and of silk.
And if your mind be so inclined
  To offer them your arm,
Pull out a handsome purse of gold,
  They can't resist the charm.

𝔄 𝔖𝔬𝔫𝔤.

The tune *Robin Rowser*.

FROM "Westminster Drollery, or, a choice collection of the newest Songs and Poems both at Court and Theaters, by a Person of Quality, with additions. London, Printed for H. Brome at the Gun in St Paul's Churchyard, near the West End, 1671," 16mo.

Leonard Macnally of the Irish bar, author of several dramatic pieces, and of the popular song "The Lass of Richmond Hill," wrote a comic opera called "Robin Hood, or Sherwood Forest," performed at Covent Garden with immense success in 1784 and subsequently, in which a song occurs as sung by Annette "the tiny foot-page," so closely resembling our present ballad that we insert it here, illustrative as it is of Puff's observation in the *Critic* that "two geniuses have hit upon the same thing, only Shakespeare made use of it first, that's all."

> My name is little Harry, O,
> Mary I will marry, O ;
> In spite of Nell or Isabel,
> I'll follow my own vagary, O.
> > With my rigdum jigdum airy, O.
> > I love little Mary, O,
> > > In spite of Nell,
> > > Or Isabel,
> > I'll follow my own vagary, O.
>
> Smart she is and handy, O,
> Sweet as sugar candy, O ;
> > Fresh and gay,
> > As flow'rs in May,
> And I'm her Jack-a-dandy O.
> > With my, &c.
>
> Soon to church I'll have her, O,
> Where we'll wed together, O ;
> > And that, that done,
> > Then we'll have fun,
> In spite of wind and weather, O.
> > With my, &c.

1. My name is honest Harry,
And I love little Mary,
In spite of Cis, or jealous Bess,
I'll have my own vagary.

2. My love is blithe and bucksome
   And sweet and fine as can be :
Fresh and gay as the flowers in May,
   And looks like Jack-a-dandy.

3. And if she will not have me,
   That am so true a lover,
I'll drink my wine and ne'er repine,
   And down the stairs I'll shove her.

4. But if that she will love me,
   I'll be as kind as may be;
I'll give her rings and pretty things,
   And deck her like a lady.

5. Her Petticoat of Satin,
   Her Gown of Crimson Taby,
Lac'd up before and spangled o'er,
   Just like a *Bartlemew Baby*.

6. Her Waistcoat is of Scarlet,
   With ribbons tied together,
Her stockins of a bow-dy'd hue,
   And her shoes of Spanish leather.

7. Her smock o' th' finest Holland,
   And lac'd in every quarter :
Side and wide, and long enough,
   And hangs below her garter.

8. Then to the Church I'll have her,
   Where we will wed together :
So come home when we have done.
   In spight of wind and weather.

9. The Fidlers shall attend us,
And first play, *John come kiss me;*
And when that we have danc'd a round,
They shall play, *Hit or miss me.*

10. Then hey for little Mary,
'Tis she I love alone, Sir ;
Let any man do what he can,
I will have her or none, Sir.

NO DOMINIES FOR ME.

THIS has been printed from a Broadside, circa 1817, a verbatim reprint from Herd's Ancient and Modern Scotish Songs, 1786. In Peter Buchan's "Gleanings of Scarce old Ballads," Peterhead, 12mo, 1825, a more lengthened version occurs. The additional stanzas given by him will be found as footnotes. For the sake of "country gentlemen" we may mention that the appellation "Dominie" is that bestowed by the common people of Scotland upon Schoolmasters, private Tutors, and Probationers. "The author of this excellent song," remarks Mr Buchan, "was the Rev. John Forbes, Minister at Deer, Aberdeenshire. This eccentric character was born at Pitnacalder, a small estate near Fraserburgh, of which his father was proprietor." Hence he was commonly called Pitney !—"Nae Dominies for me" was written before he became incumbent of Deer, and is believed to have been founded upon an incident personal to himself. In after life he took the greatest delight in singing it and hearing it sung. He published in 1757 a collection of Spiritual songs, which in point of poetical composition do not possess anything like the merit of his first effort. "He was a rigid Presbyterian, and was said by some to possess the gift of prophecy." He died in 1769. Forbes forms the subject of a ballad called "By the side of a Country Kirk wall," written by the Rev. John Skinner, Longside near Peterhead (one of Burns' Correspondents), in which he is characterized as "a sullen whig minister."—This Ballad will be found with its relative music, in Hogg's Jacobite Relics, 2d. series, Edin., 1821.

The Ballad "No Dominies for me" has been preserved in the form of a broadside, printed apparently about the year 1740. Mr Stenhouse states that he was credibly informed it "was written by the late Rev. Mr Nathaniel M'Kie, minister of Crossmichael in the Stewartry of Kirkcudbright, but as Mr M'Kie, according to the Scots Magazine, died

in January 1781 in the 66th year of his age, this credibility is open to
extreme doubt, inasmuch as in 1740 he was only fifteen, and he must
indeed have been an extraordinary youth to have written such a song at
so early an age.

On referring to " A new Book of old Ballads," Edin., 12mo, 1844
(Maidment), I find a different song entitled "No Dominies for me, Lady"
with these observations :—" In the new edition of Johnson's Musical
Museum, vol. 5, page 504, there is a copy of a ballad entitled 'No
Dominies for me, Laddie,' said to be taken from Yair's Charmer, vol.
2, p. 347, Edin. 1751. Ritson, who inserted it in his collection, was
unable to discover the tune ; but the late James Balfour, Esq., accountant
in Edinburgh, communicated the original melody, and it has been given
in Johnson. It is said to have been written by the Rev. Nathaniel
Mackie, minister of Cross-Michael, who died on the 26th January, 1781,
aged 66, but the editor has a broadside of the ballad, printed certainly
not later than 1700, and the copy from the Hamilton MS. is at least as
early in date. In Buchan's Gleanings, the Rev. John Forbes, minister
of Deer, is said to be the author. He died in 1769, in the 80th year of
his age. He must therefore have been eleven years of age in 1700, the
date of the Hamilton MS.—a fact which militates against the claim of
authorship set up for him. Perhaps one or other of these Rev.
gentlemen may have had a hand in altering the original ballad."

We have referred to the Broadside mentioned in this note, and find
several additions, which are given at the end of the ballad.

No Dominies for me, Laddie.

I chanced to meet an airy blade,
  A new made pulpiteer, laddie,
With a cocked up hat and powdered wig,
  A black coat and cuffs fu' clear, laddie.
A long cravat at him did wag,
  And buckles at his knees, laddie,[a]
Says he, my heart, by Cupid's dart,
  Is captivate to thee, lassie.

I'll rather choose to thole grim death,
  So cease and let me be, laddie ;
For what ? says he, good troth, said I,
  No dominies for me, laddie.

Ministers' stipends are uncertain rents
   For ladies' conjunct fee, laddie,
When books and gowns are all cried down,
   No dominies for me, laddie.

But for your sake, I'll fleece the flock,
   Grow rich as I grow old, lassie,
If I be spared I'll be a laird,
   And thou's be madam called, lassie.
But what if you should chance to die,
   Leave bairns ane or twa, laddie,
Naething would be reserved for them
   But hair-mould Books to gnaw, laddie.

At this he angry was I wat,
   He gloomed and looked fu' hi', laddie,
When I perceived this, in haste
   I left my dominie, laddie.[b]
Fare ye well, my charming maid,
   This lesson learn of me, lassie,
At the next offer hold him fast
   That first makes love to thee, lassie.[c]

Then I returning hame again,
   And coming doun the toun, laddie,
By my good luck I chanced to meet
   A gentleman dragoon, laddie.[d] ,
And he took me by baith the hands,
   'Twas help in time of need, laddie,
Fools on ceremonies stand,
   At twa words we agreed, laddie.

He led me to his quarter house,
   Where we exchanged a word, laddie,[e]
We had no use for black gowns there,
   We married o'er the sword, laddie.

X

Martial drums are music fine,
    Compared wi' tinkling bells, laddie,
Gold red and blue is more divine
    Than black, the hue of hell, laddie.

Kings, queens, and princes crave the aid
    Of my bra' stout dragoon, laddie,
While dominies are much employed
    'Bout queans and sackcloth gowns, laddie.
Awa' wi' a' the whinging loons,
    They look like let-me-be, laddie,
I've now delight in roaring guns,
    No dominies for me, laddie.

----

a The old broadside as well as Mr Buchan's version commences, and
carries on as follows, down to this point :—

[As I went forth to take the air,
    Into an evening clear, laddie ;
I met a brisk young handsome spark,
    A new made pulpiteer, laddie.
An airy blade, so brisk and braw,
    Mine eyes did never see, laddie ;
A long cravat at him did wag,
    His hose girt 'boon the knee, laddie.

By and out o'er this young man had
    A gallant douse black gown, laddie ;
With cock'd up hat and powder'd wig,
    Black coat and muffs fu' clean, laddie.
At length he did approach me nigh,
    And bowing down fu' low, laddie ;
He grasp'd me as I did pass by,
    And would not let me go, laddie,

Said I, pray friend, what do you mean ?
    Canst thou not let me be, laddie ?
Says he, my heart, &c.]

ᵇ In the old Ballad these stanzas here occur. A garbled portion of them are also in Mr Buchan's version.

[Then came I hame to my step-dame,
　By this time it was late, laddie;
But she before had barr'd the door,
　I blushed and looked fu' blate, laddie.
Thinks I, maun I lie in the street,
　Is there no room for me, laddie?
And is there neither plaid nor sheet
　Wi' my young dominie, laddie?

Away I went, cam till this door,
　And knocked with my foot, laddie,
But he was ly'n down before,
　He heard me not at first, laddie.

Then with a humble voice I cried,
　Pray open the door to me, laddie,
But he replied, "I sleep by guess,
　So cease, and let me be, lassie."
"The sooner that you let me in,
　You'll be the more at ease, laddie;
And on the morrow I'll be gone,
　Or married as you please, laddie."

"And what if I should chance to die,
　Leave bairns ane or twa, lassie,
Naething would be reserved for them,
　But hair-mould books to gnaw, lassie.
Ministers stipends are uncertain rents
　For ladies conjunct fee, lassie;
When books and gown are a' cried down,
　Nae dominies for me, lassie."]

ᶜ Another interpolation.

[I would have cursed my doleful fate,
　If it had been my lot, laddie,

For to have match'd with such as you,
A good-for-nothing sot, laddie.
Necessity, no love it was,
Caused me come to thee, laddie,
Plague on thy face so scant of grace,
No pity had on me, laddie.]

 d These lines are from the old broadside. They are not reprinted by Buchan.

[Says he, " Fair maid what aileth thee ?
Canst thou not stay and speak, lassie?"
I ran as fast as I'd been chas'd,
My modesty to keep, laddie.
He chased me to my father's door,
As dogs do wild fowls hunt, laddie ;
The door was barred, defied I was,
I blusht and lookt full blunt, laddie.]

e The old broadside has,
" Of each other we gat words, laddie."

Maggie's Tocher.

A version of this lively Scotch song has been printed by Ramsay in the Tea-table Miscellany, 1724, a copy of which, with the music, occurs in Thomson's Orpheus Caledonius, London, 1723, 8vo, and in "a collection of Scots Songs, adapted for a Voice and Harpischord; Edinburgh, printed and sold by Neil Stewart at his shop, Parliament Square," circa 1790. It will also be found in Old Ballads, 3 vols. 1725, "to its ain tune." We have also met with a somewhat questionable broadside ballad of five stanzas upon a like theme entitled, "We'll a' cuddle thegither," the burthen of which is to this effect :—

" We'll a' lye thegither,
We'll a' cuddle thegither,
We'll hae nae beds but ane,
Until it be warmer weather."

In a song called "Miss Cuddy," to be found, with the music, in vol. vi. of Durfey's Pills, p. 268, a similar chorus occurs, and what is very remarkable, the last stanza is identical with the same stanza in the common and coarser version of our present ballad.

"Ramsay," Stenhouse remarks, "by the usual signature in his

Tea Table Miscellany, the letter Z, testifies that this ballad in his time was known to be very ancient." He continues, "a rich vein of genuine broad humour runs through the whole of the old song, and the air, although in a minor key, is remarkable both for its antiquity and sprightliness."

The meal was dear short syne,
　　We buckled us a' thegither;
And Maggie was in her prime,
　　When Willie made courtship till her.
Twa pistols charged by guess,
　　To gie the courting shot;
And syne came ben the lass
　　Wi' swats drawn frae the butt.
He first speer'd at the gudeman,
　　And syne at Giles the mother,
" And ye wad gi'es a bit land,
　　We'd buckle us e'en thegither, Jo."

" My dochter ye shall hae,
　　I'll gi'e ye her by the hand:
But I'll part wi' my wife, by my fai,
　　Or I part wi' my land.
Your tocher it sall be gude,
　　There's nane sall hae its maik:
The lass bound in her snood,
　　And crummie wha kens her stake;
With an auld bedden o' claes
　　Was left me by my mither,
We've sorted a' the flaes;
　　Ye may cuddle in them thegither."

" Ye speak richt weel, gudeman,
　　But ye maun mend your hand,
And think o' modesty,
　　Gin ye'll no quat your land.
We are but young, ye ken,
　　And noo we're gaun thegither;

A house is a but and a ben,
    And Crummie will want her fother.
The bairns 'll be coming on,
    That pits me in a swither;"
" The best that can be done
    Is to cuddle them a' thegither.

" Your tocher's be guid eneuch—
    For that ye needna fear—
Twa guid stilts to the pleugh,
    And ye yoursel maun steer.
Ye shall hae twa guid pocks
    That ance were o' the tweel,
The tane to haud the groats,
    The t'ither to haud the meal.
Wi' an auld kist made o' wands,
    And that sall be your coffer,
Wi' aiken woody bands,
    An' that may haud your tocher."

" Consider weel, gudeman,
    We hae but borrowed gear;
The horse that I ride on
    Is Sandy Wilson's mare.
The saddle's nane o' my ain,
    And thae's but borrowed boots,
An' when that I gae hame,
    I maun tak to my koots;
The cloak is Geordy Watts',
    That gars me look sae crouse;
Come! fill us a cogue o' swats,
    We'll mak nae mair toom ruse."

" I like ye weel, young lad,
    For telling me sae plain;
I married when little I had
    O' gear that was my ain.

A bargain it maun be,
" Fy, cry on Giles the mither,"
" Content am I," quo' she,
" E'en gar the hizzy come hither."
The waddin' it sune cam' aff,
    An' ilk ane paid their penny ;
The barn filled mair than half,
    Ilk Jockey he brought his Jenny.

The fiddlers they played wi' birr,
    For a' the lave got frisky,
And they keept up sic a stir
    As they handed aboot the whisky.
The gudeman cam tumbling in,
    And the minister kissed the mither ;
The bride took aff her shoon,
    An' they a' got fuddled thegither.
They cleekit, they crossed, they set,
    The groom got the length o' his tether,
When he cried " we've no dune yet,
    For we'll a' cuddle thegither."

Hame the guests they coudna gang,
    For the rain cam' on wi' a blatter ;
And the wind it blew sae strang,
    And the roof let in the water.
So helter skelter they ran,
    Gaed head ow'r heels through ither,
Till the roof it fell in wi' a bang,
    An' huddled them a' thegither.

See you Johnny Coming ?

BURNS remarks of this Song (see Reliques)—" For genuine humour in
the verses, and lively originality in the air it is unparalleled. I take it to
be very old." Stenhouse, in his Illustrations "of the Lyric Poetry and

Music of Scotland," says "this observation had been hastily made, for the air, either when played or sung slowly, as it ought to be, is exceedingly pathetic, not lively.   Burns afterwards became sensible of this; for, in one of his letters to Thomson, inserted in Currie's edition of his works, he says, 'I enclose you Fraser's set of this tune; when he plays it slow, in fact he makes it the language of despair.   Were it possible in singing to give it half the pathos which Fraser gives it in playing, it would make an admirable pathetic song.'"   And proceeding upon this idea he wrote the song of "Thou hast left me ever, Jamie," which commends itself to the lovers of Scotch melody more on account of the music than of the words, it being, like many of Burns' songs, the merest commonplace.   Mr Thomas Fraser, to whom Burns makes allusion, was an excellent musician.   He was a native of Edinburgh, and was celebrated there for many years as the principal oboe concerto player.   He died in 1825.   See note in Chambers' Scottish Songs, Edin. 1829, 2 vols. 8vo.

According to Whitelaw (see his Book of Scotish Song, Glasgow, 1845, small 4to.), this song, which usually commences "Saw ye Johnny Coming?" made its first appearance in Herd's Collection, 1776.   That version is in four stanzas only, in argument similar to the first four of our version; and it has been reprinted in Cromek's Select Scotish Songs, 1810; Motherwell's Harp of Renfrewshire, 1819; and in numerous other popular collections.   Our version is from a chap copy, "Three excellent new songs: 1. The Gawkie; 2. A New Mason's Song; 3. See You Jonny Coming, printed in the year 1784."   Miss Joanna Baillie has altered, but not improved, Herd's version of this song, for which see Dr Rogers' "Modern Scottish Minstrel."

"See you Jonnie coming," quoth she,
See you Jonnie coming,
Wi' his coat of hodden gray,
And his dogie running?
See him coming o'er the lee,
And his dogie wi' him,
Wi' his bonnet cocked ajee,
Fee him father, fee him," quoth she,
"And for a merk of mair fee dinna stand wi' him."

"What wad you do wi' him, hussie,
What wad ye do wi' him?
For deil a pair o' breeks he has,
And ye hae nane to gi'e him."

" I hae twa coaties in my kist,
    And ane of them I'll gi'e him."
    Then fee him father, fee him," quoth she,
" And for a merk of mair fee dinna stand wi' him.

    For he's a bonny tall young man
      And a weel-doing,
    And the work about the house
      Gaes weel on when I see him.
    I'll spin a hesp of mair yarn
      Every day I see him.
    Then fee him father, fee him," quoth she,
" And for a merk of mair fee dinna stand wi' him."

    " Will he work if I fee him," quoth he,
      Will he work if I fee him?"
    " Deed, father, there's nae fear o' that,
      If routh o' meal ye gi'e him;
    He'll ha'd your plough, thrash in your barn,
      And crack wi' me at e'en.
    Then fee him father, fee him," quoth she,
"And for twa merk of mair fee for lord's sake stand nae wi' him.

    " But gin you winna fee him," quoth she,
      " Gin you winna fee him,
    I'll kilt my coats aboon my knee,
      And I'll awa' wi' him,"
    " If you'll stay I'll fee him," quoth he,
      " If you'll stay I'll fee him,
    If he'll thrash in the barn all day,
      Muckle gear I'll gi'e him."

    " Come awa' and fee him," quoth she,
      " Come awa' and fee him,
    He shall thrash in your barn all day,
      But crack wi' me at e'en."

" Then I'll be kind to him, hussie,
    I'll be kind to him,
    If he thrash in my barn all day,
    And crack wi' you I'll loe him."

" Come awa' till him," quoth she,
    " Come awa' till him,
    A' that's within our pantry door,
    Shall a' be got to fill him."
" Come and let us do it, hussie,
    Come and let us do it,
    The best we hae within the house,
    He's aye be welcome to it."

O'ER THE HILLS AND FAR AWAY.

THE version here printed is from "the Dairy Maid ; or, Vocal Miscellany, being a collection of choice Songs, Scots and English, with a variety of Toasts and Sentiments. Edinburgh, Printed by A. Robertson, and sold at his shop in Niddry's Wynd, 1784," 12mo. It has been collated with another in a " collection of old Ballads corrected from the best and most ancient copies extant," 1723, vol. 2, p. 237.—It is therein titled " Distracted Jockey's Lamentation ; or, O'er the Hills and far away," and is introduced as a Scotch song, but all the Scotch words (if they ever appeared in an earlier edition) are Anglicised. The air was very popular during last century. It is introduced in "Gay's Beggar's Opera " 1728, and in "Farquhar's Recruiting Officer," 1705. In the former it is sung slowly and with pathos, in the latter briskly. Both are highly effective. The words in both instances are written *apropos* of the respective dramatic situations in which they have been placed. The difference in the readings of Distracted Jockey's Lamentation as compared with the present version is given in the foot-notes.

There is a song in Herd's Scotish Songs, vol. 1, p. 179, entitled " Ranting Roving Laddie," the first stanza of which runs thus :

"My love was born in Aberdeen,
    The bonniest lad that e'er was seen ;
    O he is forced frae me to gae
    Over the hills and far away."

Stenhouse in his Illustrations of the Lyric Poetry and Music of Scotland, remarks :—" The title of this old pipe tune is 'O'er the Hills and far awa',' of which a MS. copy of considerable antiquity is in the possession of the Editor. It is probable that this, with many other Scotish melodies and Songs, was introduced into England about the year 1603, when James VI. left his native country to ascend the English throne." He then proceeds to refer to the old Ballad in the Pepysian collection of " The wind hath blown my plaid awa, or a discourse betwixt a young maid and the Elfin Knight " which he says "seems to have been composed about this time," and argues that, as the burthen is "The wind has blown my plaid awa'," "from the peculiar structure of the stanzas, and the broad dialect of the burthen line, the author of this Ballad must have heard both the tune and words of the silly old Scotish ditty 'Its o'er the hills and far awa.' "—Now, as allusion is made to the Elfin Knight in "the Complaynt of Scotland," this probability, we humbly submit, is in favour of it being the older Ballad of the two. David Webster, well-known about forty years ago to the antiquarians of Edinburgh as the judicious publisher of a limited impression of various reprints &c. of ancient prose and poetical tracts of value, printed a version of " The Elphin Knight " thus prefaced : " This Ballad is printed partly from an old copy in Black Letter, and partly from the recitation of an old lady, which appears to be the Scotish version, and is here chiefly adhered to. We do not recollect to have seen it printed in any of our modern collections of old songs." The Pepysian copy, according to Stenhouse, consists of twenty stanzas, while Webster's has twenty-one, the concluding one running thus :—

> "My plaid awa', my plaid awa',
> And owre the hills and far awa',
> And far awa' to Norrowa' ;
> My plaid shall not be blown awa'."

A copy of the Pepysian version will be found in the Appendix to Motherwell's Minstrelsy, Glasgow, 1827, 4to.

Stenhouse further remarks, "the song entitled ' O'er the Hills and far away' beginning 'Jocky met with Jenny fair,' is not a genuine Scotish production. It was made by one of the Grub Street Poetasters, about the year 1700, and afterwards inserted with the music in the fourth volume of the ' Pills to Purge Melancholy.' It is there called 'Jockey's Lamentation,'" and is the same version as that subsequently reprinted in the old Ballads above referred to. Immediately following this song in Durfey's book (which by the way occurs in the fifth, not the fourth volume) comes "The Recruiting Officer; or, the merry Volunteers; being an excellent new copy of verses upon raising recruits. To the foregoing tune." Another song of "Over the Hills and far away" entitled "The wind has blawn my plaid away" is in the Appendix Part I. to the second series of Hogg's Jacobite Relics.

O'er the hills and far away.

Jocky met with Jenny fair,
Aft by* the dawning of the day,
But Jocky now is fu' of care,
Since Jenny staw† his heart away.
Although she promised to be true,
She proven has alake unkind,
Which gars poor Jocky aften rue‡
That e'er he lo'ed a fickle mind.
  And its o'er the hills and far away,
  Its o'er the hills and far away,
  Its o'er the hills and far away,
  The wind has blown my plaid away.

Now Jocky was a bonny lad,
As e'er was born in Scotland fair,
But now poor man he's e'en gane wud,§
Since Jenny has gart him despair.
Young Jocky was a piper's son,
And fell in love when he was young,
But a' the springs‖ that he could play
Was o'er the hills and far away.
  And she's o'er the hill, &c.

* Betwixt.   † Stole.

‡ The which does make poor Jocky rue
  That Jenny's fickle as the wind.

§ But now poor Jockey has run mad
  For Jenny causes his despair.

‖ Tunes.

He sung—when first my Jenny's face*
I saw, she seemed sae fu' of grace,
With meikle joy my heart was filled,
That's now, alas ! with sorrow killed.
Oh ! was she but as true as fair,
'Twad put an end to my despair,
Instead of that she is unkind, †
And wavers like the winter wind.
    And its o'er the hills, &c.

Ah ! could she find the dismal wae,
That I for her sake undergae,
She couldna chuse but grant relief,
And put an end to a' my grief.
But oh ! she is as fause as fair,
Which causes a' my sighs and care,‡
And she triumphs in a proud disdain,
And takes pleasure in my pain.§
    And its o'er the hills, &c.

Hard was my hap to fa' in love
With ane that does so faithless prove,
Hard was my fate to court a maid
That has my constant heart betrayed.
A thousand times to me she sware
She wad be true for ever mair,
But to my grief, alake ! I say
She staw my heart and ran away.
    And its o'er the hills, &c.

  * When first I saw my Jenny's face
    She did appear with such a grace.

  † But oh ! alas! this is unkind,
    Which sore does terrify my mind.
      'Twas o'er the hills, &c.,
        That Jenny stole my heart away.

  ‡ My sad despair.
  § And takes delight to see my pain.

* Since that nae pity she will take,
I maun gae wander for her sake,
And in ilk wood and gloomy grove,†
I'll sighing sing adieu to love.
Since she is fause whom I adore,
I'll never trust a woman more,
Frae a' their charms I'll flee away,
And on my pipe I'll sweetly play
O'er the hills and far away.
   O'er hills and dales and far away,
   O'er hills and dales and far away,
   O'er hills and dales and far away,
   The wind has blown my plaid away:‡

* [Good gentle Cupid take my part,
  And pierce this false one to the heart,
  That she for once may feel the woe
  That I for her do undergo;
  Oh make her feel this raging pain,
  That for her love I do sustain;
  She sure would then more gentle be,
  And soon repent her cruelty.]

† Into the woods and shady grove,
  And bid adieu to my false love.

‡ [There by myself I'll sing and say,
  'Tis o'er the hills and far away,
  That my poor heart is gone astray,
  Which makes me grieve both night and day,
  Farewell! farewell! thou cruel she,
  I fear that I shall die for thee;
  But if I live this vow I'll make,
  To love no other for your sake.]
    'Tis o'er the hills and far away,
    'Tis o'er the hills and far away,
    'Tis o'er the hills and far away,
    The wind has blow'd my plaid away.

Ꭲꭷꬲ ꬲꭶꭒꭶꬲ ꭵꬲ ꭵꪧ ꭟꭵꪧ.

FROM a MS. found with others in the repositories of a family in
Dumfrieshire. Its date is evidently about 1770. We have a copy of the
same song with several verbal differences in the MS. collection previously
noticed as having been obtained at an auction in Leicester Square. It
is therein set down as "a new song sung by Miss Stephenson," who was
a popular vocalist at Vauxhall about the time we have mentioned.

Young Colin declares I'm his joy and delight,
He's ever uneasy when I'm from his sight;
He wants to be with me wherever I go,
The deuce sure is in him for teazing me so.
    The deuce, &c.

His pleasure all day is to sit by my side,
He pipes and he sings tho' I frown and I chide;
I bid him begone, but he, smiling, says " no !"
What mortal but Colin could plague a maid so?

He often requests me his pains to relieve,
I ask him what favours he hopes to receive ?
His answer's a sigh, while in blushes I glow—
The deuce, sure, is in him for teazing me so.

This breast-knot he yesterday brought from the wake,
And softly entreated I'd wear't for his sake ;
Such trifles 'tis easy enough to bestow,
I sure deserve more for his teazing me so.

He hands me each morn from the cot to the plain,
He meets me at eve to conduct me again ;
But what's his intention I wish I could know,
For I'd rather be married than plagued with him so.

𝔓𝔦𝔠𝔨𝔦𝔫𝔤 𝔏𝔦𝔩𝔦𝔢𝔰.

FROM a chap copy of "Four excellent new songs, 1. The Captain's
Frolic ; 2. Picking Lilies ; 3. The distressed Sailors on the rocks of
Scylla ; 4. The Generous Gentleman." Circa 1782.

This is a good specimen of a peculiar kind of ballad, which, some
years ago, used to fascinate the minds of sentimental damsels whose
notions of poetry were rather limited.

Down in yon meadow fresh and gay,
Picking lilies fresh and gay,
Picking lilies red and blue,
I little thought what love could do.

Where love is planted there it grows,
It buds and blossoms like any rose,
It has such a sweet and pleasant smell,
No flower on earth can it excel.

There is thousands, thousands in a room,
My love she carries the brightest bloom,
She surely is some chosen one,
I will have her or I'll have none.

I saw a ship sailing on the sea,
As deeply loaded as she could be,
But not so deep as in love I am,
I care not whether I sink or swim.

Must I go bound, shall she go free ?
Must I love one that loves not me ?
Why should I act such a childish part,
As to love one that would break my heart ?

I put my hand into a bush,
Thinking the sweetest rose to find,

But I pricked my finger to the bone,
And left the sweetest rose behind.

If roses be such a prickly flower,
They should be gathered when they are green,
For he that weds with an unkind love,
I'm sure he strives against the stream.

If my love were dead and gone to rest,
I'd think on her that I love best,
I'd wrap her up in the linen strong.
And I'd think on her when she's dead and gone.

Labour in Vain.

From a chap copy of "Three excellent new songs, 1. The rock and a wee pickle tow ; 2. The Tankard of Ale ; 3. Labour in vain." Circa 1794.

In pursuit of some lambs from my flocks that had stray'd,
   One morning I ranged o'er the plain ;
But, alas ! after all my researches were made,
   I perceived that my labour was vain.

At length growing hopeless my lambs to restore,
   I resolv'd to return back again ;
It was useless, I thought, to seek after them more,
   Since I found that my labour was vain.

On this my return, pretty Phœbe I saw,
   And to love her I could not refrain ;
To solicit a kiss, I approach'd her with awe,
   But she told me my labour was vain.

But, Phœbe, I cried, to my suit lend an ear,
   And let me no longer complain ;
She reply'd with a frown, and an aspect severe,
   Young Colin, your labour's in vain.

Y

Then I eagerly clasp'd her quite close to my breast,
And kiss'd her and kiss'd her again :
O Colin, she cry'd, if you're rude, I protest
That your labour shall still be in vain.

At length, by entreaties, by kisses, and vows,
Compassion she took on my pain ;
She now has consented to make me her spouse,
So my labour has not been in vain.

The Misfortunate Clown.

From a chap book titled "The Clown, to which is added, Poor
Allan, the Pedler. Cape of Good Hope. Falkirk, printed by T.
Johnston 1801." It has been collated with a copy about ten years
earlier in date, in which the tune is stated to be, "As Patie cam' up
through the Glen." The argument of the ballad is one that has been
frequently dealt with both by Scotish and English song-writers—that of a
suitor making up his mind to go upon a courting expedition, and meeting
with a rebuff. The Scotish poetasters, however, are not content that
the lady should simply dismiss the presumptuous fellow, but they cause
him to be maltreated. The English treat the matter with a better grace.
The marked contrast is shown in this and the English ballad which
follows.

It is possible that some of those fictitiously philanthropic young ladies,
who, in the grand question so frequently mooted of late in the London
papers, as to how little it is possible for a married couple to live upon,
have avowed their partiality for love in a cottage if productive only of
bread and cheese and kisses, might be induced to think that the pos-
sessions which "The Misfortunate Clown" enumerates as his, would
be more than sufficient to form the nucleus of a grand establishment.

There once was a clown in a stead,
    What think ye but he'd hae a wifie
To manage his meal an' his bread,
    For his siller it was na sae rifey.
A laird o' the neist barn-town
    Had dochters an' siller in plenty,

Thinks he, gif the nest be na flown,
　Rejoice! for my chance shall be dainty.
　　　　　Fal tol de ral de, &c.

He puts on his braw plaiding trews,
　An' scrapes aff his beard wi' a whittle,
Slips on the best o' his blues,
　An' rubs up his bonnet fu' muckle.
He taks the wide-teethed stable kame
　An' gies his rough head a bit clautie,
He maist tore the hide frae the bane,
　For O, it was terribly tautie.
　　　　　Fal tol, &c.

His head piece puts on aboon a',
　His cheeks in a cog fu' o' water;
Thinks he, O I'm bonny an' braw,
　An' I'm sure o' the lass an' her tocher.*
A staff in his han' fadam long,
　A knock o't right sair it wad bruize† ye;
He lilted awa' and he sang,
　" Noo, I'm sure that she canna refuse me."
　　　　　Fal tol, &c.

Arriv'd at the gentleman's door,
　No kenning the ways o' the gentry,
He lean'd a' his weight till't an' mair,
　An' fell wi' a blad in the entry.
The dochters an' servants cam' ben,
　To wonder and gaze upon Johnny,
He fixes his e'en on Miss Jean,
　For O she was wonderous bonny.
　　　　　Fal tol, &c.

Miss Jeany, to haud up the joke,
　She oxtered him ben to her cham'er,
　　* Cutter.　　　　　　　　　† Muse.

An' O how he stutterd an' spoke,
    As he tell'd her, " Ye shine just like am'er."
Quoth he, " Lass, my errand to you
    Is to mak ye a kind o' half marrow,
To wait on my housie, my doo,
    When I'm at the plough an' the harrow.
                   Fal tol, &c.

I've nae less than twa pair o' stools,
    A fitgang, a bed, an' an am'ry,
A bink for our bickers an' bowls,
    Faith I break them right aft whan I'm angry.
I've likewise twa guid horn spoons,
    A flesh fork, a pat, an' a ladle,
A girdle for toasting our scones,
    Baith pokers an' tangs, an' a padle.
                   Fal tol, &c.

You'll get parritch an' milk i' the morning,
    An' butter an' cheese to your dinner,
The same again night for your corning,
    Ye'll grow buxom like auld luckie Genner.
For I've thretty pound Scots ilka year,
    Twa pecks o' guid meal, an' a sixpence
Comes in ilka Saturday clear,
    Sent me down bye frae auld Andrew Dickson's.
                   Fal tol, &c.

Besides I've a sonsy milk-cow,
    A' thae things 'll aye haud us breathing,
Twa pigs an' a dainty bred sow,
    They get a' their grazing for naething.
Sae tell me in ye're comin' hame,
    An' dinna appear in a swither,
For gin ye winna tak me, my dame,
    I'm just gaun ow'r to anither."
                   Fal tol, &c.

" Dear Johnny !" said she, with a smile,
" I cannot accept of your offer,
Ane higher than you must beguile,
    Ere my father will part with my tocher.
If I were to give my consent,
    I would merit my father's displeasure,
So Johnny, lad, just be content
    At losing this beautiful treasure."
                                    Fal tol, &c.

Her father this while at the door,
    Lap in wi' an angry complexion,
An' O how he curst an' he swore
    He would brat him, an' bruise him, an' vex him.
Poor Johnny maist coupit the creels
    To get awa off in a hurry,
They hounded the dogs at his heels,
    An' then was sic scurry and worry.
                                    Fal tol, &c.

They hooted, they pelted him sair,
    As ower the lea rigs he stumbled ;
An' just as he couldna rin mair,
    In the dyke-seuch head foremost he tumbled.
In the dirt thus he landed at last,
    An' his braw new plaid trews met their ruin ;
How and when he got hame he ne'er said,
    But he swore he'd nae mair gang awooin'.
                                    Fal tol, &c.

Dick's Courtship.

From the press of W. Armstrong, Banastre Street, [Liverpool].

Last new-year's day, so blythe and gay,
I mounted on my dapple grey,

And away I went to Stanley Green
To court the parson's daughter, Jean.
    Laddie fal lee.

My buckskin breeches I put on,
My country clogs to save my shoon,
And my oldest hat upon my head,
Bound round about with ribbons red.

Straightway I went into the hall,
And for Mistress Jean aloud did call,
Some trusty servant let me in,
That I the courtship might begin.

" Well, now you're come, without delay
Pray tell me what you've got to say?"
" Why, don't you ken me, Mistress Jean?
I am poor Dick from Stanley Green.

" My father sent me here to woo,
And I can fancy none but you—
If you love I as I love you,
What need I make so much ado?"

" If I consent to be your bride,
Pray, what for me can you provide?
For I can neither card nor spin;
How much a-week do you bring in?"

" Why, I can plough and I can sow,
And can besides both reap and mow,
And to market go with father's hay,
And earn my sixpence every day."

" Sixpence a-day will never do,
I must have silks and satins too,

Besides a coach to take the air."
"Oh! dang the woman, she maks me stare.

Besides, yon house which stands hard by,
Is all my own when father does die.
If you'll engage to marry me now,
I'll feed you as fat as father's old sow."

"Your compliments, Dick, are so polite,
You make the company laugh outright ;
And if you have no more to say,
Pray, mount old Dobbin and ride away."

𝔜oung 𝔯oger of 𝔱𝔥e 𝔐ill.

This also bears the imprint of W. Armstrong, Liverpool.

Young Roger of the Mill, one morning very soon,
Put on his best apparel, new hose, and clouten shoon,
And he a wooing went, to bonny buxom Nell,
"Adzooks! said he, can thou fancy me, for I like thee
wondrous well, well,

For I like," &c.

It was early the next morning and on a holiday,
Young Roger drest his horses and he gave them corn and
hay,
"I am come to speak my mind, what say'st thou bonny Nell?
Adzooks! says he, can thou fancy me, for I like thee
wondrous well, well."

"I thank you for your offer," the damsel she replied,
"But I am not in such a haste to be a ploughman's bride,
For I do live in hopes to marry a farmer's son."
"If that be so, farewell, I'll go," said Roger, "for I have
done."

"Your horses you have dress'd, I think I've heard you say,
Made all in readiness, and having come this way
Just sit and chat a-while ;" "No, no indeed, not I,
For I cannot sit, and cannot chat, as I've other fish to fry.

"Go take your farmer's son, with all my honest heart,
For though my name be Hodge and I drive the plough and
    cart,
I need not tarry long before I get a wife,
There's buxom Joan 'tis very well known, she loves me as
    her life."

"And Oh, what is buxom Joan, cannot I suit as well?
For she has ne'er a penny, not so has bonny Nell,
I have got fifty shillings," the money made Hodge to smile,
He bowed his head, and he drew a chair, and he vowed he'd
    chat a-while.

"So now, my dearest Nell, against next quarter day,
If thou hast fifty shillings, why need we longer stay,
For I have fifty more, the money a cow will buy,
So we'll join our hands in wedlock's bands, and there's
    none like you and I."

The Governing Fair.

From Chap Copy of Songs—"Mounseer Nong Tong Pas, to which
are added, John Anderson my Joe ; The Governing Fair ; The Mariner's
Wife." Printed by G. Miller, High Street, Dunbar, 1800.

I am a brisk young lively lass,
    A little more than twenty,
And by my comely air and dress,
    I can have sweethearts plenty.
But I'll beware of wedlock's snare,
    Tho' dying swains adore me ;

The men I'll teaze, myself to please,
My mother did so before me.

In rich brocades and diamonds bright,
Like gayest spring's delighting,
My parts and humour shall unite
To make me more inviting.
For I'll advance and learn to dance,
To please shall be my glory;
I'll learn to trace each step with grace,
My mother did so before me.

I'll dress as fine as fine can be,
My pride shall be my pleasure;
And though the neighbours envy me,
To mind them I've no leisure;
I'll take delight, both day and night,
To be reviewed in story;
I'll have it said—" There shines a maid !"
My mother did so before me.

To park and play I'll often go,
To spend each leisure hour;
I'll walk and talk with every beau,
And make them feel my power.
But if a dart should pierce my heart,
From one that does adore me,
We'll wed and kiss, what harm's in this?
My mother did so before me.

Then will I manage, when I wed,
My husband to perfection,
For, as good wives have often said,
" Keep husbands in subjection."
No snarling fool shall o'er me rule,
Or e'er eclipse my glory;
I'll let him see I'll mistress be,
My mother did so before me.

MR LOWE AND MISS CUNDY.

THIS Song is from the Catnach press, and is advertised to be "sold by Marshall, Bristol ; Inkpen, Lewes ; T. Batchelor, 14 Hackney Road Crescent ; and Mrs Boyse, Brighton. Also by Pierce, Southborough.

The superstitious allusion in the last stanza, "never cut your toe-nails on a Sunday," may be illustrated by the following *Nursery rhyme as to cutting one's nails.*

> Cut them on Monday,
>   You cut them for health ;
> Cut them on Tuesday,
>   You cut them for wealth :
> Cut them on Wednesday,
>   You cut them for losses ;
> Cut them on Thursday,
>   You cut them for crosses ;
> Cut them on Friday,
>   You cut them for sorrow ;
> Cut them on Saturday,
>   You'll see your beau on the morrow.

Another version has it thus :—

> Monday for health,
> Tuesday for wealth,
>   Wednesday the best day of all ;
> Thursday for losses,
> Friday for crosses,
>   Saturday no luck at all.

Mr Lowe and Miss Cundy.

A spruce Linen Draper, one Mr John Lowe,
    Walked the Custom-house quay one Sunday,
His dress was the pink of the fashion and go,
    When he met with the charming Miss Cundy.
Her beautiful eyes took him quite by surprise,
    And so queer was the state that he felt in ;
He tried all in vain to tell her his pain,
    For his heart was really a melting.
But alas ! who can look into Fate's book of Laws?
Mr Lowe would have married Miss Cundy,

He lost her ! he lost her ! and only because,
He cut his toe-nails on a Sunday !

The next time he met her his love he made known,
Her person he thought all perfection ;
He pressed her with speed to be bone of his bone,
She blushed, and—had no objection :
He gaily did sing, went and purchased the ring,
And the next Sunday was the bespeak day,
For that day would chime, and agree with his time,
Much better than having a week day.
     But alas, &c.

On the blest Sunday morning he got up with glee,
(Little thinking what mischief was hatching),
Took out his pen-knife his toes to make free,
At night to prevent them from scratching;
But the knife slipt, and gave his great toe such a wound,
(Sweet wedlock there's surely a fate in)
He could not put it at all to the ground,
Though he knew sweet Miss Cundy was waiting.
     But alas, &c.

Oh, words can't describe all his trouble and woe,
Only think of his sad situation,
A surgeon was sent for, who dressed his great toe,
And talked about amputation.
Laid up for a month, while Miss Cundy so smart,
Disappointed of having this short knight,
Without delay got her another sweetheart,
And married in less than a fortnight.
So young men, if love has got into your heart,
Recollect Mr Lowe and Miss Cundy;
And whatever you do before you get wed,
Never cut your toe-nails on a Sunday.

Moll Boy's Courtship.

A copy of this Ballad occurs in "the Dairy Maid; a Vocal Miscellany," Edin 1784. It is there called "Honest Mall Boye." There are several variations, but not of much moment.

Noble Sir Arthur a hunting doth ride
With his hounds at his feet, and his sword at his side.
As he was a riding by chance he did spy
A charming brown girl, her name was Moll Boy.

O charming Moll Boy, my butler shall be
To draw the red wine betwixt you and me,
I'll make you a lady of highest degree,
If you will but love me my charming Molly.

I'll deck you with ribbons, and many fine things,
I'll cover your fingers with jewels and rings,
Of satin and silk shall your petticoats be,
The pride of my heart, my darling Molly.

I'll have none of your ribbons, nor none of your rings,
Nor none of your jewels, nor of your fine things,
For I have gotten petticoats suits my degree,
I'll ne'er love a married man till his wife die.

O lovely Moll Boy, lend me your penknife,
And I will go home and kill my old wife,
I'll kill my old wife and come unto thee,
If you will but love me my charming Molly.

O noble Sir Arthur, you must not do so,
Go home, love your own wife; let no body know,
For seven long years I'll wait upon thee,
But I'll ne'er love a married man till his wife die.

Seven long years were long gone and past,
And the old woman went to her long home at last,
That day she was buried a blythe man was he,
And he soon came a courting his charming Molly.

O fairest Moll Boy give me but your hand,
And all I possess shall be yours at command,
For my wife she is buried, I come unto thee,
Say thou wilt but love me my charming Molly.

Oh charming Moll Boy has given consent,
Straightway to the Church to be married she went,
Now charming Moll Boy in her coach she doth ride,
With maids to attend her, her man by her side.

It's all ye young women take warning by me,
Never love a married man until his wife die.

THE WILLOW TREE.

THIS bears the imprint of W. Armstrong, Banastre Street, [Liverpool]. The air of "The Willow Tree" forms No. 95 of Mr Chappell's Collection of National English Airs. He remarks : "This is one of the common ballad tunes, still sung about the counties of Derbyshire, Warwickshire, and Lancashire. The verse printed with the music is from a ballad of the same title in Percy's Reliques of Ancient Poetry, but we have no reason to believe in their identity. The following is a specimen of the original words :—

> 'Oh, this willow tree will twist,
>   And this willow tree will twine ;
> And I wish I was in that young woman's arms,
>   That once had a heart of mine,
>   That once had a heart of mine.' "

He further observes : "This tune is in Forbes' Cantus (1682), in a manuscript 1639 now in the Advocates' Library, Edinburgh, and in the Skene MS. The words are in a small black-letter collection entitled 'The Golden Garland of Princely Delights,' and in Percy's Reliques." Among the King's Pamphlets in the British Museum, vol. v., occurs a ballad, called "A Justification of our brethren in Scotland." Tune, "Under the Willow Tree," 1647.

The tune in Forbes' Cantus, to which Mr Chappell refers, can neither be wedded to the words of "Willow, Willow, Willow," in Percy's Reliques, from which Shakespeare has derived his song of the Willow in Othello, nor to the words of our present song. The Ballad in the Cantus begins thus :—

" How now, shepherd, what means that?
Why wears't thou willows in thy hat?
Are thy scarffs of green or yellow
Twin'd to branches of green willow?
They are changed, so am I ;
Sorrows live when joys do dye :
It is Phillis, only she,
That makes me wear the willow tree."

The Willow Tree.

O take me to your arms, love,
    For keen the wind does blow,
O take me to your arms, love,
    For bitter is my woe.
She hears me not, she cares not,
    Nor will she list to me ;
Whilst here I lie alone to die,
    Beneath the willow tree.
            Whilst here I lie, &c.

My love has wealth and beauty,
    The rich attend her door,
My love has wealth and beauty,
    And I, alas ! am poor.
The ribbons fair that bound her hair,
    Is all that's left to me,
Whilst here I lie alone to die
    Beneath the willow tree.
            Whilst here I lie, &c.

I once had gold and silver,
    I thought 'em without end,
I once had gold and silver,
    And thought I had a friend.
My wealth is lost, my friend is false,
    My love he stole from me ;
And here I lie alone to die
    Beneath the willow tree.
            And here I lie, &c.

Jack Robinson.

ALSO from the press of J. Catnach, 2 Monmouth Court, 7 Dials.

A deservedly eminent and very successful Scotish artist, with whom this song is a great favourite, and who occasionally delights his more select friends with a taste of its quality in a style which few can imitate, has assured us that it is a Ballad of the last century, and that he remembers to have seen in early youth a very old copy stitched up in a canvas cover, with several other songs of that period;—the collection evidently of some seafaring man.

This gentleman's version differs occasionally in the arrangement and in words. These are noted below.

The perils and dangers of the voyage past,
And the ship in Portsmouth arrived at last,
The sails all furl'd, and the anchor cast,
    The happiest of the crew was Jack Robinson.
For his Poll he had trinkets and gold galore,
Besides of prize money quite a store,
And along with the crew he went ashore,
    As cockswain to the boat, Jack Robinson.
                Tol de rol, &c.

He met with a man and said, " I say,
Mayhap you may know one Polly Gray,
She lives somewhere hereabouts," the man said " Nay !
    I do not indeed," to Jack Robinson ;
Says he to him, " I've left my ship,*
And to all my messmates given the slip,
Mayhap, you'll partake of a good can of flip,†
    For you *are* a civil fellow," says Jack Robinson.
                Tol de rol, &c.

In a public-house then they both sat down,‡
And talked of admirals of high renown,
And drank as much grog as came to half-a-crown,
    This here strange man and Jack Robinson.

    * Jack says, "D'ye see, I've left my ship."
    † "Mayhap you'll take a share of a right good can of flip."
    ‡ " Into a grogshop they went and they both sat down,
        And convers'd about admirals," &c.

Then Jack called out the reck'ning to pay,
The landlady came in, in fine array,
"My eyes and limbs, why here's Polly Gray,*
　　Who'd thought of meeting here?" says Jack Robinson.
　　　　　　　　Tol de rol, &c.

The landlady she stagger'd against the wall,
And said at first as how she did not know him at all,
"Shiver me," says Jack, "why, here's a pretty squall!
　　Damme, don't you know me?—I'm Jack Robinson!
D'ye see this here handkerchief as how you giv'd to me
Full three years ago, before I went to sea?
Every day I look'd at it and then I thought of thee,
　　Upon my soul, I did," says Jack Robinson.
　　　　　　　　Tol de rol, &c.

Says the landlady, says she, "I've changed my state,"
"Why you don't mean," says Jack, "as how you've got a mate;
You know you promis'd me." Says she, "I couldn't wait,†
　　For no tidings could I gain of you, Jack Robinson.
When one day somebody comed to me and said,
That somebody else had somewheres read
In some newspaper as how that you was dead,"
　　"I han't been dead at all," says Jack Robinson.
　　　　　　　　Tol de rol, &c.

Then he turn'd his quid and finish'd his glass,
Hitch'd up his trowsers, and said, "alas! alas!‡
That ever I should live to be made such an ass!
　　To be bilk'd by a woman!" says Jack Robinson.

---

* "When Jack he call'd out, the reck'ning to pay,
　　In came the landlady in fine array;
　　'Why, bless my heart!' says Jack, 'if here aint Polly Gray,
　　Who'd 'a thought of meeting you here?' says Jack Robinson."
† "You know," says she, "you promised, Jack; and you know I
　　couldn't wait."
‡ Then he hitch'd up his trousers and finished his glass,
　　And turn'd his quid," &c.

But to fret and stew about it now is all in vain,
I'll get a ship and off I'll go to Holland, France, and Spain,
No matter where :—to Portsmouth I'll ne'er come back
    again,"
And he was off before they could say Jack Robinson.
           Tol de rol, &c.

THE OLD MAID'S LAMENT FOR A HUSBAND.

From a Chap copy.   "Falkirk, printed by T. Johnston, 1817."

STENHOUSE remarking in his "Illustrations of the Lyric Poetry and Music of Scotland" on the song, "My Father has Forty good Shillings" says : "Mr Ritson informs us that there is an old English ballad in the black letter, entitled 'The Maiden's sad complaint for want of a husband ; to the new west country tune, or Hogh, when shall I be married? By L. W.' Mr Ritson annexes the following stanzas :—

> O when shall I be married,
>   *Hogh, be married?*
> My beauty begins to decay :
> 'Tis time to find out somebody,
>   *Hogh, somebody,*
> Before it is quite gone away.
>
> My father hath forty good shillings,
>   *Hogh, good shillings,*
> And never a daughter but me ;
> My mother is also willing,
>   *Hogh, so willing,*
> That I shall have all if she die."

The Old Maid's Lament for a Husband.

> My new gown's away to make,
>   My sark 'tis no fair worn yet,
> My spencer's o' the silk sae black,
>   And no an inch o't torn yet.
> But what ails a' the lads at me?
> 'Tis mair than I can guess or see,
> I'm feared a maiden auld I'll be
>   And live a life forlorn yet.

z

My sister Kate was ne'er so tight,
    Nor frank, nor half so bonnie, O,
To my surprise last new year's night,
    Was buckled unto Johnny, O.
Whilst I, poor lass, maun stay at hame,
And cauld and sleepless lye my lane,
And sab and greet wi' grief and shame,
    For fear I'll ne'er get ony, O.

I'm sure I gang baith braw and clean,
    And look aye blyth and cheery, O,
Nae straughter legs had Burns's Jean,
    But ne'er a lad comes near me, O.
My hair is papered every night,
And oiled to make it sleek and bright,
Wi' mindin' it my prayers I slight,
    Unless to send some dearie, O.

My heart is vexed, tears blind my e'en,
    To see bare-headed lassies, O,
Get men before they be nineteen,
    And for douce wives then passes, O.
Since I did count years thirty-twa,
The deil ane speirs my price ava',
Or makes an errand great or sma'
    To treat me wi' caresses, O.

I courted lang wi' Willie Glen,
    But 'cause he had nae tocher, O,
I thought the warld aye my ane,
    And slighted his kind proffer, O.
'Cause I was saucy, he was proud,
That time o' lads I had a crowd,
But mony a time since syne I've rued
    I didna take his offer, O.

There's nane mair keener to be wed,
Tho' a' my friends misca' me sair,
There's nane mair fear'd to die a maid,
For troth I'm maist at my last prayer.
There's nane deaves me like aunty Nell,
'Cause she cuist a liggan gird hersel,'
Cries, " lass take gude tent o' yoursel',
And ne'er trust men though they should swear."

But let them flyte or let them frown,
Or let them a' be friendly, O,
I'll do my best to get a man,
And dress myself fu' finely, O.
If ony lad would come my road
And bid me gang, wi' wink or nod,
Aff I would go at the first bode
And ever would prove kindly, O.

THE LAIRD OF COCKPEN.

COCKPEN is a small estate in the County of Edinburgh, which belongs
to the heirs of the Marquis of Dalhousie. It had previously been acquired
either by Baron Cockburn, or his father, who was a respectable haber-
dasher in Edinburgh. The former, owing to his marriage with one of
the daughters of Captain Rannie (the owner of Melville Castle) acquired a
considerable sum of money, but, what was much better, became connected,
by the marriage of his sister-in-law, with Henry Dundas, afterwards
Lord Advocate for Scotland, and better known as the first Viscount
Melville, through whose powerful patronage he, having been bred to the
bar, obtained the comfortable situation of one of the Barons of Exchequer.
He was the father of the late Lord Cockburn who sometimes ventured to
boast of his family. Upon one occasion, when old Mr Horner, the
father of Leonard Horner and of Francis Horner, M. P., was dining with
a large company at Bonally, where Henry Cockburn resided both before
and after his elevation to the Bench, his host took an opportunity,
during a pause in the conversation, to ask his guest, (who be it observed,
was a linen manufacturer himself), whether he remembered his (Cockburn's) grandfather? " Very well indeed," was the answer ; " he was a

very decent man. I have seen him often in his shop in the Lucken-booths." This malapropos disclosure of the origin of the family, did not seem very agreeable to Master Harry, who had not expected that his guests would have been in this way so far enlightened about his ancestry. He had anticipated a glowing eulogy upon the virtues of his grandfather, instead of a revelation of the fact that he had soiled his fingers by humble trade.

We believe that the Ballad has no reference to any of the Cockburn family, and that the name was selected by the Baroness Nairn (the authoress) from its singularity. It was rendered popular for a while during the lifetime of Charles Mackay, the celebrated performer of Bailie Nicol Jarvie, and was first introduced by him to public notice about the year 1821. The concluding stanza was not originally sung, until it was felt that poetic justice had not been quite done to the Laird, as there was no reason why he should have been allowed to remain an unsuccessful wooer. In all probability Mr Murray, the manager of the Edinburgh Theatre, supplied the deficiency. "Dr Rogers, however, remarks in his Modern Scottish Minstrel, Edin. 1855, cr. 8vo., vol. i. The modern Ballad has been often attributed to Miss Ferrier, the accomplished author of 'Marriage' and other popular Novels. She only contributed the last two stanzas."

This humorous and highly popular song, he goes on to say, was composed by Lady Nairn towards the close of the last century, in place of the older words connected with the air, "When she came ben, she bobbit," which Dr Rogers conceives "to be a composition of the reign of Charles II.," without any further evidence than the well-known anecdote of his Majesty's affection for the air of "Brose and Butter," which a Cockpen of that time, who excelled in playing it, made the means of a restoration of his inheritance. See Hone's Table Book, vol. i. p. 411, also Notes and Queries, 2d series, vol. viii., p. 123.

The older words thus referred to will be found in Herd's Scots Songs, vol ii., p. 206. The first stanza runs thus :—

When she cam ben, she bobbit,
And when she cam ben, she sobbit,
And when she cam ben, she kissed Cockpen,
And then denied that she did it.

A paraphrastic edition of the same ballad will be found in "Select Scotish Songs, Ancient and Modern," with critical observations and Biographical notices by Robert Burns, edited by R. H. Cromek, F.A.S.E. London 1810, cr. 8vo., 2 vols.

Lady Nairn, third daughter of Laurence Oliphant of Gask, in Perthshire was, according to Dr Rogers, born in 1766. In her youth she is said to have been remarkably pretty so much so that she was known throughout her native district as "the flower of Strathearn." She was married in 1806 to her cousin William Nairn, Esq., Assistant Inspector of Barracks in Scotland, who became Baron Nairn in 1824, by the removal of the attainder of the second Lord Nairn of 9th Feb. 1715 (1716), and of a subsequent attainder in 1746 of the second Lord's son, John Nairn, who had taken upon himself the title. The removal of this attainder, and of those of the Earl of Mar, Viscount Kenmure, and the Viscount Strathallan, were occasioned by the desire of his Majesty, King George IV. to show to the people of Scotland in some degree, how much he had been gratified by the enthusiastic reception accorded him during his visit to Scotland in 1822. Subsequent restorations took place at a later period, but it does not appear to have originally been the Royal intention to extend the clemency of the crown beyond the immediate descendants of the persons attainted, in which position the two Viscounts and Lord Nairn stood, they being the direct male representatives of the attainted. Lord Mar's case is peculiar. As Lord Erskine, he could not have obtained the benefit of that act, because he was only the male representative of the Lords Erskine—a collateral Peerage—but he got over this difficulty by the fact of his ancestress having been the daughter of the attainted Earl, and the peerage being an ancient territorial Earldom, the title was inherited by the Erskines through females.

Upon the death of the restored Baron Nairn, which took place in 1830, he was succeeded in the Peerage by his only son William, born in 1808, who survived him only seven years. The title was then claimed by the Countess Flahault, who was in her own right Baroness Keith, as a descendant and representative of Mercer of Auldie, who, it is said, was covered by the patent as heir-general of the Nairn family. How this stands we do not presume to say, but it appears from the Edinburgh Almanack that her Ladyship's daughter, now Marchioness of Lands-downe, has taken also the title of Baroness Nairn. These explanations are necessary, as the dowager baroness has sometimes been confounded with Lady Keith.

It is remarkable that by the act of 1746, the father and grandfather of the Dowager Lady Nairn were also attainted. This attainder it is understood is still in operation, for when some years since the late Mr. Oliphant of Gask preferred a claim to the dormant Barony of Oliphant, he was met by the objection that however good his case might otherwise be, the existing statute effectually prevented his success. This was before George IV.'s visit, when there were no expectations of any of the attainted families being rehabilitated. If any existing male Oliphant could prove his descent from one of the older Oliphants of Gask, there is every probability now of the claim being sustained.

After the death of her son, the Baroness Nairn resided chiefly on the Continent, until within two years of her own death, which occurred at

Gask in 1845. For sometime 'she had devoted much attention to many praiseworthy acts of benevolence.

She was, it is believed, a contributor to "the Scotish Minstrel,"—a collection of Scotish Melodies published periodically under the editorial care of Mr R. A. Smith, and which was completed in six royal 8vo volumes in 1824. Sometime after her death several of her Lyrics were published in a volume entitled, "Lays from Strathearn," arranged by Finlay Dun.

Dr Rogers, in his notice of Lady Nairn, makes this strange statement as to the removal of the attainder. "This measure is reported to have been passed on the strong recommendation of George IV.; his Majesty having learned, during his state visit to Scotland in 1822, that the song of 'The Attainted Scotish Nobles' was the composition of Lady Nairn;" and adds: "the song is certainly one of the best apologies for Jacobitism." How such a report ever obtained is strange, as acts of grace in such cases are not apt to be performed by crowned heads upon such slender considerations. But, apart from this, if any one will take the trouble to read the verses referred to (and which will be found at page 232, vol. 1 of Dr Rogers' Book) he will be staggered to think that either the Baroness Nairn could have penned, or his Majesty could have expressed admiration of such doggrel. It is paying a very poor compliment to the poetic powers of the Baroness to charge her with having written such lines, and to the taste of the most accomplished gentleman in Europe if he could have been attracted by them.

The Laird of Cockpen.

The Laird o' Cockpen he's proud and he's great,
His mind is ta'en up wi' affairs o' the state;
He wanted a wife his braw hoose to keep,
But favours in wooin' are faschious to seek.

Near yonder dykeside a leddy did dwell—
At his table-head he thocht she'd look well—
MacLeish's ae dochter o' Claversha' Lea,
A penniless lass wi' a long pedigree.

His wig was well poothered and as gude as new,
His doublet was red, and his hose they were blue;
He put on a ring, a sword, and cock'd hat,
An' wha could refuse the Laird wi' a' that?

He mounted his naig, and he rode cannilie,
And when he arrived at Claversha' Lea,
" Gae tell Mistress Jean to come speedily ben,
She's wanted to speak wi' the Laird o' Cockpen."

Mistress Jean she was makin' the Elder-flower wine,
"What brings the Laird here at sic an ill time?"
She's put aff her apron, put on a silk goun,
A mutch wi' red ribbons an' cam awa' doun.

An' when she cam ben he bowed fu' low,
An' what was his errand he sune let her know,
Astonished was he when the leddy said " Na !"
An' wi' a low courtesy turned her awa'.

Dumbfounder'd was he, but nae sigh did he gie,
He mounted his naig and he rode cannilie,
An' often he thocht, as he jogged through the glen,
" She was daft to refuse the Laird o' Cockpen."

Noo after the Laird his exit had made,
Miss Jean she reflected on what she had said,
" For ane I'll get better, for waur I'll get ten,
I was daft to refuse the Laird o' Cockpen."

Next time that the Laird an' the Leddy were seen,
They were gaun arm in arm to the Kirk on the Green;
Noo, she sits in the ha' like a weel-tappit hen,
But nae chickens as yet hae appeared at Cockpen.*

* There is another reading of this concluding stanza, which is as
follows :—

> Jean gaed to the kirk ruing sair a' the while,
> The Laird he was there, sae she gied him a smile,
> And sune was she perched, like an auld tappit hen,
> As mistress and mair in the ha's o' Cockpen.

IMPROBABILITY.

THE ballad which follows is from a broadside, printed in Scotland about 1809, and is a reproduction, in a garbled form, of "a song" to be found in Durfey's Pills, 1719, vol. 5, p. 36.   It is curious, as showing how over a long period of years ballad literature travels from one country to another. Substantially the songs are identical, and the lines, in many instances, precisely similar.   The arrangement is very different, and two stanzas have not been adopted in any form.   The first is this stanza in Durfey, in reply to the friend's desire, "To tell her when I meant to marry:"—

> "Sweet heart?" quoth I, "if you would know,
>   Then hear the words, and I'll reveal it ;
> Since in your mind you bear it so,
>   And in your heart you will conceal it."
> She promis'd me she'd make no words,
>   But of such things she would be wary ;
> And thus in brief I did begin
>   To tell her when I meant to marry.

The next is his concluding stanza:—

> "Good sir, since you have told me when
>   That you've resolved for to marry ;
> I wish with all my heart till then
>   That for a wife you still may tarry.
> But if all young men were of your mind,
>   And maids no better were preferred ;
> I think it were when the d—l were blind,
>   That we and our lovers should be married."

A similar sentiment to that which pervades our ballad prevails throughout numerous lyrics.   One we remember hearing when a child, which commenced :—

> "When gooseberries grow on the stem of a daisy."

And there is a sonnet in the *John Bull Magazine*, a clever but shortlived periodical of the year 1824, edited by Dr Maginn, beginning :—

> "When golden Phœbus, rising in the west,"

which, after enumerating several impossibilities, leads to this conclusion:—

> "Then, Tailor dear, I'll pay this bill of thine,
>   Which in the meantime serves my pipe to light."

We have also a dreamy recollection of a second sonnet, commencing :—

> "When lobsters sing hymns in the palace at Windsor."

Here is another to the same purpose, from the volume of Durfey just quoted, which is titled, "Song set by Mr Jeremiah Clark. Sung by Mr Leveridge:"—

When maids live to thirty yet never repented,
When Europe's at peace and all England contented,
When gamesters won't swear, and no bribery thrives,
Young wives love old husbands, young husbands old wives;
When landlords love taxes, and soldiers love peace,
And lawyers forget a rich client to fleece ;
When an old face shall please as well as a new,
Wives, husbands, and lovers will ever be true.

When bullies leave huffing and cowards their trembling,
And courtiers, and women, and priests their dissembling ;
When these shall do nothing against what they teach,
Pluralities hate, and we mind what they preach ;
When vintners leave brewing to draw the wine pure,
And quacks by their medicines kill less than they cure ;
When an old face shall please as well as a new,
Wives, husbands, and lovers will ever be true.

Improbability.

As I was walking in a grove
   All by myself, as I supposed,
My mind did ofttimes me remove,
   But by no means could be composed.
At length by chance a friend I met,
   Which caused me long time to tarry ;
And much of me she did entreat,
   To tell her when I would her marry.

When saffron grows on every tree,
   And every stream flows milk and honey ;
When sugar grows in carrot fields,
   And usurers refuse their money ;
When country men for judges sit,
   And Michaelmas falls in February ;
When millers do their toll forget,
   O then, my love and I'll be married.

When women know not how to scold,
  And Dutchmen leave off drinking brandy;
When cats do bark and dogs do mew,
  And brimstone's taken for sugar-candy;
Whenever Whitsunday does fall
  All in the month of January;
When cobblers work without an awl,
  O then, my love and I'll be married.

When Shrovetide falls in Easter week,
  And Christmas in the month of July;
When lawyers plead without a fee,
  And tailors deal both right and truly;
When all deceit is quite put down,
  And truth by all men is preferred;
When indigo dyes red and brown,
  O then, my love and I'll be married.

When men and beasts the ocean plough,
  And fishes in green fields are feeding,
And cockles in the streets do grow,
  And swans upon dry banks are breeding;
When mussels sell for diamond rings,
  And glass to gold may be compared;
When gold is made of grey goose wings,
  O then, my love and I'll be married.

When candlesticks do serve for bells,
  And frying-pans are used for ladles;
When in the sea they dig for wells,
  And porridge pots are used for cradles;
When all maids to their loves prove true,
  And horses on men's backs are carried;
When mice are seen with cats to play,
  O then, my love and I'll be married.

Indifference; or, a Rap at the Door.

The last time I came o'er the muir,
It was to see my love to be sure,
It was to see my love to be sure,
And she bade me rap at the door, door,
And she bade me rap at the door, door,
It was to see my love to be sure,
And she bade me rap at the door, door,
And she bade me rap at the door.

"Open the door and let me in,
Coming to see you, I've broken my shin,
Coming to see you, I've broken my chin,
And the pain it feels wondrous sore, sore,
And the pain it feels wondrous sore, sore."
" Broken your chin ! how sorry am I,
I can't find out the way for to cry,
But I will find out the way by and by,
And I'll tease you ten times more, more,
And I'll tease you ten times more."

" Tell your father and mother too,
That I'm your lover come to court you,
That I'm your lover come to court you,
And I pray you to open the door, door,
And I pray you to open the door, door."
" If I were to open the door to you,
It would only be for a minute or two
It would only be for a minute or two
My father and mother they'd you endure,
And they'd beat me wondrous sore, sore,
And they'd beat me wondrous sore.

" O my lad, I'm up to your tricks,
For you have beguiled five or six,

For you have beguiled five or six,
And I myself will not be the next,
You may stand and rap at the door, door,
You may stand and rap at the door, door."
" If I've beguiled six or seven,
Eight, or nine, ten, or eleven,
Eight, or nine, ten, or eleven,
You yourself will make a round dozen,
So I'll rap no more at your door, door,
So I'll rap no more at your door."

" The trees are high, the leaves are green,
The days are past that we have seen,
The days are past that we have seen,
There's another in the place where you should have bee
So you may stand and rap at the door, door,
So you may stand and rap at the door, door."
" If the trees are high the leaves are not shaken,
Although I'm slighted, I'm not heart-broken,
Although I'm slighted, I'm not heart-broken,
As long's there another true love to be gotten,
I'll rap no more at your door, door,
I'll rap no more at your door."

" O young man, I value you not,
Although the hangman had your coat,
Although the hangman had your coat,
And yourself in a bottomless boat,
With the devil to row you ashore, ashore,
With the devil to row you ashore."

Courting too Slow.

It was on a Monday morning, and oh ! it was soon,
I bought pretty Betty a pair of new shoon,

A pair of new shoon and slippers also,
But I lost pretty Betty by courting too slow.

I bought pretty Betty a garland of green,
With ribbons and jewels most rare to be seen,
And the rings on her fingers were of the bright shining gold,
But I lost pretty Betty by not being bold.

It was on a Tuesday evening, and oh ! it was late,
I fain would have kissed her, but I was too blate,
Still thinking to gain her consent to be true,
But I lost pretty Betty, by courting too slow.

For in came a sailor with his tarry trews,
And he went to the chamber where my love was,
He kissed her, and clapped her, and flattered her so,
And he won the day by my courting too slow.

It's all ye young men, pray, take my advice,
When you go a courting pray don't be too nice,
But kiss the pretty girls and give them to know,
You don't mean to lose them by courting too slow.

My Minnie Ment my Auld Breeks.

THIS ballad is by Alexander Rodger, the author of " Behave yourself
before folk," and other popular lyrics.

The air it is sung to is that of the "Corn-clips," an old Scotch song,
the words of which are not quite suited to "ears polite." Two versions of
the "Corn-clips" are to be found in the first volume of the Bannatyne
Club Garlands, printed in 1826. The first stanza, which is the same in
both, runs thus :—

> " My mither ment my auld brekis,
> An' vow but yai wer duddy ;
> An' sente me out to wede ye coirne
> Upoune ye bankis o' Logie."

The hero of the song leans upon his corn-clips to view a damsel passing through a ford in his immediate vicinity, for which offence he is had
up before the kirk-session and severely "rebukit."

My minnie ment my auld breeks,
  And wow but they were duddy;
And sent me to get shod our mare
  At Robin Tamson's smiddy.
The smiddy stands aside the burn
  That wimples through the clachan;
I never yet gang by the door
  But aye I fa' a lauchin'.

For Robin was a walthy carle,
  And had ae bonny dochter;
But ne'er would let her tak a man,
  Tho' mony lads had sought her.
But what think ye o' my exploit?
  The time our mare was shoeing,
I slippet up beside the lass,
  And briskly fell a-wooing.

And aye she e'ed my auld breeks
  The time that we sat crackin';
Quo' I, "my lass, ne'er mind the clouts,
  I've new anes for the makin'.
But gin ye'll just come hame wi' me,
  And leave the carle, your father,
Ye'se get my claes to keep in trim,
  Mysel' an' a' thegither."

"'Deed lad, quoth she, your offer's fair,
  I really think I'll tak it;
Sae gang awa', get oot the mare,
  We'll baith slip on the back o't;
For gin I bide my faither's time,
  I'll wait till I am fifty;

But na—I'll marry in my prime,
    An' mak a wife fu' thrifty."

Wow! Robin was an angry man,
    At losing o' the dochter ;
Thro' a' the kintra side he ran,
    And far and near he sought her.
But when he came to our fire-end,
    And fand us baith thegither,
Quo' I, " Gudeman, I've taen your bairn,
    And ye may tak my mither."

Auld Robin girned and shook his pow,
    " Guid faith," quo' he, " you're merry ;
But I'll just tak ye at your word,
    And end this hurry burry."
Sae, Robin and our auld gudewife,
    Agreed to creep thegither ;
Now, I hae Robin Tamson's pet,
    And Robin has my mither.

O were I King o' Fairy-Land.

This song is from " The Gaberlunzie," a Scotish comedy in three acts,
printed at Edinburgh in 1839. The comedy, which is in Scotish verse,
is extremely well written. The plot is simple, being founded upon one
of the exploits of "the gudeman of Ballengeich." The author is, we
understand, a gentleman resident in the north of England.

O were I king o' fairy-land,
    Here I wad mak my bower,
Beneath the coltfoot's spreading leaf,
    To fend me frae the shower.
Or hide amang the primrose leaves,
    Beside the crystal well,

Where morn and e'en I'd constant wait
   To see thy bonny sel.

The freshest lily's snawy breast
   Can ne'er wi' thine compare!
Yon fleecy cloud, like winter's drift,
   It is na half sae fair.
The cloudless beauty o' the lift
   Will never match thy een;
O were I king o' fairy-land
   Nae ither wad be queen.

MARRIAGE; OR THE MOUSETRAP.

MARRIED life has been a subject which from time immemorial has furnished Poets, Dramatists, and all writers of fiction, with food for satire; and in most cases, whether justly or unjustly we shall not presume to say, their shafts have been directed against the weaker vessel. At the same time the more philosophic extol "a Bachelor's merry life," and with some show of reason, as the verses which follow "shall," as Launcelot Gobbo says, "frutify unto you:"

VERSES ON FRUIT TRENCHERS.

Contributed to Notes and Queries by Mr John Piggot, Junr., who mentions that he copied them from some fruit trenchers which once belonged to Queen Elizabeth, and which are now in the Bodleian Library, Oxford:—

> If that a bachelor thou bee,
>   Keepe thou so, still be ruled by mee,
> Leaste that repentance all to late,
>   Reward thee with a broken pate.

> Content thyselfe withe thyne estat;
>   And send no poore wight from the gate,
> For why this councell I thee give
>   To learne to die and die to lyve.

> Thou gapest after deade men's shoes,
>   But bare foote thou art like to goe;
> Content thyselfe, and doo not muse,
>   For fortune saithe it must be soo.

> Iff thou bee younge then marie not yett,
>   Iff thou bee olde thou haste more wytt.
> For younge menn's wyves will not be taught,
>   And olde men's wyves be good for naught.

IN PRAISE OF THE JOYFUL LIFE OF A BACHELOR.

From Sir J. Hawkins's History of Music, reprinted in Ritson's Ancient Songs.

> The bachelor most joyfullye,
>   In pleasant plight doth pass his daies,

2 A

Good fellowshipp and companie
He doth maintaine and keipe alwais.

With damsels braue he maye well goe,
The married man cannot doe so,
If he be merie and toy with any,
His wife will frown, and words geue manye :
His yellow hose he strait will put on,
So that the married man dare not displease his wife Joane.

We find the term " Yellow " thus interpreted in Grose's " Classical
Dictionary of the vulgar tongue," London, 8vo. 1785, " to look yellow—
to be jealous "—for, as Pope has it, " all seems yellow to the jaundiced
eye ;" and again in Halliwell's " Dictionary of Archaic and Provincial
words," Lond. 1752, 8vo.—we have " Yellow-Stockings.   To anger
the yellow-stockings, *i.e.* to provoke jealousy."

There is " a merry jest of John Thomson and Jackaman his wife,
whose jealousy was justly the cause of all their strife, to the tune of
Pegge of Ramsay," which will be found *ad longum* at page 132 of the
letterpress portion of Chappell's National English airs.   In it the
yellow-stocking figures prominently thus :—

When I was a bachelor,
   I liv'd a merry life,
But now I am a married man,
   And troubled with a wife,
I cannot do as I have done,
   Because I live in fear ;
If I but go to Islington,
   My wife is watching there.
Give me my yellow hose again,
   Give me my yellow hose,
For now my wife she watcheth me,
   See yonder where she goes.
     .   .   .   .

Thus marriage is an enterprise
   Experience doth show,
But scolding is an exercise
   That married men do know ;
For all this while there were no blows,
   Yet still their tongues were talking,
And very fain would yellow hose
   Have had her fists a walking.
     Give me my yellow hose, &c.
     .   .   .   .

This maketh bachelors to halt
So long before they wed,
Because they hear that women now
Will be their husbands' head.
And seven long years I tarried
For Jackaman my wife,
But now that I am married,
I'm weary of my life.
Give me my yellow hose, &c.

For yellow love is too too bad,
Without all wit or policy,
And too much love hath made her mad,
And filled her full of jealousy.
She thinks I am in love with those
I speak to passing by ;
That makes her wear the yellow hose
I gave her for to dye.
Give me my yellow hose &c.,

The concluding incident of this ballad has been adopted by Wilson, the ornithologist, in his popular Scotish Poem of " Watty and Meg ; or, the Wife Reformed." So troubled is John Thomson with the unceasing jealousy of his better half that in despair he says ·—

I will get a soldier's coat
And sail beyond the seas, —

An announcement which brings Jackaman to her senses, and it is agreed that she shall turn over a new leaf, and behave herself better in future.

Sir John Harrington, in his " brief view of the state of the church," says : " In a wedding sermon, Dr Chadderton is reported to have made this comparison, and to have given this friendly caveat : That the choice of a wife was full of hazard, not unlike, as if one in a· barrel full of serpents, should grope for one fish ; if (said he) he escape harm of the snakes, and light on a fish, he may be thought fortunate ; but let him not boast, for perhaps it may prove an eel."

From " Merry Drollery," London 1670.
Some wives are good and some are bad,
Reply. Methinks you touch them now.
And some will make their husbands mad ;
Chorus. And so will my wife too ;
. And my wife, and my wife,
And my wife so will do !

	Some women love to breed discord ;
Reply.	Methinks, &c.
	And some will have the latter word ;
Chorus.	And so will, &c.

	Some women will spin, and some will sew ;
Reply.	Methinks, &c.
	And some will to the tavern go ;
Chorus.	And so, &c.

	Some women will ban, and some will curse ;
Reply.	Methinks, &c.
	And some will pick their husband's purse ;
Chorus.	And so will, &c,

	Some women will brawle, and scold, and grieve ;
Reply.	Methinks, &c.
	And some their husbands will deceive ;
Chorus.	And so will, &c.

	Some women will drink, and some will not ;
Reply.	Methinks, &c.
	And some will take the other pot ;
Chorus.	And so will, &c.

	Thus of my song I make an end :
Reply.	Methinks, &c.
	Hoping all women will amend ;
Chorus.	And so, &c.

Captain John Stevens, the well-known Spanish Scholar, translated into English (London 12mo, 1697) from the Portuguese of Don Francisco Manuel, a Book which he entitled "The Government of a Wife ; or, wholesome and pleasant advice for married men : in a letter to a friend." This Book treats of wives of various humours, conditions, and temperaments, with the best modes of dealing not only with the author's countrywomen, but with those who have come under the observation of the English translator.   After discoursing of jealous women, foolish women, extravagant wasteful women, and many others, "What shall I say," argues the Don, "of those wilful women, who will be positive and absolute in their own opinions?   These for the most part are either very foolish or very proud.   I cannot allow of arguing with a wife, for this is granting them an equality of judgment and authority which must be carefully avoided.   She must be made sensible it is not her part to understand but to obey, and to be led not to lead.   Let her sometimes be put in mind, that having in marriage resigned her will to her husband, it is now a crime to make use of what is not her own."   Again, he observes: " I cannot forbear speaking one word of a certain sort of matrons, who right or wrong will wear the breeches and be absolute within doors. These ground their pretensions to that usurped power on being very vertuous, very wise, or of very great birth ; and sometimes when the husbands are mild, good-natured, or loose livers, they compass it without alledging any of those titles. If once the husband discovers any such design in his wife, let him look narrowly to her; for if once she gets the upper hand of him, she will never give over till he entirely becomes her slave. I knew one, who finding his wife upon these terms, said to her, ' Madam, I will carry you home to your father, and then will take a course at law with him to recover my wife ;' and she asking of him ' Why he said so?' he answered, ' Because you are not my wife, but my Husband !' An ingenious and pleasant married man used to tell me, it was impossible but women would command their husbands ; but that all a good man could do was to endeavour it should be as late as possible. For my part, I can no way allow it should ever come to pass : no man of sense will allow of it ; and no woman that loves her husband desires it."

Don Manuel is particularly severe, and, to our mind, not unjustly so, on "those who paint their faces"—a practice which does not unhappily subside as the world grows older.

That satirical rogue, Douglas Jerrold, has put into the mouth of Gold-thumb, the old trunkmaker of his clever comedy, " Time Works Wonders," this reflection on women:—"when they're maids they're mild as milk. Once call 'em wives and they set their back against their marriage certificate, and defy you."

Although the generality of writers characterize the married state as a state of servitude and vexation, more particularly to the unhappy husband, there are others who take a more roseate view of the matter, we mean of matrimony. Mr. Payne Collier gives, as one of the parts of his Illus-trations of Early English popular literature, a tract from the text of Wynkyn de Worde titled, " here begynneth the Complaynt of them that ben to late maryed," wherein the author observes :—

> Yf there be yll women and rebell,
>   Shrewed, dispytous, and eke felonyous,
> There be other fayre and do full well,
>   Propre, gentyll, lusty and joyous,
>   That ben full of grace and vertuous ;
> They ben not all born vnder a sygnet :
> Happy is he that a good one can get.

Also in Mr Collier's " Broadside Black Letter Ballads, printed in the sixteenth and seventeenth centuries," 4to, 1868, is a Ballad called " Salomon's Housewife ; or, the praise of a Good Wife, as set forth in his Proverbs," which thus begins :—

He that a gratious wife doth finde,
  Whose life puts vertue chief in ure,
One of the right good housewife kinde,
  That man may well himselfe assure,
And boasting say that he has found
The richest treasure on the ground.

Ballad literature, however, does not usually chronicle cases of this kind ; from which it is to be presumed that the Ballad makers themselves have lived in an atmosphere of such domestic disquiet, that they are ignorant of the existence of a matrimonial Elysium, or having been made aware of the absence of comfort and happiness in the homes of that class to which they have more particularly addressed themselves, have believed that the force of ridicule would tend more towards the improvement and reformation of their minds and manners than virtuous example.

𝔐arriage, or the 𝔐ouse 𝔗rap.

Made to a comical tune in the Country Wake.

THE air of this song appears in Chappell's " National English Airs," under the title of " Of all the simple things we do." It was introduced into the Beggar's Opera, The Generous Freemason, and The Patron, or an Old Man taught Wisdom. In the Dancing Master it is called " Old Hob, or The Mouse Trap." The song itself with the music will be found in Durfey's Pills to purge Melancholy, vol. i. 1719, and in the Musical Miscellany, vol. v. p. 108.
  Mr Chappell remarking upon a tune " Of all comforts I miscarried," which was introduced into the *Devil to Pay* and other Ballad Operas, quotes the first verse thus :—

  " Of all comforts I miscarried,
    When I play'd the fool and married,
    'Tis a trap, there's none need doubt on't,
    Those that are in would fain get out on't."

Of all the simple things we do,
  To rub over a whimsical life ;
There's no one folly is so true,
  As that very bad bargain, a wife ;
We're just like a mouse in a trap,
  Or vermin caught in a gin ;

We sweat and fret, and try to escape,
 And curse the sad hour we came in.

I gam'd and drank, and played the fool,
 And a thousand mad frolics more ;
I rov'd and rang'd, despised all rule,
 But I never was married before ;
This was the worst plague could ensue,
 I'm mew'd in a smoky House ;
I us'd to tope a bottle or two,
 But now 'tis small beer with my spouse.

My darling freedom crown'd my joys,
 And I never was vext in my way ;
If now I cross her will her voice
 Makes my lodging too hot for her stay ;
Like a fox that is hamper'd in vain,
 I fret out my heart and soul ;
Walk too and fro the length of my chain,
 Then forc'd to creep into my hole.

The Scolding Wife.

New Sett by Mr. Akcroyd.

FROM Durfey's Pills, vol. iii. p. 141, 1719, (with music). Burns wrote
a short humorous song for Johnson's Scots Musical Museum, beginning
"I married a scolding wife the fourteenth of November." He titled it
"The Joyful Widower," and adapted it to the air of Maggie Lauder.

Some men they do delight in hounds,
 And some in hawks take pleasure ;
Others joy in war and wounds,
 And thereby gain great treasure ;

Some they do love on sea to sail,
   Others rejoice in riding :
But all their judgments do them fail,
   There's no such joy as *chiding*.

When soon as day I ope mine eyes,
   To entertain the morning;
Before my husband he can rise,
   I *chide* and proudly scorn him ;
When at the board I take my place,
   Whatever be the feasting;
I first do *chide* and then say grace,
   If then dispos'd to tasting.

Too fat, too lean, too hot, too cold,
   I ever am complaining;
Too raw, too roast, too young, too old,
   I always am disdaining ;
Let it be fowl, or flesh, or fish,
   Tho' I am my own taster;
Yet I'll find fault with meat or dish,
   With maid or with the master.

But when to bed I go at night,
   I surely fall a weeping ;
For then I leave my great delight,
   How can I chide when sleeping ?
Yet this my grief doth mitigate,
   And must assuage my sorrow ;
Altho' to-night it be too late
   I'll early *chide* to-morrow.

THE POUND OF TOW.

BEFORE the introduction of machinery caused hand loom weaving to
fall to a discount, and gave the idea that it was more economical to
purchase linen and cotton fabrics than to purchase the raw material and
make them, every thrifty dame in Scotland employed her leisure time at
her spinning wheel, and kept her house well supplied with home-made
(or, as they termed it, "hamert-made") napery, of a quality that no
machinery can equal. It used also to be an understood thing that every
unmarried female, or spinster (as she was relatively designated), should, in
anticipation of marriage, spin her own "providing," that is a sufficiency
of linen to enable her to enter on housekeeping. The heroine of our
Ballad appears to have conformed to the practice of the times, but only
apparently " for uniformity's sake," for we find that all the industrious
and thrifty habits which she had entertained prior to marriage are to
"the gudeman's" justifiable disgust entirely abandoned after the "Tom
fool's knot" has been securely tied, and idleness and extravagance
instead are wildly welcomed. She, like many others of her class, has
coveted marriage as a release from labour, affording a future of inglorious
ease, and enabling her to snap her fingers at everyone, her poor "bread
winner" not excepted. We are thus reminded of the pert servant girl,
depicted by George Colman jun., in his very clever farce of "X. Y. Z.,"
who, on snappishly presenting a letter to her mistress, is asked where she
expects to get a character if she goes on in that way? " I don't want a
character !" she brusquely replies, " I'm going to be married !"

The copy of "the Pound of Tow," from which we print, is from the
press of J. Jennings, 15 Water Lane, Fleet Street.

A song, similar in sentiment, called "The Cruell Shrow ; or,
the Patient Man's Woe ; declaring the misery and great pain, by his
unquiet wife he doth dayly sustain," attributed to Lord (subsequently
Marquis of) Wharton, will be found at page 91 of the Letterpress volume
of Chappell's National English Airs. It is a reprint of a Black Letter
copy, printed for Henry Gosson.

A stanza, somewhat analogous to the sixth of the following, occurs in
the song of " Bide ye yet," as written by Miss Janet Graham of Dumfries
and originally published in Herd's Collection under the title of the
Wayward Wife, thus:—

"Sometimes the rock, sometimes the reel,
Or some piece of the spinning-wheel,
She'll drive at you, my bonny chiel,
And send you headlangs to the diel.

Sae bide you yet, and bide you yet,
Ye little ken what's to betide you yet,
The half of that will gane you yet,
If a wayward wife obtain you yet."

The Pound of Tow.

Come all ye jolly bachelors that would married be,
I'd have you be advised, and take a word from me;
A single man is free from strife, from sorrow, and from woe,
Besides your wife will plague your life with a weary pound of
 tow.

When you have a mind to marry, and that you go to woo,
I'd have you be advised, see what your lass can do,
It's she can heckle, card, and milk both cow and ewe,
And rock the cradle with her foot, and spin a pound of tow.

Before my wife was married she was a thrifty dame,
Could do all kinds of country work, make butter, cheese,
 and cream,
Could weed potatoes, flax, and corn; she could both reap
 and mow,
And every night when she'd come home she'd spin a pound
 of tow.

But now since she is married she's still more thrifty grown,
For she has learnt to scold and brawl in such a dreadful
 tone,
When in my ears she rings a peal it's out of doors I go,
Cursing the day I brought her home to spin a pound of tow.

I bought my wife a stone of flax, as good as ever grew,
And out of it she heckled me a single pound of tow,
So weary of the pound of tow I wish'd we'd ne'er begun,
I wish my wife may end her life before the tow is spun.

To imitate the quality she'll in the fashion be,
She must have every pretty thing that e'er her eyes do see,
Her idle pride for to support my cloathes to pawn do go,
Whilst through the streets she spends her time instead of
spinning tow.

Instead of hasty pudding she'll have the best of tea,
With pigeon, duck, and partridge, on the table there must be,
If her wants are not supplied to rack my pate must go,
With the poker, reel, or ladle, or the wheel that spins the tow.

If all such thrifty wives were in a boat together,
The boat for to be bottomless, without a sail or rudder,
And fifty leagues from any land, I'd leave them there to
row,
In hopes they'd ne'er return again to spin a pound of tow.

Washing Week.

Tиıs will be found in the Weekly Magazine or Edinburgh Amuse-
ment, 1771, where it is "Addressed to G—— T——."

In this, dear George, we both agree,
(You bred in camp, I bred at sea),
     That cleanliness is oft
A cursed plague about a house,
And always met our warm abuse,
     When boys with Mrs Croft.

But to the Beggar and the king,
Clean linen's a reviving thing,
     Though both these plagues don't reach ;
The beggar strips at jocund morn,
In some clear stream, and on the thorn
     Spreads out his rags to bleach.

The King, great man ! sends all his out,
Not caring for a single clout ;
   But, what's more happy still,
He's not obliged to count the rags,
Nor stuff them into canvas bags,
   Oh no !—nor write the bill.

But, Lord have mercy on us all !
Whene'er we wash all hands must fall
   To something or another ;
For madam scolds and flies about,
Now up, now down, now in, now out,
   Dabbling through wet and smother.

This cursed time all comfort flies ;
At six she starts—" Come, Ned, arise,
   And get the lines hung out."
" Yes, to be sure, my dear," I cry,
I dare as well be hanged as lie
   For fear my dove should pout.

Breakfast is got, and whipp'd away,
Because the washers want their tea,
   Before that I've half done ;
The doors all open, linen's spread,
The sky looks black—" Come hither, Ned,
   Shall we have rain or sun ? "

" My dear, you need not be in pain,
I think it does not look like rain."
   " Oh then, we'll hang out more."
When lo ! the words have hardly pass'd,
But, puff ! there comes a heavy blast,
   And all must be rins'd o'er.

Then ten-fold falls the peal on me :
" You ass, to be ten years at sea !
   See ! see the linen, do ! "

I sneak away to have a smile,
Snug, while I hear her all the while
   Calling me black and blue.
But what still troubles more my mind,
Amidst such plagues, at once to find
   The washer, as she wrings,
Cracking some jest ; then o'er the tub
Pauses awhile, and every rub
   With pleasure sweats and sings.

I hate, I must confess, all dirt,
And truly love a well-washed shirt ;
   But once a-week this reek
Is more than flesh and blood can bear ;
And him I hate—oh ! make his share
   A washing every week.

The Washing Day.

The sky with clouds was overcast, the rain began to fall,
My wife she beat the children, and raised a pretty squall ;
She bade me with a frowning look, to get out of the way,
The deil a bit o' comfort's there on the washing day,
  For it's thump, thump, scold, scold, thump, thump away,
  The deil a bit o' comfort's there on a washing day.

My Kate she is a bonny wife, there's none more free from
    evil,
Except upon a washing day, and then she is the devil !
The very kittens on the hearth, they dare not even play,
Away they jump with many a thump, on the washing day
  For it's thump, &c.

A friend of mine once asked me, how long poor Jean's been
    dead?
Lamenting the good creature, and sorry I was wed
To such a scolding vixen, whilst he had been at sea ;
The truth it was he chanced to come on a washing day ;
    For it's thump, &c.

I asked him to stay, and " come," said I, " ods bobs !
I'll no denial take—you shall," though Kate was in the suds.
But what we had to dine upon, i'faith I shall not say,
But I'll wager he'll not come again on a washing day :
    For it's thump, &c.

On that fatal morning when I rise I make a fervent prayer
Unto the gods that it may be throughout the day quite fair,
That not a gown or handkerchief may in the ditch be laid,
For should it happen so, egad, I'd catch a broken head !
    For it's thump, &c.

Unfortunate Wife.

THIS has been copied from a Broadside imprinted about the beginning
of the present century, by "J. Kendrew, Printer, Collier-gate, Yorkshire."

In " The North Country Chorister; an unparalleled variety of excellent
Songs," edited by Joseph Ritson, Durham, 1792, 12mo, the argument
of this ballad occurs in Song III., " The Joyful Maid and the Sorrowful
wife," which differs so entirely in diction as to prevent any reference here
to the various readings.   The burthen of the early portion runs thus :—

    " And then I was a maid, a maid,
      And joy came to me then ;
    Of meat and drink, and rich cloathing,
      I'm sure I wanted none."

And by contrast, this is the refrain after marriage :—

    " And then I was a wife, a wife,
      And sorrow came to me then ;
    Of care and strife and weary life,
      I'm sure I wanted none."

A maid was I, a maid was I,
  And I lived with mama at home,
I eat and I drank in my gay clothing,
  For money I wanted none.
        A maid was I, &c.

My cap was made of the finest muslin,
  And plaited neat all around,
A maid was I, and a maid was I,
  And I lived with mama at home.

My gown was made of the finest cotton,
  My stays they were of silk,
My shift was made of the finest Holland,
  Washed as white as milk.

My stockings were made of the finest cotton,
  My garters they were of silk,
My shoes were made of the best Spanish leather,
  My buckles they were gilt.

There came a young man to the garden gate,
  And asked me if I would wed,
I was just sixteen and somewhat green,
  So I took in all he said.

He was comely and full of courtesy,
  So to go with him I agreed,
In the wish to be wed, whatever betide,
  Maidens are fools indeed.

And a wife was I, and a wife was I,
  And trouble and strife came on,
Trouble and strife all the days of my life,
  For money he gave me none.
        Trouble and strife, &c.

My cap was made of the coarsest cloth,
  And never a plait all round,
And a wife was I, and a wife was I,
  When trouble and strife came on.
              Trouble and strife, &c.

My gown was made of the coarsest linsey,
  As for stays I went without,
My shift was made of the coarsest harden,
  And ragged all round about.
              A wife was I, &c.

My stockings were made of the coarsest woollen,
  As for garters I went without,
My shoes were made of old boot legs,
  And the bottoms came tumbling out.
              And a wife was I, &c.

Then brats of bairns came thick and fast,
  To curse and plague one's life,
No food for their wants, no clothes for their backs,
  Oh, who would be such a wife.
              And a wife, &c.

If you marry in haste, it's certain you will
  At your leisure most surely repent,
Love's charges are heavy, and what's one to do
  When the money's all gone and spent?
              And a wife, &c.

THE JEALOUS HUSBAND OUTWITTED.

THERE is a Ballad of the last century, called "O Rare Nell," in which
a similar plot occurs. The scene is laid "in Bristol town," and rare Nell
who is the "handsome housekeeper" of a gentleman that "oftentimes
had kissed her," frightens him, by the aid of sweeps and gunpowder

into a marriage. The idea occurred to her by his having said in one of his softer moments :—

> " He wished the Devil might take him,
>   A woeful tale to tell,
>   If ever I prove false unto
>   My charming dear Nell.
>   In about a month thereafter,
>   He turn'd her out of house,
>   He was longing for a richer,
>   So left poor Nell."

We have met with another version of "O Rare Nell," printed by Croshaw of York, entitled "The Lawyer and Nell," the locality assigned to which is in Suffolk. Nell and the sweep waylay the Lawyer at "the side of a wood, where the road it was not very wide," and "just as the clock had struck twelve, as homeward the lawyer was steering," from the house of a lady fair, to whom he had been paying court, they rush out upon him in the character of devils, and the sweep setting fire to "a parcel of crackers," the lawyer is so terrified that he exclaims :—

> " If you'll go no farther with me,
>   To-morrow I'll marry poor Nelly."

Which he accordingly does.

The Jealous Husband Outwitted.

A hosier lived in Leicester,
    As I've heard many tell,
He had a handsome witty wife,
    And loved her full well.

And he was touched with jealousy,
    As often you shall hear,
Which caused his handsome witty wife
    Many a bitter tear.

Each night he got a drinking,
    And roving up and down,
And often it was midnight
    Before he e'er came home.

2 B

Then he would call her names,
   And swear and stamp his feet,
And oftentimes he threatened
   He'd turn her to the street.

At length a scheme came in her head,
   Thinks she, I'll try the same,
Perhaps my conjuration
   His jealousy may tame.

A chimney sweeper living near,
   Straightway to him she goes,
And told to him her fancy,
   And what she did purpose.

She says, " you have two hearty boys,
   As any of their kind,
And with their help I do not fear
   That we may change his mind."

She and the sweeps went home,
   As true as it was said,
She drest herself just like Old Nick,
   And so she went to bed.

The one she placed behind the door
   To let her husband in,
The others by the fireside,
   All for to burn his skin.

So presently he did come in,
   As drunk as any owl,
He began to curse and call her names,
   And speak words very foul.

Says he, " you jade get out of bed,
   And bring to me a light !"

She with the sweeps came crawling in,
   Which did him sorely fright,

And threw this jealous husband
   Into a great surprise,
With that they let some gunpowder
   Off into his eyes.

"O spare me, master Devil,
   O spare me now, I pray,
And every fault that I have done,
   I'll mend another day.

"O spare me, master Devil,
   And you little devils all,
And if e'er I'm jealous of my wife,
   Upon me you may call."

"If you'll promise me," she said,
   "A good husband to be,
Be kind unto your loving wife,
   And use her tenderly,

"My little devils I will take off,
   And bid you all farewell,
But if e'er you're jealous of you're wife,
   You must to my dark cell."

She laid her hairy jacket bye,
   And of it took great care,
The sweeps they kept the secret close,
   That her husband should not hear.

Yet if anything should happen,
   They were to call again,
But he proves a very good·husband,
   And saves them all their pain.

THE CANNY MILLER AND HIS WIFE.

"THE Canny Miller and his Wife" has ostensibly been written to record a local event in the neighbourhood of Edinburgh, seemingly about fifty years ago.

The chief incident in this story is not unlike one mentioned by Brydon in his very amusing Travels in Sicily, where an exchange of small clothes took place between an Ecclesiastic and a Soldier. The Friar, to the great scandal of the monastery to which he belonged, appeared attired *a la Militaire*, and the unhappy soldier, in like manner, presented himself to his comrades in the greasy habiliments of a Mendicant Friar. The Prior of the Monastery being a man of the world, and having a shrewd guess as to the real facts of the case, sent to the barracks a deputation of holy men, who demanded and got back the garments which, they asserted, had been miraculously transferred to the soldier by the Holy Virgin in order to rebuke him for his immoral practices. By this arrangement the reputation both of the men of the church and the men of the sword escaped being compromised. On the contrary, the sacred inexpressibles became a source of emolument, as crowds of votaries flocked with offerings to the Virgin in honour of the miracle which, through her, had been wrought. The military wardrobe was honourably transmitted to the barracks.

We have an imperfect recollection of something like this being in the Fabliaux, but analogous anecdotes may be found in the different Books of the Facetiæ, so that we are inclined to suspect that Brydon, who was not very accurate in his facts, may have paraphrased his amusing piece of gossip from those sources.

There are other ballads upon the same subject. One called "John Lindsey" who is a common sailor, and whom his wife has come on board his ship to visit, is made love to by the Captain, who presents her with fifty guineas. Lindsey ascertains this fact, secretes himself in the Captain's Cabin, and exchanges his tarry jacket for the Captain's dress, in which he goes ashore and proceeds to visit the Captain's lady. It being late, she, mistaking him for her husband, upbraids him for staying out. Before he leaves the house she to her surprise discovers the mistake, and she and the tar adjourn to the vessel, to comfort their respective spouses. Jack gets a fifty pound note to hold his tongue, and the Captain winds up by saying :—

> "There is many a one that does match us you know
> We are four jolly funny ones all in a row."

The Canny Miller and his Wife.

In Canonmills there lived a Miller,
Who lately came by a purse o' siller,
How it fell out I'll plainly show,
But would not wish the like to you.
   O the canny miller,
   O brave miller, O.

One day the miller went from home,
That day he left his wife alone,
That night he was to watch his mill,
And he was not long gone when his wife took ill.

On the stroke of ten when she was abed,
And visions and dreams were racking her head,
A noise and a creak, and a push and a crash,
As if the window was sent to smash.

She started up and in terror cried,
As she saw a figure by her bed-side,
" Have pity on me, my own beloved,"
That voice, a former sweetheart proved.

" What brings you here ? Begone, begone,
You know I'm friendless, and alone."
" Love caused me thus to venture in,
And your kind favour I mean to win.

" I've been to market, and my store
Amounts to fifty pounds and more,
All shall be yours ! " with that the loon
Pulled off his coat and flung it down.

The miller came home to his dear wife,
Whom he adored as his life,

And loath to wake her out of sleep
In at the window he eke did creep.

But the spark he had slipt under the bed,
Which made the miller's wife afraid,
When she arose as 'twere from sleep,
With pain and fright she scarce could speak.

He says, " my dear, what is the matter?"
" I'll die," said she, " if I don't get better,
For with a curmurring I am seized,
A little gin perhaps might ease't."

He says, " there's brandy in the house,"
" But O," said she, " it's of no use ;
If you regard my life one pin,
Run to Stockbridge—bring me some gin."

The miller he had off his coat,
To find it was no easy job,
He found the spark's and put it on,
Not knowing but it was his own.

The Miller to Stockbridge did rin,
He cries, " get up, get up ! some gin !
For my wife is taken very bad,
Give me the best that can be had."

The miller's hand his pouch put in,
It was to pay the wife her gin,
He scarcely could believe his eyes,
When he beheld his golden prize.

The Miller he in haste ran home,
To find his wife of course alone,
But much ado she'd with the swain,
To send him packing as he came.

He would insist she would consent
To hold out some hopes ere he went,
And when he came again to see her,
That he would find the coast all clear,

The miller's coat he then put on,
But soon found out 'twas not his own,
He raved, he stampt, he curs'd, he swore
He would not go out o'er the door

Unless his garment he could behold,
Likewise his precious purse of gold,
The same that to her he would give,
If she his visits would receive.

" Past two o'clock ! " just then was cried,
By a policeman gruff, outside ;
The miller's clattering steps drew near,
These put our lover in mortal fear.

The miller's wife the bolt she drew,
And up the window frame she threw,
" Get out, get out, as fast's ye can,
Or you will be a murdered man."

He sat upon the window sill,
Urging his suit with right good will,
The miller's knock a tremor sent,
She gave him a shove and o'er he went.

The amorous swain gave such a cry,
For he fell right plump in the pigs' stye,
The window was shut to with a din,
And the bar was drawn as the miller came in.

And when he had named about the coat,
And the purse of money therein he'd got ;

"That coat," quoth the wife, "for your Sunday display
I coft at an auction the other day."

The miller he sat down to drink,
He says, "my wife, I freely think,
You will gain more by your broker's trade,
Than ever I by my mill have made."

The miller made a happy catch,
He found the baker's golden watch,
It helped him long to pay his rent,
And with his wife he is content.

And as for the spark who his brochan had got,
It's better things be as they are, he thought,
And he swore that never again in his life,
Would he go a courting another man's wife.

ROSEY ANDERSON.

Rose Anderson, daughter of a merchant in Perth, was at the age of sixteen married to Mr Thomas Hay Marshall, also a merchant and erewhile Provost of that city. To all appearance they lived happily together for several years, but the lady, being fond of gaiety and gadding about to balls, Card Assemblies, &c., while her husband had no taste for such pursuits, and being of a thoughtless disposition, she latterly conducted herself with such freedom as to induce suspicion of her chastity; and, very strong circumstances transpiring, a Process of Divorce was raised in which the husband was ultimately successful after a keen and protracted litigation, extending over a period of six years.

In Mrs Marshall's answers to the Bill of Advocation for her husband, it was argued that "the Respondent was educated as an only child, under the eye and with the partial fondness of too indulgent parents, accustomed, from her infancy, to give a loose to all that childish levity, and even eccentricity, which non-age, indulgence, and supposed affluence can be supposed to occasion." That her marriage was "at the urgent desire of her parents, and against her own inclination." " From her father's house being open at all times to officers, and other strangers occasionally resident in Perth, the respondent had, previous to her marriage, acquired a freedom of manner, in addition to her natural levity, which was well known to the complainer. After the respondent's marriage, the complainer was so far from checking, in any respect in the respondent, this freedom of manner, and disregard of public opinion, that he himself kept open house to all officers and others, by whose acquaintance he thought himself honoured, in whose company he found pleasure, or from whose employment or influence he expected to derive advantage." "He was hardly ever at home, unless he had company. He kept open house to many young men, whom he most commonly left the respondent alone to entertain in his absence ; and it will be shown in the sequel, that the greatest part of those alledged improprieties of conduct, of which he has now adduced a proof, although he wishes to insinuate that they took place during the course of a few weeks and in his absence, yet truly occurred while he himself was at home, residing with the respondent ; and occurred, not in the short course of a few weeks, but during a period; a period, too, wherein she was, by the neglect of her husband, most exposed to such improprieties, of upwards of two years." She alledged that the fact of her father becoming bankrupt in 1796 was the first indication she had of Mr Hay Marshall's desire to be quit of her, and that the accusations which followed were not then adduced as his reason for turning her out of doors. Of course these allegations are made in extenuation of her conduct, which, by her own admission and shewing in her further answers, does not appear in the purest light.

The unfortunate lady subsequently became so abandoned as to be compelled to seek for a living in the streets of London.

These things happened towards the close of the last, and about the beginning of the present century.

The nobleman mentioned in the ballad, who, it was admitted, had been in the habit of meeting her on Kinnoul Hill, was afterwards Ambassador to Constantinople. His first wife was Miss Nisbet of Dirleton, whom he divorced in consequence of adultery with Mr Ferguson of Raith. By his second wife, Miss Oswald of Dunnekier, he was father of the late Earl, who, it need hardly be mentioned, was the first native of this country who opened up a trade with Japan.

The lover of Mrs Hay Marshall was the individual who obtained permission from the Sultaun to remove the marbles, which were gradually perishing, from Athens to Great Britain, and which are now in the British Museum, and are commonly called "The Elgin Marbles."

Rosey Anderson.

A Favourite Song.

Hay Marshall was a gentleman as ever lived on earth,
He courted Rosey Anderson a lady into Perth ;
He courted her, he married her, made her his wedded wife,
And at that day, I dare to say, he loved her as his life.

There was an assembly into Perth, and Rosey she was there,
Lord Elgin danced with her that night, and did her heart
    ensnare,
Lord Elgin danced with her that night, she walked home on
    his arm,
Hay Marshall he came rushing in, in very great alarm.

I am all into surprise, he says, I am all into surprise,
To see you kiss my wedded wife before my very eyes.
Do not be in surprise, he says, I'm near my own abode,*
For I've conveyed your lady home, from the dangers on the road.

I did not kiss your wedded wife, nor did I with her stay,
I only brought her safely home, from the dangers of the way.
Oh had she not a maid, a maid, of what was she afraid ?
Or had she not a lantern her wayward steps to guide ?

Betsy she was called on the quarrel for to face,
I would have brought my lady home, but Lord Elgin took
    my place.
Although you be a lord he said, and I but a provost's son,
I'll make you smart for that, my lord, although you think it's fun.

He took his Rosey by the hand, and led her through the room,
Saying, I'll send you up to fair London, till all this clash
    goes down,
I'll send you up to fair London, your mother to be your guide,
And let them all say as they will, I'll still be on your side.

* Lord Elgin's lodgings were immediately opposite Mr Marshall's house.

Weeks barely nine she had not been into fair London toon,
Till word came back to Hay Marshall that Rosey play'd the
     loon,
O woe be to your roses red, that ever I loved you,
For to forsake your own husband amongst the beds of rue.

A lady from a window high was spying with her glass,
And what did she spy but a light grey gown rolling amongst
     the grass.
Hay Marshall had twenty witnesses and Rosey had but three,
Waes me, cries Rosey Anderson, alas what shall I do?

My very meat I cannot take, my clothes I wear them worse;
Waes me, cries Rosey Anderson, my life to me's a curse.
If it was to do what's done, she says, if it was to do what's
     done,
Hay Marshall's face I would adore, Lord Elgin's I would shun.

The spring it is coming on, some regiments will be here,
I hope to get an officer my broken heart to cheer.
Now she has got an officer her broken heart to bind,
And now she's got an officer and he has proved unkind,

And left her for to lie her lane, which causes her to cry:
" In Bedlam I must lie my lane, in Bedlam I must die!
Ye ladies all, both far and near, a warning take by me,
And don't forsake your own husbands for any lords you see."

A COPY OF VERSES IN PRAISE OF QUEEN CAROLINE.

CAROLINE AMELIA ELIZABETH, Queen Consort of England, was born
17th May 1768. She was the daughter of Charles William Ferdinand,
hereditary Prince of Brunswick Wolfenbuttle, and the Princess Augusta,
eldest sister of King George III. Soon after the French Revolution, the
marriage of the heir-apparent to the crown of England began to be
regarded as a subject of great national importance, and negotiations for
an alliance with the Princess Caroline of Brunswick were entered into.
On the 20th December 1794, Caroline became, by contract, Princess of

Wales, and in the month of April following, accompanied by her mother and a numerous retinue, she departed from Brunswick and was received with great magnificence at the English Court.   On the 8th of April 1795, the marriage was celebrated between George Prince of Wales, and Caroline of Brunswick.   The Royal pair, however, were not well assorted, and they lived only a short time together.   On the 7th January 1796, a daughter was born, the Princess Charlotte, who died in childbed in 1817, the wife of Prince Leopold of Saxe Coburg, who subsequently became King of the Belgians.   A few months after the birth of Princess Charlotte, a formal separation took place between the Prince and Princess of Wales, and in consequence of certain censorious reports, an investigation into the conduct of the Princess was made, which terminated in her acquittal.   In August 1814, Caroline took leave of her daughter and proceeded to Italy, whence she visited Africa, Greece, and finally passed on through Asia to Jerusalem, the Holy Sepulchre and other places.   During her travels, intelligence of her daughter's death reached her.   On the death of George III. (29th January 1820), her Royal Highness as Consort of George IV. became Queen of England.   A charge of extreme misconduct having been made against her, she went to England to stand her trial, which commenced on 17th August 1820, and continued till Friday 10th November, when Lord Liverpool, the Prime Minister, withdrew the Bill of Divorce, on the double ground of the smallness of the majority (nine), and the unconstitutionality and inex-pediency of the Bill.   Still she was virtually found guilty, inasmuch as she was not allowed to share in the coronation of his majesty George IV.   This was a grievous disappointment to her, and a great blow to her pride, the Whig portion of the community having pretended to regard her as an ill-used innocent woman, more for the purpose of enlisting the sympathy of the commonalty, to be twisted into indignation against the King and the Tory government of the day.   She became in consequence severely indisposed, and died at Brandenburg House on 7th August 1821.   On the Tuesday following, her remains were privately removed in a hearse decorated with ten escutcheons and drawn by eight horses, and, having been escorted by a squadron of dragoons to Harwich, the coffin was thence transmitted by the "Glasgow" Frigate, to be deposited in the tomb of her ancestors at Brunswick.   This trial was the means of bring-ing forward, as Attorney-General for the Queen, Mr Henry Brougham, who was afterwards raised to the Woolsack and the Peerage, and who is now known as Lord Brougham.*

It is a remarkable fact that both Mary, Queen of Scots, and Queen Caroline should have selected Italians for their private secretaries ; in all likelihood, in both instances, from a full appreciation of the morality of that country.

* Since this was written Lord Brougham has departed this life at an extreme old age

In Rush's "Residence at the Court of London, 1819 to 1825," Second series, vol i., occurs this pasage.   "November 11. Dined with the Duke de Frias, Spanish Ambassador * * * Mr * * * * * * told anecdotes of the Queen ; amongst them, that when she lived at Blackheath she had many a time played blindman's buff with Sir William Scott, Mr Canning, and others who made up her parties.   He also said that Bergami had declared that if ever he caught Alderman Wood in Italy, he would kill him, as he had been the means of making the Queen refuse fifty thousand pounds sterling a-year from the government ; of which sum, had it come into her hands, he, Bergami, would have had a handsome portion annually for life."   This indicates the familiarity which existed between the Italian and his Royal mistress.

There emanated from the press, chiefly during the progress of the trial, numerous caricatures and Poetical Squibs, illustrated by Cruick-shank, which have now become rare.   Although these were princi-pally on the part of the Queen, others on the King's side were in every respect superior in point of merit.   It is a remarkable fact that one man in this way, by his infinite wit, did more on behalf of the Crown, than the combined efforts of the democratic party against it.   We allude to Theodore Hooke, who in the pages of "John Bull," from time to time produced such a series of clever attacks upon Her Majesty and her friends as covered them with ridicule.   One of them in particular

> " Have you been to Bradenburgh,
> Hey ma'am ! ho ! ma'am ?"

had such an effect on the female portion of the Queen's friends, as actually in a great measure, to cause to be put down those absurd exhibitions, which under the name of levees and under the auspices of " Absolute Wisdom," better known as Sir Mathew Wood, her Majesty was so injudicious as to countenance.

A Copy of Verses in praise of Queen Caroline.

Ye Britons all both great and small,
    Come listen to my ditty,
Your noble queen, fair Caroline,
    Does well deserve your pity ;
Like harmless lamb that sucks its dam
    Amongst the flowery thyme,
Or turtle dove that's given to love :
    And that's her only crime.

Wedlock I ween to her has been
  A life of grief and woe,
Thirteen years past she's had no rest,
  As Britons surely know.
To blast her fame men without shame
  Have done all they could do,
'Gainst her to swear they did prepare
  A motley perjured crew.

Europe they seek for Turk or Greek,
  To swear her life away,
But she will triumph yet o'er all,
  And innocence display.
Ye powers above, who virtue love,
  Protect her from despair,
And soon her free from calumny
  Is every true man's prayer.

THE WEAVER'S SONG.

THE following has been printed, more on account of its antiquity than on any other, from "the pleasant History of John Winchcomb, in his younger years called Jack of Newberry, the famous and worthy clothier of England ; declaring his Life and Love ; together with his charitable deeds and great hospitalities, and how he set continually five hundred poor people at work, to the great benefit of the Common-wealth : worthy to be read and regarded. The fifteenth edition, corrected and enlarged by T. D. *Haud curo invidiam.* Licensed and entered according to order, London, printed for Eben. Tracy at the Three Bibles on London Bridge," 4to, *circa* 1670. The first edition was entered at Stationer's Hall, 7th March 1596. The author of this really "pleasant History" was Thomas Deloney, (a silk weaver) author of "The Gentle Craft," "Thomas of Reading," and other popular works of their day. He was termed by Kemp, in the Nine Daies' Wonder, 1600 4to, "the great Ballad maker." It is understood that he died in 1660. *See* Mr Collier's Preface to Deloney's Strange Histories, and Mr J. H. Dixon's Preface to "The Garland of Good-will," (Percy Society editions).

In Fuller's "Worthies" (Berkshire) occurs this notice of

JACK OF NEWBERRY.

John Winscombe, called commonly Jack of Newberry, was the most considerable clothier (without fancy and fiction) England ever beheld. His looms were his lands, whereof he kept one hundred in his house, each managed by a man and a boy. In the expedition to Flodden-field, against James, King of Scotland, he marched with an hundred of his own men (as well armed and better clothed than any) to shew that the painful to use their hands in peace, could be valiant, and employ their arms in war. He feasted King Henry VIII. and his first Queen, Katharine, at his own house, extant at Newbury at this day, but divided into many tenements. Well may his house now make 16 clothiers' houses, whose wealth would amount to 600 of their estates. He built the church of Newbury from the pulpit westward to the tower inclusively, and died about the year 1520, some of his name and kindred of great wealth still remaining in this county.

Mr J. Payne Collier has recently included "The Weavers' Song in the praise of Loue and Friendship, to the tune of Apelles," in "Broadside Black-letter Ballads of the sixteenth and seventeenth centuries," printed (for private circulation) by Thomas Richards, 1868, pp. 130, 4to. The Ballads in that collection, numbering 25 in all, are very uninteresting with exception of "the Weavers' Song" itself, and "the Cobbler of Colchester, a merry new song, wherein is shewed the sorrowfull cudgelling of the Cobbler of Colchester by his wife, for the eating of her apple pye. To a pleasant new tune, called Trill lill." There are one or two verbal differences in Mr Collier's copy of our ballad, but not of much moment. The more important are "cates" for "cakes" in the second stanza, and 'tune" for "tube" in the ninth stanza.

The Weavers' Song is thus introduced in Jack's pleasant History :—
"Then came his Highness" (*i.e.* King Henry VIII.) "where he saw a hundred looms standing in one room, and two men working in every one, who pleasantly sung in this sort :"—

The Weavers' Song.

When Hercules did use to spin,
    And Pallas wrought upon the loom,
Our trade to flourish did begin,
    When Conscience went not selling broom ;
Then Love and Friendship did agree
To keep the bands of Amity.

When Princes' sons kept sheep in field,
    And Queens made cakes of wheaten-flour,
The men to lucre did not yield,
    Which brought good cheer to every bower.
Then Love and Friendship did agree
To hold the bands of Amity.

But when the gyants huge and high,
    Did fight with spears like weavers' beams,
Then they in iron beds did lye,
    And brought poor men to hard extreames.
Yet Love and Friendship did agree
To hold the bands of Amity.

Then David took his sling and stone,
    Not fearing great Goliah's strength ;
He pierced his brains and broke the bone,
    Though he were fifty feet of length.
For Love and Friendship did agree, &c.

But while the Greeks besieged Troy,
  Penelope apace did spin ;
And weavers wrought with mickle joy,
  Though little gains were coming in.
For Love and Friendship did agree, &c.

Had Helen then sate carding wool,
  (Whose beauteous face did breed such strife)
She had not been Sir Paris's trull,
  Nor caused so many to lose their life,
Yet we by love did still agree, &c.

Or had King Priam's wanton son
  Been making quills with sweet content,
He had not then his friends undone,
  When he to Greece a gadding went,
For Love and Friendship did agree, &c.

The cedar trees endure more storms
  Than little shrubs that sprout on high,
The weavers live more void of harms,
  Than Princes of great dignity.
While Love and Friendship doth agree, &c.

The shepherd sitting in the field
  Doth tune his pipe with hearts' delight ;
When Princes watch with spear and shield,
  The poor man soundly sleeps all night,
While Love and Friendship doth agree, &c.

Yet this by proof is daily try'd,
  For God's good gifts we are ingrate,
And no man through the world so wide,
  Lives well contented with his state.
No Love and Friendship can we see
  To hold the bands of Amity.

THE WEBSTER OF BRECHIN'S MARE.

THIS "old merry song," as it is designated in the Chap book from which it has been extracted, is not without humour of a peculiarly Scotish nature. The Chap-book bears the imprint of the well-known Flying Stationer of Falkirk, T. Johnston, and is dated 1815. In Stenhouse's Illustrations of the Lyric Poetry and Music of Scotland it is remarked, in reference to a specimen of this song given in Johnson's Scots' Musical Museum, "this is only a fragment of a long ballad frequently heard at country firesides entitled ' The Brechin Weaver.' It possesses some traits of humour, though not of the first order. The specimen in the Museum is certainly quite enough. The tune to which the ballad is chaunted, however, is very pretty."

The Webster of Brechin's Mare.

In Brechin did a Webster dwell,
  Who was a man of fame,
He was the deacon o' his trade,
  John Steinson was his name.
A mare he had, a lusty jade,
  Sae sturdy, stark, and strang,
Baith Lusty and trusty ;
  And he had spared her lang.

The webster bade his mare go work,
  Quoth she, " I am not able,
For neither get I corn nor hay,
  Nor stand I in a stable.
But hunts me and dunts me,
  And dings me from the toun,
And fells me and tells me,
  I am not worth my room."

The webster swore a horrid oath,
  And out he drew a knife,
If one word come out of thy head,
  I vow I'll take thy life.

The mare ay, for fear ay,
   Fell fainting to the ground,
And, groaning and moaning,
   Gaed in a deadly swoon.

They clipped her and nipped her,
   They took from her the skin,
The haunches and the paunches,
   They quickly brought them in.
" Make haste, dame," said he,
   " And wash this grease and dry't,
For I will hazard on my life,
   The Doctor's wife will buy it."

They rumbled her, they tumbled her,
   They shot her o'er the Brae,
With rumbling and tumbling,
   She to the ground did gae.
But the night being cauld,
   And the mare wanting her skin,
And darkness came out o'er the land,
   And fain would she been in.

She rapped and she chapped,
   With her twa forther hooves,
They heared and feared,
   And thought it had been thieves.
The webster's son was stout in heart,
   He ran unto the door,
And thrust a spear into the mare,
   Five quarters lang and more.

The door ay, with more ay,
   They closed hastily,
All trembling and shaking,
   And then for help did cry.

"What ails thee, my son," says he,
  "O tell me if thou can,"
"Ah, and alas! father," he says,
  "For I have killed a man.

"If magistrates and senators,
  Get knowledge of this deed,
They'll hang us and fine us,
  Without any remede."
Then they ran unto the door,
  To bury the man for fear,
But when they came unto the door,
  They found it was the mare.

"Go haste you, I request you,
  And tell my father, dear,
What will we or shall we do
  With this wicked mare?"
"O hold thy tongue, my son," he says,
  "I think you are a fool,
I wish we had her hung in cords,
  We'll eat her against yule.

"We'll wash her and we'll dash her,
  She's a' smeared o'er wi' dub,
We'll wring her and fling her,
  An' saut her in a tub.
"And we'll cry in our neighbours all,
  And bid them all come in,
John Dunkinson, John Davidson,
  And kind Patie Grinn."

On Christmas day the greasy pack
  Did a' convene in haste,
The haill tribe of yarn stealers
  Came a' unto the feast.

They ate and drank and made a rant,
The end no man can tell;
In terms good I do conclude,
And bid you now farewell.
*   *   *   *   *
The weaving craft it is renowned so,
That rich nor poor without it cannot do.

BONNY PAISLEY.

From a Chap copy "Entered according to order," 1795. Those
who are familiar with the Irish song set to the beautiful air of "The
Meeting of the Waters," and entitled "The Boys of Kilkenny," which
was wont, about forty years ago, to be sung with such unction at the
Edinburgh Theatres by Weekes (the very stout Irish Comedian), will re-
cognize several of the stanzas in the following.

A copy of "The Boys of Kilkenny" will be found in the Popular
Songs of Ireland. Edited by T. Crofton Croker, Lond. cr. 8vo. 1839.
In his introduction to the Ballad in question, Mr Croker gives three
reasons for believing that Thomas Moore was the author, but in a subsequent footnote he observes "by good authority" he is wrong in ascribing
the song to Mr Moore.

Bonny Paisley.

OVER hills and high mountains,
I have oftentimes been,
Through hedges and broad ditches
I wandered all alane.
There is nothing that doth grieve me,
Or troubles my mind,   ..
As the leaving of my sweetheart
In Paisley behind.

O Paisley is a fine town,
It shines where it stands;
The more I think on it,
The more my heart warms,

For if I were in Paisley,*
    I would think myself at home,
For there I have a sweetheart,
    But here I have none.

O the weavers in bonny Paisley,
    They are clever young blades,
When they do go a-courting
    Of pretty young maids ;
They will kiss them and clap them,
    And spend their money free ;
Of all the towns in Scotland,
    O Paisley is for me.

O the lasses in bonny Paisley,
    They are pretty young maids,
For they love the jolly weavers,
    And despise all other trades.
And if any other tradesman
    Should cast a loving eye,
To the arms of a jolly weaver
    She will suddenly fly.

For it is up into the Hoxiehead—[Hawkhead?]
    I will build my love a bower,
Where neither Duke nor Lord
    Shall over her have power.
But if anybody ask you,
    " My dear what is your name ?"
Tell them that I'm your jolly weaver,
    And you're my dearest swain.

The Weaver and the Tailor.

As I was a-walking
    Down by yon shadey grove,
I heard a couple talking,
    It was concerning Love.
The young man being a weaver,
    The maid she proved coy,
And he knew full well, by her discourse,
    She loved a tailor boy.

" My dear, for to maintain you
    I'll make my shuttle fly,
I'll wear my fingers to the bone,
    New fashions for to buy.
I'll buy you silks and satins,
    And all things you do choose,
I'll buy you all new fashions
    That you read of in the news."

" O how can you maintain me,
    And you a journeyman?
How can you maintain me
    When you have ne'er a loom?
With your lee and your rubbing bone,
    Your knife instead of sheers ;
But I'll go and wed the tailor boy
    That needs neither read nor gear."

" If you do wed the tailor boy,
    At his back you'll have to run,
You'll have to dig potatoes,
    For work he can do none.
You'll have to carry in the peats
    In a basket or a creel,
While the tailor he sits on his bench
    Threading a bar of steel."

" Hold your tongue of my tailor boy,
   He'll not do so to me,
For when that he does go abroad,
   I'll take my liberty.
And I will go a-gossiping
   In all places thro' the toun,
And I will please my tailor boy
   When he comes home at noon."

" When your tailor boy does come home,
   He'll clip off both your ears,
He'll beat you with his lapping board,
   And snip you with his shears.
He'll chide you for your idleness,
   The length of the whole day,
And an iron goose you'll have to pluck,
   And cook in cabbage whey."

" Hold your tongue of my tailor,
   He'll not do so to me,
For Adam was a tailor
   When the world began to be.
For Adam he made aprons
   Out of the leaves so fine,
So ever since the world began,
   The tailor trade doth shine."

" But if you saw your tailor lad
   When he sits all alone,
You would take him for an ornament,
   For legs you can see none.
Like a frog upon a beating stone
   He sits the live-long day,
While the weaver he goes neat and trim,
   Amongst the ladies gay."

" Oh ! ever since the world began,
The tailors were the beaux,
For at such fragments of a man,
Girls ne'er turn up their nose."
" I would not be a tailor's wife,
For they are roving blades,
And if you'd live a happy life,
Look out in other trades."

RAGGED, AND TORNE, AND TRUE.

The learned and ingenious Mr Payne Collier in " A Book of Roxburghe Ballads," which he edited (4to, Lond. 1847) says, "we may
conjecture from internal evidence that this capital old Ballad was first
published while Elizabeth was still on the throne ; the Broadside we
have used was ' printed for the Assignees of Thomas Symcocke,' who in
the reign of James I. had a patent for publications occupying only 'one
side ' of paper or parchment." (See Collier's *Hist. Engl. Dram. Poetry
and the Stage*, iii. 383). "Symcocke," he goes on to say, "granted
deputations to others, and by one of his ' assigns,' the present impression
of an older production was put forth." Of all evidence to adduce as to
the date or authenticity of old Ballads, that of "internal evidence " is the
worst, inasmuch as having been transmitted and retransmitted orally,
they, long before being chronicled by the Printer, like the story of "the
three black crows," come out from the alembic of a hundred tongues
entirely different from their original design. It is highly probable that
Mr Collier's conjecture is correct as to the era of this spirited Ballad
being that of the golden days of good Queen Bess, although it would be
somewhat difficult to determine that from the Text alone. Irrespective
of its antiquity, the intrinsic merit of " Ragged and Torn and True "
has secured for it a place in this collection.

Ragged, and Torne, and True.

I AM poore man, God knowes,
And all my neighbours can tell,
I want both money and clothes,
And yet I live wondrous well.

I have a contented mind,
   And a heart to beare out all,
Though Fortune (being unkind)
   Hath given me substance small.
Then hang up sorrow and care,
   It never shall make me rue ;
What though my backe goes bare,
   I'me ragged, and torne, and true.

I scorne to live by the shift,
   Or by any sinister dealing ;
I'le flatter no man for a gift,
   Nor will I get money by stealing :
I'le be no knight of the post,
   To sell my soule for a bribe,
Though all my fortunes be crost,
   Yet I scorne the cheater's tribe.
Then hang up sorrow and care,
   It never shall make me rue ;
What though my cloake be thread-bare,
   I'me ragged, and torne, and true.

A boote of Spanish leather
   I have seen set fast in the stocks,
Exposed to wind and weather,
   And foul reproach and mocks,
While I in my poore ragges
   Can passe at liberty still :
O, fie on these brawling bragges,
   When money is gotten so ill !
O, fie on these pilfering knaves !
   I scorne to be of that crue,
They steale to make themselves brave ;
   I'me ragged, and torne, and true.

I have seen a gallant goe by
   With all his wealth on his backe,

He look't as loftily
  As one that did nothing lacke ;
And yet he hath no means
  But what he gets by the sword,
Which he consumes on queanes,
  For it thrives not, take my word.
O fie on these high-way theeves !
  The gallowes will be their due:
Though my doublet be rent i' th' sleeves,
  I'me ragged, and torne, and true.

Some do themselves maintaine
  With playing at cards and dice :
O, fie on that lawlesse gaine
  Got by such wicked vice !
They coozen poore country-men
  With their delusions vilde,
Yet it happens now and then
  That they are themselves beguilde :
For if they be caught in a snare,
  The pillory claimes its due.*
Though my jerkin be worne and bare,
  I'me ragged, and torne, and true.

I've seene some gallants brave
  Up Holborne ride in a cart,
Which sight much sorrow gave
  To every tender heart :
Then have I said to my selfe,
  What pity it is for this,
That any man for pelfe
  Should do such a foule amisse.

* This stanza is particularly applicable, in modern times, to Stock-jobbers, Stockbrokers, and all that despicable crew who "repose and fatten" on the gambling practised on the Stock Exchange; and for whose sakes, as a body, it is a pity that the Pillory is no longer an institution of our country.

O, fie on deceit and theft !
   At the last it makes men rue ;
Though I have but little left,
   I'me ragged, and torne, and true.

The pick-pockets in a throng,
   At a market or a faire,
Will try whose purse is strong,
   That they may the money share ;
But if they are caught i' th' action,
   They are carried away in disgrace.
Either to the House of Correction,
   Or else to a worser place.
O, fie on these pilfering theeves !
   The gallowes will be their due :
What need I sue for repreeves ?
   I'me ragged, and torne, and true.

The hostler to maintaine
   Himself with money in's purse,
Approves the proverbe true,
   And sayes, Gramercy, horse :
He robs the travelling beast,
   That cannot divulge his ill ;
He steals a whole handfull at least
   From every halfe-peck he should fill.
O, fie on these coozening scabs,
   That rob the poore jades of their due !
I scorne all theeves and drabs,
   I'me ragged, and torne, and true.

'Tis good to be honest and just,
   Though a man be never so poore ;
False dealers are still in mistrust,
   Th'are afraid of the officers' doore :
Their conscience doth them accuse,
   And they quake at the noise of a bush,

While he that doth no man abuse
For the law needs not care a rush.
Then wel fare the man that can say,
I pay every man his due :
Although I go poore in array,
I'me ragged, and torne, and true.

Munro's Tragedy.

From a Chap Book of Songs.   Circa 1778.

When the sons of North Britain were used to range,
To see foreign countries and lands that are strange,
Among that same number was Donald Munro,
Who to America likewise did go.

Two sons with his brother he caused to stay,
Because for their passage he could not then pay ;
But seven long winters having past by and gone,
They went to their uncle one day when alone,

And asked his permission to cross o'er the sea,
Where they with their parents in plenty might be.
But their uncle replied and answered them, no !
That they'd got no money, therefore could not go.

Being thus disappointed no comfort they find,
Till the thoughts of the army did run in their mind ;
So leaving their uncle they came where they found
A regiment of foot-men for America bound,

With whom they enlisted and soon took the main,
In hopes for to see their dear parents again ;
But when they were landed in that country wide,
Rebellion and murder in triumph did ride.

With humble submission then both of them went
One day to their Captain and begged his consent,
To go up the country their parents to see,
To which the good Captain was pleased to agree.

So leaving the camp with a boy for their guide,
They came to the place where their friends did reside,
And walking with pleasure, these words they did say,
" O, could we but find our dear parents to day !

" How it would surprise them to see us so near,
As they of our listing never did hear."
So going on farther they spyed a grove,
Where the trees and the bushes all seemed to move.

It being two rebels who lurked in the wood,
Who pointed their pieces where the two brothers stood,
Soon lodged their two bullets into their two breasts,
And ran to their prey like most ravenous beasts.

To take all their money and strip off their clothes,
Not being quite dead they gave them some blows,
One of them expiring, did lift up his eyes,
And seeing the murderer approaching, he cries :

" O cruel monsters ! O blood-thirsty hounds !
How could you thus kill us till once we had found
Our father whom we have sought with such care ?
If he hears of our fate he will die in despair.

He left us in Scotland seven twelvemonths ago,
Perhaps you may know him, his name is Munro ;
The old man on his person then fixed his eyes,
His heart was soon seized with grief and surprise.

He cried out with sorrow, " what is this I have done ?
O cursed be these hands, I have murdered my son !"

"Are you really my father?" the son then did cry,
" I'm glad that I've seen you before that I die."

Being sorely disturbed, the old man replied,
" What is he, that young man that lies there by your side?"
" O ! he is my brother and your loving son,
Your loss had been less had 1 fallen alone.

"O how is our mother, and is she yet well ?
If she hears of our death her heart it will fail,
But farewell, dear father," the son did reply,
"Since you've been our ruin contented we die !"

When this he had spoken down dropped his head,
His father observed him and found he was dead ;
The sight was so shocking he fell to the ground,
The thoughts of the murder his heart did confound.

He cursed his misfortune and that fatal day,
And kissed their dead bodies as cold as the clay.
" O could I recall you and make you to live,
My life for your ransom I freely would give.

" Why joined I these rebels to assist their bad cause,
And murder my children against nature's laws ?
I took you for others, O fatal mistake,
Sure I was bewitched, my sons, for your sake.

" I'll sink beneath sorrow, give way to despair,
I will breathe my life out till death end my care,
Then shall I meet you on a happier shore,
Where I will be able to kill you no more."

BUNG YOUR EYE.

WE print from "a Garland of New Songs. The Banks of Clyde. The Victory of Barossa. Bung your Eye. The Stranger. Printed by J. Marshall, Old Flesh Market, Newcastle, where may also be had a large and curious collection of Songs, Ballads, Tales, Histories, etc.," *circa* 1812.

The air is of somewhat ancient date. The editor has in his possession a small MS. volume of popular airs transcribed apparently shortly after the beginning of last century. Among them is one titled " Bung your Eye."

" Bung your Eye" was a cant term for a species of gin, a liquor which has rejoiced in more figurative appellatives than any other. During the fast days of Tom and Jerry, *i.e.*, about 1821, gin received many names which stuck to it afterwards. There was " Flash-of-lightning," " Blue Ruin," " Dead Eye," " Knockmedown," and numerous others. Cant names were applied to the beverages used by the common people in London so far back as 1698. A specimen of these will be found in the collected edition of the Original Works of William King, LL.D., 3 vols., London 1776, in a travestie of Doctor Lister's Journey to London.—We have "humtie-dumtie," "three-threads," "four-threads," "old Pharoah," "Knockdown," "hugmetee," "clamber crown," "fox-comb," etc.

" Old Tom " as applied to gin dates from the beginning of the past century, at which period the distillery of Hodges was situated at Millbank.

It derived its appellation from Old Tom Chamberlain, his relative and partner. Old Tom managed the operations of the distillery while Hodges gave his attention to the commercial part of the business. He had a private apartment where he always had a small supply of superior gin, flavoured in a particular way. Ordinary customers when they gave their orders were treated to a glass of common gin, the better class whom it was desirable to propitiate were invited by Old Tom into his sanctum and favoured with a glass of his " particular." The superiority of the contents of this private bottle soon became known, and when a customer was asked what he would have, he of course preferred "a glass of Old Tom." This decided the firm in manufacturing that especial good quality of gin for the trade, and they gave it the name of Old Tom.

An incident similar to that which forms the subject of the present ballad, occurred about thirteen years ago in a Railway carriage on the Eastern Counties' Line. It was chronicled in verse by Thackeray, and appeared in the pages of " Punch " at a time when the writers in that periodical had some pretensions to wit. We cannot refrain from quoting a stanza or two from " the Lamentable Ballad of the foundling of Shoreditch :"

*   *   *   *   *

And on reaching Marks Tey Station, that is beyond Colchest-
Er, a lady entered into them most elegantly dressed.

She entered into the carriage all with a tottering step,
And a pooty little Bayby upon her bussum slep ;
The gentlemen received her with kindness and siwillaty,
Pitying the lady for her illness and debillaty.

She had a fust class ticket, this lovely lady said,
Because it was so lonesome she took a secknd instead.
Better to travel by secknd class, than sit alone in the fust,
And the pooty little bayby upon her breast she nust.

A seein of her cryin, and shiverin and pail,
To her spoke this surging, the Ero of my tail ;
Saysee, you look unwell, ma'am, I'll elp you if I can,
And you may tell your case to me, for I'm a mediccle man.

*   *   *   *   *

When at Shoreditch tumminnus at lenth stopped the train,
This kind mediccle gentleman proposed his aid again,
"Thank you, sir," the lady said, "for your kyindness dear ;
My carridge and my osses is probibbly come here.

Will you old this baby, please, vilest I step and see?
The Doctor was a famly man ; "that I will," says he,
Then the little child she kist, kist it very gently,
Vich was sucking his little fist, sleeping innocently.

*   *   *   *   *

Some vent in a Homminibus, some vent in a cabby,
The Capting and the Doctor vaited vith the babby,
But never, never back again did that lady come
To the pooty sleeping Hinfut a suckin of his Thum !

Going back to a remoter date of some two hundred years ago, there
was a book issued at " London, printed by R. Wood for Eliz. Andrews,
at the White Lion, near Pye-Corner, 1664," called " A Royal Arbor
of Loyal Poesie, consisting of Poems and Songs digested into Triumph,
Elegy, Satyr, Love, and Drollery, composed by Tho. Jordan," in which
occur " Representations in parts to be habited, sung. and acted, as they
have been often times with great applause performed before the Lord
Mayor and Sheriffs of London." We would more particularly refer to
" The Cheaters cheated. A Representation in four parts to be sung.
Nim, Filcher, Wat, and Moll ; made for the Sheriffs of London."

2 D

Wat comes up to London from Zomerzetzhere to evade the consequences of a rustic intrigue.   In a song he avows his intention "to
buy new vashions," with " fifty pound, che took't away from vather."
Filcher and Nim, two of fortune's minions, overhear him, and resolve to
make themselves master of his money.   The question is, "how shall we
get his hands out of his pockets?" to which Filcher replies :—

> "Let me alone for that : I lately bought a glass
> Wherein all several colours may
> Be seen that ever was,
> If held up thus with both hands.

Nim.   A pretty new design :
This trick will fetch his fingers out.

Fil.   And, hey, then in go mine."

*   *   *   *   *

Wat.   I cannot zee a colour yet.

Nim.   Thou dost not hold it high.

Wat.   Che hav't it, che ha't, ch'av got it now !

Nim.   I' faith, and so have I. [*Picks his pocket.*

Wat.   Here's black, and blew, and gray, and green,
And orange-tauny white ;
And now Ich ave lost all agen.

Fil.   In troth y' are in the right. [*Filch picks t'other pocket.*

Wat proposes to purchase the glass, but the rogues will not hear of
payment, and allow him to carry it away.   Rejoicing in the possession
of their booty, they are utterly dismayed when on opening the purse they
find "nothing but nails in't," and on investigating the contents of the
parcel from "t'other pocket," they are staggered to find "nought but
bread and cheese in't."   They go off resolving to be even with "the
Bomkin."   Moll Medlar then enters with a basket, and is singing and
dancing when Wat comes on the scene.   He addresses her.   She tells
him she loves him.

Wat.   Then sweet Mol, come buss thy Wat :
Let us twain be merry.

Mol.   I could nimbly dance, but that
My basket makes me weary.

He takes the basket and "both dance to their own singing," when
Mol under this pretence,

> "I have too much strained my throat ;
> I prathe, sing a little, *She doth dance off.*"

Wat, after indulging in a song, "turns about and misseth her." He "sets down the basket and looks into it," and finally "pulls a childe" out of it. After "hushing" it and offering it to the audience, he "puts it in agen to the basket and exit." The two rogues then enter and lament their run of ill-luck. "They retreat to several corners," as Wat again makes his appearance, "with a little Trunck on a stick hanging at his back." He sings a farewell to London, in which he takes occasion to state:—

> "In plush and in zatten a vynely wrought
> Ich chave laid out forty pound every groat.
>
>   *   *   *   *   *
>
> Here's zilk, and gold, and zilver strings,
> Here's gloves, silk hozen, points and rings."

Filcher and Nim overhearing this come forward and draw upon him, whereat he runs off leaving the trunk. They then quarrel and are fighting as to the entire possession of the trunk when Moll enters and parts them. She enquires the cause:—

> *Fil.*   I'll tell you then how the quarrel did rise,
>   This fellow and I have took a rich prize.
> *Nim.* And now he denies me my share in't. *Fil.* He lies.
>   We agreed that the sword should decide it.
>
>   This trunk is well furnish'd, as e'er it can hold,
>   With silk and with velvet, with silver and gold.
> *Moll.* Turn't all into money, and when it is sold,
>   You equally may divide it.

Nim proposes to open the trunk.
"Faith," says Filcher, "open't or shut it, 'tis all one to me,
    I vow I'll have all or none." *Moll opens the trunk,*
And taking out the child, Nim exclaims: "I vow 'tis a child.
    You swore you'd have all or none."
To which Filcher replies:—"I'll stand to my bargain, for I will have none."

Moll then explains how she had tried to dupe the countryman, and presents the babe to Filcher, exclaiming,

> Come kiss it, and love it, for faith 'tis your own,
>   *   *   *   *   *
> You said you would wed me and live by your trade.

To which Filcher says, "I'll presently make thee my wife," and the representation terminates with the three resolving to turn over a new leaf :—

>   *Fil.*   I never will quarrel, or swagger, or roar.
>   *Nim.*   Then make the poor simpletons pay all the score.
>   *Moll.* I never will do as I have done before.
>   *All.*   We every one will mend.

Bung your Eye.

As a buxom young fellow was walking the street,
A certain fair maiden he chanced to meet,
And as she drew near him she said, will you buy?
Pray what do you sell? she replies, Bung your eye.

To be serious, fair maiden, what have you got there?
Would you wish for an answer both kind and sincere?
'Tis Holland's Geneva, called by the bye,
As a nick-name, my friend, it is Bung your eye.

If you be a gentleman, as you do appear,
To sell all my Geneva I need not to fear.
While I speak to some neighbours as they pass by,
So I'll leave you the care of this Bung your eye.

The woman being gone it was his intent
To look into her basket he was fully bent,
In a few minutes after the young child did cry,
Instead of Geneva found a young Bung your eye.

O curse this bad woman! what has she got here?
I have bought her Geneva, I vow, very dear,
I'm afraid all the lasses as they pass me by,
Will call me the father of young Bung your eye.

Bung your eye he took home as I have heard say,
To have the child christen'd without more delay ;
Says the parson, I'll christen the child by and bye,
What name will you give him? he said, Bung your eye.

Bung your eye, said the parson, it is an odd name !
O yes, Sir, he said, and an odd way it came,
I'm afraid all the lasses as they pass me by,
Will think me the father of young Bung your eye.

Come all you young fellows that walk in the street,
Beware of those maidens you chance for to meet,
For Holland's Geneva put me in surprise,
Believe me, my girls, it bunged up both my eyes.

The Heart oppressed wi' Sorrow.

FROM the Gaberlunzie, a Scotish Comedy, referred to at page 367.

The merry birds may hail the dawn,
 The hills and glens adorning,
And joyfu' spring, on early wing,
 To meet the dewy morning ;
The fairest flowers frae sunny showers
 New tints o' beauty borrow ;
But nature's smile can ne'er beguile
 The heart oppress'd wi' sorrow.

The burnie laves wi' crystal waves,
 The snaw-white pebbles near me ;
And youthfu' day, wi' gladdening ray,
 Maks a' things bright to cheer me.
The blushing rose her bosom shows,
 Just opening to invite me ;
In vain their art to sooth my heart ;
 Nae langer they delight me.

THE INDEPENDENT WESTMINSTER ELECTOR'S TOAST.

IN MEMORY OF THE GLORIOUS TWO HUNDRED AND TWENTY.

To the Tune of " Come let us prepare," &c.

THE date of the Westminster Election to which this refers was 1742. Sir Charles Wager, and William Lord Sundon, who had sat for West-minster during the eighth Parliament after the Union, which extended from June 13, 1734, to April 28, 1741, were, after a strong opposition, returned for the ninth Parliament which was summoned for June 25, 1741.

Sir Charles Wager was gazetted Admiral in 1738. He had been knighted by Queen Anne for his gallant behaviour in the West Indies, in attacking, taking one, and destroying some rich galleons. He was Treasurer of the Navy, and first Lord of the Admiralty. He died in 1743. Lord Sundon had entered Parliament as William Clayton, Esq., and, while a Lord of the Treasury, in 1735 was created " Lord Sundon " in Ireland. His wife was a favourite of the Queen (Caroline).

A petition having been presented, at the instance of several inhabitants, on behalf of the unsuccessful candidates, Edward Vernon and Charles Edwin, Esquires, their Election was declared void, on 22d Dec. 1741, on these grounds:—"the King's menial servants, not having proper houses of their own within the city, have not a right to vote." Also that Mr John Lever, High Bailiff [the returning officer] at the last Election, acted in an illegal and arbitrary manner, inasmuch as "it appears to this house that a body of armed soldiers, headed by officers, did, on Friday the 8th day of May last, take possession of the Church Yard of St Paul, Covent Garden, near the place where the poll was taken, before the said Election was ended. Resolved, that the presence of a regular body of armed soldiers at an Election of Members to serve in Parliament, is an high infringement of the liberties of the subject, a manifest violation of the Freedom of Elections, and open defiance of the Laws and Constitution of this Kingdom: and Mr Lever (the High-Bailiff), Nathaniel Blackerby, George Howard, and Thomas Lediard, Esquires, Justices, who ordered the soldiers to attend, were ordered into custody by the Sergeant-at-arms."* A new Election followed, when Edward Vernon was again unsuccessful, and John Viscount Percival and Charles Edwin, Esq. were declared duly elected.

John, Viscount Percival, was the eldest son of the first Earl of Egmont, an Antiquarian, who was one of the principal authors of a

* See Beaton's Parliamentary Register, vol. i., p. 112.

"Genealogical History of the House of Yvery in its different branches of Yvery, Luvel, Percival, and Gournay," London, Woodfall, 2 vols., 4to, 1742. The Member for Westminster was at the expense of printing it, and as the book was not sold, it is now amongst the rarest of Genealogical works, and fetches a most extravagant price when a copy occurs for sale at an auction. Lord Orford, in his Memoirs of the reign of King George the Second, (edited by Lord Holland), London, 3 vols. 8vo, 1846, says: "The collecting and consulting records and genealogies, and engraving and publishing cost him (as the Heralds affirm) near £3000. He endeavoured afterwards to recall it, and did suppress a great many copies." From the same authority we learn that Percival in his youth had a scheme of assembling the Jews and making himself their King. He gained his reputation in Parliament by opposing the mutiny bill. His great talent was indefatigable application. Away from the atmosphere of the House, he was humane, friendly, and as good-humoured as it was possible for a man to be, who was never known to laugh. Once, indeed, it is recorded, he was seen to smile, and that was at chess. Towards the decline of Sir Robert Walpole's power, he had created himself a leader of the Independents, a knot of tradesmen, many of whom had been converted to Jacobitism by having been fined at the Custom-house for contraband practices. It was by this influence he got into Parliament on the expulsion of Lord Sundon and Sir Charles Wager. "He was personally brave," says Walpole, "as brave as if he were always in the right." He was born at Westminster on 24th Feb. 1710-11, married (15th Feb. 1736-7) the Lady Catherine Cecil, second daughter to James, fifth Earl of Salisbury, and died 20th Dec. 1772, his wife having died 16th Aug. 1752. He married a second time in 1756, Catherine, daughter of the Honourable Charles Compton, fourth son of George, fourth Earl of Northampton. On his father's death on 1st May 1748 he became Earl of Egmont, and while Member for Bridgewater in 1762, he was called to the House of Peers by the title of Lord Luvel and Holland of Enmore in the county of Somerset, both of which Baronies had been forfeited by the attainder of Francis, Viscount Lovel, I. Henry VII.

Charles Edwin was the son of Samuel Edwin, Esq., of Lanvihangel, in the County of Glamorgan by Lady Catherine, third daughter of the Earl of Manchester. His grandfather was Sir Humphrey Edwin, Lord Mayor of London. Charles Edwin sat five years as one of the members . for Westminster. He subsequently sat for Glamorgan County.

"Bubb," referred to in the concluding stanza, is George Bubb Doddington, of whom we have the following account :—

George Bubb Doddington, Baron of Melcombe Regis, the son of an Apothecary in Dorsetshire named Bubb, was born in 1691, and appears to have been educated at Oxford. In 1715 he was elected Member for

Winchelsea, and soon after appointed Envoy extraordinary at the Court of Spain, where he continued till 1717. By the death of an uncle, George Dodington of Eastbury, on 28th March 1720, he came into possession of a very large estate in the county of Dorset, he having previously by the Statute 4 George 1st obtained power to alter his surname. In the year following he was appointed Lord Lieutenant of the county of Somerset ; in 1724 he was constituted a Lord of the Treasury and obtained the lucrative office of clerk of the Pells in Ireland, being then Member for Bridgewater. He became closely connected with Sir Robert Walpole, and in 1726 published, in folio, a poetical epistle addressed to that Minister, which is only remarkable for its servility. It was reprinted in Dodsley's collection of Poems, vol. vi., p. 129. In 1736-7 he took part in the contest between George II. and the Prince of Wales (heir apparent), in the question about the augmentation of the Prince's annual allowance, which led to a coolness with Sir Robert, and he was dismissed from the Treasury in 1740. On the downfall of the Minister, which he had helped to compass, his expectations of preferment not being gratified, he took part against the new Administration, and on the next change was rewarded on 25th Dec. 1744 with the post of Treasurer of the Navy, and shortly afterwards was sworn as a Member of the Privy Council. The Treasurership of the Navy he resigned in 1749, when the Prince of Wales asked him to become Treasurer of the Chambers with the reversion of a Peerage. The death of the Prince, however, on the 21st March 1750-51 put an end to his expectations and to those of many, who, through him, had entertained visions of greatness when the Prince should become Monarch. For some years after he endeavoured in all humble and servile ways, but in vain, to regain the King's favour. Through the instrumentality of the Duke of Newcastle, he obtained, in 1755, his former post of Treasurer to the Navy. This he lost the following year, regained the offer in 1757, but, by his vacillation, he again lost it. On the accession of George III., he was received into the confidence of Lord Bute, and on 3d April 1761 was advanced to the Peerage. He died, unmarried, on 28th July 1762. He was understood to have had some hand in a Dramatic Entertainment called "The Wishes," which he took some pains to have produced at Drury Lane the year before his death. While it was in rehearsal, he invited all the performers to his seat at Hammersmith, and had it acted *al fresco* in the garden. Sam Foote, who was of the party, took that occasion to inform himself of the peculiarities of his Lordship, and under the name of Sir Thomas Lofty introduced him into his comedy of the Patron, which was brought before the public in 1764. Lord Melcombe is allowed to have been, in private life, generous, magnificent, and convivial ; but, in the course of his political life, he was insincere and faithless. His reigning passion was to be regarded well at Court. To this object he sacrificed every circumstance of his life.   His talents do not appear to have been distinguished by much brilliancy, but he was reflective and of a cool judgment.   The principal performance by which Lord Mel-combe is known was his " Diary," which was published long after his death from his own MS., under the Editorship of a distant relative Mr. Peregrine Wyndam, who in his Prefatory address exhibits a just, but somewhat unfriendly appreciation of his Lordship's true character. This Diary "unveiled the nakedness of his mind and has left him to be viewed as a courtly compound of mean compliance and political pro-stitution."   See *Walpole's Catalogue* of Royal and Noble Authors, Park's edition, 8vo, Lond. 1806, vol. iv., p. 248, also *European Magazine* for June 1784, in which there is a portrait of his Lordship, a vulgar-looking countenance, with thick lips, and a broad nose, somewhat *retroussée.*

In the Appendix to vol. i. of Lord Orford's Memoirs of the reign of King George the Second, occurs "a brief account of George Bubb Doddington," being from his Lordship's annotated copy of the Diary. He observes that Doddington's wit was very ready, and relates this anecdote : " Lord Sundon was Commissioner of the Treasury with him and Winnington, and was very dull.   One Thursday, as they left the Board, Lord Sundon laughed heartily at something Doddington said ; and when gone, Winnington remarked, 'you are very ungrateful, Doddington ; you called Sundon stupid and slow, and yet you see how quick he took what you said.'   'Oh !' replied Doddington, 'He was only laughing now at what I said last Treasury day.'"   He goes on to say, " Doddington was married to a Mrs Behan, whom he was supposed to keep.   Though secretly married he could not own her, as he then did, till the death of Mrs Strawbridge, to whom he had given a promise of marriage under the penalty of £10,000.   He had long made love to the latter, and at last, obtaining an assignation, found her lying on a couch.   However, he only fell on his knees, and after kissing her hand for some time, cried out, 'Oh ! that I had you but in a wood !'   'In a wood !' exclaimed the disappointed dame, 'What would you do then ?   Would you *rob* me?'"   It was on this lady that was made the ballad :—

> My strawberry, my strawberry
> Shall bear away the bell."

To the air of which Lord Bath, many years afterwards, wrote his song on "Strawberry Hill."

Doddington had no children.   His estate descended to Lord Temple, whom he hated.

His want of taste and his tawdry ostentation were displayed in his dress and furniture.   "At Eastberry, in the great bed-chamber, hung with the richest red velvet, was pasted on every pannel of the velvet, his crest

(a hunting-horn supported by an eagle) cut out of gilt leather. The
foot-cloth round the bed was a mosaic of the pocket-flaps and cuffs of
all his embroidered clothes. At Hammersmith, his crest, in pebbles,
was stuck into the centre of the turf before his door.* The chimney-
piece was hung with spars representing icicles round the fire, and a
bed of purple, lined with orange, was crowned by a dome of peacock's
feathers. The great gallery, to which was a beautiful door of white
marble, supported by two columns of *lapis lazuli*, was not only fitted
with busts and statues, but had, I think, an inlaid floor of marble ; and
all this weight was above stairs. One day, showing it to Edward, Duke
of York, Doddington said, "Sir, some persons tell me that this room
ought to be on the ground,"—"Be easy, Mr Doddington," replied the
Prince, "it will soon be there."

Doddington was very lethargic : falling asleep one day after dinner,
with Sir Richard Temple, Lord Cobham, the General, the latter
reproached Doddington with his drowsiness. Doddington denied having
been asleep, and, to prove he had not, offered to repeat all that Lord
Cobham had been saying. Cobham challenged him to do so. Doddington repeated a story, and Lord Cobham owned he had been telling it.
"Well," said Doddington, "and yet I did not hear a word of it ; but
I went to sleep because I knew that about this time of the day you
would tell that story."

My Westminster Friends.

My Westminster friends,
Now we've gained our ends,
Here's a Health, and I'm sure, 'twont repent ye :
With gratitude think.
To the health let us drink
Of the Glorious Two Hundred and Twenty.

Come honestly on,
Give your votes as you've done,
When you voted for Edwin and Vernon ;
Like Britons be bold,
Laugh at power and gold,
Else Slavery comes, and will spare none.

* His mansion at Hammersmith was afterwards better known as
Brandenburgh House. It was the residence for a while of the Mar-
gravine of Anspach, and subsequently of Queen Caroline.

The Army so grand,
For the good of the Land,
That is annually chose its Protectors,
A new trade have got,
And without Scott or Lot :
Are now all become our Electors.

The Justices, too,
Will soon have their due,
As well as that R[ogu]e, the High-Bailey,
Though you strut and look big,
With your sword and tye-wig,
The Parliament soon will to jail wi' ye.

Brave Edwin, for you
Did all he could do,
As at the last Poll ye remember,
Now, all of ye shou'd
To him be as good,
And choose him once more for your Member.

An honest good Lord,
To find out, how hard,
At this time, let any man think, Sir !
Yet all do agree,
Lord Perceval's he !
Then Edwin and Perceval drink, Sir.

Besides his brave spirit,
My Lord has his merit
With us, that *Guts* * hates him to death, Sir,

* Sir Robert Walpole, Prime Minister.   The following Epigram
upon this able Statesman, appeared in the *Craftsman*, 1727 :—
What strange resemblance can your fancy see,
'Twixt Walpole's fame and Wolsey's infamy ?
In vain through Greece and Italy you roam,
In vain explore our annals here at home;
In vain you conjure up old shades from Hell;
For as friend Theobald hath expressed it well,
None but himself can be his parallel.

He has swore "Zounds! and Blood!"
That my Lord never shou'd
Be a member so long as he'd Breath, Sir,

Then under his nose,
These brave men we will choose,
To show we don't fear, but despise him,
We'll laugh and we'll flout,
At the Rabble at Court,
Who, for what they can get idolize him.

The P[arliamen]t just,
And firm to their trust,
Have giv'n you another Election,
Then your liberty use,
These honest men choose,
And rely on their steady Protection.

Vernon's self will rejoice,
When he hears of our choice,
And is told how we've routed the old-ones,
Then join hand in hand,
To each other firm stand,
For success always follows the Bold-ones.

But, if any more,
B[ub]b shou'd do as before,
Or by fraud or by violence cheat you,
In numbers then go
And demolish your Foe,
Ye're Fools if again he Defeat you.
But if any more, &c. [*Chorus.*

THE COURTIER.

THE hero of the following Ballad is unmistakeably the Honourable Anne Poulett, who for four successive Parliaments sat as Member for the Borough of Bridgewater. He was first elected in 1769, when he petitioned against the election of J. James Viscount Perceval, and claimed the seat ; secondly in 1774 ; thirdly in 1781, when his return and that of Benjamin Allen, Esq., were petitioned against, and he was found by a Committee of the House to have been duly elected, but that John Ackland, Esq. ought to have been returned in place of Mr Allen ; and fourthly in 1784. See *Oldfield's Representative History*, 8vo. 1816, vol. 4th, pp. 442-3.

In Dodsley's Annual Register, of date 24th March 1784, we find this paragraph ;—"The Right Honourable Charles James Fox was presented by the Mayor, Aldermen, and capital burgesses, with the freedom of the Borough of Bridgewater, Somerset ; and therewith chosen Recorder for the same, in the room of Vere Poulett, brother to Anne Poulett, member for the said Borough," &c. Two days afterwards, Mr Fox was elected member for the northern district of the Boroughs in Scotland.

Mr Vere Poulett is the gentleman referred to in the opening stanza, who "first bought the place." He was one of the members for Bridgewater from 1741 to 1747, when he retired in favour of an elder brother Peregrine. The Honourable Peregrine, and the Honourable John Poulett (twins) were born 10th Dec. 1708. They were second and third sons of the first Earl Poulett by Bridget, daughter and co-heir to Peregrine Bertie of Waldershare in Kent, brother of the Earl of Lindsay, and uncle to Robert, Duke of Ancaster. Peregrine died member for Bridgewater, 26th August 1752. John, the second Earl, Lord Lieutenant of Somerset, dying a bachelor on the 5th Nov. 1764, the Earldom devolved on his next surviving brother, Vere, who, on the 16th of the same month, was chosen Recorder of Bridgewater. He died 14th April 1788, aged 78.

Hinton House, to which allusion is made in the second stanza, was the family seat.

The youngest son of the first Earl, and brother of the three last mentioned Pouletts, was, by command of the Queen, his Godmother, christened Anne. He was born 11th July 1711, and died 5th July 1785.

The title still exists in the male descendant of Vere, the third Earl. The family seat is still Hinton St George.

The second son of Vere, also the Honourable Vere Poulett, sat for Bridgewater during the seventeenth Parliament after the Union, and during the third Imperial Parliament. He was a Major-General in the army.

The date of this ballad is 12th Nov. 1784, and *apropos* of that year, here are some stanzas from "the Theatre of Fun ; or, Roderick Random in high glee." Lond. 1784, 12mo :—

A TOUCH ON THE TIMES.

By Mrs Spencer.

Hail ! happy year ! hail ! Eighty-four !
  Of Englishmen the glory ;
Such virtuous times and deeds before
  Were never heard in story.

Hail ! happy husbands ! happier wives !
  Forgot each vice and passion,
Ye lead most chaste and charming lives,
  E'en keeping's out of fashion.   ·

No more men wound bless'd Virtue's ear
  With loose or free discourses ;
No more we constant women hear
  Of parting or divorces.

Thank Heaven ! this age is prudent grown,
  Fine ladies scorn deceit ;
And Lords, no more to falsehood prone,
  Are wise, and good, and great.

The courtier scorns the double tongue,
  Which former courtiers knew ;
And great and small, and old and young,
  Are each as good as true.

At playhouse now no crowds are seen,
  To gape at Folly's treat ;
But churches are so full, I ween,
  You scarce can get a seat.

Provisions are so wondrous cheap,
  The poor have peace and plenty ;
And Magistrates such order keep
  The prisons all are empty.

Venality and faction now,
  Are banished from the nation,
We all are patriots and avow
  We hate dissimulation.

In short such virtue, void of crimes,
  Was never known before,

Until the present glorious times :
 () happy eighty-four !

Yet should you think I'm not sincere,
 To irony inclined ;
Reverse the picture and, I fear,
 The very truth you'll find.

Mr Fox, of whom mention is made in stanza four, being in the spring
of 1785 at the Levee, the King passed by him in the Drawing-Room
with a "How do you do, Mr Fox ?" and walked on without waiting for
an answer.   Fox seeing Lord Mansfield, asked him if his Lordship knew
what he had done to the King that had made his majesty so abrupt and
laconic.   "My good friend" (replied Lord Mansfield, with a smile)
"if you expect that the king shall make long speeches to you in the
Drawing-Room, you must make short speeches in St Stephen's Chapel."

The Courtier.

In good Sir Robert's golden days,
 When Brib'ry had no harm in't,
My brother Vere first bought this place,
 And sought for Court preferment :
And Hinton House, unto this hour,
 Doth hold it mortal sin, sir,
To side with him that's out of pow'r ;
 Or turn from him that's in, sir.
 And this is law, I will maintain,
 Until my dying day, sir,
 Whatever minister shall reign,
 I will be in his pay, sir.

When Scotish Councils rul'd this land,
 And tarnish'd England's glory,
I join'd Lord Bute with heart and hand,
 And was a rank old Tory.
I stuck by North, when North came in,
 Thro' his Administration,
Voted with him through thick and thin,
 And help'd to damn the nation.
 And this is law, &c., &c.

When good Lord Rockingham appeared,
    And honest men looked big, sir ;
With this new wind about I veer'd,
    And would have been a Whig, sir ;
To him I wing'd, and made my Court,
    But found 'twas all in vain, sir,
He scorned such paltry mean support,
    So I whipp'd back again, sir.
        And this is law, &c., &c.

When Fox and North at length agreed
    To turn all blunderers out, sir,
I then, in duty to my creed,
    Once more turned North about, sir.
Receipt-tax, India-Bill, and all,
    With them I stoutly voted ;
At backstairs' Council learn'd to bawl,
    And secret influence hooted.
        And this is law, &c., &c.

When North disdained all views of power,
    I left such politicians,
And turn'd to Thurlow, Pitt, and Gower,
    Yet curs'd all coalitions :
For this once more the Treasury
    Have back'd me at Bridgewater ;
And Master Pitt my man shall be,
    Until the times shall alter.
        And this is law, &c., &c.

_____

THE TIMES HAVE ALTERED.

THIS Ballad, which may date about 1820, is curious as contrasting the
domestic system then pursued by farmers and tillers of the soil, with
that which had been in practice some time before.   The high prices for
farm produce which had subsisted for several years prior to the termination of the war in 1815, had caused farmers, particularly those resident

in the North of England and the South of Scotland, to become wealthy in spite of everything. They held extensive areas of land at a compara- tively low rental, yet without the aid of artificial manures, and in the face of high wages required by the then limited population of the country who were willing to engage as farm servants and hinds, even the most slovenly conducted farms yielded a handsome revenue. When Peace was accomplished, and intercourse with more remote places became more frequent, foreign customs and foreign fashions began to pervade the land, and notions of equality with superiors to take possession of the minds of mere traders; chivalry waned towards its dotage, and was pushed on one side by meaner spirits whose idol was the golden calf. By the change thus effected, farmers (or rather their more ambitious helpmates), finding themselves in a very comfortable position, began to imagine themselves as good as their landlords, and they therefore proceeded to imitate the landlords' style of living in so far as lay in their power. The great differ- ence which took place in their habits is correctly enough depicted in the Ballad, although done in rather an envious and bitter spirit in conse- quence of a supposed grievance,—a reduction in wages paid to farm servants in conformity with the natural fall in prices, and the greater supply of labouring men by reason of the demand for soldiers having subsided. Farmers now drove to market in their phaetons, in place of riding on horseback, with, when occasion required it, their wives on the pillions behind ; the wives visited their neighbours in carriages in place of carts, and their sons aped the dandy, and followed the hounds in the hunting field in hunting costume, as good as any lord. The style then adopted by farmers to emulate the country gentlemen is still in too many instances followed up, notwithstanding the ruin which always attends undue extravagance, and which in cases of this kind has so frequently shown itself. Still, if circumstances are not pushed to the extreme, a farmer may carry on for nearly a lifetime, educate his children as well as the children of a squire, keep his carriage, and live sumptuously upon a small commencing capital, so small that if employed in trade it would barely yield him a subsistence.

In a very interesting paper in the Edinburgh Magazine, by "An old Farmer, Selkirkshire, 25th June 1818," after giving some particulars of his grandfather's time, he proceeds to say :—"A description of our common mode of living in my father's time will give you a pretty accurate idea of the system that prevailed about the middle of last century. A long stout table stood near the window of the kitchen, or 'Ha',' (as it was frequently termed). At meals the gudeman took his seat at the head of the table, next him sat his own family and relations, and below them the servants. . . . The close of Autumn was celebrated by a *kirn*, or harvest home, when all the shearers, servants, and cottars were regaled with supper, in which the 'the great chieftain of the pudding race' always formed a prominent dish, with a moderate libation of home brewed beer and whisky. Music and dancing sometimes concluded the entertainment, but not in my father's house, he, being a staunch adherent to the most rigid form of Presbyterianism, had unrelentingly proscribed all 'promiscuous dancing' in his family, as one of the worst of these worldly fashions 'which are not convenient.' For similar reasons Halloween was forbidden to be held in our house. Yet, besides the kirn, a few old holidays were still partially observed by us, and, among these, Hansel Monday. . . . . Except among relatives, or near friends, nothing of what is now understood by visiting, was then practised. Formal dinners and tea parties were equally unknown. The use of tea, indeed, among people of our rank, was very limited. . . . You may probably be apt to suppose that the life of a farmer must have been very dull and stupid in those times. Nothing could be more erroneous. We had, in fact, much more leisure and inclination also, to be merry, than is permitted to us now. Spring and autumn were the only seasons that required arduous labour, in the old system of farming; and then, these seasons came round to us with an air of more festivity, had more of a heart-stirring aspect about them, and their toils were encountered (if I may so express it) with more of a military ardour, than in those days of regular *rotations*, machinery, and summer fallow. At other times of the year we took matters easy enough. The *winning* of peats and hay, ewe-milking, sheep-shearing, and the management of the horned cattle, occupied the lightsome days of Summer. In Winter our leisure was still greater, and our enjoyments more diversified. Field sports were eagerly followed by both masters and servants in the intervals of labour, or after the short winter yoking was over. Many a time, too, have I seen my grave worthy father toss down the football, or the *kitti-cat*, to us and the servant-lads, and sometimes take a hearty bout at these games himself. In Winter we beguiled the long evenings with story-telling, ballad-singing, tales of bogles and witches, (in which all devoutly believed); and to these the wandering beggar and the pedlar, always welcome guests, added other varieties of entertainment. Some of these amusements were rather childish, perhaps, and fit only for a rude state of society; yet, with all our modern improvements, I am inclined to consider it at least doubtful if *all* that has been abandoned of our former manners has been equally well replaced, and whether some part of our present knowledge and refinement has not been purchased by the sacrifice of qualities still more valuable."

The following apropos anecdote is told by Cobbett :—"An old farmer who lives at Burghclare, under the north Hampshire Hills, observed to me last year, when we were talking about the corruption and degeneracy of the times, that it was the fine words, and the flattery of men to the farmer's wives that had done all the mischief; "for," said he, "when 'twas *dame* and *porridge*, 'twas real good times ; when 'twas *mistress* and *broth*, 'twas worse a great deal ; but when it came to be *ma'am* and *soup*, 'twas d——d bad."

The Times have Altered.

Come all you swaggering farmers, whoever you may be,
One moment pay attention and listen unto me ;
It is concerning former times, as I to you declare,
So different to the present times if you with them compare.
Chorus—For lofty heads and paltry pride, I'm sure it's
  all the go,
For to distress poor servants and keep their wages low.

If you'd seen the farmers wives 'bout fifty years ago,
In home-spun russet linsey clad from top to toe ;
But now a-days the farmer's wives are so puffed up with pride,
In a dandy habit and green veil unto the market they must
 ride.
Chorus—For lofty heads, &c.

Some years ago the farmer's sons were learnt to plough and
 sow,
And when the summer-time did come, likewise to reap and
 mow ;
But now they dress like Squire's sons, their pride it knows
 no bounds,
They mount upon a fine blood horse to follow up the hounds.

The farmers' daughters formerly were learnt to card and spin,
And, by their own industry, good husbands they did win;
But now the card and spinning-wheel are forced to take their
 chance,
While they're hopped off to a boarding-school to learn to
 sing and dance.

In a decent black silk bonnet to church they used to go,
Black shoes, and handsome cotton gown, stockings as white
as snow,
But now silk gowns and coloured shoes they must be bought
for them,
Besides they are frizzed and furbelowed just like a freizland
hen.

Each morning when at breakfast, the master and the dame
Down with the servants they would sit, and eat and drink
the same,
But with such good old things, they've done them quite away;
Into the parlour they do go with coffee, toast, and tea.

At the kitchen table formerly, the farmer he would sit,
And carve for all his servants, both pudding and fine meat,
But now all in the dining-room so closely they're boxed in,
If a servant only was to peep, it would be thought a sin.

Now, in those good old fashion'd times, the truth I do
declare,
The rent and taxes could be spared, and money for to spare,
But now they keep the fashion up, they look so very nice,
Although they cut an outside show they are as poor as mice.

When Bonaparte was in vogue, poor servants could engage
For sixteen pounds a year, my boys, that was a handsome
wage,
But now the wages are so low, and what is worse than all,
The masters cannot find the cash, which brings them to the
wall.

When fifty acres they did rent, then money they could save,
But now for to support their pride, five hundred they must
have ;
If those great farms were taken and divided into ten,
Oh! we might see as happy days as ever we did then.

CALTON JESS.

ALTHOUGH this Ballad is titled "Calton Jess" its only evident object is to ridicule the prevailing follies in dress of the time, which may date from 1818 till ˙about 1821. As the locality called "the Calton" in Edinburgh is pretty much the same as "the Calton" in Glasgow, not of the most aristocratic order, the ballad-maker in satirizing the Dandies and Dandyzettes of the day, who arrogated to themselves the position of the elite of rank and fashion, has no doubt adopted for his title the name of some character well-known in either of these cities, who, moving in the lowest sphere, could, with popular effect, be contrasted with them in their extreme pretensions.

The terms "Dandy," (male) and "Dandyzette," (female) were introduced into the "forcible vernacular" of this country about, or shortly before, the period already indicated. Dandy is synonymous with the more ancient "Beau," "Buck," "Coxcomb," "Dainty Gallant," "Petit Maitre," "Macaroni," "Blood," "Fop," "Exquisite," "Choice Spirit," "Quat," &c., and with the appellation now prevalent of "Swell." These, although used originally as terms of reproach, have, in consequence of the general taste for slang, lost their true significance, and have become conventional expressions.

The etymology of "Dandy" has been deduced from "Dandiprat," a small silver coin of little value, struck by Henry VII., and hence, Bishop Fleetwood observes, " the term is applied to worthless and contemptible persons." In Middleton's "More Dissemblers besides Women," Dandolo says of Lactantio's page, "there's no fellowship in this dandiprat, this dive-dapper." In the same play Cinquepace says, "who would be plagued with a dandi-prat usher," &c. In Massinger's "Virgin Martyr," Hircius, speaking of Dorothea's attendant, thus soliloquizes : " The smug dandi-prat smells out whatever we are doing." Marston and Dekker also use the word, which seems to have been in common request in the age of Queen Elizabeth, as an epithet of reproach. The word "Quat," is explained in the Canting Dictionary, 1737, as "a pimple," and the same authority gives us, "Chit, a Dandiprat or Dergen, a little tufting fellow." " Dandy-prat, a little puny fellow."

In point of dress, the dandy or swell has ever been *outré*. The costume which formed the subject of so much ridicule previous to and after the date of our ballad, is admirably depicted in the various contemporaneous caricatures by the inimitable Cruikshank. The dandy wore a blue swallow-tailed coat, tight fitting in the sleeves, and very short in the waist (to resemble the ladies' gown boddice then in vogue), a buff or other waistcoat, also short, met by a pair of tight pantaloons,

which were continued by silk stockings, and followed up by shallow tapering pointed shoes. The gloves were bright yellow, fashioned from chamois
leather. The collar was a stand-up collar—a modern Shakesperian collar
reversed—called "dog's ears," while the neck was encased in a huge
neckcloth or bandana. The hair was frizzled, and whiskers, which had
just come in, extended half-way down the cheek to the edge of the
collar. The wristbands were voluminous, and turned up over the cuff
of the coat. The hat was low in the crown. The Dandy wore stays,
and an eye-glass. A bunch of seals depended by a ribbon from his fob,
and he invariably carried an umbrella with a long ferule. Occasionally
the costume was varied by a pair of wide trousers reaching to the calf,
and overhanging the top of his Hessian boots, and a hat of the Kevenhuller
shape, i.e., wider at the crown than at the bottom, and rather wide in
the brim. There was another species of hat in use, the exact reverse of
this, tapering from the brim to the top, which bore a very small crown.

The mania for absurd costume, originally imported from France, was
not entirely confined to this country. We find the following in a New
York Paper, in the days of Dandyism.

"*Dandy-hats.* Our City has been much amused with a low tripod-
kind of a hat, made of fine beaver, and worn by our bang-ups. Some
call them 'the Touch,' others 'the Gape and Stare ;' the real name is
' Bolingbroke.' It is about six inches in crown, and four in rim, shaped
like an inverted cone. It is a real tippy. We yesterday saw one of the
fancy, dressed quite unique; blue frock, black silk Wellington cravat,
buff waistcoat, cassock pantaloons, high-heel boots, black ribbon and
eye-glass, bushy hair frizzed, and surmounted with one of those tippy
hats. He looked like an hour-glass, and minced his steps along
Broadway in the real Jemmy Jumps style. The ladies were highly pleased,
and more glasses were directed towards him than would have been to
the Emperor Iturbide, had he just landed ; while our Blood, insensible
to all curiosity, danced up the street, humming the favourite air of
' Look, dear ma'am ! I'm quite the thing, natius hay, tippity ho.'"

The character, Sir Francis Faddle, in Dimond's Musical Drama of
"For England, ho !" was written to ridicule the Dandy, chiefly in his
affected mode of speaking. "Above all things, it is necessary that the
Independent Dandy should adopt a peculiar tone of utterance, winding
some words out to an indefinite length, and snapping others right off in
the middle, before they get half-way through his mouth, at the same
time intermixing as many 'a—a—a's' as he finds convenient."* Mr
Jones, erewhile the light comedian in Mrs Henry Siddons' Company
at the Edinburgh Theatre, dressed and acted the part of Sir Francis

* Article "the Independent Dandy," in "Dandymania, being a Dissertation on
Modern Dandies, by a Jackey Dandy." Published by Duncombe, Little Queen Street
Holborn.

Faddle in the most perfect manner. He was, however, a capital actor otherwise. " Lord Dundreary " is a spurious imitation of Sir Francis Faddle.

The principal features in the costume of the Dandyzette of the period to which we chiefly refer consisted of an immense Leghorn bonnet with broad flaps, adorned with ribbons of a bright shining colour, a short-bodied gown, very full, made close up to the neck, a full skirt reaching to the ancles, and sleeves like great balloons. The immediate descendants of the Dandyzette will be found in those girls of the period termed "fast."

The Velocipede was a kindred invention,and Dandies and Dandyzettes are, in caricatures, represented as almost perpetually riding on it. It consequently obtained the name of "the Dandy Hobby."

"The She and He Dandy" are thus described in the Epilogue to the Tragedy of Brutus, produced in London in 1818 :—

> But bless me—what two nondescripts together !
> 'Tis SHE—a pile of ribband, straw, and feather ;
> Her back a pillion, all above, and on it,
> A church bell ? cradle? tower? no, faith, a bonnet !
> Aye, and an actual woman in it.
>
> .   .   .   .   .
>
> What straps, ropes, steel, the aching ribs compress,
> To make the Dandy beautifully less !
> Thus, fools, their final state of folly cast,
> By instinct to strait waistcoats come at last.
> Misjudging Shakespeare ! this escaped thine eye,
> For though the brains are out, the thing won't die.

Referring to a work published at London in 1814, entitled "Portraits of Fops," who were the immediate predecessors of Dandies, the following remarks in reference to Foppery occur in the Preface :—

"Successive ages have established and extended its empire. It not only inhabits the palace of the sovereign, and the mansions of the noble, but has descended to take up its residence in the dwellings of industry, the habitation of the artizan, and cottage of the peasant. Pervading every class of the community, it finds a thousand methods to display itself, and supports myriads of the labouring classes in providing the means for the indulgence of its ever-varying, but never-ending caprice. Sprung from immortal parents, it partakes itself of their immortal nature, and appears only to acquire fresh vigour from the lapse of ages. It mingles in the devotional exercises of religion, poisons the streams of morality, perverts science, gives a tinge to art, infects the Senate, the coffee-room, and the pot-house ; shines at all periodsand in every sphere ; and though by all affected to be despised, is in fact, practised, imitated, loved, and supported by all. Wisdom itself, yielding to the general disorder, has suffered itself to be contaminated by *Foppery ;* and the consequence has been, the introduction of a spurious kind of taste, and an adulterated species of morality, from which still more alarming results than have yet been witnessed may be ultimately expected to proceed."

Calton Jess.

THERE'S Calton Jess, a bonny lass,
  She's blythsome, brisk, and a' that,
Her skin's no black like Widow Watt,
  Nor toothless, deaf, and a' that.
For a' that, and a' that,
  The want o' cash and a' that,
But Jess and I before we die,
  Will laugh at dandies a' yet.

Wi' little art I've gained her heart,
  She's yielding, kind, and a' that,
Tho' I to her ne'er gae a chair,*
  Nor Brandy drams, and a' that.
For a' that, and a' that,
  Her sugar lips and a' that,
They sweeter are to me by far,
  Than dandyzettes and a' that.

Although nae dashin' seals I hae,
  Nor diamond rings and a' that,
Nor quizzin' glasses e'er sae fine,
  I'll ne'er loss heart for a' that.
For a' that, and a' that,
  Their frizzled hair and a' that,
But Jess will take me as I am,
  And daut me weel for a' that.

* This word, which does not occur in the Scotish tongue, is presumed to be "cheerer," an expression in use in Northumberland to signify a glass of whisky toddy, or of any other powerful stimulant of a kindred nature.

I'm no sae vain as hae a cane
  To hook up gloves and a' that,
I'll run nae risk to burst my stays
  Wi' loutin' down and a' that.
For a' that, and a' that,
  Their crooked staves and a' that,
An aiken rung is better far
  Than dandy canes and a' that.

My sarks they are baith stout and strong,
  Nae pricked up necks and a' that,
Nae Tippy coats wi' swallow tails,
  Nor straight laced stays and a' that,
For a' that, and a' that,
  Their smooth shirt necks and a' that,
Tho' deil a sark be on their back,
  Troth ! dandies maun na fa' that.

Their waists sae sma' and hats sae braw
  And ruffles fine and a' that,
Blood horses ye would think them a',
  They bridles need and a' that.
For a' that, and a' that,
  Their stiffeners, braid, and a' that,
And napkins tight about their necks,
  And cocked up chins and a' that.

Wi' trousers short and head a-cock,
  And Wellingtons and a' that ;
If they had been at Waterloo
  They'd fight the French and a' that.
For a' that, and a' that,
  Their frightsome dress and a' that,
They've chance to swagger when they swing,
  The sport o' men and a' that.

TUGAL M'TAGGER.

This was a very popular song in Glasgow about forty years ago. It used to be sung by Mr Livingstone, at the Theatre Royal there.

The jealousy between the Highlanders and the Lowlanders which then existed, and which has not yet entirely died out, caused the latter to sneer at and satirize their Gaelic brethren, at least such of them as hived into the principal towns in the Lowlands, generally the worst specimens of their nation, whose object it was to get forward in the world by putting out better men. They were regarded as half savages, full of low cunning, fawning to abject servility upon those from whom they might gain anything, and capable of the meanest actions,—characters even worse than that which Sir Walter has depicted in the Dougal Creature. There is a phrase still in use to indicate their want of skill as handicraftsmen, which is applied to anything that is tolerably well done :—" It's no sae Heeland."

Tugal M'Tagger.

Would you'll ken me, my name is Tugal M'Tagger,
She'll brought hersel' doun frae the braes o' Lochaber,
Shust to learn her nainsel to pe praw Habberdaber
　　Or fine Linen Traper, the tane o' the twa.

She'll pe a stranger, she'll look unco shy-like,
She's no weel acquaint wi' your laigh kintra dialect ;
But hough! never heed,—she's got plenty o' Gaelic,
　　She comes frae ta hoose at ta fit o' Glendhu.

But her kilt she'll exchange for ta praw tandy trowser,
An' she'll learn to ta leddy to scrape an to pow, sir.
An' say to ta shentlemans, " how tid you'll to, sir,"
　　An' then she'll forgot her poor freens o' Glendhu.

An' when she'll be spoket ta laigh kintra jabber,
She'll gie hersel' oot for ta laird o' Lochaber
Shust come for amusements to turn Habberdaber,
　　For tat will pe prawer tan herdin' ta cow.

She'll get a big shop, an she'll turn'd a big dealer;
She was caution hersel', for they'll no sought no bailer.
But Tugal M'Tagger hersel' maks a failure,
They'll call her a bankrumpt, a trade she'll not know.

They'll call'd a great meeting, she'll look unco quate, noo,
She'll fain win awa but they'll tell her to wait, noo;
They'll spoket a lang time apoot her estate, noo;
I'll thocht that they'll thocht me the Laird o' Glendhu.

They'll wrote a lang while noo apoot a trust deeder,
She'll no wrote a word for hersel' couldna read her,
They'll sought compongzition, hough! hough! never heed her;
There's no sic a word 'mang the hills o' Glendhu.

But had she her dirk, hersel' would come ower them;
They'll put her in jail, but she'll stood there before them;
But faith, she'll got oot on a hashimanorum,
An' noo she's as free as ta win's o' Glendhu.

JOHNNY LAD.

EVIDENTLY a Nurse's song "sung to its own proper tune" to amuse
her charge "Johnny."—It is merely a collection of nursery rhymes
strung together without reason, but presenting a succession of jingle
grateful to the youthful ear, and of pictures pleasing to the youthful
fancy. Mr Peter Buchan has printed it in his Ancient Ballads and
Songs of the North of Scotland, Edin., 8vo, 1828, vol. ii. He innocently remarks :—"Among all the ballads or songs of this name, and
they are not a few, to be met with in modern collections, this one has
never made its appearance, at least I have never seen it. It is very old,
and, as far as I can learn, the original of all the others; although it does
not altogether agree with my ideas of the composition of ancient song.
The old air to which it is sung is truly beautiful."

There occurs in Ramsay's Tea Table Miscellany a song of like construction, termed "The Nurse's Song," the tune of which was "Yellow
Stockings." It is merely a string of fragments of nursery rhymes. It
begins, "Hey my kitten, my kitten." In Herd's Scotish Songs there
is also "The Nurse's Song," commencing :—

> How dan dilly dow,
>   How den dan,
> Weel were your minny
>   An' ye were a man, &c.

And in the same collection occurs :—
> When I was a wee thing,
>   And just like an elf,
> All the meat that e'er I gat,
>   I laid upon the shelf, &c.

Tune—"John Anderson my Jo."

Johnnie Lad.

> I bought a wife in Edinburgh
>   For a bawbee,
> I get a farthing in again
>   To buy tobacco wi'.
> We'll bore in Aaron's nose a hole,
>   And put therein a ring,
> And straight we'll lead him to and fro,
>   Yea! lead him in a string.
> *Chorus*—And wi' you, and wi' you,
>   And wi' you, Johnnie lad,
> I'll drink the buckles o' my sheen
>   Wi' you my Johnnie, lad.

> When auld Prince Arthur ruled this land,
>   He was a thievish king,
> He stole three bolls of barley meal,
>   To make a white pudding.
>   And wi' you, &c.

The pudding it was sweet and good,
    And stored weel wi' plumes,
The lumps o' suet into it
    Were big as baith my thooms.
        And wi' you, &c.

There was a man in Nineveh,
    And he was wondrous wise,
He jumped into a hawthorn hedge,
    And scratched out baith his eyes.
        And wi' you, &c.

And when he saw his eyes were out,
    He was sair vexed then,
He jumped intill another hedge,
    And scratched them in again.
        And wi' you, &c.

O Johnnie's no a gentleman,
    Nor yet is he a laird,
But I would follow Johnnie lad,
    Although he were a caird.
        And wi' you, &c.

O Johnnie is a bonny lad,
    He was ance a lad o' mine,
I never had a better lad,
    And I've had twenty-nine.
        And wi' you, &c.

L'Envoy.

Our task is ended, and aside we fling
The minstrel's harp to rest its wearied string.
And so, goodnight! since we our say have said,
Shut up the volume and proceed to bed;
And dream, dear reader, of a future, when
The Pedlar may shake hands with you again.

APPENDIX.

CAPTAIN WARD AND THE RAINBOW, p. 1.

SIR WALTER SCOTT, when he left this country in Sept. 1831, in the hopeless pursuit of restored health, sent a version of this ballad, which differs most materially from ours, in the following letter to his friend, the Secretary of the Bannatyne Club, for insertion in the "Bannatyne Club Garland," where it appeared in 1848:—

" DEAR SIR,—I find among my papers the enclosed ballad, prepared for your chronicle of sundry unconsidered trifles. It has never, that I know, been taken notice of, though it occurs in stall copies, and was popular when I was a boy. It is, I think, well written, and on an interesting subject. You will judge for yourself as to using it. Farewell for a long while, and best wishes.—Yours very truly,

WALTER SCOTT.

In Sir Walter's Introductory notice to the ballad, he mentions that in his boyhood he "remembers it as one of the popular ditties which were learned by heart by the youngsters of the period, whose fashion it was to go from house to house disguised with shirts over their clothes, and fantastic vizards, which were termed in Scotland *guisarding* and in England *mumming*." He further observes :—"It is not to be found in any approved collection of ballads, either of modern or ancient times, and is hidden amongst the stall-copies of the present day." He acknowledges that he is not "acquainted with the authentic account of the engagement between 'Captain Ward and the Rainbow.'"

In the catalogue for December 1867 of Messrs T. & W. Boone, New Bond Street, is :—

"909. Newes from sea of two notorious Pyrats, Ward the Englishman, and Danseker the Dutchman, with a true relation of all or the most of piracies by them committed unto the sixt of April 1609. Black Letter. *Woodcut in title of their execution at the main-yard.* 4to, half

morocco, fine clean copy—very rare, £3, 3s. Printed by N. Butter 1609."
Into whose hands this rare volume has fallen we have been unable to
trace.

PAUL JONES, p. 32.

The following notice is from the Scots Magazine, in which also will
be found an account from time to time of the various progresses of our
hero :—

"Amsterdam, Oct. 8th [1779].—Tuesday last, Paul Jones, with the
prizes the Serapis and Countess of Scarborough entered the Texel, and
this day he appeared on the Exchange. He was dressed in the American
uniform, with a Scotch bonnet edged with gold; is of a middling stature,
stern countenance, and swarthy complexion."

THE FRENCH SQUADRON, p. 39.

The "Sir John" referred to in the sixth stanza was not Sir John
Halket, as we had conjectured, but Sir John Anstruther, who, when Paul
Jones anchored off Pittenweem, imagining that his fleet were ships
expected to return about that time from an exploring expedition to the
coast of Africa, sent off one of his boats with a basket of vegetables
and a parcel of newspapers for the voyagers. His present was accepted,
and the basket was returned filled with powder, accompanied by a
recommendation to Sir John to defend his house. Andrew Paton, a
Pittenweem pilot, who was in the boat, was the only person allowed on
board. He was retained, as his services were required along the Scotish
coasts. Subsequently he was landed in Holland with a handsome
remuneration. These events were contemporaneously recorded in a thin
4to pamphlet, called "Paul Jones ; or, the Fife Coast Garland : a serio-
comical poem." See "The East Neuk of Fife. By the Rev. Walter
Wood, A.M., Elie. Edin. 1862," cr. 8vo.

This "serio-comical poem " does not evince any extraordinary wit on
the part of its author.

The Scotch clergyman, who took the credit of having been the
means of expelling the squadron of Paul Jones from the Frith of Forth,
figured also as a small scribbler of his time. Here is the title-page of
one of his pamphlets :—

"A Death-bed Dialogue ; Being a series of Conversations between
Mr Shirra and Mr Lister, late Minister of the Gospel at Dundee.
Together with the duty of the survivors, in three parts, written by Robert
Shirra, Minister of the Gospel at Kirkcaldy. Edin., printed by John
Gray and Gavin Alston. Sold at their Printing House in Jackson's
Close, 8vo, N.D."

CAPTAIN GLEN, p. 47.

Allusion is made to this ballad in the Scotch Song, called "The Totums," in which "auld Johnny," while "breaking whinstones at the side of a dyke," is depicted, among other things, to 'whistle Captain Glen.'"

THE RUNAWAY BRIDE, p. 84.

"*The Runaway Bride.*—This comic song, beginning 'a laddie and a lassie dwelt in the south countrie,' is preserved in Yair's collection, vol. ii., Edin. 1751, and in Herd's collection, 1776. The lively air to which the words are adapted was communicated to Mr Clarke by a gentleman from Roxburghshire, who sung the song with great humour and spirit." *Stenhouse's Illustrations of the Lyric Poetry and Music of Scotland*, Edin. 1853, 8vo.

Archibald M'Laren, serjeant Dumbartonshire Highlanders, who for many years prior to, and for many years after, the beginning of the present century, was a writer of dramatic pieces of considerable merit, nearly one hundred in number, which he usually published by subscription, is the author of "the Runaway Bride; or, the New Marriage Act repealed: a farce, with songs," Lond. 1823. It does not, however, bear any reference whatever to the ballad.

VALIANT M'CRAWS, p. 88.

The Estates of the last Lord Seaforth devolved upon his daughter, Lady Hood, who, after the death of her first husband, married her relative Mr Stewart Mackenzie. She sold the Island of Lewes to Mr James Mathieson, who had realized a large fortune in the East by the sale of opium to the Chinese, and who was afterwards created a baronet, and is the present member of Parliament for the County of Ross. Lady Hood Mackenzie was a friend and correspondent of Sir Walter Scott, and within the last few years has privately printed, under the title of "the Seaforth Papers," a most interesting volume consisting entirely of letters written to or by members of this family. It was never published; but in one of the numbers of the *North British Review* many very interesting extracts have been inserted relative both to political and literary matters.

A graphic account of the mutiny of the 78th regiment will be found in the "Memorials of Edinburgh Castle," by James Grant, the deservedly popular Scotish novelist.

The picture from which "the death of Major Pierson" was engraved is well known. It was painted by Copley, the father of Lord Lyndhurst. A drama, called "The Battle of Jersey," in which this picture formed the design for the concluding tableau, and brought down the curtain amid tremendous applause, was produced at Guernsey in May 1868.

WOUNDED NANCY'S RETURN, p. 94.

Female Soldiers and Sailors.

We find the following Broadside Ballads on this subject among our gatherings:—

The Rambling Female Sailor.—(Born at Gravesend).

The Female Smuggler.—(Printed by Fordyce, Dean Street, Newcastle.)

The Female Sailor; "Ann Jane Thornton, born in Gloucestershire."

The Female Drummer.

Mary in Search of her Lover.—(A sailor),

William and Phillis.—(Also sailors).

The Female Cabin-boy; or, Row among the Sailors.

Lovely Molly's Valour in the Wars.

The Faithless Sea Captain; or, the betrayed Virgin's Garland, in 3 parts.

An older ballad than any of these will be found in "Percy's Folio MS." It is entitled "the Valourous Acts performed at Gaunt by the brave bonnie lass Mary Ambree, who, in revenge of her lover's death, did play her part most gallantly. The tune is the Blind Beggar."—Mary Ambree is frequently referred to by Ben Jonson, by Fletcher in his "Scornful Lady," and by Butler in his "Hudibras."

BONNET OF BLUE, p. 101.

In another copy of this song, there are these lines which come in as verse third :—

His cheeks are like the roses, his eyes like the sloes,
He is handsome and proper and kills where he goes ;
He is handsome and proper and comely for to view,
He's a bonny Scotch lad and his bonnet so blue.

There is a song in two parts, which will be found in "An Antidote against Melancholy ; made up in Pills composed of Witty Ballads, Jovial Songs, and Merry Catches," Lond. 1661, 4to. It has been reprinted in Fairholt's Satirical Songs and Poems on costume from the 13th to the 19th Century—in the publications of the Percy Society, 1849. It is also in Evans' Old Ballads, Vol. 4, p. 264, Lond. 1784, and is entitled, "Blew-cap for me ; or

A Scotch Lasse her resolute chusing,
Shee'l have bonny Blew-cap, all other refusing."

The "Scotch Lasse," who lived "in Faukeland towne," avows it to be her determination :

> " Gif ever I have a man,
> Blew-cap for me."

Various suitors appear—an Englishman, a Welchman, a Frenchman, an Irishman, " a dainty spruce Spaniard," " a haughty high German," and "a Netherland Mariner."

> "These sundry sutors of seuerall lands,
>   Did daily solicite this lasse for her fauor,
> And euery one of them alike vnderstands,
>   That to win the prize they in vain did endeauour.

> .   .   .   .   .

> At last came a Scottish man (with a blew cap),
>   And he was the party for whom she had tarry'd,
> To get this blithe bonny lasse 'twas his gude hap,
>   They gang'd to the kirk and were presently married ;
> I ken not weel whether
>   It was lord or leard,
> They caude him some sike
>   A like name as I heard,
> To chuse him from all
>   She did gladly agree,
> And still she cry'd "Blew-cap !
>   Thou'rt welcome to me."

True Blue.—There is a saying in Warwickshire "He is true Coventry Blue," which Grose thus explains in his "Provincial Glossary." Lond., 1787, 8vo. " Coventry was formerly famous for dying a blue that would neither change its colour nor could it be discharged by washing. Therefore the epithets of Coventry blue and true blue were figuratively used to signify persons who would not change their party or principles on any consideration."

Pliny informs us, that blue was the colour in which the Gauls clothed their slaves ; and blue coats, for many ages, were the liveries of servants, apprentices, and even younger brothers, as it is now of the Blue Coat Boys and of other Blue Schools in the Country. Hence the proverb in Ray "He is in his better blue clothes," as applied to a person in low degree when dressed very fine.—*Edin. Review.*

Chaucer in his " Court of Love," mentions blue as the emblem of constancy :—

Lo, yonder folk, quoth she, that kneel in blue,
They wear the colour, ay, and ever shall,
In sign they were, and ever will be true,
Withouten change.

BATTLE OF WATERLOO, p. 106.

We have seen a copy of this ballad, printed at Stirling and sold by M,
Randall, which is thus described in the title:—"The Battle of Waterloo.
Composed by two soldiers of the Highland Brigade."

EVERY ONE TO HIS OWN TRADE, p. 121.

"THE CRAFTSMAN."—Written by Lord Bolingbroke, W. Pultney,
and other writers, in opposition to Sir Robert Walpole's measures. It
commenced Dec. 5th, 1725. Such was the popularity of these essays,
that ten or twelve thousand were frequently sold in one day. 1737,
12mo, 14 vols. 1731, 12mo, 14 vols.—*Lowndes' Bibliographer's Manual
of English Literature.*

FEMALE ROBBER, p. 123.

This song is titled in a Chapbook, "The Female Robber.—Turpin's
Sister."

EXPLANATION OF THE TERMS USED IN THE CANTING SONGS.

CANTER'S HOLIDAY, p. 141.

Canters, or Canting-Crew, thieves, beggars, gypsies and others using
the canting lingo.
Maunder, a beggar.
Harmanbeck, a beadle.
Cuffin-queere, a Justice of the Peace, also a churl.

THE THIEF-CATCHER'S PROPHECY, p. 142.

Tour you well, look well out; have your eyes about you.
Rubbed up to the Nubbing-cheat, sent to the Gallows.
Nubbed, hung; *nub* means the neck.
Padder, a highwayman on foot.
Millken, a housebreaker,
Glazier, one who breaks windows and show-glasses, to steal goods
exposed for sale.

Pinch the lurry, to steal money, watches, rings or other moveables.

File-cly or bungnipper, a pickpocket,

Cully, a fop, a dupe to women.

Budge, a sneaking thief; one who slips into houses in the dark to steal cloaks or other clothes.

Bulk, one accompanying a File, whose business it is to jostle the party to be robbed, while the File picks the pocket.

Hick, a countryman.

Napt, caught unexpectedly.

Angler, a pilferer or petty thief, who with a stick having a hook at the end steals goods out of windows, &c.

Shoplift, one who steals while pretending to purchase goods in a shop.

Bob, his assistant who receives and carries off the stolen goods.

Bubber, a thief that steals plate from public houses.

Beautrap, a sharper, well dressed, who lies in wait for raw Country Squires or ignorant fops.

Cull, a good-natured quiet fellow.

Cole, money.

Famble, one who trades in gloves and in counterfeit rings; rings or gloves.

Mob, a wench.

Sweet, easy to be imposed on.

Cog, anything dropped by the sweetner to entice his intended dupe.

Prancer, a horse jobber.

Horse-coursing, bartering or exchanging horses. Properly, according to Grose, Horse-cosing.

Noozed, hanged.

Sheepnapper, sheep-stealer.

Caught in the Cove, he's marked for a sheep; if caught in the act, he is considered by his associates as a sorry sneak.

Dunaker, a stealer of cows and calves.

Kidnapper, originally one who stole or decoyed children or apprentices from their parents or masters to send them to the Colonies; called also "spiriting."

Tips them the pike, allows them to run away.

Prigger of Cacklers, one who steals fowls.

Thief-catcher, those who make a trade of helping people (for a consideration) to their lost goods, and sometimes for interest or envy betraying the rogues themselves, being usually in fee with them, and acquainted with their haunts. The reward thus obtained is termed "blood-money."

Craftsmen, members of the canting crew.

DARKMAN'S BUDGE, p. 144.

Darkman's budge, one who slides into a house in the dark of the evening, and hides himself, in order to let some of the gang in at night to rob it.

Bit the blow, stolen the goods.

Rubs us to the whit, sends us to Newgate.

Make, a halfpenny.

Darbies, fetters.

Boozing-ken, a tavern.

Fenced his hog, spent his shilling.

Mort, a woman.

Chive, knife.

Bing out, run out.

Been Morts, good wenches.

Tour and tour, look out, look out.

Duds, clothes.

Binged avast, stolen away.

Been cove, a good fellow.

Lour, money.

Dell, a buxom wench.

Benship to my watch, went in with my views.

Stall and cly, steal and pocket.

This doxy dell can cut been whids, this beggar wench can give good words.

Drill, entice well.

Win, a penny.

Benshiply, excellently.

Deuseaville, the country.

The booth being raised, the house being alarmed.

Plant in Ruffman's Row, hide in the woods, hedges, or bushes.

Strowling ken, receiving house.

Cheats, sharpers of all denominations.

Duds and ruffpeck, clothes and bacon.

Stow what you stall, hold your tongue as to what you acquire.

Rum-coves what so quire, to rogues that are base.

Bucksom dell that snilches well, the merry girl on the look out.

A jybe well jerk'd, tick Rome-confeck, get a license with a counterfeit seal.

Back by Glimmar to maund, as if undone by fire, to beg.

Mill each ken, to break each house.

Cove bing then, man run then.

Through ruffmans, jague, or laund, through hedge, ditch, and field.

Crampings quire tip cove his hire, base shackles give the man his deserts.

Quire-ken, the jail.
Old ruffler mill, may the devil take.
Quire-cuffin, a Justice of Peace.
Booze, mort, and ken, been darkmans then, drink, wench, and ale-house,
then goodnight.
On cheats to trine, on the gallows to hang.
Rum-coves dine, by great rogues betrayed.
Long lib, long-home.
Romeville, London.

THE STROWLING MORT'S PRAISE, p. 147.

Strowling-morts, pretended widows who frequently travel the country
making laces upon yews, Beggars tape, &c. They are the forty-ninth
order of Canters, are light-fingered, hypocritical, and often dangerous to
meet, especially when a Ruffler is with them.
Clapperdogeon, a beggar born and bred. The forty-first order of
varlets. Brought up in a habitual course of idleness and beggary, they
are generally the most to be apprehended as thieves and robbers whenever they have opportunity.
Kinchin cove, a little man.
Rumpad, the highway.
Quarrons, body.
Stamps, legs.
Dimber-Damber, The top-man or prince among the canting crew.
Also the chief rogue of the gang, or the completest cheat.
Palliards, beggars born, the offspring of Clapperdogeons. The
seventh rank of the canting crew, whose hint it is to create artificial
sores upon their body, and by pretending to be in great pain impose on
the tender-hearted passers by, whom, when occasion offers, they would
not hesitate to rob or even murder.
Glymmer, fire or light.
Cramprings ne'r didst scour, never required to run away from bolts or
shackles.
Harmans, the stocks.
Toure, swear.
Thou still didst loure, thou still hadst money.
Cank and dommerar, dummy and madman.
Rum-maunder, a beggar who pretends to be silly.
Abram-cove, a lusty strong rogue barely clothed ; a tatterdemalion.
Jybes well jerked, passes well sealed.
Crackmans, hedges.
Quacking cheat, a duck.

Tib o' the Buttery, a goose.
Redshank, a duck, or mallard.
Ruffpeck, bacon.
Grannam, corn.
Lap and poplars, buttermilk and porridge.
Bughar, a dog.
Skew, wooden dish,
Filch, a staff with a hole through and a spike at the bottom to pluck
clothes from a hedge, or anything out of a casement.
Jybes, or gybes, any writing or pass sealed.
Togeman, a gown or cloak.

THE BEGGAR'S CURSE, p. 148.

Ruffin, the Devil.
Cly, take or steal.
Pannan, bread.
Poplars of Yarum, milk porridge.
Lightmans, day.
Stamps fast in the Harmans, legs in the stocks.
Heave, rob.
Cly the jerk, to be whipped.
Niggle or mill, to attempt to steal from, or to actually steal from.
Nip a bung, cut a purse.
Dup the gigger, open the door with a picklock.

RETOURE, MY DEAR DELL, p. 150.

Toute, observe.
Surtoute, survey.
Panter, heart.
Glaziers, eyes.
Patri-coe, or pater cove, the fifteenth rank of the canting tribe; strolling
priests that marry people under a hedge without gospel or prayer-book,
the couple standing on each side of a dead beast are enjoined to live
together till death does them part; so shaking hands the wedding
terminates.
Redshanks and tits, ducks and geese,
Whiddle, to tell, or discover.
Squeck, to confess, to peach, or turn stag.
Colquarron, a man's neck.

JACK SHEPHARD, p. 153.

Priggs that snabble the prancers strong, horse-stealers.
Peter-lay, to be on the peter-lay is to be on the track to steal boxes
or portmanteaus from behind coaches or waggons.

Bowman, a dexterous cheat, or noted housebreaker.
Rumbo-ken, a prison house.
Rum Cull, a rich fool, easily cheated, especially by a wench.
Scran, refreshments.
A famble, a tattle, and two pops, a ring, a watch, and a pair of pistols.
Diddle shops, gin shops.

YE SCAMPS, YE PADS, YE DIVERS, p. 159.

Scamps, pads, divers, highway robbers and pickpockets.
The lay, enterprise.
Tothilfield's sheepwalk, the prison-yard at Tothilfields.
Jigger-dubber, Turnkey.
Mill doll, beat hemp in Bridewell.
Kiddy, a familiar appellation given to a friend; *kid* is a child.
Shiners, cash.
Daddlers, hands.
Flashy, bewigged.
Bub, drink.
Jazy, a wig.
Garnish, money customarily spent among the prisoners on first coming in.

BEGGARS, p. 137, *et seq.*

We glean the following from Balfour's " Practicks ; or, a system of the more ancient Law of Scotland," folio, Edin. 1754.

ANENT BEGGARIS.

The king hes statute, be consent of the haill parliament, ripelie avisit, that na thiggaris be tholit to beg, nouther to brugh nor to landwart, betwix fourtene and threscoir ten zeiris, bot thay be sene be the counsall of the townis, or of the land, that thay may not win thair leving uther-wayis : and thay that sall be tholit to beg, sall have ane certane takin on thame, to landwart of the Schiref ; and in the burrowis thay sall have takin of the Alderman or of the Baillies : and all utheris persounis havand na takinnis, nouther of land, na of burgh, sall be chargit be opin proclamatioun, to labour and pass to craftis, for winning of thair living, under the pane of birning on the cheik, and banishing of the countrie. *Ja. 1., fol. 5., c. 27., 26 Maij., 1424.* . . . . *Item.* That the statute of king James the first, maid upon stark beggaris, be observit and keipit ; and that the Schireffis, Provestis, Baillies within burrowis, baith of rialtie and regalitie, spiritualitie and temporalitie, see that this act be execute and keipit ; and that thay thole nane to beg within thame except crukit folk, seik folk, impotent folk and waik folk, under the pane of payment of ane merk for ilk uther beggar that beis fundin. *Ja. IV.*, *fol.* 104, *c.* 104, 11 *Mart.* 1503, *Ja I.*, *fol.* 18, *c.* 114, 1 *Mart.* 1427.

Item. For refraning of the multitude of maisterfull and strang beggaris, it is ordanit that na beggaris be tholit to beg in ane parochin that are born in ane uther ; and that the heidisman of ilk parochin mak takinnis, and give to the beggaris thairof, and that they be sustenit within the boundis of that parochin; and that nane utheris be servit with almous within that parochin bot they that beris that takin allanerlie, under the panis contenit in the said Act.—*Ja.* v., *fol.* 121. *Act* 24, 7 *Junij* 1535, *Mar. R. fol.* 5, 1 *Feb.* 1551. *Mar. R. fol.* 168. *Act* 38, 20 *Junij* 1555.

Item. That na lipper* folk enter na come in a burgh of the realme bot thrise in the oulk, that is to say, ilk Monounday, Wednesday, and Friday, fra ten houris to twa efternoon ; and quhair fairis and mercattis fallis in thay dayis, that they leif thair entrie in the burrowis, and gang on the morn to get thair leving. *Item.* That na lipper folk sit to thig,† nather in kirk na in kirk-zaird, na uther place within the burrowis, bot at thair awin hospitall, and at the port of the town, and at uther placis outwith the burrowis. *Item.* That the Bischopis, Officiallis, and Denis inquire diligentlie, in thair visitatioun of ilk paroche kirk, gif ony be smittit with lipper ; and gif ony sic be fundin, that thay be deliverit to the King, gif thay be Secularis; and gif thay be Clerkis, to thair Bischopis. *Ja.* I., *fol.* 18, *Act* 118, 1 *Mart.* 1427.

Gif ony person that dwelt in the burgh, or wes born in it, be put out of the samin for leprosie, and he have gudis and geir sufficient for his cleithing and sustentatioun, he sall be put in the hospitall ; and gif he hes not of his awin quhairon he may live and be clad, the burgessis of the toun sall make ane gaddering amongis thame, quhairon he may be swa sustenit. *Item.* Na lipper nor missell‡ folk sall enter within the town, bot in the throw-passing, and sall not gang fra dure to dure, bot thay sall sit at the throw-gangis of the brugh, without the portis thairof, to ask almous fra thame that passis in and out : and thairfoir na man sall tak on hand to herberie lipper folk, under the pane of ane unlaw. *Leg. burg. c.* 62.

Item. It is statute, that na lipper folk enter within the portis of the burgh ; and gif ony happinis to enter, he sall in continent be cassin furth be the Serjand of the burgh : and gif ony lipper folk dois in the contrare of this our inhibitioun, and usis to enter within the burgh, the cleithing of the bodie sall be takin fra him and brint, and he beand nakit, sall be put furth of the burgh. It is in like wayis statute, that sum honest men of the burgh sall gadder almous, to be gevin and distribute to all lipper folk in ony meit and convenient place without the burgh. *Stat. Gild.*, *c.* 16

* *Lipper*, leprous.   † To beg.   ‡ Leprous.

Divers ordinancies maid anent beggaris. *Vide in libro impresso. Ja.* VI., *fol.* 5. *Act.* 7. 20 *Octob.* 1579 *Ja.* VI., *parl.* 10, *c.* 16, 10 *Decemb.* 1585. *Ja.* VI. *parl.* 12, *c.* 147, 5 *Junij* 1592. *Ja* VI., *parl.* 15, *c.* 288, 19 *Dec.* 1597.

AULD EDDIE OCHILTREE, p. 166.

Edinburgh Beggars in 1774.—The Magistrates of Edinburgh in 1744 issued a proclamation interdicting all beggars from appearing in the streets, under pain of being apprehended and confined in one of the vaults under the new bridge, there to be fed on bread and water. This arbitrary order was carried into effect, and these wretched holes were for some time tenanted by beggars, until, as I have been told, this species of incarceration was put an end to by a melancholy event. An unfortunate creature, whose mental incapacity ought to have placed him in a fitting lunatic asylum, was picked off the streets and summarily placed in one of these abominable cells, where he was overpowered and partly devoured by the rats, which had from time to time increased to a formidable extent. This fatal event led to an investigation, which caused the magistrates for the future to close the vaults as a place for receiving unfortunate beggars. This "new bridge" is at present known as the North Bridge, and connects, in the east, the old and new portions of the city. The Theatre Royal, now replaced by the Post-Office, stood nearly at the north end, on the east side.—J. M. in *Notes and Queries.*

INNS OF COURT, p. 172.

For a graphic description of the Inns of Court and their festivities, see Knight's "London." And there will be found in Payne Collier's "Broadside Black Letter Ballads, printed in the sixteenth and seventeenth centuries," 4to, 1868, one titled "The Honour of the Inns of Court Gentlemen ; or, a brief recitall of the magnificent and matchlesse show that passed from Hatton and Ely house in Holborne to Whitehall, on Monday night, being the third of February, and the next day after Candlemas. To the tune of our noble King in his Progresse." The procession of the barristers and students is thus described :—

> A various crew of anticks all,
> With seuerall humours
> In shape did represent,
> The number of them was not small,
> Which to the spectators
> Gaue wonderful content ;
> Each one in his due posture
> Did shew exceeding sport,
> To the honour of those gentry
> That liue at the Inns of Court.

A hundred sweet young gentlemen,
That all vpon great horses
Were mounted gallantly,
Clad in white cloath of tissue then,
And red and white feathers
Most glorious to the eye ;
In equipage most sumptuous
They past in solemne sort :
These were the braue young gentry,
That liue at the Inns of Court.

MAD SONGS, p. 172, *et seq.*

A ballad of ten stanzas, printed without a title in Jordan's "London Triumphs" 1677, has been reprinted in Fairholt's Civic Garland (Percy Society 1846) under the title of "The Mad Sectary." "It was sung," he observes, "in Guildhall, after dinner, to the tune of 'Tom-a-Bedlam,' by 'one of the city musicians, being attired like a New-Bedlamite, with apt action, and audible voice.' It gives a curious detail of the many forms of belief which distracted the religionists of the Cromwellian age." The first stanza runs thus :—

I am the woful'st madman,
That e'er came near your knowledge ;
I thrice have in
New Prison been,
And twice in Bedlam Colledge :
In hunger, cold, and darkness,
I was a verysad man,
But I will show,
And tell you how
I first became a madman :
Then give me room, give me breath, give me hearing,
My name is Captain Pigeon,
When English-men
Fell out, I then
Did alter my religion.

Another mad song, "Bess of Bedlam," will be found with its relative music in Purcell's Orpheus Britannicus, folio, Lond. 1698. It begins thus :—

From silent shades and the Elizium groves,
Where sad departed spirits mourn their loves,
From chrystall streams, and from that country where
Joue crowns the fields with flowers all the year,

Poor senseless Bess, cloath'd in her raggs and folly,
Is come to cure her love-sick melancholy.

In the same book there is a version, with music, of the " Mad Song "
(page 185) it is there titled "A Song in the fourth Act of the Fool's
Preferment," and goes thus :—

I'll sail upon the Dog-star,
    And then pursue the morning ;
I'll chase the moon till it be noon,
    But I'll make her leave her horning.

I'll climb the frosty mountain,
    And there I'll coyn the weather ;
I'll tear the rainbow from the sky,
    And tye both ends together.

The stars pluck from their orbs too,
    And crowd them in my budget ;
And whether I'm a roaring boy,
    Let all the nation judge it.

This song has been transferred by Ramsay to his Tea-Table Miscellany,
1724, with the last line altered to

"Let Gresham College judge it : "

and this additional stanza :—

While I mount yon blue celum,
    To shun the tempting gipsies ;
Play at football with sun and moon,
    And fright ye with eclipses.

Another "Tom of Bedlam" figures in Ritson's " Ancient Songs from
the time of King Henry the Third to the Revolution," Lond. 8vo, 1790;
p. 265. It is in eight stanzas of which this is a specimen :—

From the top of high Caucasus,
    To Paul's wharf near the tower,
In no great haste, I easily past
    In less than half an hour.
The gates of old Byzantium
    I took upon my shoulders,

And them I bore twelve leagues and more,
In spight of Turks and soldiers.
Sigh, sing, and sob, sing, sigh, and be merry,
Sighing, singing, and sobbing,
Thus naked Tom away doth run,
And fears no cold nor robbing, &c.

Ritson, in the same collection, has a comical ballad called "John and Joan; or, a mad couple well met, to the tune of the Paratour,"—from a Black-letter copy in Major Pierson's collection, the authorship of which he attributes to "Martin Parker, a Grub-street scribbler and great ballad-monger of Charles the First's time." There is a method in the madness of John and Joan, described as "a mad phantastic couple," who resolve that "neither will be vext," whatever the other may do, and :—

" Whatever did the goodman,
His wife would do the like,
If he was pleas'd, she was appeas'd,
If he would kick, she'd strike.
If quean or slut he called her,
She called him rogue and knave ;
If he would fight, she'd scratch and bite,
He could no victory have.

If John his dog had beaten,
Then Joan would beat her cat.
If John in scorn his hand would burn,
Joan would have burnt her hat.
If John would break a pipkin,
Then Joan would break a pot ;
Thus he and she did both agree
To waste all that they got.

Matters proceeded for a long while in this very comfortable manner.

But mark now how it chanced,
After a year or more,
This couple mad all wasted had,
And were grown very poor :
John could no more get liquor,
Nor could Joan purchase drink ;
Then both the man and wife began
Upon their states to think.

So leaving those mad humours,
Which them before possest,
Both man and wife do live a life
In plenty, peace, and rest.

SOUTH SEA BUBBLE, p. 190.

Poem upon a lady's being offered a purse by one of the late Directors of the South Sea Company. *By a Lady.* From a Broadside "Printed at Edinburgh by William Adam, Junior, A.D. 1719."

> Curse on thy bribes ! shall female love be stain'd
> With impious dross from ruin'd Britons drain'd ?
> Shall we be added to the publick shame ?
> Beauty be sold to a detested name ?
>
> Know, monstrous wretch, our bitter souls disdain
> Thy horrid spoils and execrable gain ;
> Our hearts are tender, and shall ever scorn
> To joy in that which made our country mourn.
>
> But oh ! if we a patriot soul could view,
> That would revenge his nation's cause on you ;
> With pride we'll meet the brave, well-meaning breast,
> Wake all his joys, and lull his cares to rest.
>
> In blessing him we'll waste each precious hour,
> And cursing thee and thy once fatal power.

THE POYAIS EMIGRANT, p. 207.

The authorship of this song is ascribed to Ebenezer Picken, a Scotch poet of very considerable merit, and author of a Dictionary of the Scotish Language. Picken was born at Paisley in 1769 or 1770. His father was a silk weaver. While prosecuting his studies at the College of Glasgow he published a thin octavo volume of poems. These, with many additions, were republished in two volumes, 12mo., at Edinburgh in 1813.

BUBBLES OF 1825, p. 208.

"*New Companies.*—It has been estimated that the different new schemes now in agitation amount to 114, and the Capitals to be more than £105,000,000 ; viz., Railroads, 20, capital £13,950,000 : Banking, Loan Investment, &c., 22—£36,760,000 ; Gas Companies, 11—£8,000,000 ; British and Irish Mines, 8—£3,600,000 ; Foreign Mines, 17—£11,565,000 ; Shipping and Dock Companies, 9—£10,580,000 ; Miscellaneous, 27—£11,070,000."—*Dublin and London Magazine, March* 1825.

BACCHANALIAN SONGS, p. 214, *et seq.*

Cambden, in his Annals under the year 1581, has this observation, "The English, who hitherto had, of all the northern nations, shewn themselves the least addicted to immoderate drinking, first learned, in their wars in the Netherlands, to swallow a large quantity of intoxicating liquor, and to destroy their own health by drinking that of others."
More than one of the writers of the present day who pen those dreary productions for the London Stage, which they erroneously characterize as "Burlesques," have greedily seized upon Cambden's clever remark, and without any compunction taken forcible possession of it "to garnish their lean wit withal." Thus they render it: "By drinking others' healths, I've lost my own."

COME! COME! COME! p. 216.

"To the sweeter soil
Of fair Exus Isle," &c.

"Exus Isle" is presumed to be the island of Naxus, the largest of the Cyclades, where Bacchus met Ariadne, after she had been cruelly forsaken by Theseus, and married her.

PRAISE OF ALE, p. 220.

This Ballad occurs in the 3rd Vol. of Old Ballads, 1725, under the title of " The answer of Ale to the challenge of Sack." "The Praise of Hull Ale" is embodied in a song to the tune of "Greensleeves" in Durfey's Pills, vol. vi. p. 223.

THE TANKARD OF ALE, p. 224.

According to Lord Bacon "the Ex-ale-tation of Ale" has been ascribed, by several judicious people, to Bishop Andrews.

COME CHEER UP YOUR HEARTS, p. 226, AND
FROM GOOD LIQUOR NE'ER SHRINK, p. 228.

These have been reprinted, *with the music*, in "the Convivial Songster," printed for John Fielding, No. 23 Paternoster Row. 12mo., *circa* 1780.

LOVE OR LIQUOR, p. 229.

The air of "Steer her up and haud her gaun" will be found at page six of " A Collection of Scots' Tunes, some with variations for a violin, hautboy, and German flute, with a bass for a violoncello or harpiscord, by William M'Gibbon, Edinburgh, printed and sold by R. Bremner at the Harp and Hautboy." *Circa,* 1740.

THE PITCHER, p. 234.

We now find that this song has been printed in "The Edinburgh Miscellany; a collection of the most approved Scotch, English, and Irish songs, set to music," 2 vols. 12mo., Edin. 1808.

'TWAS MERRY IN THE HALL, p. 250.

Romance of Alexander.—A copy of this romance is in the Bodleian Library. The illuminator appears to have taken nearly six years over the paintings which embellish this precious volume, as he has noted down the date when he had completed his work,—the date when the transcriber finished his task had previously been entered.

The romance was composed about the year 1200; this copy was made in 1338.

There is also a splendid MS. of this romance, with rich and delicate illuminations, in the British Museum, Bib. Reg., 15 E. 6.—It is in prose.

TOBACCO, p. 257.

"Raphael Thorius," commonly called Thoris, (referred to at p. 258), "a Frenchman born, was, in his younger days, conversant among the Oxonians in the condition of a sojourner, and made considerable progress in the faculty of medicine, but took no degree therein, only was numbered among those of the physic line. Afterwards he settled in London, practised that faculty with good success, and was in his time accounted *Coryphæus Medici gregis;* and as a physician famous, so no vulgar poet. The words which he hath written are many, but none were published till after his death."—*Wood's Athen. Oxon.* ii. 378, *Edn. Bliss.*

"Hymnus Tabaci" is very scarce. A copy in Longman's Bibliotheca Anglo-Poetica was some years ago priced £1 1s.

Hausted wrote two comedies, viz., The Rival Friends, 4to, 1632, and Senile Odium, 12mo, 1633.

A report has just been published in Berlin relative to the cultivation of tobacco in Germany. During the year 1867 the extent of land planted with tobacco was 77,270 German acres—28,553 acres in Prussia, 25,876 in Baden, 18,221 in Bavaria, 3192 in Hesse, and the rest in the other countries of the Zollverein. The total weight of the tobacco produced (in the dry leaf) was 530,934 cwt., of which 197,401 cwt. came from Prussia. The average production was 6·87 cwt. per acre, the maximum

being 19 cwt., and the minimum half-a-hundredweight. The highest
price paid for a cwt. of German tobacco was 20 thalers (75f.), and the
lowest only one thaler.

The contention as to the baleful effects of tobacco upon the human
frame has recently been revived, and many facts, deduced from observation and experience, have been advanced to prove how hurtful the weed
is. Professor Christison of Edinburgh, some years ago, treated of
tobacco in his famous work on Poisons. "The empyreumatic oil of
tobacco," he observes, "is well-known to be an active poison, which
produces convulsions, coma, and death. The plant itself, according to
Botanists, called *Nicotiana Tabacum* belongs to the same natural order
as *Atropa Belladonna* or deadly nightshade, and the *Datura Stramonium*
or thorn-apple, both of which are among the most powerful and deadly
of the acro-narcotic poisons." Dr Rees, editor of the Cyclopedia, has
said, "a drop or two of the chemical oil of tobacco being put on the
tongue of a cat, produces violent convulsions, and death itself in the
space of a minute." It is also used to destroy the tick in sheep, and very
frequently with bad effects to the health of the animal.

Catherine de Medicis is supposed to have been the first female snuff-
taker. In consequence of this Queen having used tobacco it obtained
the distinguished appellations of *Herba Catherinæ Medicæ* and *Herba
Reginæ*.

It is a remarkable fact that snuff-takers form a large portion of the
inmates of Lunatic Asylums.

Cambden the historian, in noticing the introduction of tobacco into
England, regards the habit of smoking as barbarous and degenerating.

Joshua Sylvester, a poet of James the First's time, wrote a poem
against tobacco, called "Tobacco Battered and the Pipes Shattered
(about their ears that idly idolize so base and barbarous a weed, or, at
leastwise, over-love so loathsome a vanitie), by a volly of holy shot
thundered from Mount Helicon." Like many others, Sylvester seems
to have considered tobacco a provocative to intemperance in liquor.
He further goes on to say :—

> Of all the plants that Tellus' bosom yields,
> In groves, glades, gardens, marshes, mountains, fields,
> None so pernicious to man's life is known
> As is tobacco, saving *hemp* alone.
> If there be any herb in any place
> Most opposite to God's good herb of grace,
> 'Tis doubtless this; and this doth plainly prove it,
> That, for the most part, graceless men do love it,
> Or rather dote most on this withered weed,
> Themselves as withered in all gracious deed.

If then tobacconing be good, how is't
That lewdest, loosest, basest, foolishest,
The most unthrifty, most intemperate,
Most vicious, most debauched, most desperate,
Pursue it most? the wisest and the best
Abhor it, shun it, flee it as the pest.

"The Tabaco and his great vertues" are discoursed of in a very rare
and curious book of Dr J. N. Bonardus, entitled "Ioyfvll Newes out of
the New-found VVorlde. Wherein are declared, the rare and singuler
vertues of diuers Herbs, Trees, Plantes, Oyles and Stones, with their
applications, aswell to the vse of Phisicke, as of Chirurgery: which being
well applyed, bring such present remedie for all diseases as may seeme
altogether incredible: notwithstanding by practice found out to be true.
Also the portrature of the said Hearbs, verie aptly described: Englished
by John Frampton, Marchant. Newly corrected as by conference with
the olde copies may appeare. Wherevnto are added three other Bookes
treating of the Bezaar Stone, the herb Escuerconera, the properties of
Iron and Steele in Medicine, and the benefit of Snow. London, Printed
by E. Allde, by the assigne of Bonham Norton, 1596." 4to.

The author describes Tabaco, as "an hearbe of much antiquitie, and
knowen amongst the Indians, and inespecially among them of the Newe
Spaine, and after that those countries were gotten by our Spaniardes,
being taught of the Indians, they did profite themselves with those
thinges, in the woundes which they receiued in their warres, healing
themselves therewith to their great benefite." It is presented as a salvo
for most of the "ills which flesh is heir to," and, particularly in venom
and venomous wounds, it "hath great commendation, which hath beene
knowne but a short time since, for when the wilde people of the Indias
which eate men's fleshe doe shoote their arrowes, they anointe them
with an hearb or composition made of many poysons, with the which
they shoote at al things that they would kill, and this venom is so strong
and pernicious that it killeth without remedie, aud they that bee hurte
die with great paines and accidents, and with madnes, vnlesse that there
be found remedy for so great an euill. A fewe yeeres past they laid to
their wounds *Sublimatum,* and so were remedied, and surely in those
partes they haue suffered much with this vexation of poyson. A little
whiles past, certaine wilde people going in their Boates to S. John de
Puerto Rico, to shoote at Indians or Spaniards (if that they might find
them), came to a place and killed certain Indians and Spaniards, and did
hurt many, and as by chaunce there was no *Sublimatum* at that place to
heale them, they remembred to lay upon the wounds the juice of the
Tabaco, and the leaves stamped. And God would, that laying it vpon
the hurts, the griefs, madnes, and accidents wherewith they died were

mitigated, and in such sorte they were deliuered of that euill, that the strength of the venom was taken away, and the wounds were healed, of which there was great admiration."

"Within these few yeeres there hath beene brought into Spayne of it more to adornate gardens with the fairenesse thereof, and to giue a pleasaunt sight, then that it was thought to haue the meruelous medicinable vertues which it hath."

"It is growen in many parts of the Indias, but ordinarilie in moyst and shadowie places, and it is needeful that the grounde where it is sowen be well tilled, and that it be a fruitefull grounde, and at all times it is sowen in the hot countries. But in the colde countries it must bee sowen in the moneth of Marche, for that it may defende itselfe from the frost. The proper name of it amongst the Indians is *Picielt*, for the name of Tabaco is giuen to it by our Spaniards by reason of an Island that is named *Tabaco*."

"The Indians of our Occidentall Indias, doo use the Tabaco to take away wearinesse, and for to make lightsomenesse in their labour, for in their daunces they bee so much wearied, and they remaine so wearie, that they can scarcely stirre ; and because that they may labour the next day and returne to that foolish exercise, they receiue at the mouth and nose the smoke of the tabaco, and remaine as dead people : and being so, they be eased in such sorte that when they be awakened out of their sleepe, they remaine without wearinesse, and may returne to their labour as much as before."

In travelling " by any desert or dispeopled country where they shall finde neither water nor meate, they receiue thereof little balles which they make of the tabaco; for they take the leaues of it, and chew them, and as they goe chewing of them, they goe mingling with them certaine pouder made of the shelles of cockels burned, and they mingle it in the mouth altogether vntill they make it like dowe, of the which they frame certaine little balles, little greater then Peason, and lay them to drie in the shadow, and after they keep them and vse them in this forme following :—When they vse to trauel by the wayes where they finde no water nor meate they take a little ball of these, and put it betweene the lower lippe and the teeth, and goe chewing it all the time that they trauell, and that which they chew they swallow downe, and in this sort they journey three or four dayes without hauing neede of meate, or drinke, for they feele no hunger, drieth, nor weaknesse, nor their trauell doth trouble them."

Tobacco, when introduced into France, was styled Nicotiane, "of the name of him that gaue the first intelligence thereof vnto this realme. Some haue called this hearbe the Queene's hearbe, because it was firste sent vnto her; Maister John Nicot, Counsellor to the King, being Embassadour for his Maiestie in Portugall, in the yeere of our Lorde

1559-60-61, went one day to see the prysons of the King of Portugall;
and a gentleman, being keeper of the said prysons, presented him with
the said hearb, as a strange plant brought from Florida. The same
Maister Nicot, hauing caused the said hearb to be set in his garden,
where it grewe and multiplyed maruellously," was by accident discovered
to cure ulcers and wounds, so that Nicot, when he found "that the Coun-
tesse of Ruffe had sought for al the famous Phisitions for to heale
her face, vnto whom they could giue no remedy, thought it good to
communicate the same into France and did sende it to King Frauncis the
Seconde and to the Queen Mother, and to many other Lords of the
Court, with the manner of ministering the same."

BALLAD OF THE SEVENTEENTH CENTURY, p. 276.

" *Of the Salmon.* A Salmon, called in Latin *Salmo*, has different
names, according to its different ages. Those that are taken in the
river Ribble in Yorkshire, in the first year are called *Smelts*, in the
second *Sprods*, the third *Morts*, the fourth *Forktails*, the fifth *Half-fish*,
and in the sixth, when they have attained their proper growth, they are
thought worthy of the name of *Salmons*.

Their greatest magnitude is much the same in most parts of Europe,
and when they are largest they weigh from 36 to 40 pounds.

.   .   .   .   .

"The Salmon chuses the rivers for his abode about six months in the
year. They enter the fresh-water about February or March, where they
continue till the autumnal season, at which time they cast their spawn
and soon after return to the sea. But directly the contrary of this is
reported of the river Ex in Devonshire, and the rivers Wye and Usk in
Monmouthshire, where the Salmon are said to be in season during the
other six months; and what is still more remarkable, if true, is that
they never frequent the Wye and Usk in the same year, for if they are
found in one of those rivers they are sure to be wanting in the other.
But, however this be, it is certain the salt water best promotes their
growth, and the fresh chiefly constitutes to make them fat.

.   .   .   .   .

"There is a remarkable Cataract on the river Tivy in Pembrokeshire,
where people often stand wondering at their strength and slight which
they use to get out of the sea into the river; on which account it is
known in those parts by the name of the Salmon-leap. On the river Wear,
near the city of Durham, there is another of this kind, which is accounted
the best in England. Likewise at Old Aberdeen, in Scotland, there is
another, where such great plenty of Salmon has been caught that they
have been accounted the chief trade of the place; and there is an obsolete
law which obliged them to sell none to the English but for gold coin.

"Whenever their passage to the sea is intercepted by weirs, or any other contrivance, they soon grow sickly, lean and languid, losing their beautiful spots; and if they are caught in that condition, when they come to the table they prove tasteless and insipid. In the second year they pine away and die. It is worth observation that the Salmon not only is desirous of returning back to the rivers, but to that very river where it was spawned. The Salmon is of a very quick growth, and much more so than any other fish.

⁂

"The river Lone, which glides through Lancashire, is so overstocked with Salmon, that the servants make an agreement that they will not eat it above twice a-week;* the same thing is reported of some parts of Scotland. However this is certain, that they are so plentiful in the Tyne, that near Biwell Castle, in Northumberland, I have bought one which weighed twenty pounds, alive, out of the Weirs for two shillings. But this is still exceeded by Lough Erne, in Fermanagh, a province in Ireland, for this water abounds so much in salmon, that the only fear the fishermen have is of too great a draught, by which their nets are often broken.

⁂

"In some places they fish for salmon in the night time by the light of torches or kindled straw, which the fish, mistaking for the daylight, make towards, and are struck with the spear, or taken with the net, which they lift up with a sudden jerk from the bottom, having laid it the evening before opposite to the place where the fire is kindled.† In some parts of Scotland it is said they ride a-fishing up the rivers, and when they espy them in the shallows they shoot them with fire-arms."—*Art of Angling*, 18mo, Lond. 1743.

THE TOWN GALLANT, p. 299.

We find that this song has been reprinted in "the Civic Garland, a Collection of Songs from London Pageants." Edited by F. W. Fairholt, F.S.A., and printed for the Percy Society, 1845. Mr Fairholt thus prefaces it:—

"*The Epicure.*—From Jordan's 'Triumphs of London,' 1675. I have

---

* This was also the case at the Tyne and Tweed. A similar rule is understood to have existed in the North of Scotland, where the servants stipulated that they should not be obliged to feed on salmon above thrice a-week.

Sykes in his Local Records, Newcastle, 1824, 8vo, chronicles at various times several extraordinary draughts of salmon from the Tyne and Tweed, of which the most remarkable was on 1st Sept. 1814, when "there were upwards of 10,000 salmon in Berwick Market, which had been caught in the river Tweed."

† This system of "spearing," as it is designated, is forbidden by the Tweed Act, but it is sometimes now resorted to by poachers in the narrower parts of the river above Kelso.

mentioned (Pageants, part I., p. 84), that Ritson had printed this song in his collection of 'Ancient Songs,' but I omitted to say that the verses there are transposed, the sixth taking the place of the fourth, &c., while the two concluding verses are entirely omitted. He speaks of 'a copy of it, with considerable variations, and some additional stanzas, in the valuable collection of Major Pearson,' which was no doubt printed for the use of the ballad-singers, as many of Jordan's songs were of a popular character, and much sung in his own day. Ritson entitles it 'The Town Gallant;' in the Pageant it is called 'The Epicure; sung by one in the habit of a Town Gallant,' and is thus introduced :— ' His Lordship and the guests being all seated, the city musick begin to touch their instruments with very artful fingers, and after a lesson being played, and their ears as well feasted as their mouths; an acute person with a good voice, good humour, and audible utterance, (the better to provoke digestion), sings this new droll.'—I have adopted a few of Ritson's readings where they improve the sense."

Mr Fairholt gives these additional stanzas :—

Your usurer that in the hundred takes twenty,
Who wants in his wealth, and doth pine in his plenty,
Lays up for a season which *he* ne'er shall see,
The year of one thousand eight hundred and three;
His wit, and his wealth, his law, learning, and sense,
Shall be turned into nothing a hundred years hence.

Your most Christian Mounsieur, who rants it in riot,
Not suffering his more Christian neighbours live quiet;
Whose numberless legions that to him belongs,
Consists of more nations than Babel has tongues:
Though num'rous as dust, in despight of defence,
Shall all lie in ashes a hundred years hence.

We mind not the counsels of such bloody elves,
Let us set foot to foot, and be true to ourselves;
Our honesty from our good fellowship springs,
We aim at no selfish preposterous things,
We'll seek no preferment by subtle pretence,
Since all shall be nothing a hundred years hence.

THE PRODIGAL'S RESOLUTION, p. 301.

This has also been reprinted in Mr Fairholt's Civic Garlands, "from Thomas Jordan's 'London Triumphant,' where it is simply called 'A Song.'" He has two additional and concluding stanzas, which are not worth inserting here. Those who are curious about them may consult Mr Fairholt's book.

THE ENJOYMENTS OF TOWN, p. 307.

Rackets.—So called from *raquette*, the instrument in the form of a perforated battledore with which the ball is struck at tennis. Tennis Courts were common in England in the Sixteenth Century, and were greatly patronized by the nobles. Henry VII. was fond of the game. In the accounts of expenditure during his reign is an entry: "Item, for the King's loss at tennis, twelve pence." Henry VIII., according to Stow, added "divers fair tennis courts" to Whitehall. James I. speaks of tennis as a princely game. Charles II. had a particular costume in which he played. Hand-tennis was called Fives by reason of it being played by five competitors on either side. "When Queen Elizabeth was entertained at Elvetham, Hampshire, by the Earl of Hertford, after dinner, about three o'clock, ten of his lordship's servants, all Somerset-shire men, in a square greene court before her majestie's windowe, did hang up lines, squaring out the forme of a tennis-court, and making a cross line in the middle; in this square they played *five to five* with hand-ball, at bord and cord as they tearme it, to the great liking of her highness."—See Nichol's Progresses of Queen Elizabeth, 4to. 1788-1807.

Tennis was a favourite game in Edinburgh for sometime after the beginning of the present century. The Racket, or Fives Court, was situated in Rose Street in the new town of Edinburgh, and was kept by one Hallion, who was a "utility" man at the Theatre Royal. In those days the nobility and gentry of Scotland had their town residences in the Scotish metropolis, and the Tennis court and the Theatre were consequently very well patronized. The desire, however, of their successors in the present day to identify themselves in some degree with the Court, has caused them to abandon their own country, and to regard its soil only as a means to enable them to keep up their establishment in the south, where they oftentimes foolishly attempt to vie with the magnates of England, and so impoverish themselves to the injury of those who come after them, as well as to the injury of Scotland itself.

LONDON IS A FINE TOWN, p. 309.

In one of B. Gilpin's sermons, preached at Greenwich (1580), is this passage :—" When Christ suffered his passion, there was one Barabbas; St. Matthew calleth him a notable thief; a gentleman thief, such as rob now-a-days in velvet coats; and other two obscure thieves, nothing famous. The rustical thieves were hanged, and Barabbas was delivered; even so now-a-days, the little thieves are hanged that steal of necessity, but the great Barabbases have free liberty to rob and spoil without measure, in the midst of the city."

It is worthy of notice, that there is "A New Ballad" in a 12mo volume, printed at London in 1714 "By a Lover of his Country," called "Political Merriment : or, Truths told to some tune," which commences thus :—

"The world's a frantic whimsy and Britain is a farce,"

to the tune of "Oh, London is a fine Town."

A SONG, TO THE TUNE OF ROBIN ROWSER, p. 317.

This has been reprinted in Ritson's English Songs, vol. i. p. 149. '

"A Bartlemew Baby," which is cited as a simile in verse 5, is thus explained by inference in Grose's Classical Dictionary of the Vulgar Tongue, Lond. 1785.

"*Bartholomew Doll* — A tawdry overdrest woman, like one of the childrens' dolls sold at Bartholomew fair."

THE WILLOW TREE, p. 349.

Nicholas Rowe writes a song to "his lady" in her sickness, which begins thus :

> To the brook and the willow that heard him complain,
> Ah, willow, willow.
> Poor Colin sat weeping, and told them his pain,
> Ah, willow, willow ; ah willow, willow.
> Sweet stream, he cry'd sadly, I'll teach thee to flow,
> Ah, willow, &c.
> And the waters shall rise to the brink with my woe.
> Ah, willow, &c.

JACK ROBINSON, p. 351.

The conventional expression "Jack Robinson" is thus explained in Grose's Classical Dictionary of the Vulgar Tongue, 1785. "Before one could say Jack Robinson : a saying to express a very short time, originating from a very volatile gentleman of that appellation, who would call upon his neighbours and be gone before his name could be announced."

—"Jack Robinson" is a familiar appellation by which seamen are frequently addressed. There is a character of that name introduced in Moncrieff's Drama called "The Cataract of the Ganges," which was produced in London in 1823. He is a youth, enamoured of the adventures of Robinson Crusoe, by which he is induced to go to sea and to imitate as far as he can in Oriental latitudes the great object of his admiration. The wit of his character consists 'n his saying on every occasion, "I will [do so and so], as sure as my name's Jack Robinson," a phrase which, being often repeated, fails not in the end to provoke a laugh.

A story is told of Sheridan that, at a debate on a Bribery Bill, which had been introduced into Parliament by a member, named John Robinson, he, having some idea that Robinson himself, like the majority of the members, had not obtained his own seat without some kind friend having administered "the oil of palms" to the more needy of his constituents, rose to say that there was at least one member in the house who could not conscientiously affirm that bribery had not been used in his election. "Name! name!" was the immediate cry on all sides. "I decline," replied Sheridan, "to give any names, although I could do so as easily as say Jack Robinson."

Apropos of this:—The wife of the Prince Talleyrand, who was a very beautiful but a very ignorant woman—the divorced wife of a person of the name of Grant—was one day told by her husband that he had invited to dinner the celebrated traveller and explorer of the antiquities of Egypt (Denon), and requested her, before that gentleman came, to possess herself of all information regarding him by reading his published work, which she would find on the library table. She accordingly proceeded to the library, where finding a French translation of Robinson Crusoe, she without further consideration arrived at the conclusion that that was the book to which her husband had referred. Captivated with the interest of the early portion of the narrative, she very soon mastered its leading features and appeared at the dinner table, fully primed with, as she thought, all particulars respecting the doings of her distinguished guest. Every attention was paid to him by the lady, and many questions were put, to him somewhat mysterious, but which he answered in the best way he could. At last the Princess, with a most benevolent look, innocently asked, " Pray how did you leave Monsieur Friday?" This brought matters to a crisis, and led to an explanation by which the lady was undeceived as to the identity of her guest with the hero of Defoe's romance. This story has been generally accredited; but a similar occurrence is said to have taken place very many years previously. A gentleman of the name of Robinson, very tall in stature, and dressed after the English fashion, was present at a dinner party at which was also Madame du Barri, who was much struck with his appearance, and who, hearing him addressed as Monseiur Robinson, jumped at the conclusion that he was the veritable Robinson Crusoe, and upon that supposition, she asked him many questions which rather puzzled him to answer. At length, after in vain endeavouring to elicit the desired information, she, perceiving there was some unaccountable mistake, exclaimed " Mon dieu! are not you the Robinson Crusoe so famed in history ?"

IMPROBABILITY, p. 360.

A poetical effusion of seven verses bearing upon this subject, will be found in "The Parlour Portfolio," selections from Magazines and

Newspapers, 2 vols. 8vo, 1820. It is called "Prophetical Improbabilities ; or, England, woe to thee ! addressed to the numerous croakers in Great Britain and Ireland." And goes thus :—

> When roasting-jacks are water-mills,
> And milk-pails worsted stockings :
> When mountains change to small mole-hills,
> And serious truths are mockings :
> When silver spoons are leather thongs,
> And pickled salmon milk ;
> When muslin bonnets are tea-tongs,
> And copper saucepans silk.
>   Then England, woe to thee !

CALTON JESS, p. 4

"A true-bred English beau has indeed the powder, the essence, the tooth-pick, the snuff-box ; and is as idle ; but the fault is in the flesh— he has not the motion, and looks stiff under all this. Now a French fop, like a poet, is born so, and would be known without clothes; it is in his eyes, his nose, his fingers, his elbows, his heels. They dance when they walk, and sing when they speak. We have nothing in that perfection as abroad."— BURNABY.

The Beau's Character.—From the comedy called Hampstead-Heath, written by Thomas Baker, 1706. Set and sung by Mr. Ramsden. Reprinted in Durfey's Songs Compleat, Pleasant, and Divertive, vol. 5, 1719, and in Fairholt's Satirical Songs on Costume, 1849.

> A Whig that's full,
> An empty scull,
> A box of Burgamot ;
> A hat ne'er made
> To fit is head,
> No more than that to plot.
> A hand that's white,
> A ring that's right,
> A Sword, Knot, Patch, and Feather
> A gracious smile,
> And grounds and oyl,
> Do very well together.
> A smatch of French,
> And none of sense.
> All conquering airs and graces

A tune that thrills,
A lear that kills,
Stol'n flights and borrow'd phrases,
A chariot gilt,
To wait on jilt,
An awkward face and carriage ;
A foreign tour,
A sly amour,
And mercenary marriage.

A limber ham
Good gracious ma'am.
A smock-face tho' a tann'd one ;
A peaceful sword,
Not one wise word,
But state and prate at random.
Affiliations,
Duns, quotations
From Cælia and Amadis ; *
Toss'd up a Beau,
That grand ragout,
That hodge-podge for the ladies.

THE BEAU.

From Poems on several occasions, by C. Arnold, Lond. 1757, 4to.

.   .   .   .   .

Draw him just as when I saw
The dear one shine at Ranelagh ;
Let his hat be very small,
Of the finest beaver all ;
Light as feather, emblem plain
Of his levity of brain ;
On his head a bag toupèe
Frizzled a la mode Pari :
Short, that so may full appear
The enchanting Brunette ear ;
Grace his neck debonnair,
With the modish solitaire ;
Of the blackest ribband sleek,
Let it flutt'ring tap his cheek ;

* Two popular romances of the day.

Draw the lock that's in his pole,
Give the wanton eye its roll ;
Don't forget the patch and dimple,
Patch that's placed to hide a pimple ;
And be sure the coat you load
With golden tassels a la mode ;
Blue, too, of the finest die,
Just to cover half the thigh ;
Satin waistcoat white as milk,
Breeches of the finest silk ;
Nor a wrinkle let there be,
Short, too, just about the knee ;
Let the Dresden ruffles shew,
Hand as white as any snow ;
Bright his sword, his buckles too,
Softest Spanish for his shoe,
Hose the finest he puts on,
As e'er laborious silkworm spun,
O'er all his form, with art disclose
An air-like dancing as he goes ;
Take these hints without delay,
To the world this thing display ;
The Beau shall then with shame confess
That e'en his better part is dress.

Macaroni.—Folengio Theophilus of Mantua, known also by the title of Merlin Coocaye, an Italian poet, wrote a poem, the name of which was long after adopted for all trifling performances of the same species. It consisted of buffoonery, puns, anagrams, wit without wisdom, and humour without good grace, and was called "The Macaroni," from the Italian cakes of the same name, which are sweet to the taste, but have not the smallest degree of alimentary virtue ; on the contrary, they pall the appetite and clog the stomach. These idle poems soon became the reigning taste in Italy and in France. They gave birth to Macaroni academies, and, reaching England, to Macaroni Clubs, till at last, everything insipid, contemptible, or ridiculous, in the character, dress, or behaviour, of both men and women, was summed up in the despicable appellation of a "Macaroni," which was long, in particular, the common appellation of that most insipid, contemptible, and ridiculous character, an effeminate coxcomb.—*The Collector*, 1798.

The Macaronis figured in London in 1772. An account of the costume of "the Macaroni," and of "the female Macaroni," will be found in the introductory notices to two songs bearing those titles, which appear in "Satirical Songs and Poems on Costume : from the 13th to the 19th century." Edited by Mr Fairholt for the Percy Society,

London 1849, cr. 8vo. In this excellent collection will also be found other songs respecting beaux and belles, and their style of costume at different periods of time.

The following jeu d'esprit, from the Westminster Magazine, sums up pretty accurately the qualifications and uselessness of the genus "dandy:"—

THE EPITAPH OF A MODERN FINE GENTLEMAN, 1775.

HERE LIES
without any hopes,
and
Equally useful in death, as life,
The flimsy carcase
of
A VERY FINE GENTLEMAN,
vulgarly called
A MACARONI.
The only proofs of his existence
were,
That he picked his teeth at Almack's,
and
Ruined himself at the Scavoir Vivre.
Though born to a great fortune,
With a good understanding,
He made the worst use of 'em,
Turning blesses into curses;
And, tho' young,
Outlived them both.
At school he learnt to be vicious;
By travel he was made ridiculous;
Returned from abroad without any
acquisitions,
But a thorough contempt of his
own country,
And with every vice and folly of those
he had seen.
He gamed to kill time,
Married to live single,
Wandered from place to place,
Because he was miserable every
where;
at last,
By refining away every moral and

social virtue,
Without desire, passions, inclinations,
or affections,
almost without senses,
He lived despising, and despised,
and dy'd,
Without fortune, friends, or faith,
Returning from the nothingness he
sprung,
And in which he remain'd
During the short term of his unna-
tural life.
READER !
Though thou be blessed with extensive
knowledge,
And the warmest imagination,
Thou hast never read of, or canst fancy,
A more insignificant and contemptible
Being
than that
WHICH LIES HERE.

—————

Finis coronat opus.

Edinburgh:
Printed by Turnbull & Spears.

www.ingramcontent.com/pod-product-compliance
Lightning Source LLC
Chambersburg PA
CBHW032311290326
41932CB00068B/340